Have you been to our website?

For code downloads, print and e-book bundles, extensive samples from all books, special deals, and our blog, please visit us at:

Rheinwerk Computing

The Rheinwerk Computing series offers new and established professionals comprehensive guidance to enrich their skillsets and enhance their career prospects. Our publications are written by the leading experts in their fields. Each book is detailed and hands-on to help readers develop essential, practical skills that they can apply to their daily work.

Explore more of the Rheinwerk Computing library!

Philip Ackermann
JavaScript: The Comprehensive Guide
2022, 1292 pages, paperback and e-book
www.rheinwerk-computing.com/5554

Jürgen Wolf
HTML and CSS: The Comprehensive Guide
2023, 814 pages, paperback and e-book
www.rheinwerk-computing.com/5695

Philip Ackermann
Full Stack Web Development: The Comprehensive Guide
2023, 740 pages, paperback and e-book
www.rheinwerk-computing.com/5704

Christian Wenz, Tobias Hauser
PHP and MySQL: The Comprehensive Guide
2025, approx. 1081 pp, paperback and e-book
www.rheinwerk-computing.com/6022

Johannes Ernesti, Peter Kaiser
Python 3: The Comprehensive Guide
2022, 1036 pages, paperback and e-book
www.rheinwerk-computing.com/5566

www.rheinwerk-computing.com

Kerem Koseoglu

SQL

The Practical Guide

Editor Rachel Gibson
Acquisitions Editor Hareem Shafi
Copyeditor Doug McNair
Cover Design Graham Geary
Photo Credits iStockphoto: 184339322/© t_kimura; 157329060/© enot-poloskun
Layout Design Vera Brauner
Production Eric Wyche
Typesetting SatzPro, Germany
Printed and bound in the USA, on paper from sustainable sources

ISBN 978-1-4932-2679-5
1st edition 2025

© 2025 by:
Rheinwerk Publishing, Inc.
2 Heritage Drive, Suite 305
Quincy, MA 02171
USA
info@rheinwerk-publishing.com

Represented in the E.U. by:
Rheinwerk Verlag GmbH
Rheinwerkallee 4
53227 Bonn
Germany
service@rheinwerk-verlag.de

Library of Congress Cataloging-in-Publication Control Number: 2024057966

All rights reserved. Neither this publication nor any part of it may be copied or reproduced in any form or by any means or translated into another language, without the prior consent of Rheinwerk Publishing.

Rheinwerk Publishing makes no warranties or representations with respect to the content hereof and specifically disclaims any implied warranties of merchantability or fitness for any particular purpose. Rheinwerk Publishing assumes no responsibility for any errors that may appear in this publication.

"Rheinwerk Publishing", "Rheinwerk Computing", and the Rheinwerk Publishing and Rheinwerk Computing logos are registered trademarks of Rheinwerk Verlag GmbH, Bonn, Germany.

All products mentioned in this book are registered or unregistered trademarks of their respective companies.

No part of this book may be used or reproduced in any manner for the purpose of training artificial intelligence technologies or systems. In accordance with Article 4(3) of the Digital Single Market Directive 2019/790, Rheinwerk Publishing, Inc. expressly reserves this work from text and data mining.

Contents at a Glance

1	Introduction	15
2	Basic Elements of Relational Databases	29
3	Setting Up the Environment	71
4	Data Definition Language	99
5	Data Manipulation Language	155
6	Transaction Control Language	221
7	Data Query Language	253
8	Data Control Language	421
9	Conclusion	447

Dedication

To my dearest wife, Ozge,
for your endless love and unwavering support.
This is my first book since I met you.

In Loving Memory

Of my parents, Peyman and Yaman, who are no longer with us—
I know you would be proud to see this book published.
This is my first book since I lost you.

Contents

1 Introduction — 15

1.1 Relational Databases — 17
1.2 What Is SQL? — 20
1.3 Target Audience — 23
1.4 What You'll Learn from This Book — 24
1.5 Tips for Reading This Book — 26

2 Basic Elements of Relational Databases — 29

2.1 Fundamentals — 29
    2.1.1 Databases — 30
    2.1.2 Database Products — 30
    2.1.3 Schemas — 34
2.2 Structures — 38
    2.2.1 Tables — 38
    2.2.2 Data Types — 43
    2.2.3 Views — 46
2.3 Keys and Indexing — 49
    2.3.1 Primary Keys — 49
    2.3.2 Foreign Keys — 52
    2.3.3 Indexes — 55
2.4 Normalization — 59
    2.4.1 First Normal Form — 59
    2.4.2 Second Normal Form — 60
    2.4.3 Third Normal Form — 61
    2.4.4 Results — 61
2.5 Operations — 62
    2.5.1 Stored Procedures — 63
    2.5.2 Triggers — 65
2.6 Authorization — 68
2.7 Summary — 70

Contents

3   Setting Up the Environment   71

3.1   Our Database of Choice 73
3.2   Local Database Setup 75
    3.2.1   Windows Installation 75
    3.2.2   macOS Installation 81
3.3   SQL IDE Setup 83
    3.3.1   pgAdmin 84
    3.3.2   Visual Studio Code 92
3.4   Summary 97

4   Data Definition Language   99

4.1   Database Manipulation 100
    4.1.1   Database Creation 100
    4.1.2   Database Modification 101
    4.1.3   Database Deletion 106
4.2   Schema Manipulation 107
    4.2.1   Schema Creation 107
    4.2.2   Schema Modification 108
    4.2.3   Schema Deletion 112
4.3   Table Manipulation 115
    4.3.1   Table Creation 115
    4.3.2   Table Modification 134
    4.3.3   Table Deletion 145
4.4   View Manipulation 147
    4.4.1   View Creation 149
    4.4.2   View Modification 151
    4.4.3   View Deletion 152
4.5   Common Pitfalls of Data Definition Language 153
    4.5.1   Renaming Objects 153
    4.5.2   Deleting Objects 153
4.6   Summary 154

5 Data Manipulation Language — 155

5.1	**Building a Data Manipulation Language Playground**	156
5.2	**Data Manipulation Language Operations**	162
	5.2.1 Insert	162
	5.2.2 Update	174
	5.2.3 Delete	185
	5.2.4 Common Pitfalls of Data Manipulation Language Operations	190
5.3	**Data Manipulation Language Automation**	191
	5.3.1 Stored Procedures	192
	5.3.2 Triggers	199
5.4	**Summary**	219

6 Transaction Control Language — 221

6.1	**Building a Transaction Control Language Playground**	222
6.2	**Why Is Transaction Control Language Necessary?**	228
6.3	**COMMIT and ROLLBACK**	230
6.4	**Save Points**	235
6.5	**Locks and Concurrency**	241
	6.5.1 Locks	242
	6.5.2 Transaction Isolation	248
6.6	**Common Pitfalls of Transaction Control Language**	251
6.7	**Summary**	251

7 Data Query Language — 253

7.1	**Building a Data Query Language Playground**	254
	7.1.1 Master Data Tables	255
	7.1.2 Order Tables	258
	7.1.3 Delivery Tables	260
	7.1.4 Invoice Tables	264
	7.1.5 Complaint Tables	269
	7.1.6 Mock Data	270

7.2	**Single Table Queries**		273
	7.2.1 Selecting All Columns		274
	7.2.2 Selecting Some Columns		276
	7.2.3 Filtering Rows with WHERE Conditions		278
	7.2.4 Ordering Results		293
	7.2.5 Partial Selection		297
	7.2.6 Unique Selection		299
	7.2.7 Null Values		301
	7.2.8 Aggregate Functions		303
7.3	**Multitable Queries**		312
	7.3.1 Refresher on Relationships between Tables		312
	7.3.2 INNER JOIN		315
	7.3.3 Using Aliases		322
	7.3.4 OUTER JOIN		325
	7.3.5 Self-Join		334
	7.3.6 Subqueries		337
	7.3.7 Set Operations		349
7.4	**String Functions**		358
	7.4.1 Concatenation		358
	7.4.2 LEFT and RIGHT		361
	7.4.3 Length		363
	7.4.4 LOWER and UPPER		365
	7.4.5 LTRIM, RTRIM, and TRIM		366
	7.4.6 REVERSE		368
	7.4.7 SUBSTRING		368
	7.4.8 Regular Expressions		369
7.5	**Math and Numeric Functions**		373
	7.5.1 Math Operators		373
	7.5.2 ABS		376
	7.5.3 RANDOM		379
	7.5.4 ROUND, FLOOR, and CEILING		380
	7.5.5 SIGN		383
7.6	**Temporal Functions**		383
	7.6.1 Interval Calculations		384
	7.6.2 Current Date and Time		385
	7.6.3 Date Differences		385
	7.6.4 Extracting Date Parts		387
	7.6.5 Time Zones		388

7.7	Window Functions			389
	7.7.1	RANK		390
	7.7.2	DENSE_RANK		393
	7.7.3	ROW_NUMBER		395
	7.7.4	LEAD		401
	7.7.5	LAG		404
	7.7.6	NTILE		405
	7.7.7	FIRST_VALUE		407
7.8	Miscellaneous Functions			410
	7.8.1	CAST		410
	7.8.2	CASE		411
	7.8.3	COALESCE		414
	7.8.4	Common Table Expressions		415
7.9	Summary			418

8 Data Control Language   421

8.1	Building a Data Control Language Playground		422
8.2	User and Role Manipulation		424
	8.2.1	Users	424
	8.2.2	Roles	426
	8.2.3	User Manipulation	429
	8.2.4	Role Manipulation	430
8.3	Granting Access		431
	8.3.1	Granting Access Directly	432
	8.3.2	Granting Access Through Roles	436
	8.3.3	Granting Access through Role Hierarchies	439
8.4	Revoking Access		440
8.5	Reporting Privileges		441
8.6	Summary		446

9 Conclusion   447

Appendices 449

A	**Entity-Relationship Diagrams**		451
	A.1	Entity-Relationship Diagrams and Their Significance	452
	A.2	Entities	453
	A.3	Relationships Among Entities	457
	A.4	Entity-Relationship Diagrams Exercises	465
	A.5	Summary	470
B	**Tips and Tricks**		471
	B.1	SQL Injection	471
	B.2	Application-Level Authorization	473
	B.3	Sensitive Data	476
	B.4	Logical Deletion	477
	B.5	Indexes versus Summary Tables	478
	B.6	Legal Concerns	479
	B.7	Primary Key Determination	480
	B.8	Logging	482
	B.9	Backup and Recovery	482
C	**About the Author**		485

Index 487

Chapter 1
Introduction

This chapter introduces readers to relational databases and the Structured Query Language (SQL) programming language. It sets the stage for the rest of the book by explaining who the book is for, what readers will learn, and how readers might approach the topics in the book.

Hello there, and welcome to this exciting book on SQL: an ever-viable subject! We'll journey together through the pages, learning the most essential features of SQL, learning new skills, and gaining insights into how to apply those skills to everyday technical requirements. As the author, I am thrilled to have the honor of accompanying you on this journey.

In today's world, you can find countless resources and much documentation on any technical subject. It's even possible to use AI for assistance in learning, but nothing can replace the wisdom gained from years of hands-on experience. Being a professional developer who's worked with databases for many decades, I intend to provide not only technical guidance on SQL but also certain insights into how to approach technical requirements and apply the appropriate techniques to gain the best results.

Examples in this book will be based on real-world scenarios as well as typical cases that you're likely to encounter at some point during your development journey. We may simplify some cases because we don't want to shift our focus from learning SQL to understanding a complex example. Human attention is a limited resource, and it's best to spend it on what really matters.

The realistic nature of our examples will enable you to grasp the logic and purpose of SQL features in such a way that you'll be able to quickly apply them to your daily requirements. That was a personal frustration of mine during my novicehood: some resources provided sterile and unrealistic cartoon examples—involving cats, dogs, tomatoes, potatoes, and all. While the resources explained the technical topics at hand, it required significant effort on my part to apply the examples to the practical cases in my projects.

> **Learning and Application**
> Learning the theory of a feature is one thing, but the ability to apply the feature in real life is what makes it worthwhile. Going over realistic case studies typically helps readers in both respects.

1 Introduction

Real-world examples will certainly be cleansed of any company specific process or content due to privacy concerns. Sample contents of database tables will mostly be random mock data, not test or live data from any party. It's unavoidable, though, that some mock data will resemble real-life people or companies. If you encounter such a case, be aware that this is purely coincidental and not intentional.

Speaking of examples, all code samples in this book are available online! You can find all SQL code in this book at *https://github.com/keremkoseoglu/sql*, which can be useful throughout the book. Instead of manually writing code samples into your editor, you can simply copy and paste from the repository.

SQL has some resemblance to board games like chess or go, in which the rules are simple but game play can get very complex. This book will guide you through the syntax, features, and typical applications of SQL, which you'll surely learn well and apply to your daily requirements. But be aware that business scenarios can get really complex in some cases where experience matters. In such cases, we recommend that you consult with senior developers to learn best practices honed by experience instead of attempting to reinvent the wheel. It will help you immensely on your learning journey and prevent you from developing some bad habits.

Obviously, we need a playground in which to develop examples, create database objects, and execute queries against them. We've picked PostgreSQL as our database of choice. It's a community-owned database that's free and open source. It's very popular, works across platforms, and has advanced features to future-proof your journey. PostgreSQL also supports all the functionality covered by this book.

No worries, though—the SQL knowledge you'll gain in PostgreSQL won't lock you into it. Although SQL syntax varies from database to database in some cases, PostgreSQL is known to have a very portable SQL syntax that hews very closely to ANSI SQL standards and is identical to them in many cases.

> **American National Standards Institute Structured Query Language**
> The American National Standards Institute Structured Query Language (ANSI SQL) is a standardized database query language that provides the general standards of SQL, meaning it defines the de facto SQL syntax. Although vendors are expected to support ANSI SQL in their database products, some deviate from it and add new features, including special syntax elements that are unsupported by other databases. Therefore, portability of SQL code between database systems is not always a simple matter of copying and pasting code. Some adaptation might be required.

Most of the case studies in this book will avoid database-specific features and focus on universal features expected to be supported by any relational database. That brings us to the next topic: what is a relational database?

1.1 Relational Databases

SQL is the de facto language targeting relational databases, so it's appropriate to give an overview of the latter. In a nutshell, a *relational database* is a type of database that organizes data into tables with rows and columns, which we can imagine as a set of spreadsheet pages. Those "sheets" refer to each other and become "related" as needed to prevent data duplication.

You'll encounter these concepts and much more in due course. As an early sneak peek, you can refer to Figure 1.1, which gives an example of the basic structure of a relational database with sales data and the following other characteristics:

- The spreadsheet-like customer table contains master data on all customers, including their IDs, names, phone numbers, and addresses.
- The spreadsheet-like invoice table contains data on invoices issued by the company, including invoice IDs, dates, amounts, and currencies. This table contains the ID of each corresponding customer as well. When we need to see the details on an invoice customer, we can simply peek inside the customer table and look for their ID. There's no need to duplicate customer data in the invoice table.
- The spreadsheet-like table payment table contains payment data, including transaction IDs, payment amounts, and currencies. This table contains the invoice ID for each payment, and when we need to see the details of the corresponding invoice, we can simply peek inside the invoice table with the invoice ID in hand. There's no need to duplicate invoice data in the payment table.

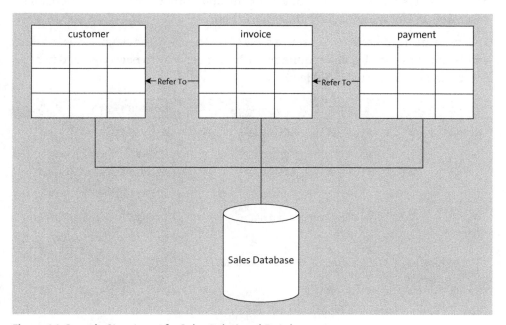

Figure 1.1 Sample Structure of a Sales Relational Database

17

1 Introduction

Easy, right? It's just like a set of Excel spreadsheets with superb VLOOKUP functionality.

The concept of relational database was first defined by E. F. Codd in "A Relational Model of Data for Large Shared Data Banks," which was a research paper he published in 1970. His raw ideas evolved over time and were turned into many different ACID-compliant relational database products.

> **Atomicity, Consistency, Isolation, and Durability**
>
> Atomicity, consistency, isolation, and durability (ACID) are the expected features of any competent database product. They ensure that database transactions are processed correctly and reliably. The meaning of each of the four components is as follows:
>
> - **Atomicity**
>   The entire transaction completes successfully or doesn't happen at all.
> - **Consistency**
>   Datasets must be consistent before and after the transaction.
> - **Isolation**
>   Multiple transactions can occur in parallel, without interference.
> - **Durability**
>   Once a transaction is committed, changes are permanently stored, even in the event of a system crash.

Data storage used to be a straightforward topic. There were a few options to store data, and developers and architects would pick the appropriate solution. Relational databases were one of the few solid options back then.

Today, we are in different circumstances. We are in the age of the cloud, big data, and AI, and as time has gone by, new requirements have given way to new types of databases. Some examples are listed in Table 1.1.

Database Types	Descriptions	Examples
Relational	Organizes data into tables with rows and columns	PostgreSQL MySQL Microsoft SQL Server Oracle Database
NoSQL	Handles unstructured data	MongoDB (document stores) Redis (key-value stores)
Time-series	Optimized for time-stamped data	InfluxDB TimescaleDB

Table 1.1 Various Database Types

1.1 Relational Databases

Database Types	Descriptions	Examples
Object-oriented	Stores data in objects	ObjectDB Actian
Graph	Focuses on relationships between data points	Neo4j ArangoDB
Cloud	Hosted on cloud platforms, focuses on scalability	Amazon RDS Azure SQL DB
In-Memory	Stores data in RAM	SAP HANA
Spatial	Optimized for spatial data, such as geographic information systems	PostGIS Oracle Spatial

Table 1.1 Various Database Types (Cont.)

Delving into the details of each database type is beyond the scope of this book. The purpose of Table 1.1 is to demonstrate the breadth of alternatives for handling data. But does this mean that relational database management systems (RDBMS) are out of fashion? Not at all.

> **Old but Gold**
> Don't let the gray hair fool you! Although a relational database is an aged concept, it has aged well and is still a solid and valid technology used throughout the industry. Classics are bound to be old, anyway—they can't become classics until they age and stand the test of time.

According to multiple sources, relational databases are still the most widely used databases in the entire industry. They are still relevant, going strong, and powering countless systems on the planet—such as ERPs, websites, mobile applications, flight systems, financial institutions, health care systems, telecommunications, and social media platforms. If you can imagine your data as a set of structured spreadsheets, then a relational database is one of the most solid alternatives for you to store your data, due to its benefits.

In Table 1.2, you can see some of the significant benefits of relational databases—and having SQL as a reliable industry-standard language is one of them. Learning how to use SQL to query and manipulate data in relational databases is still a solid career investment.

1   Introduction

Benefits of Relational Databases	Descriptions
Structured	Relational databases provide well-defined and easy-to-understand schemata, which organize data into rows and columns.
Data integrity	You can enforce data integrity in multiple tables through constraints and transactions.
Standardized language	You can use SQL throughout the system for operations like data manipulation and queries.
Scalability	As data grows over time, databases can scale accordingly.
Mature ecosystem	Documentation, best practices, forums, experts, community support, etc., are widely available.
Security	You can maintain data security with user authentication and authorizations.

Table 1.2 Some Benefits of Relational Databases

Besides, many other database types support SQL in enabling developers to reuse their existing skills, so an investment in SQL can open doors for you into other databases as well.

Now, let's put SQL under the magnifying glass.

1.2   What Is SQL?

Since you're holding this book in your hands (or viewing it on your screen), you already have an idea of what SQL is all about that made you pursue the goal of learning about it in detail. We've already gone over SQL "informally," so it's time for a formal introduction.

Structured Query Language (SQL) is a programming language that's used to manage, manipulate, and query contents of relational database systems. SQL was one of the first languages to target E. F. Codd's relational model, which we mentioned in Section 1.1. It was initially developed in the 1970s by IBM, and it evolved into an American National Standards Institute (ANSI) and International Organization for Standardization (ISO) standard in the 1980s. The language is obviously a success—even today, it's easily the most widely used database language.

Mind you that SQL is not a general-purpose language like Python, Java, or Rust. It's rather a domain-specific language (DSL) tailored to a specific goal. In our case, the goal of SQL is to manage and query relational databases, nothing more. But since SQL is the de facto standard for that purpose, it's widely used in conjunction with general-purpose languages. For example, a developer might code the business logic of their app in Python while coding the data manipulation part in SQL.

In the typical approach (depicted in Figure 1.2), Python code is the central executable of the app. As data manipulation is needed, the appropriate SQL statements are be generated by the Python code and executed against the database.

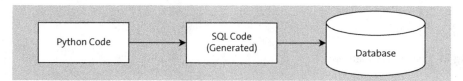

Figure 1.2 SQL as the "Middleman" between Database and Application

However, you don't need to be a programmer to enjoy SQL! Many nonprogrammers simply use a database app or tool to connect to a database and execute handwritten SQL code to achieve the results they want. For instance, business users and data scientists often query databases to extract meaningful data to support their tasks (as sketched in Figure 1.3). The declarative nature of SQL makes it approachable by a wide audience.

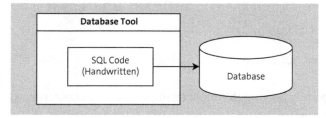

Figure 1.3 SQL Written Manually by the User

> **Declarative versus Imperative Programming Languages**
>
> *Declarative programming languages* enable the programmer to specify "what" the program should accomplish, without explicitly coding the steps for "how" to achieve it. SQL and HTML are examples of such languages, which provide a high level of abstraction that makes them arguably more approachable. The programmer simply says what they want, using relatively simple statements, and the target framework does the heavy lifting for them.
>
> *Imperative programming languages*, on the other hand, enable the programmer to explicitly code "how" the program should accomplish the desired task. Python and Rust are examples of such languages, which enable a high level of control and flexibility at the cost of a steeper learning curve. The programmer can enjoy an increased level of technical granularity in their algorithms, which is necessary in many cases.

1 Introduction

Listing 1.1 shows what a basic SQL statement looks like.

```
SELECT
    emp_name,
    department,
    hire_date
FROM
    employee
WHERE
    salary > 60000;
```

Listing 1.1 Basic SQL Statement

See? The statement itself is almost in plain English. We "declare" to the database system what we want: a name, a department, and the hire dates of employees with salaries higher than $60,000. We don't need to give any technical details on how to achieve this goal because our target database happily processes the statement and gives us the results we want, as shown in Table 1.3.

emp_name	department	hire_date
John Doe	Engineering	2021-01-15
Jane Smith	Marketing	2020-06-01
Emily Johnson	Sales	2019-03-23

Table 1.3 Sample Result Set of Basic SQL Statement

In this book, we'll obviously go way beyond this basic example and learn how to make the best of SQL to achieve our goals.

Although SQL itself is a complete set of standards, it consists of *sublanguages*, which define distinct groups of SQL statements that serve different purposes.

Sublanguages	Definitions	Purposes
DDL	Data definition language	Schema manipulation Table manipulation View manipulation
DML	Data manipulation language	Data entry creation Data entry updates Data entry deletion
TCL	Transaction control language	Consistent data manipulation on multiple tables

Table 1.4 Sublanguages of SQL

Sublanguages	Definitions	Purposes
DQL	Data query language	Data extraction from tables
DCL	Data control language	User and authorization management

Table 1.4 Sublanguages of SQL (Cont.)

If some (or even all) of the sublanguages in Table 1.4 are foreign to you, no worries! That's why we're here! We deal with each sublanguage in the later chapters of this book, and we'll go over all of them.

It ought to be said though that DQL is arguably the most used sublanguage of them all. Database tables are created once, and each entry is also created once, but the huge stack of entries in various tables is queried all the time to extract information from raw data. Our example in Listing 1.1 is also a DQL showcase.

Now that we've seen that SQL is approachable by a large audience, let's talk about the target audience of this book in particular.

1.3 Target Audience

So, who exactly is this book for? First, the good news: you don't need any significant experience in programming or relational databases to benefit from this book! We'll go through an overview of relational databases and even provide guidance on how to set up a small exercise database on your personal computer, so you'll be equipped with the technical framework to go through this book and develop your SQL skills.

There are some unavoidable prerequisites, though:

- Basic computer literacy
- Basic experience with spreadsheets (such as Microsoft Excel)
- Fundamental knowledge of databases (no hands-on experience needed)
- Basic understanding of programming (no hands-on experience needed)
- A computer with a recently released operating system
- Rights to install software to the computer or access to a remote database

Most (if not all) readers of this book have these prerequisites anyway, so we don't ask for much!

Our target audience includes, but isn't limited to, the following:

- Programmers looking for an extensive guide on SQL to fill their knowledge gaps
- Testers who are required to query data
- Data analysts who want to use SQL to analyze and interpret data
- Corporate staff who need to query business data

1 Introduction

- Database administrators looking to deepen their understanding of SQL for more effective management
- Educators looking for a structured curriculum and study guide
- Students learning SQL
- Hobbyists and startup enthusiasts who need to use SQL in their personal projects

We won't judge your motivation—anyone with an interest in SQL is most certainly welcome! Now that we've defined our audience, let's go over what we are offering in this book.

1.4 What You'll Learn from This Book

Being a book on SQL, this book will teach you the necessary technical skills to conduct operations on relational databases.

For starters, we'll go over the basic elements of relational databases. We'll highlight common relational database terms, concepts, and features. This will help you—especially if you're a beginner—understand what's fundamentally possible with relational databases and get to know the terminology that we'll use throughout the rest of the book.

In case you don't have access to a remote database, you'll be guided through the steps of installing and setting up a local PostgreSQL database on your local computer. This will be your playground, where you'll be able to write SQL code, experiment with this book's SQL code, and try out SQL features.

Once we are through with the fundamentals, we'll set sail to the sublanguages of SQL, which is the primary focus of this book. As stated in Section 1.2, SQL has several sublanguages that serve distinct purposes. We'll follow the logical sequence of these languages, starting with data definition language (DDL).

DDL is used to create database objects like schemas and tables. Before you can create or query data, you must have tables—and before you can create a table, you must have a schema. So, this will be your first logical step: you'll learn to create and alter database objects that will contain data in the future.

Sample DDL keywords include the following:

- CREATE TABLE
- ALTER TABLE
- DROP TABLE

With database objects in place, your next logical step is to put data into tables and learn to modify data when needed. Using data manipulation language (DML), you'll learn to insert, update and delete data. We'll also go through some automation options with triggers, which are set up to execute upon data insertion, modification, and deletion in a table and are used to automatically alter data in related tables. Stored procedures are similar mechanisms, but they aren't executed automatically—they need to be called manually.

> **Stored Procedures**
>
> Every database has a unique language for procedures, which means that developing stored procedures is a topic distinct from SQL and beyond the scope of this book. We'll only briefly explore the role of stored procedures in databases and show some basic examples.

Sample DML keywords include the following:

- INSERT
- UPDATE
- DELETE

Transaction control language (TCL) will be your next logical step. Sometimes, there's a need to modify multiple tables, and these modifications should either be saved together or not saved at all. This is known as atomicity, as we discussed in Section 1.1. TCL provides this very functionality! If you need to update ten tables and an error occurs after you update the first six tables, the resulting data inconsistency will probably cause application errors. TCL helps eliminate such risks. You'll learn how TCL works and walk through code examples to help you understand how to take advantage of TCL mechanisms.

Sample TCL keywords include the following:

- COMMIT
- ROLLBACK
- SAVEPOINT

Once you can create data entries successfully, it's time to query them to transform raw data into information. Data query language (DQL) is arguably the most common database feature, and it's used to query data from database tables. You'll learn about data queries from single tables or a combined set of tables. We'll cover data filters, string and math operations, date- and time-based calculations, and advanced ranking functionalities (window functions). You'll be able to use this knowledge to query data in your own databases to generate knowledge.

Sample DQL keywords include the following:

- SELECT
- JOIN
- WHERE

1 Introduction

Some databases contain sensitive data, and data access should be limited to some users or user groups. Data control language (DCL) is used to organize data access and authorizations. We'll discuss the necessity of DCL, explore its use cases, and go through SQL code examples to configure database authorizations.

Sample DCL keywords include the following:

- GRANT
- REVOKE

We also have some bonus content beyond core SQL!

You'll learn about entity-relationship diagrams (ERDs), which are an industry-standard set of visual symbols. They are used to demonstrate different relationship types among database tables, and they'll appear throughout this book. You'll learn ERD symbols and their meanings, which will help close any knowledge gaps you might have.

We'll also go through some tips and tricks to help improve your initial database designs. We'll cover some satellite concepts revolving around SQL, which will be helpful to anyone from a seasoned developer to a database freshman.

You might be wondering how to make the most of this book. Is it better to read from the first page to the last, or should you tailor a custom reading order to yourself? We'll discuss this next.

1.5 Tips for Reading This Book

Different readers may approach this book from different angles. Let's go through some suggestions and see what works best for you.

Some of you may need a holistic grasp of SQL, covering everything it has to offer. Technical people, such as programmers and testers, may fall into this category:

- If you feel like a complete newbie or think you might have gaps in your knowledge, no worries! This book is designed to guide you through a logically ordered curriculum, equipping you with all the necessary skills without leaving any significant gaps. You can go through this book by following its natural chapter sequence and become ready for your SQL adventures!
- Alternatively, you might lack knowledge in only some areas of SQL. In that case, it's perfectly fine to skip some chapters and focus on those that are most useful to you. We recommend adding our tips and tricks appendix to your reading list, though!

Some of you may only be interested in data queries, using DQL. Functional people, such as data analysts and business users, may fall into this category:

- If you feel like you lack knowledge of core database concepts, you can go through the initial chapters to have a stronger grasp of relational databases in general.

- Once or if you feel like you have gotten a good overview of relational databases, you can jump to DQL and go through the content to learn the commands, techniques, and subtleties of query database tables.

A smaller percentage of our readers may be educators. If you fall into this category, you can use the curriculum order of this book as a reference and make use of its content to support your courses.

Mind you that ERDs are used in diagrams throughout this book. Although ERDs are not directly bundled into SQL, knowing ERD symbols will help you understand our diagrams better. If you're not familiar with them, you can squeeze our appendix on ERDs into the early stages of your reading order. No worries: it's a quick read, and the symbols are as intuitive as it gets!

Now, if you've decided on your personal reading order, let's set sail!

Chapter 2
Basic Elements of Relational Databases

Although different relational databases provide different functionalities, they're foundationally similar. This chapter will highlight common relational database terms, concepts, and features. The chapter helps readers—especially beginners—understand what's fundamentally possible with relational databases and get to know the terminology that we'll use throughout the rest of this book.

SQL is the de facto language of relational databases. It's used to create, modify, delete, and query operations over database components.

To accurately understand SQL statements and their effect on the database, we naturally need to have an understanding of the relational database itself. Otherwise, we might find ourselves in the same situation as a mechanic who's holding a big toolbox but doesn't know anything about car engines! But once we get to know the "engine," we can use our "tools" to make it behave the way we need to.

If you already have a good understanding of relational databases, you can skip this chapter and jump to the SQL chapter of your interest. However, we recommend taking the time to go through this chapter to ensure that you have an adequate grasp of relational databases and the logic behind their components. You can always revisit this chapter to refresh your knowledge!

We'll start from the most basic, fundamental concepts—like databases, database products, and schemas—and follow a logical path toward relatively high-level components, such as normalization and operations.

2.1 Fundamentals

In this section, we'll go over the bare bones of any relational database. If this were a book on construction, we'd be talking about the foundations of buildings. Beyond the hardware and operating system, the fundamentals are the lowest-level components we can imagine from SQL's point of view.

2.1.1 Databases

Let's start with a formal definition: a *database* is an organized collection of data. The name *database* suggests the same, right? It's a base where data resides. The most common abbreviation of this term is *DB*.

So, how is a relational database different from any other database? If all databases are bases of data, what makes relational databases special?

A *relational database* is a type of database that stores data in tables, where each table enforces a spreadsheet-like structure of columns and rows. So basically, you can imagine a relational database as a huge Excel file with many interconnected sheets, where each sheet stores a certain type of data.

We'll talk about tables and their components in Section 2.2, so there's no rush! At this point, it's enough to imagine a relational database as a spreadsheet file on steroids.

We've already discussed that there are different types of databases. Within the scope of this book, the term *database* will refer to relational databases unless stated otherwise.

2.1.2 Database Products

A *database product* is the software that you install on a computer or server, which will host databases.

There are many companies offering commercial relational database products, such as Microsoft SQL Server and Oracle Database. However, there are also free and open-source alternatives, such as MySQL and PostgreSQL. As long as its technical and licensing aspects match your requirements, you can pick any relational database that works for you and install it on your system.

> **Knowledge Portability**
>
> Although each database product has its own pros and cons and offers some distinct features, each also shares a vast common ground with the others—which is good news for SQL developers! Your know-how on relational databases and SQL will be mostly portable.

Typically, a database product has different versions targeting different operating systems. PostgreSQL, for instance, has different downloadable versions for Windows, Linux, and MacOS, but their functionality is mostly the same. As is evident in Figure 2.1, installing a basic local database product is not too different from installing any other application—just run the installer and follow the installation wizard.

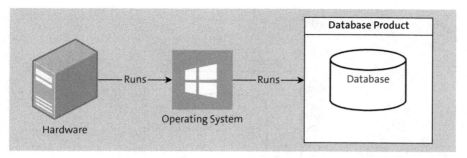

Figure 2.1 Overview of Database Product Running on Computer

After the installation is complete, you'd typically start the database service—and voila! You have a database product running! Most database products also offer a nice user interface, in which you can configure databases, see stored data, and even execute SQL code.

> **Local Database Installations**
> In Chapter 3, we'll go over the steps of how to install a local database product on your personal computer. This will be the playground where you'll learn and test SQL.

Installation, configuration, management, and scaling of a production database used for live transactions on a public server is a whole different story, though—and certainly beyond the scope of this book! We're here for SQL, so we leave such topics to system experts. It's enough to know that such a comprehensive database product is basically still an installed application on top of a server or operating system.

In a common, straightforward approach, a distinct server or operating system would run only a single instance of a database product. Case in point: you'd install only one instance of the PostgreSQL application on your local computer, just like you'd install only one instance of Microsoft Excel.

Although relatively new technologies like virtualization and containers enable different interesting architectures, we'll not go there at this time.

It's a common practice for companies to have multiple database product instances installed on different servers, though. In Figure 2.2, you can see a sketch of a company with some distinct databases.

2 Basic Elements of Relational Databases

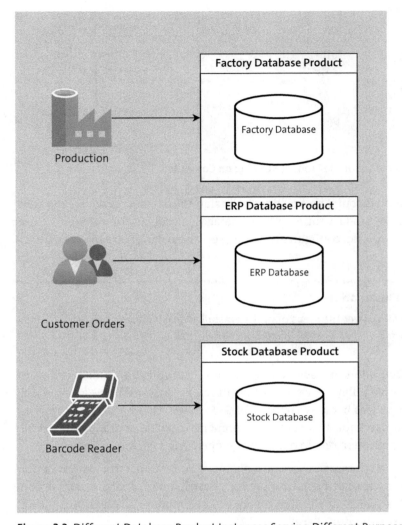

Figure 2.2 Different Database Product Instances Serving Different Purposes

However, a database product instance can also contain and host multiple databases. Figure 2.3 demonstrates an architecture where the plant database product instance hosts factory and stock databases simultaneously.

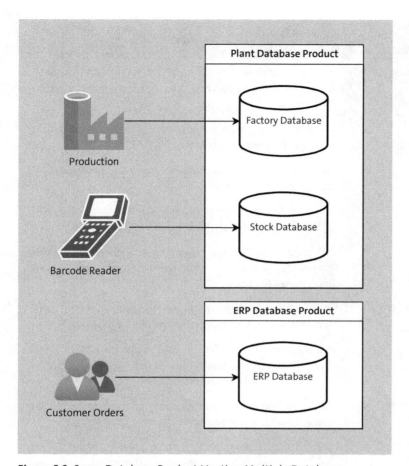

Figure 2.3 Same Database Product Hosting Multiple Databases

In these simplified examples, the following are true:

- The factory database is used to store production-related data.
- The ERP database is used to store order-related data.
- The stock database is used to store warehouse-related data.

You might wonder why a company would use multiple databases instead of setting up a big central database and storing everything there. Well, that centralized approach might work for some companies, but as the number of operations and volume of data grow, having multiple distinct databases can have some advantages. Table 2.1 explains some of them.

Advantages of Having Multiple Databases	Explanations
Separation of concerns	Different databases can be used for different business functions and configured according to the requirements of each business unit.
Scalability	Distributing data to different servers can help handle data load and improve performance.
Security	Sensitive data can be stored in dedicated databases with stricter access controls.
Damage control	In the event a data breach or hardware failure, the area of effect will be limited to the affected database only.
Legal concerns	Some countries have laws regarding data storage and quality standards. Having distinct databases for legally regulated subjects makes life easier.
Geographical distribution	Companies operating in multiple regions can find local databases useful for improving performance for local users.
Legacy systems	Some companies have legacy systems that have fallen behind in the tech race. Multiple databases allow for making new developments on more recent platforms.
Development and testing	It's a common practice to have distinct databases for development, testing, and production.
Data warehousing	Having dedicated databases for data warehousing, analytics, and reporting can lift this burden off transactional databases, improving their performance.

Table 2.1 Some Possible Reasons to Host Multiple Databases

The concepts of databases and database products are the broadest ones we need to understand and differentiate. Now, we'll step into a single database and learn about schemas.

2.1.3 Schemas

A database contains multiple components, such as tables, views, and even executable code in the form of stored procedures. We'll put those components under the microscope in Section 2.2, so bear with us.

It's certainly possible to imagine a database like a huge box that holds all such components together. Figure 2.4 demonstrates a simple human resources (HR) database in which employees, departments, and vacations are stored in distinct tables—just like spreadsheet pages.

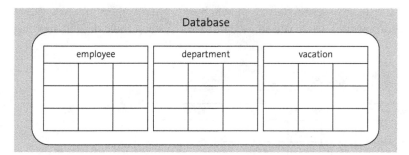

Figure 2.4 Simple HR Database

Now, imagine the maintenance staff knocking on our door and telling us that they need to use a database of measured room temperatures. They want to keep track of rooms, thermometers, and measurements. How can we give them what they need, in addition to hosting the HR database?

Using our knowledge so far, we have two options.

Figure 2.5 demonstrates the first option, in which we create a new maintenance database. HR gets to use their own database containing their own tables, while the maintenance department gets to use their database containing their own tables.

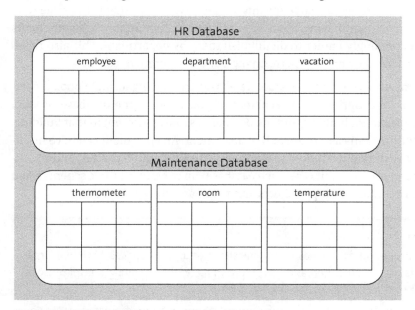

Figure 2.5 Distinct Databases for Distinct Purposes

Although this solution is viable, it's not always desirable. The advantages of having multiple databases were mentioned in Section 2.1.2, but they often come with compromises, such as increased system complexity and higher costs, especially if multiple database product instances are present.

Figure 2.6 demonstrates the second option, in which we cram all tables into a common single database. Both parties share the same database but keep their data in separate sets of tables.

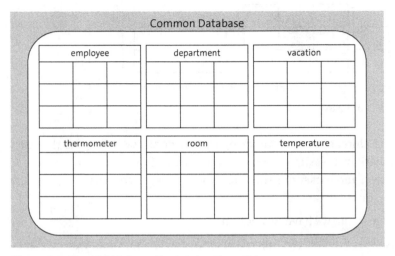

Figure 2.6 Single Database Containing Everything

Although this solution seems viable for this simple case, it certainly won't scale well. Imagine each department having hundreds of tables! As the number of components grows, it gets exceedingly harder to distinguish them by department. This also raises further concerns like data privacy, performance, and development conflicts.

Between the extremes of having separate databases and having a single pooled database, we have a third option: using schemas. If you imagine the database product instance as an apartment building and the database as one apartment in that building, you can imagine a schema as a room in that apartment. An apartment can have multiple rooms, and each room can hold many objects, like furniture, clothes, and instruments. It's the same logic in our case: each database can contain multiple schemas, and each schema can contain multiple objects, like tables and stored procedures.

> **Namespaces**
> Experienced programmers can easily imagine schemas as namespaces. Both help organize elements into a structured and logical grouping, while providing a level of isolation. Naming conflicts are also prevented in both cases.
>
> If you don't know about namespaces, no worries! It's just a technical metaphor, so you didn't miss anything.

Going back to our example, it's possible to use a common database for both departments while separating their database objects into distinct schemas. Figure 2.7 demonstrates this approach.

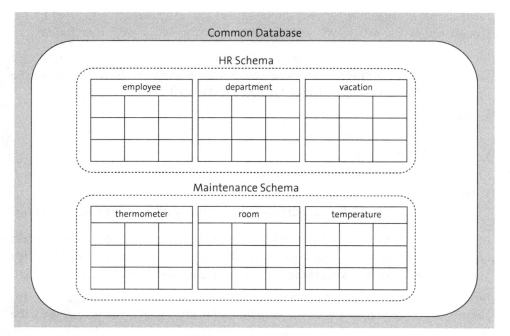

Figure 2.7 Single Database Containing Distinct Schemas

Isn't that beautiful? We can host both stakeholders on the same database, while ensuring that their database components will never get mixed up or cause conflicts.

In this picture, when a user wants to access a table, they should express the schema name and the table name together. In other words, the employee table should no longer be called employee; it should be called HR.employee whenever we need to access it. Following the same logic, the room table should no longer be called room; it should be called Maintenance.room from now on. The same would apply to further database components as well; they should be called out by including the name of the schema they belong to.

> **Fully Qualified Names**
>
> Just like calling a person by their first and last names, you can call a database component (such as a table) by its full name: [schema_name].[table_name]. This becomes a complete identifier that specifies the exact location of the component within the database hierarchy and prevents any possible conflicts.
>
> In some cases, you can also include the database in the fully qualified name and express it as [database_name].[schema_name].[table_name].

This convention even enables us to have namesake objects in both schemas. If both departments want to create their own log table, no problem! HR.log and Maintenance.log can exist simultaneously because the uniqueness of their names is ensured by the schema prefix.

It ought to be said that most databases come with a default schema. If you don't create distinct schemas for different purposes, you'll still be working under a schema—the default one. The following is a list of databases and their default schemas:

- **PostgreSQL**
  The default schema is `public`.
- **Microsoft SQL Server**
  The default schema is `dbo`, which stands for *database owner*.
- **Oracle**
  Each user of this database has a default schema that has the same name as the user.

In a SQL statement, if you mention a table without specifying the schema, the database engine will assume that you're targeting the default schema. To prevent conflicts, it's good practice to express the schemas' fully qualified names, such as `Maintenance.log`.

Now that we've learned about databases and schemas, we can move forward and learn about what they can hold. We've talked about tables already, so it's time to get into the details.

2.2 Structures

In this section, we'll learn about database components, which are directly responsible for containing our data. If we imagine the database as an apartment and the schema as a room in that apartment, we're about to talk about the cabinets, closets, and drawers in the room, which are the *structures* holding our everyday household items.

2.2.1 Tables

Tables are arguably the very center of the concept of relational databases, and it's very important to understand them. A big part of SQL revolves around tables, as we'll see in due course. But no worries—the concept of tables is also one of the easiest ones to grasp!

To understand tables, we can follow a metaphor of spreadsheets. You can imagine a database as a folder on your computer, so let's assume that the folder is initially empty, as shown in Figure 2.8.

In this approach, we can imagine the database schema as a Microsoft Excel file we create in our folder. Let's assume that the file is initially empty, as shown in Figure 2.9.

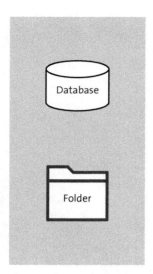

Figure 2.8 Database Imagined as Empty Folder

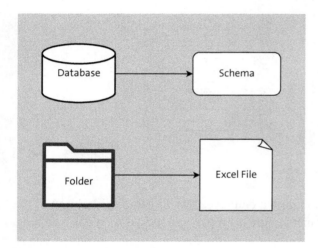

Figure 2.9 Schema Imagined as Empty Excel File

Obviously, you can have multiple Excel files in the folder if you want—just like you can have multiple schemas in the database. Logically, it's the same thing. But we'll go forward with a single file/schema at this time.

Arriving at the last step of our metaphor, we can imagine database tables as pages in our Excel file. It's that simple!

Following our example in Section 2.1.3, if you had to keep HR data in an Excel spreadsheet, you'd most probably create a new page for each data type, right? In our case, you'd create three pages, as demonstrated in Figure 2.10.

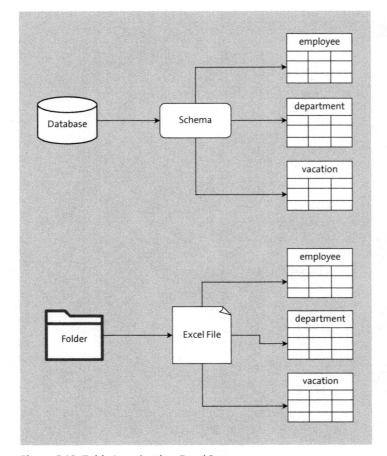

Figure 2.10 Table Imagined as Excel Page

The first Excel page, employee, would hold employee master data. Each column of the table would correspond to a distinct feature of employees, such as ID, name, surname, or birthday.

Table 2.2 is exactly what the employee database table would look like. After creating the database table, we'd insert the master data of employees into it, and we'd query the table whenever we needed information about our employees.

id	name	surname	birthday	...
1	Frank	Williams	1982-05-25	...
2	Diana	Brown	1982-04-26	...
3	Michael	Krueger	1983-04-18	...
...	...	...	...	...

Table 2.2 Sample Page of employee Database Table

> **Spreadsheets and Tables**
>
> Spreadsheet pages and database tables are very similar concepts. If you can imagine structured data on an Excel page, you can imagine structured data in a database table. They're logically identical.

The second Excel page, `department`, would hold department master data. Each column of the table would correspond to a distinct feature of departments, such as ID, name, or floor.

Table 2.3 is exactly what the `department` database table would look like. If we query the entries of this SQL database table (which we'll do many times in due course), the results set will look identical to a spreadsheet page.

id	name	floor	...
101	Accounting	1	...
102	Sales	2	...
103	Human Resources	3	...
...	...	...	...

Table 2.3 Sample Page of department Database Table

The third Excel page, `vacation`, would hold the vacation records of employees. Each column would correspond to a distinct feature of a vacation, such as vacation ID, employee's ID, start date, end date, or paid/unpaid category.

You know the drill by now: Table 2.4 looks exactly what the `vacation` database table would look like.

id	employee_id	start_date	end_date	paid	...
1001	1	2024-07-24	2024-07-30	true	...
1002	2	2024-09-15	2024-09-25	false	...
1003	1	2024-11-10	2024-11-15	false	...
...	...	...	...	...	...

Table 2.4 Sample Page of vacation Database Table

Although database tables resemble spreadsheet pages, there are some fundamental differences between them.

Table 2.5 basically implies that a database table should be imagined like a less flexible spreadsheet page that consists of a single set of columns with fixed data types.

Features	Spreadsheet Pages	Database Tables
Content	You can put anything into a spreadsheet page, like text, formulas, graphics, and multiple tables.	Tables accept structured and standardized sets of data entries, and nothing else.
Data types	Rows can contain different types of data in the same column. You can insert a number, text, and a date, sequentially.	Rows must contain a predefined type of data in the same column. For example, you can't put a number in a date column.
Entry counts	A spreadsheet page typically has a limit on row count.	Tables don't limit row count; they can scale up as data grows.

Table 2.5 Some Differences between Spreadsheet Pages and Database Tables

> **Why Databases?**
>
> If spreadsheets are so similar to databases and arguably even more flexible, why bother using databases at all? Can't we all just get along with our spreadsheets?
>
> Well, no. The two correspond to different requirements.
>
> Spreadsheets provide a flexible and user-friendly interface; they're best suited to personal use on small datasets. Databases have the upper hand if a more structured, scalable, and robust solution for multiple users is required, due to the fact that they have the following advantages:
>
> - **Scalability**
>   Databases can handle large datasets efficiently.
> - **Data consistency**
>   Strict rules and relationships on databases enforce clean data.
> - **Concurrency**
>   Multiple users can access and modify data on databases simultaneously.
> - **Querying**
>   Complex data operations can be conducted on databases using SQL.
> - **Development**
>   Databases support stored procedures and triggers for purposes like automation.
> - **API**
>   Custom development is possible on databases using many programming languages.

2.2.2 Data Types

In Section 2.2.1, we discussed the fact that database tables enforce uniform data types in each column. Now, we're going to delve a little deeper into this subject and learn about basic data types we can use.

Let's look at the mock data in Table 2.6, which showcases members of a social media platform.

id	name	surname	birthday	is_active
NUMERIC	TEXT	TEXT	DATE	BOOLEAN
256	Olivia	Thompson	1987-03-14	true
257	Ethan	Carter	1992-07-22	false
258	Ava	Martinez	1978-11-05	true

Table 2.6 Data Snapshot of member Database Table

In this case, the following apply:

- The id column can contain only numeric values. We can't enter text or date values there.
- The name and surname columns can contain only text values. We can't enter numeric or date values there.
- The is_active column can contain only the Boolean values true or false. We can't enter any other values there.

This enforcement ensures that we have clean, usable, and predictable data in the member table. Without such enforcement, we could end up having dirty data like a disorganized spreadsheet page, as demonstrated in Table 2.7.

id	name	surname	birthday	is_active
256	Olivia	Thompson	1987-03-14	Yes
member_257	Ethan	Carter	07/22/1992	false
two five eight	Ava	Martinez	5th November 78	Correct

Table 2.7 Imaginary Dirty Data in member Database Table

Imagine having millions of unstructured entries, like in Table 2.7, and trying to run a simple query, like picking active members and calculating their average age. Good luck with that! The same operation is very easy with SQL when you have clean data, like in Table 2.6, as we'll see in due course.

2   Basic Elements of Relational Databases

> **Clean Data**
>
> Dirty, unorganized, and unstructured data is the bane of data-oriented operations, such as analytics, reporting, and machine learning algorithms. Data type standardization in relational databases helps with clean data and makes the lives of clients much easier.

So, how many data types can we use in our columns? The short answer is ... plenty! Table 2.8 showcases some of the most significant data types we can use.

Data Types	Targets	Examples
Numeric	Columns with numeric content, such as quantities, measurements, scores, and temperatures	`integer`, `decimal`, `real`
Monetary	Columns with currency amounts	`money`
Text	Columns with text content, such as names, descriptions, addresses, comments, e-mails, and URLs	`varchar`, `char`, `text`
Temporal	Columns with date and time content, such as birthdays, entry time stamps, and expiration dates	`date`, `time`, `timestamp`
Boolean	Columns with TRUE or FALSE content, such as checkboxes, approvals, and enablements	`boolean`
Binary	Columns with binary content, such as images, audio files, and PDFs	`bytea`
Complex	Columns with standardized content, such as XMLs and JSONs	`xml`, `json`, `jsonb`
User-defined	Columns with custom data types (domains)	N/A

Table 2.8 Significant Data Type Categories

As you can see, there's something for everyone! Relational databases have evolved and improved over time, and you can find an appropriate data type quite easily.

> **Abundance of Data Types**
>
> There are many more data types beyond the ones on this short list, and each database product provides its special data types. Also, the same data type may have different

> names in different database products. For example, PostgreSQL provides the `text` data type to store large amounts of text, and the same functionality is called the `varchar(max)` data type in Microsoft SQL Server and the `clob` data type in Oracle Database.
>
> Since this is a SQL book, this section merely aims to highlight the differentiation of data type categories. We won't put each data type under a microscope and discuss its differences from the others, so please consult the documentation of your database product if you need that information.

Considering the strictness of relational databases, we obviously need to be careful about picking the right data type. For example, once we define a table column as `numeric` and insert numeric entries, we can't simply change the column type to `date`. The database wouldn't know what to do with the numeric values of existing entries.

Relational databases provide mechanisms to allow type changes in some cases, though. For example, if you have a `text` column that contains nothing but numeric characters, you can execute a special SQL statement to change the column type to `numeric` while converting all entries from text to numbers (which we'll learn about in Chapter 4). Check the entries in Table 2.9—even if `card_number` was initially defined as a text column, you can convert it to a number column without data loss.

member_id	name	surname	card_number
5832	Laura	Anderson	3748291056
5833	James	Mitchell	5967832140
5834	Emma	Thompson	4892167354

Table 2.9 Sample Data on Golf Club Members

Or maybe you've defined a column as `varchar(10)`, which means that you intended to store up to ten characters of text there. But if you now need to store more than ten characters there, you can extend the length of the column relatively easily by converting it to `varchar(20)`, using a simple SQL statement (as we'll explain in Chapter 4). The `surname` column in Table 2.9 is a good example of how increasing the column capacity doesn't hurt any existing entries. On the other hand, changing `surname` to `varchar(5)` would hurt existing entries by cropping surnames and causing data loss, so we need to be very careful and mindful of type changes. Besides, changing data types may not always be possible, so it's best to determine the correct data type in advance and make it right during the table definition phase.

2.2.3 Views

Now that we're familiar with tables, columns, and rows, understanding views is going to be a breeze!

A *view* is a virtual table that combines and displays data from underlying real tables. A view doesn't store data itself, but anytime it's called, it gathers corresponding data in real time and presents it as if the view were a real table.

This concept will become clear in the following example of a bookstore. Table 2.10 presents a table containing author master data.

id	name
101	John Doe
102	Jane Smith

Table 2.10 Sample Bookstore author Table

On the other hand, Table 2.11 presents a table containing book master data.

id	title	author_id
1	The Great Adventure	101
2	Learning SQL	102
3	The Great Mystery	101

Table 2.11 Sample Bookstore book Table

If you take a close look, you'll see that `book.author_id` refers to `author.id`. In other words, for each entry in the book table, we should be able to find a corresponding entry in the author table, as follows:

- Book 1 (*The Great Adventure*) was written by author 101 (John Doe)
- Book 2 (*Learning SQL*) was written by author 102 (Jane Smith)
- Book 3 (*The Great Mystery*) was written by author 101 (John Doe)

Figure 2.11 summarizes this information as an ERD.

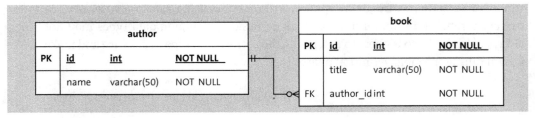

Figure 2.11 Bookstore ERD

> **Entity-Relationship Diagrams**
>
> This is the first time in this book that we've encountered an ERD, which is a diagram format that demonstrates table relationships. If the diagram makes sense to you and you understand the symbols, great! Otherwise, you'll be pleased to know that we have an appendix on ERDs. It's a quick read, and you can squeeze it into your default reading order.

Now that we've built our framework, we can move forward and prepare a view that combines both tables.

As we'll see in Section 2.4 in greater detail, it makes sense to have authors and books in separate tables. The best practices of relational databases also encourage this approach.

However, business users often have nontechnical points of view that are based on practicality. Imagine that the bookstore manager insists on seeing book and author names in a single combined table to provide a better overview of inventory. It's a reasonable request, and sometimes, all you need is a simple list of names!

To achieve this result, we can easily define a view called book_auth_name (or any other name we want). We'd tell the database that's using SQL to create the view under this name, which will combine book names with their corresponding author names. Figure 2.12 demonstrates the logic behind this view.

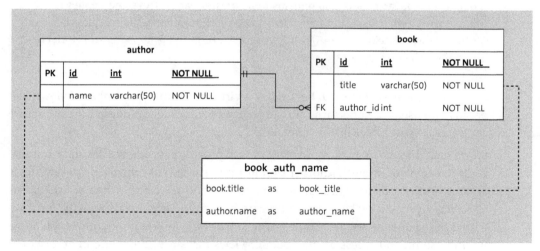

Figure 2.12 ERD of book_auth_name View Containing Book and Author Names

Once we create this view, we can call it to see its contents as if we're calling a table. Our relational database will happily process the book and author records in real time, combine them, and display the results as shown in Table 2.12.

book_title	author_name
The Great Adventure	John Doe
Learning SQL	Jane Smith
The Mystery Novel	John Doe

Table 2.12 Results of Calling book_auth_name View

It's worth mentioning again that book_auth_name is not a table and doesn't hold any data. You shouldn't think that it keeps copied or duplicate data from its underlying book and author tables. Instead, every time the view is called, it gathers and combines table data in real time and displays them. Don't let book_auth_name trick you into thinking that it's a real table—even if it looks very much like one.

Even if you delete a view, nothing happens to the underlying data because you didn't touch the master table (book or author) where the data actually resides. A view is simply a data mirror, nothing more.

> **Pivot Tables**
>
> Spreadsheet experts can imagine database views like Excel pivot tables. Pivot tables gather, filter, summarize, and display data from other spreadsheet pages. Even if you delete a pivot table, data still remains in its master pages. The same applies to database views—when you call them, they gather, filter, summarize, and display data from other database tables. Even if you delete a view, nothing happens to the data—it remains in its master tables.

Note that a database table can be used by a virtually unlimited number of views. Just because we used book and author in our book_auth_name view, it doesn't mean that we can't access those tables in any other view.

We've seen that the main purpose of views is to provide data summaries and combinations to people of interest. Another significant purpose is to centralize our table logic and provide a facade for guest programmers. Imagine a database schema with dozens of tables—it would make sense to prepare easy-to-understand views with intuitive names based on various table combinations. That way, a guest programmer could easily understand and access a small pool of views instead of drowning in an ocean of tables.

In Chapter 4, we'll see how to create, access, and delete views using SQL. For now, let's move to our next topic.

2.3 Keys and Indexing

Now that we've gone through the database components that are responsible for containing data, it's time to go through the components that are responsible for data identification. Most of the concepts under this umbrella revolve around keys.

The term *key* may be misleading for some newcomers. Although it may connotate pieces of metal used to unlock doors, it means something different altogether in SQL, so be aware that we don't use them to unlock database tables or anything like that. Instead, a key is a value that uniquely identifies an entity. For instance, in a school full of students, *student number* would be the key of each student. Having this key helps the faculty uniquely identify each student and keep their records without any confusion. Even students who share the same name are safe because their records are filed under their keys (student numbers) instead of their names.

Table 2.13 clarifies our view of keys with further examples from our daily lives.

Entities	Keys (Unique Identifiers)	Sample Values
Book	International Standard Book Number (ISBN)	978-1493214648
Vehicle	Vehicle identification number (VIN)	1HGBH41JXMN109186
Customer	Account number	CUST-8472-5619
Airplane seat	Row and seat number	18C
Hotel room	Room number	301
Parking space	Space identifier	P24
Movie theater seat	Seat number	F7
Restaurant table	Table number	12

Table 2.13 Examples of Keys in Daily Life

Clear, right? Let's move forward and see how keys help us in database tables.

2.3.1 Primary Keys

In a database table, the primary key (PK) is the unique set of columns, which identifies each row uniquely. Although some databases may allow otherwise, each database table ought to have a PK or we won't be able to pinpoint a row.

> **Primary Keys**
> Each relational database table must have a PK! When designing a table, one of the first things to consider is the PK of the table, which will identify each row uniquely for the entire lifetime of the table.

2 Basic Elements of Relational Databases

Following up on our examples in Table 2.13, let's demonstrate some database tables and spot their primary keys. Table 2.14 shows a table with hotel rooms.

room_no	size	has_jacuzzi	smokeable	bed_count
301	12	true	false	2
302	15	true	false	2
303	6	false	false	1

Table 2.14 Sample room Table of Hotel Rooms

Now, which column uniquely identifies each hotel room? Obviously, room_no is the answer—and in technical terms, room_no is the PK of the room table. Figure 2.13 demonstrates the ERD of this table.

	room		
PK	room_no	int	NOT NULL
	size	int	NOT NULL
	has_jacuzzi	boolean	NOT NULL
	smokeable	boolean	NOT NULL
	bed_count	int	NOT NULL

Figure 2.13 ERD for room Table

Let's get some fresh air by going through an example of a table with airplane seats. Table 2.15 showcases a snapshot of seats on an airplane.

plane_id	row_no	seat_letter	class_id	is_exit_row	is_window	is_aisle
GH789	1	A	BUS	false	true	false
GH789	1	B	BUS	false	false	false
GH789	1	C	BUS	false	false	true
...	...	...	...	...	...	...
PQ567	1	A	ECO	false	true	false

Table 2.15 Snapshot of seat Table

2.3 Keys and Indexing

plane_id	row_no	seat_letter	class_id	is_exit_row	is_window	is_aisle
PQ567	1	B	BUS	false	false	false
PQ567	1	C	BUS	false	false	true

Table 2.15 Snapshot of seat Table (Cont.)

Table contents should be intuitive, and it's safe to assume that we all have experience with airplanes. Our objective here is to uniquely identify an individual airplane seat. Remember, we must be able to pinpoint each table row uniquely, using a single column or a *combination of columns*.

That's the exact case here: a combination of columns!

Imagine a technician being assigned to repair a broken seat. They would need to pinpoint the exact seat first, right? Table 2.16 contains the questions the technician would ask for that purpose.

Questions	Corresponding Columns	Possible Answers
Which airplane has the broken seat?	`plane_id`	PQ567
Which row is the broken seat in?	`row_no`	1
What's the letter of the broken seat?	`seat_letter`	B

Table 2.16 Questions to Ask to Pinpoint Broken Seat

So, only a combination of airplane ID, row number, and seat letter can uniquely identify a certain seat. In our database correspondence, a combination of `plane_id`, `row_no`, and `seat_letter` can uniquely identify a row in the seat table. Thus, we build our PK, as demonstrated in Figure 2.14.

> **Singular versus Composite Primary Keys**
>
> We can sometimes define a PK by using a single column, which we would call a *singular key*. We used this in our hotel room sample case.
>
> In some cases, though, we can only define a PK with a combination of multiple columns, which we would call a *composite key*. We used this in our airplane seat sample case.

Be aware that PKs are also important in performance considerations. If you know the PK of the row you're looking for and provide it in your SQL statement, the database will find this row extremely fast! On the other hand, if you search for entries without knowing their PKs, the database will have to scan through all entries in the table, making the search slower. Indexes can help here, though, and we'll introduce them in Section 2.3.3.

51

2   Basic Elements of Relational Databases

		seat	
PK	plane_id	varchar(10)	NOT NULL
PK	row_no	int	NOT NULL
PK	seat_letter	char(1)	NOT NULL
	class_id	char(3)	NOT NULL
	is_exit_row	boolean	NOT NULL
	is_window	boolean	NOT NULL
	is_aisle	boolean	NOT NULL

Figure 2.14 ERD for seat Table

This concludes our overview of PKs. Now, we can advance towards the next key type: foreign keys.

2.3.2   Foreign Keys

A small disclosure first: you already saw foreign keys (FKs) in action in Section 2.2.3, when we referred to the author table from the book table. Now that you have a solid grasp of PKs, we can give you a formal introduction to FKs.

Conceptually, *foreign keys* are nothing more than rows in different tables that refer to each other.

Now, how would a technician refer to an airplane? By its unique ID, right? They could say, "Airplane GH789 is parked next to airplane PQ567," and everyone would understand accurately which planes they're talking about because they've mentioned the unique identifiers (the PKs) of the airplanes.

However, if the technician said, "The big airplane is parked next to the dirty airplane," it would be ambiguous because there could be multiple big or dirty airplanes. So, PKs are of the essence for unique identification.

In database terms, an FK is a column (or a set of columns) in one table that uniquely refers to a row in another table.

Enhancing the example of airplanes, Table 2.17 demonstrates possible contents of the database table containing airplanes. Let's call this table plane.

While we're at it, let's create the ERD for this table too (see Figure 2.15).

2.3 Keys and Indexing

plane_id	brand	model	manufacture_year	capacity
GH789	BOEING	737	2015	180
PQ567	AIRBUS	A320	2018	150
SS839	BOEING	747	2012	400
BZ123	EMBRAER	E175	2020	88

Table 2.17 Snapshot of plane Table

	plane		
PK	plane_id	varchar(10)	NOT NULL
	brand	varchar(10)	NOT NULL
	model	varchar(5)	NOT NULL
	manufacture_year	int	NOT NULL
	capacity	int	NOT NULL

Figure 2.15 ERD for plane Table

Do you remember that our seat table in Table 2.15 contains the plane_id for each seat entry? By making seat.plane_id an FK, we can refer it to plane.plane_id and make sure each seat entry has a correspondence to the plane table, as shown in Figure 2.16.

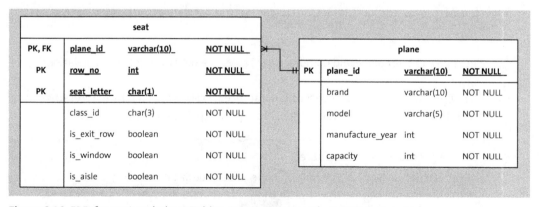

Figure 2.16 ERD for seat and plane Tables, Demonstrating Their FK Relationship

This surely helps with data integrity; you can only create seat rows for airplanes that actually exist in the table plane, and other people can much more easily understand our data structure!

> **Data Types of Foreign Keys**
>
> Relational databases generally enforce the requirement that FKs have the same data type as the PKs they reference. In our example, seat.plane_id and plane.plane_id have the exact same data type: varchar(10), and this is no coincidence! Since those fields contain the exact same values, they must have the exact same data type.

In this example, seat.plane_id is a PK of seat. However, this is not a necessity! There may also be cases in which the referring column is not a PK, as illustrated in Figure 2.17.

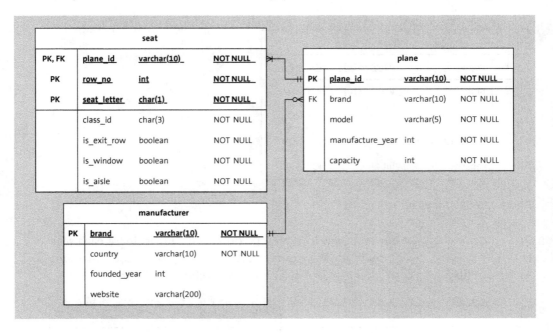

Figure 2.17 ERD for plane and manufacturer Tables, Demonstrating Their FK Relationship

Although plane.brand is not part of manufacturer.brand's PK, it can still refer to manufacturer.brand with an FK relationship. This is perfectly legit and quite normal.

> **Primary Keys in Referred Tables**
>
> The referred-to field in the master table should be a PK. In our example, manufacturer.brand can be referred to as an FK by other tables because it's a PK, but manufacturer.founded_year shouldn't be referred to as an FK. This makes sense, too, because a key must be a unique identifier, and a unique identifier would be the PK of the master table anyway.
>
> If that sounds a bit too complicated, no worries! In due course, we'll go over many examples, and you'll gain intuition regarding key relationships. Just keep reading!

Defining FK constraints is technically optional, but in practice, it's required by development standards in many cases. Also, there are many advantages to defining FK constraints, as listed in Table 2.18.

Advantages	Explanations
Data integrity	FKs ensure that data references are based on existing master data, preventing inconsistent orphan records. The `plane` table can't have a row without a corresponding `manufacturer` row.
Data uniqueness	FKs prevent data duplication. In Figure 2.17, we don't have to duplicate `manufacturer` columns into `plane`. Following the FK constraint between `plane.brand` and `manufacturer.brand`, we can access the master data of the corresponding manufacturer when needed.
Clarity	FKs make data structures much easier to understand. Even a brand-new employee can follow the data structure in Figure 2.17 and understand the logic.
Development	Many development applications provide tools for data visualization or code generation, which work dependent on FK definition.

Table 2.18 Some Advantages of FK Constraints

This concludes our content regarding FKs. Now, we'll move forward to a relatively optional topic: indexes.

2.3.3 Indexes

An *index* is actually not a database key type, but keys and indexes are loosely related concepts, so we'll cover them here.

To help you understand indexes, we'll sail through an example of customer orders. Figure 2.18 demonstrates our corresponding tables.

	order			
PK	id	int	NOT NULL	
FK	customer_id	int	NOT NULL	
	order_date	date	NOT NULL	
	total_amount	numeric(12, 2)	NOT NULL	
	currency	varchar(3)	NOT NULL	

	customer		
PK	id	int	NOT NULL
	name	varchar(50)	NOT NULL
	email	varchar(50)	
	is_active	boolean	NOT NULL

Figure 2.18 ERD for Customer Orders

2   Basic Elements of Relational Databases

The customer table stores the master data of our customers, while the order table stores the orders they placed over the entire history of our company. So, the number of rows in the order table may get really big over time. Table 2.19 shows some entries on the order table to give you a better idea.

id	customer_id	order_date	total_amount	currency
ORD001	7438	2024-07-20	170.75	USD
ORD002	8393	2024-07-21	89.50	USD
ORD003	8392	2024-07-22	230.00	EUR
ORD004	7438	2024-07-23	312.20	USD
ORD005	1002	2024-07-24	75.00	EUR

Table 2.19 Content Snapshot of order Table

Now, imagine an actual customer calling a sales representative and asking about the total price of an order they placed last week.

If the customer can provide their order number, the sales representative can spot the record immediately. Practically speaking, when the representative enters the order number into their screen and hits **Search**, their program will access order using order.id, which is its PK.

Now, let's warm up to SQL a little. Listing 2.1 contains the simple SQL statement to access an order table row by its PK.

```
SELECT
    *
FROM
    order
WHERE
    id = 'ORD005';
```

Listing 2.1 Order Query Using PK

Table 2.20 demonstrates the *only* result that would be returned from this statement. There can be only one result because a PK value may correspond to only one unique row.

id	customer_id	order_date	total_amount	currency
ORD005	1002	2024-07-24	75.00	EUR

Table 2.20 Result of PK-Based Query

Relational databases love PKs! Whenever you can provide them, they get back to you with blazing fast results in most cases. PK access is arguably the fastest way to find a row.

Now, there may also be cases in which the customer doesn't remember the order ID but remembers the date on which they placed the order. This is very common in customer service, so practically speaking, when the representative enters the order date into their screen and hits **Search**, their program will access order by using order.order_date—which is *not* its PK.

In such cases, the poor database engine will have to scan through all the rows in the order table and return entries that have the provided order_date value. Listing 2.2 contains a simple SQL statement to access an order table row by a date.

```
SELECT
    *
FROM
    order
WHERE
    order_date = '2024-07-24';
```

Listing 2.2 Order Query Using Date

If the order table contains only a handful of rows, this query may still run fast. However, in a table with millions of rows, such queries may take a very long time to complete and frustrate both customers and sales representatives!

That's where indexes come in play. Our relational database gives us the option to create an index for order.order_date. Upon initial creation of the index, the database will automatically create a secondary data structure for order.order_date, which it will then use like a book index to find order rows quickly whenever the order table is searched by date. And whenever an order table row is updated or deleted, the database engine will modify the index accordingly.

Book Indexes

Just as their name suggests, database indexes work like book indexes. You can find certain topics in a book by using the index at the very end, instead of reading through the entire book. The same applies to database indexes—you use them to find corresponding rows instead of reading through the entire table.

In Chapter 4, you'll see appropriate SQL statements that you can use to create indexes. For now, let's just focus on their purpose.

In most cases, the speeds of queries with indexed columns are not comparable to those without indexed columns. Indexed columns will almost always execute much faster, and the thing is, you don't even need to explicitly tell the database to make use of the index! When you execute Listing 2.2, the database will find and use the `order.order_date` index automatically, returning rows very quickly.

> **Index Hints**
>
> Many database products allow programmers to provide hints on which index to use. If you don't trust the database to pick the correct index, you can still make it use your index of choice by mentioning it in your SQL statement. But most of the time, databases make good decisions and use the appropriate indexes.

In our example, we went through an index containing a single field: `order.order_date`. However, it's also possible to create composite indexes containing multiple fields, just like the composite PKs seen in Section 2.3.1.

If indexes speed stuff up dramatically, then why don't we create dozens of indexes for each database table, just in case? That approach doesn't work that well because indexes come with compromises. Some of the most significant costs of using indexes are as follows:

- **Disk space**
  Just like a book index occupies additional pages, a database index occupies additional disk space. That can sometimes be a problem on large tables.
- **Performance overhead**
  Although indexes speed up some read operations, they slow down some other operations. Every time a record is created, changed, or deleted, the database must change the table itself and all indexes of the table—which has a performance cost during runtime.
- **Maintenance effort**
  Over time, indexes can become fragmented and even degrade performance, so periodic maintenance like reindexing may be needed.
- **Complexity**
  With many indexes present, the database engine may perform poorly because it can't pick the most efficient index.

Therefore, it's advisable to have a reasonable approach towards indexes. Some cases in which an index may not be desirable are as follows:

- Small tables, where read operations are fast anyway
- Tables with high write frequencies
- Columns with a low number of distinct values, such as `boolean` types
- Columns with long text or binary data

Building an accurate index plan requires some developer experience. When used appropriately, though, indexes speed up queries and improve users' quality of life! So don't be afraid of using indexes—just be mindful of not overusing them when they may not be needed in the first place. You don't want to over-engineer things by providing solutions to nonexistent problems.

2.4 Normalization

Normalization is actually not a component of relational databases, but it's so common and prevalent that it's as inseparable from relational databases as their components. Therefore, it makes sense to talk about it here.

Normalization is a development inquiry through standardized steps involving best practices of relational data organization. Once we go through these steps and modify our data structures accordingly, we can expect to end up with an improved blueprint.

Senior developers can usually design normalized data structures on their first attempts—that comes with years of practice and experience. However, it's good to have a guideline for novice developers to check their structures against!

Now that we know about tables and their relationships, the best way to understand normalization is to see it in action. Table 2.21 contains our starting point. It's a table containing a company's drivers, their managers, and the plate numbers of cars they're allowed to drive.

driver_id	driver_name	manager	manager_ext	car_1	car_2	car_3
1022	Jordan Lee	Alex Mitchell	345	XJ4P2T9	B9R3L7Q	M6V1H8Z
1023	Casey Morgan	Jamie Carter	123	XJ4P2T9	K2S8N4R	L1K4P8S

Table 2.21 Initial Look of Driver Data

This is what a basic spreadsheet page of drivers could look like. Can you spot the problems on this table already? If not, keep reading!

2.4.1 First Normal Form

According to the first normal form (1NF), tables should have only two dimensions. We should therefore get rid of repeating columns that cause multidimensionality in the table.

Our initial table features such a case: `car_1`, `car_2`, and `car_3` are repeating columns. What we need to do in 1NF is to break it down into a flat structure, listing each car in a different row. Table 2.22 shows the end result.

2 Basic Elements of Relational Databases

driver_id	driver_name	manager	manager_ext	car
1022	Jordan Lee	Alex Mitchell	345	XJ4P2T9
1022	Jordan Lee	Alex Mitchell	345	B9R3L7Q
1022	Jordan Lee	Alex Mitchell	345	M6V1H8Z
1023	Casey Morgan	Jamie Carter	123	XJ4P2T9
1023	Casey Morgan	Jamie Carter	123	K2S8N4R
1023	Casey Morgan	Jamie Carter	123	L1K4P8S

Table 2.22 First Normal Form Applied to Driver Data

As you can see, our table is two dimensional now. It looks nicer and cleaner, but not nice and clean enough! Let's try to improve our data structure further.

2.4.2 Second Normal Form

According to the second normal form (2NF), redundant data should be eliminated. We need to break columns causing redundancy into distinct tables.

In our example, the car column has redundant data because we had to duplicate driver master data for each car the drivers can drive. Instead of having single rows for drivers **1022** and **1023**, we have three of each, making six in total.

Table 2.23 showcases the table we need. We ought to store driver-car assignments in a separate table.

driver_id	car
1022	XJ4P2T9
1022	B9R3L7Q
1022	M6V1H8Z
1023	XJ4P2T9
1023	K2S8N4R
1023	L1K4P8S

Table 2.23 Driver-Car Assignments after Second Normal Form

Our driver master table is free of cars now and contains only one row per driver without any redundancies, as shown in Table 2.24.

Now, we're almost there. Just one more step!

2.4 Normalization

driver_id	driver_name	manager	manager_ext
1022	Jordan Lee	Alex Mitchell	345
1023	Casey Morgan	Jamie Carter	123

Table 2.24 Driver Master Data After Second Normal Form

2.4.3 Third Normal Form

According to the third normal form (3NF), we ought to eliminate columns that don't belong to the table PK.

If we look at Table 2.24 closely, it's is supposed to be a driver table, but we see manager data there, such as their names and extension numbers. That's not good. Drivers should have their own table, and managers should have their own table.

Let's start by giving managers a dedicated table, as shown in Table 2.25.

manager_id	manager_name	manager_ext
34	Alex Mitchell	345
35	Jamie Carter	123

Table 2.25 Manager Master Data after Third Normal Form

Now that we have a distinct manager table, we can simply refer to it as a FK. Table 2.26 shows the final driver data form.

driver_id	driver_name	manager_id
1022	Jordan Lee	34
1023	Casey Morgan	35

Table 2.26 Driver Master Data after Third Normal Form

2.4.4 Results

By going through the minimum steps of normalization, we've arrived at the ERD shown in Figure 2.19, which is free from redundancies and potential conflicts!

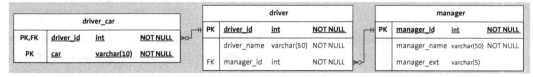

Figure 2.19 Final ERD of Normalized Tables

2 Basic Elements of Relational Databases

We can go even further and create a distinct master data table for cars, but let's stop here.

Mind you that having a normalized data structure is not a luxury—it's one of the fundamental expectations from a decent developer, and for good reason too! Normalized data structures feature many benefits, such as the following:

- Elimination of data redundancy
- Improvement of data integrity
- Enhanced query performance
- Simplified database maintenance
- Improved data relationships

> **Further Normal Forms**
>
> 1NF, 2NF and, 3NF are the minimum steps of normalization. Once our tables align with those forms, their structure will provide a good degree of redundancy prevention while maintaining manageable complexity.
>
> There are further forms, such as the Boyce-Codd normal form (BCNF), the fourth normal form (4NF) and the fifth normal form (5NF). Since this book is focused on SQL, we won't delve deeper into those topics. Understanding the basics of normalization is enough for us, but feel free to do more research if you want to!

Now that we've grasped the basics of normalization, we can move forward with further database elements.

2.5 Operations

We all know that relational databases are crucial for application development—they're a robust option for data storage. Also, end users rarely access databases directly, if ever. Instead, they typically interact with applications powered by relational databases and developed by programmers.

Since databases are under the spotlight of programmers, it makes sense for programmers to have multiple development options. One option is to steer the database using one-time SQL statements, and another option is to access the database by using your preferred programming language (such as Python) and executing autogenerated SQL statements.

Additionally, most relational databases feature internal mechanisms for special tasks. They are stored procedures and triggers, which we'll discuss in the following sections.

2.5.1 Stored Procedures

A stored procedure is basically a SQL subroutine written for a special task; it's saved on the database and waiting to be executed. Whenever the stored procedure is executed, all SQL statements within it are processed and executed sequentially.

A good example is a stored procedure that archives old data. Imagine a requirement in which we need to archive order table rows that are more than a year old by moving them to another table called order_archive. Figure 2.20 showcases these tables.

order			
PK	id	int	NOT NULL
	customer_id	int	NOT NULL
	order_date	date	NOT NULL
	total_amount	numeric(12, 2)	NOT NULL
	currency	varchar(3)	NOT NULL

order_archive			
PK	id	int	NOT NULL
	customer_id	int	NOT NULL
	order_date	date	NOT NULL
	total_amount	numeric(12, 2)	NOT NULL
	currency	varchar(3)	NOT NULL
	archive_timestamp	timestamp	NOT NULL

Figure 2.20 ERD for order and order_archive Tables

If this were a one-time task, we could do it manually by using custom SQL statements. Figure 2.21 demonstrates the flowchart of this task.

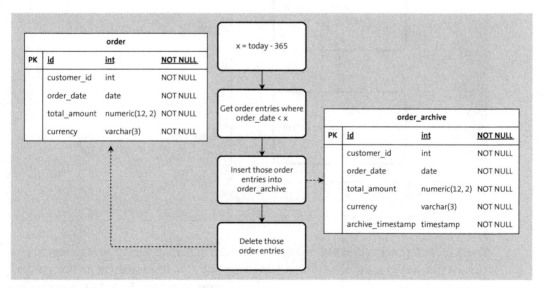

Figure 2.21 Flowchart of Custom SQL Code

But what if we have to execute this archiving task daily? Do we have to write and execute the same SQL statements every day?

2 Basic Elements of Relational Databases

Although doing the manual labor is a possibility, we have a better alternative: we can write our chain of SQL statements only once and save them as a stored procedure in the database. Let's call it `archive_old_orders`. Figure 2.22 contains the flowchart of this stored procedure, which is identical to our custom SQL code!

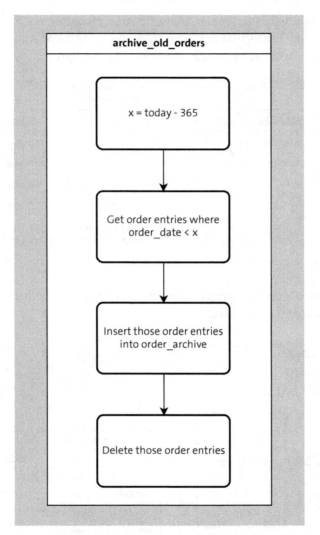

Figure 2.22 Flowchart of archive_old_orders Stored Procedure

The only difference is that we've consolidated our SQL statements under a stored procedure and stored it in the database. Now, whenever we need to archive those orders, all we have to do is to execute the stored procedure. We don't have to rewrite redundant code again and again. If the orders need to be archived periodically, we can also schedule this stored procedure to be executed daily, weekly, monthly, etc.

> **Subroutines**
>
> Stored procedures are basically database subroutines. Different programming languages give different names to subroutines, so you can imagine a stored procedure as a method, function, procedure, routine, action, form, block, or whatever you want!
>
> Using subroutines in databases provides the same benefits as any other programming language. These include reusability, modularity, reduced redundancy, and maintainability.

Although SQL is supported in stored procedures, most databases add further syntax elements and define their own SQL-based procedure language. Some examples are listed in Table 2.27.

Databases	Languages
Microsoft SQL Server	T-SQL
Oracle Database	PL/SQL
PostgreSQL	PL/pgSQL
SAP HANA	SqlScript

Table 2.27 Procedure Languages of Some Databases

Although pure SQL is mostly transportable between different database products, stored procedures are not. Each procedure language has a different syntax and features different command sets. Beyond their coincidental similarities, you can't expect them to be interoperable. For example, copy-and-pasting Oracle PL/SQL Code into Microsoft SQL Server is like copy-and-pasting Java code into a C# editor. Although some syntax elements seem similar, it simply won't run.

In Chapter 5, we'll go over the steps to create stored procedures for PostgreSQL. Now, let's move on to the next topic.

2.5.2 Triggers

Stored procedures are units of code, waiting to be executed. We can execute them manually or on a schedule. *Triggers* offer a similar functionality, but with an important difference. They're executed automatically as a reaction to a predefined data event, such as a data update in a table.

As a case study, we'll go through a requirement involving salaries. Every time a salary is updated, we need to keep a copy of the previous amount in another table for reporting and auditing purposes.

2 Basic Elements of Relational Databases

Figure 2.23 features the ERD of our salary table, containing the current salaries of our employees.

	salary		
PK, FK	employee_id	int	NOT NULL
	salary	numeric(12, 2)	NOT NULL
FK	currency	varchar(3)	NOT NULL

Figure 2.23 ERD for salary Table

The table is very intuitive. We have each employee's employee_id as our PK, and we keep their salary in the salary and currency fields.

Now, let's see our history table as well in Figure 2.24.

	salary		
PK, FK	employee_id	int	NOT NULL
	salary	numeric(12, 2)	NOT NULL
FK	currency	varchar(3)	NOT NULL

	salary_history		
PK,FK	employee_id	int	NOT NULL
PK	history_pos	int	NOT NULL
	salary	numeric(12, 2)	NOT NULL
FK	currency	varchar(3)	NOT NULL
	hist_timestamp	timestamp	NOT NULL

Figure 2.24 ERD for salary Table and Its History

Every time a row in the salary table is changed, we need to insert a new historical row into salary_history, storing the former salary before the change. Our history table has employee_id and a sequential history_pos number as its composite PK, and each new salary_history entry will have the next sequential history_pos value for that employee.

Now, how can we do that?

It's possible to achieve this functionality by using external code—let's say in Python. Anytime we need to insert a new entry into salary, we start the operation by writing the former salary data into the salary_history table.

But it's also possible to achieve the same functionality by using triggers, without external support. We can simply create a trigger containing the appropriate SQL code, which will be executed automatically whenever a row is updated in the salary table. The trigger's code would fetch the former data in the salary table and insert it into the salary_history table automatically. Figure 2.25 demonstrates the architecture of such a trigger.

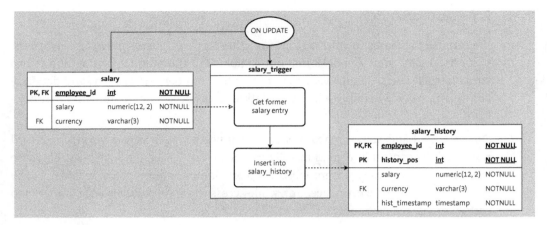

Figure 2.25 Flowchart of salary_trigger

> **Stored Procedures or Triggers?**
>
> Stored procedures and triggers offer similar functionality, and they mostly differ in how they're initiated. In cases where you need to execute a code manually or periodically, using stored procedures is the way to go. On the other hand, if you need to execute a code as a reaction to a transaction in a database table, using triggers is the way to go.

Although showcases a trigger executed upon data insertion, it's possible to set a trigger upon further events. Table 2.28 contains common types of triggers.

Trigger Types	Executed Upon
INSERT	Row creation
UPDATE	Row modification
DELETE	Row deletion
TRUNCATE	Deletion of all rows

Table 2.28 Common Trigger Types

A database table can have multiple triggers that respond to multiple events as well. In our case, we could create a second trigger of the INSERT type, which would execute whenever a new row is inserted into the salary table. But we won't. In Chapter 5, we'll learn how to define our custom triggers in PostgreSQL.

2.6 Authorization

We can use databases to store all kinds of data. Some databases may store harmless, noncritical data, such as books in a public library or the product catalog of a music store. In such cases, data privacy may not be the number-one priority, and database administrators may simply allow all database users access any data without restrictions.

On the other hand, some databases store sensitive data, such as passwords, credit card numbers, VIP contact information, salaries, and private images. In such cases, database administrators typically prefer to restrict access. Some common database tables will be accessible to anyone with an account, while access to sensitive tables will be limited to certain privileged users only.

Database administrators can make such settings via the authorization mechanisms of relational databases. By calling the appropriate SQL statements, they can grant or deny user access to certain database tables. They can even specify the operations a user can execute on a table, such as SELECT, INSERT, and UPDATE.

Figure 2.26 demonstrates a sample authorization plan for Taylor Morgan, a company intern. Taylor is allowed to read customer master data from the customer table but is not allowed to access the credit_card table in any way due to reasons of privacy and security.

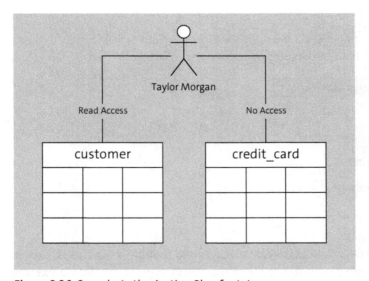

Figure 2.26 Sample Authorization Plan for Intern

Following the same logic, we can set up authorization plans for any number of individual users targeting various tables of our database. However, things start to get complicated when we have a large number of users. Imagine a big company with multiple employees in the finance, sales, and development departments. It would be very cumbersome to set individual authorizations for each user, and imagine creating new tables for each one! Do we have to go through all users and redundantly set individual authorizations for the new table to each of them?

Of course not, because relational databases allow us to create roles. In relational databases, a *role* is a group of permissions that can be assigned to users. Instead of setting individual authorizations to users, we can preset roles and assign them to users.

Case in point: Figure 2.27 demonstrates an authorization plan, which is made of the following roles instead of individual users:

- The finance_role allows read access to the customer table but no access to the credit_card table. Alex, Jordan, Taylor, and Casey inherit those authorizations because the finance_role is assigned to them.
- The sales_role allows full access to both tables. Riley, Avery, Sydney, and Jamie inherit those authorizations because the sales_role is assigned to them.
- The dev_role allows full access to the customer table but no access to the credit_card table. Quinn, Parker, Rowen, and Zoe inherit those authorizations because the dev_role is assigned to them.

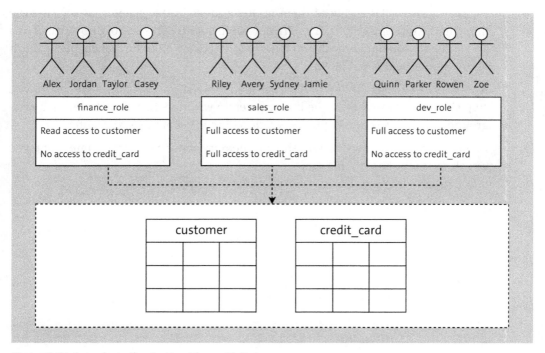

Figure 2.27 Sample Authorization Plan with Roles

If a new member joins the finance department, all we need to do is to assign the finance_role to them. Then, they'll inherit the authorizations of their peers in an instant.

If we create a new table called `customer_balances`, which needs to be accessed by the finance department, all we need to do is to grant access to that table in the `finance_role`. Then, all finance users will gain access to `customer_balances` in an instant.

It's also possible to assign multiple roles to the same user.

Setting up a sound authorization plan and setting up profiles in a big production database is a delicate process, and it's sometimes subject to audits as well. Our purpose is to learn about the basics at this point, but we'll go over the SQL statements regarding authorizations in due course.

2.7 Summary

In this chapter, we learned about the basic elements of relational databases. We went over the individual components that makes the machine work: databases, schemas, tables, views, keys, indexes, procedures, triggers, and authorizations. We also talked about normalization, which is not a technical database component but a globally accepted best practice regarding table relationships.

We mentioned ERDs and used them multiple times in this chapter, as we will keep doing in the rest of the book. If you're not familiar with ERD symbols, now would be a good time to read our appendix on ERDs before moving on to further chapters. This is your last reminder about ERDs!

Now that we've built a theoretical background for relational databases, we can move a step closer to practical SQL. The last step before writing SQL code is to set up a playground database on our computers, which is the subject of the next chapter.

In due course, if you need to refresh your memory about a database component, you can always come back to this chapter.

Chapter 3
Setting Up the Environment

In this chapter, you'll learn to install and set up a local database (PostgreSQL) on your computer, where you'll be able to write SQL code, experiment with the book's SQL code samples, and try out SQL features.

At this point, we've learned about the basics of relational databases, and we're almost ready to start with SQL! After all, that's why we're all here. But there's one final missing matter we need to address: a playground.

To make the best of this book and learn SQL effectively, you need to write SQL code yourself. Ideally, you should implement the code samples in this book yourself and take some extra exploratory steps beyond our examples to help you digest the language a little better. However, you can't do any of that without having access to a playground database. You need an environment where you can practice SQL to create tables, insert test data, query your tables—and do all the other exciting things we'll cover in this book!

This chapter will go over the steps of preparing a basic database setup. If you're like most of our readers, you'll want to install a database instance on your local computer. But don't worry, it won't cost you a thing, and you should be able to uninstall the database later if you want to. Alternatively, you can move forward with an existing database instance.

> **Corporate Policies**
>
> If you're using a corporate computer, mind you that some companies have strict policies on application installation: they simply won't allow you to do so. If you encounter a permission error preventing you from installing the database, you may have to consult with your IT department and ask for help.

Since our examples will be based on PostgreSQL, it would be ideal for you to have the same playground database product and conduct your learning journey on PostgreSQL. But don't fret if you have another database product, such as MySQL, Microsoft SQL Server, or Oracle Database. You can execute most of the code examples on other databases as well, with some occasional minor code adaptation.

If you'll be using an existing database, we advise you to create a separate schema for yourself and do all your work there. This will greatly reduce the risk of damaging neighboring data structures. In due course, you'll learn how to create a schema.

3   Setting Up the Environment

If you feel a bit confused and can't decide on how to proceed, no worries—we've got you covered! Figure 3.1 contains a fun flowchart of our playground recommendations that will guide you to the correct choice.

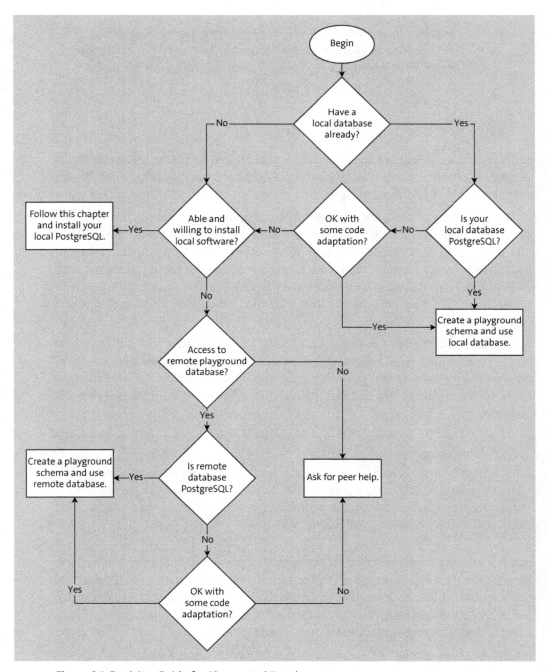

Figure 3.1 Decision Guide for Playground Database

> **Don't Use a Production Database**
>
> Since this will be your learning phase, it's OK to make some mistakes. It's totally normal and expected, we can't be experts without being rookies first, and even experts make mistakes! However, a production database with sensitive data is the last place you want to make a mistake. One wrong SQL statement can cause data loss or inconsistencies, which could cost you dearly. Therefore, we strongly recommend not using a production database as a playground. The safest place to learn SQL is a database instance meant to be a playground.

Once you decide on the strategy that works best for you, you can proceed!

> **Updates**
>
> It's inevitable that "living" applications get updated over time, and the guidance and screenshots in this chapter correspond to the most recent software versions on the date this book was written. Future updates may represent different GUI elements or require different installation steps, and in such cases, you can always refer to official installation documents and follow published guidelines.
>
> Websites are also updated all the time. Some updates are minor content modifications, while others may include a complete overhaul. Although a base domain like *www.postgresql.org* is unlikely to change, the URLs of certain pages (such as download pages) may change over time.
>
> To preserve the accuracy of this chapter over time, we'll provide section names instead of direct URLs. You can easily spot the mentioned section under the base domain and proceed from there.

3.1 Our Database of Choice

As mentioned, the playground database product of this book will be PostgreSQL. You can use another relational database product if you must, but we recommend using PostgreSQL for the highest degree of code compatibility.

You might wonder why we picked PostgreSQL from among the alternatives. Let's go over the reasons for our decision.

First of all, PostgreSQL is a community-owned relational database product that's free and open source. Its current approach allows you to use it for any purpose you want, without license costs. Installing a local instance for personal education is definitely allowed, and that's the purpose of this book.

PostgreSQL is also a very popular database product with strong community and documentation support. If you have an issue or a question regarding PostgreSQL, you're sure to find help easily. Its popularity also makes your skills valuable in the job market.

> **Popularity of PostgreSQL**
> Stack Overflow's annual survey in 2023 showcased the fact that PostgreSQL is the most popular database among professional developers, surpassing the competition. You can find the survey at *https://survey.stackoverflow.co/2023/*.

PostgreSQL is also a multiplatform database product. It's available for most common operating systems, such as macOS, Windows, and Linux. This probably covers all of our reader base, but no matter what kind of computer you're on, PostgreSQL should be available to you.

PostgreSQL also provides easy-to-use wizard-like installers, which is good news for newbies because you don't have to go through complicated installation and configuration steps to start using it. Installation is straightforward, and the default configuration allows you to start with SQL immediately!

PostgreSQL has correspondence to all SQL features we'll cover in this book, and that's naturally expected from a decent playground. PostgreSQL closely adheres to ANSI SQL standards as well, so the code you'll write for PostgreSQL will be highly portable most of the time. Beyond that, it offers advanced features, such as advanced indexing, full-text search, custom data types, extensions, and table inheritance and partitioning. Although those features are beyond core SQL and may not be covered in this book, using them can future proof your time investment in PostgreSQL. When the need arises, you can learn those features and add them to your technical toolbox.

PostgreSQL features a usable GUI application to help you manage the database and—most importantly—write SQL code. Through the provided pgAdmin application, you can start writing and executing SQL code immediately. Beyond its default GUI, PostgreSQL has a rich ecosystem, and there's a wide range of third-party extensions and tools available.

Professional developers usually connect to databases and execute generated SQL code from their favorite programming languages. Due to its popularity, PostgreSQL has ready-to-use drivers targeting many common environments, such as Python, Java, PHP, C#, Node.JS, Golang, and Rust. If you want to go beyond manual SQL and make PostgreSQL part of your next development project, you'll most likely be able to.

> **Other Databases**
> To prevent any misunderstandings, we would like to clarify that we don't mean to state that alternative database products don't have the aforementioned features at all or are inferior in any way. Quite the contrary—many relational databases share similar features but naturally differ from others on certain points.

> However, PostgreSQL provides a unique combination of the features mentioned above. This makes it our preferred choice for learning purposes, but the fact that it's our choice doesn't mean that it's objectively superior to its alternatives.
>
> Each database product has different pros and cons, and picking the most suitable one is a matter of individual case-by-case evaluation. PostgreSQL might be the best choice in some cases, while another relational database might be the best in others.

Now that we've justified our choice of PostgreSQL, let's move forward and prepare the playground database.

Our end goal is to have the following two components ready to use:

- A backend database engine
- A frontend application you can use to access the database and code SQL

3.2 Local Database Setup

If you'll use a remote database as a playground, or if you have a local database already, you can skip this topic and move on to Section 3.3. Otherwise, keep reading! Our setup guide will focus on Windows and macOS, due to their popularity.

> **Operating Systems**
> According to multiple credible sources, such as *StatCounter* and *Statista*, desktop operating systems are dominated by Windows and macOS, with a cumulative usage rate of nearly 90%. Therefore, our setup guide will focus on these operating systems.

If you're a Linux user, you'll be pleased to know that PostgreSQL is available in many common Linux distributions already. You may not have to install anything at all, so please consult the documentation of your distribution or the downloads section of the official PostgreSQL website at *www.postgresql.org*.

This website section also includes setup guides for all supported operating systems. If you have an uncommon operating system or need other installation help, then you can find guidance there.

Depending on your operating system, you can follow the corresponding section that follows.

3.2.1 Windows Installation

Visit *www.postgresql.org*, go to the **Download** section, and click on **Windows**. Find the link called **Download the installer** and download the latest PostgreSQL version corresponding to your Windows version.

3   Setting Up the Environment

The installer should contain both the engine and the GUI, so you'll be good to go with a single download! Once the download is completed, you can execute the downloaded file and follow on-screen instructions. Let's go through those steps together.

The installer will greet us as seen in Figure 3.2, so just click **Next** to continue. (You'll click **Next** on each screen to move through the individual installation steps.)

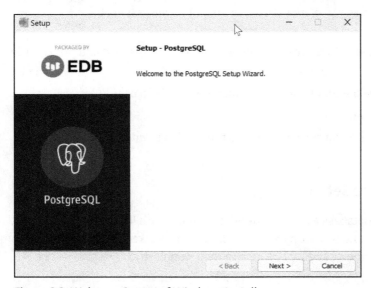

Figure 3.2 Welcome Screen of Windows Installer

The installer will ask you for a target installation directory, as shown in Figure 3.3. You can use the suggested directory or point the installer somewhere else if you need to.

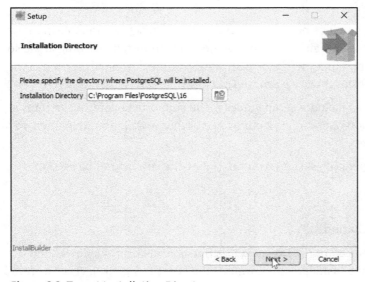

Figure 3.3 Target Installation Directory

3.2 Local Database Setup

In the next step, the installer will ask about the components to install, as shown in Figure 3.4. You can simply select everything here, and if you want to minimize the footprint, you should at least select **PostgreSQL Server** and pgAdmin.

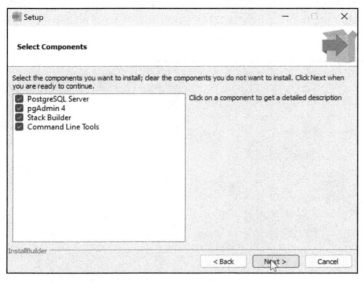

Figure 3.4 Components to Be Installed

The installer will continue by asking you to point to a data directory, as shown in Figure 3.5. This will be the place where all databases, schemas, tables, datasets, etc., will be stored. You can simply proceed with the suggested default value or select a different directory if you need to.

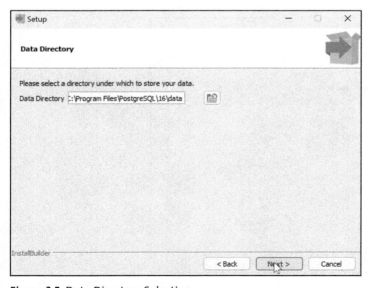

Figure 3.5 Data Directory Selection

3   Setting Up the Environment

Then, you'll be asked to provide a password for the special **postgres** account, as seen in Figure 3.6. This is a special user that can act like an administrator to setup and configure every aspect of the database. In a production environment, we advise that you use a strong password. In a local playground, you'll use for nothing else, you can proceed with an easy-to-remember password (such as **1234**). Don't forget your password since you'll need it later!

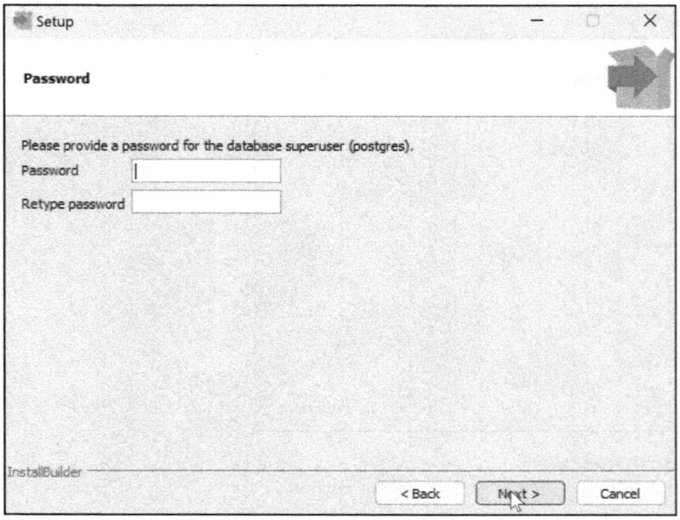

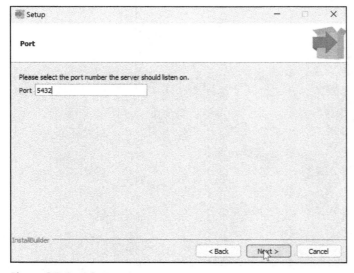

Figure 3.6 Password Request

The next screen will ask you for a database port, as shown in Figure 3.7. This will be the port on which PostgreSQL will be listening to incoming connections.

Figure 3.7 Port Request

78

In a production environment, it might be a good idea to change the default port to prevent any possible attackers from easily spotting your database. In a local playground installation, you can simply go forward with the default port, except in the unlikely case that another service is using this port already. In that case, you can pick a different port.

The next screen will ask you for the database locale you'll be using, as seen in Figure 3.8. A *locale* is a set of regional settings that determine how data is stored and displayed in a database. It contains aspects like character sets, date and time formats, and currency formats.

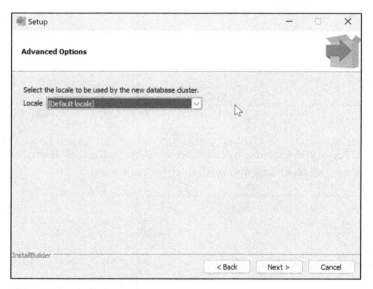

Figure 3.8 Locale Request

We recommend proceeding with the **English – US locale**. If you need a different locale, you can pick another one from the combo box.

Picking a Different Locale

In some rare cases, PostgreSQL installation may finish with an error message like **Database cluster initialization failed**. If you encounter such an error message, you can uninstall PostgreSQL and reinstall it—but this time, pick a different locale. The default locale or a regional locale may fail, but **English – US** should work OK in most cases.

Although a production database ought to be installed with the most appropriate locale, it's not a big deal in a playground database.

The next window will summarize your choices, as shown in Figure 3.9. If you see anything wrong here, you'll have the chance to go back and correct it as needed.

3   Setting Up the Environment

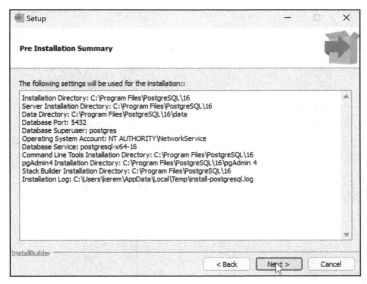

Figure 3.9 Summary of Choices

The final window will inform you that the installation is ready to start, as shown in Figure 3.10. You can simply click **Next** and wait until the process is over.

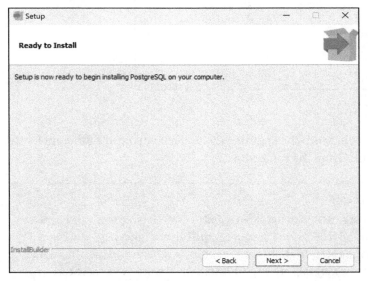

Figure 3.10 Final Window Before Installation

After the installation is completed, you may be asked if you want to set up Stack Builder. This is not needed for a playground database, so you can simply refuse to do so.

If everything has gone well so far, you should be able to find the files in the installation directory, and the PostgreSQL engine should be running as a Windows service in the background, waiting for connections and SQL statements. This service should start automatically when you restart your computer, so you don't have to worry about that.

3.2.2 macOS Installation

Although PostgreSQL can be installed as a fully featured set of packages, there's also a lightweight alternative that we're going to follow. Postgres.app is a standalone native macOS app that runs by itself without any possible headaches on the user's side. We'll simply download and install this app, and that's it—we'll have a functional playground database!

Visit *www.postgresapp.com*, go to **Downloads,** and download the latest application version corresponding to your macOS version. This installer will contain the engine. Once the download is completed, you can execute the downloaded file and follow the on-screen instructions. Let's go through these steps together.

Initially, you'll be welcomed with a window that will indicate you should drag and drop the contained **Postgres.app** file to your **Applications** folder; as shown in Figure 3.11.

Figure 3.11 Initial Welcome Window

Click the **Applications** folder and drag and drop **Postgres.app** there as requested. Once you're done, you should see **Postgres.app** among your other applications in this folder, as shown in Figure 3.12.

Figure 3.12 Postgres.app in Applications Folder

Now, double-click **Postgres.app** and start the application. The initial application window will launch with a warning like **Empty data directory**, as shown in Figure 3.13.

3 Setting Up the Environment

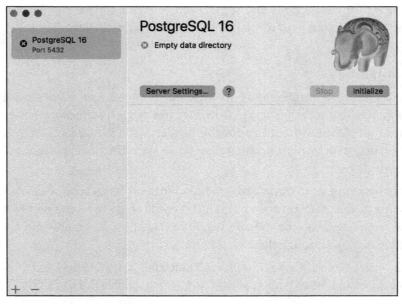

Figure 3.13 Initial Database Application

Once you click **Initialize**, the application will create its default databases and display their names, as shown in Figure 3.14.

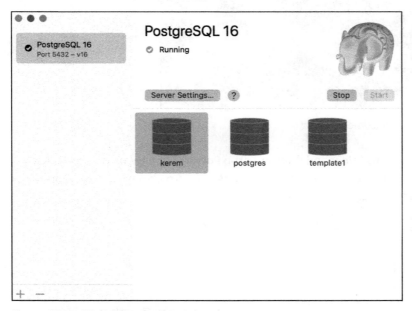

Figure 3.14 Initialized Default Databases

The postgres database will be the default database of your playground, so keep that name in mind. You can pick or create another one if you want, of course!

The database engine has been created without an administrator password, and you can keep it that way if you want—since this is just a playground, there's no sensitive data to worry about. But if you want to follow best practices and set a password, then hit **Stop**, select and then click **Server Settings,** and follow up with **Change Password**. This will bring up the prompt shown in Figure 3.15.

Figure 3.15 Setting Administrator Password

Here, you should select the **postgres** user. This is a special user that can act like an administrator to set up and configure every aspect of the database. In a production environment, we advise that you use a strong password, but in a local playground that you'll use for nothing else, you can use an easy-to-remember password (such as **1234**). Don't forget your password—you'll need it later!

Once you click **Change Password**, you're good to go! You can hit **Start** to fire up the database engine once again.

That concludes the setup of the database engine. By default, the engine will start up every time you turn on your Mac, so you don't have to worry about that.

3.3　SQL IDE Setup

Now that the engine is ready, you can move forward with the installation of a GUI application, which you'll use to connect to the database engine and write SQL statements.

If you already have a SQL IDE that you like, it means that you're an experienced reader. You can use your favorite application to connect to the playground database engine, so you can skip this section.

3   Setting Up the Environment

For the rest of us, there are different alternatives.

The pgAdmin application is the "official" PostgreSQL application to connect to servers and execute SQL code. We'll go over the steps to set up pgAdmin on your computer.

However, pgAdmin is not the only tool for the task. There are countless third-party applications and extensions that are designed for your convenience and that you can use for the same purpose. Although it's impossible to cover them all, we'll go over the setup of Visual Studio Code (VS Code) as an alternative tool. Just like pgAdmin, you can use VS Code on any common operating system. It's also free for personal use.

> **Visual Studio Code**
>
> In Stack Overflow 2023 Developer Survey, available at *https://survey.stackoverflow.co/2023*, Visual Studio Code (VS Code) came out as the most popular coding tool among developers. This makes it one of the preferred integrated development environments (IDEs) for SQL coding.

Make your choice and install your tool of choice by following the installation steps in the next sections. Feel free to install and check both and decide which one you like better.

3.3.1   pgAdmin

In this section, we'll cover pgAdmin installation on both Windows and macOS before moving on to the initial database setup and testing out SQL.

Windows Installation

The Windows version of PostgreSQL that we discussed in Section 3.2.1 already includes a copy of pgAdmin. If you've followed our local PostgreSQL installation, you don't have to install anything else; you can skip this step and proceed to pgAdmin setup. Also, if you haven't installed a local database instance, you can still follow the steps in Section 3.2.1 but select **pgAdmin** as the only installation component in Figure 3.4.

macOS Installation

If you're a macOS user, you should visit *www.pgadmin.org*, go to **Download**, find the title **pgAdmin**, click **macOS**, and download the latest application version corresponding to your macOS version. Mind you that you may need to pick a different file depending on your central processing unit (CPU). Intel users need to download the x86 version, while M* users need to download the ARM version.

Execute the downloaded the file, and you'll be greeted with the license agreement in Figure 3.16, which you should accept by clicking **Agree**.

3.3 SQL IDE Setup

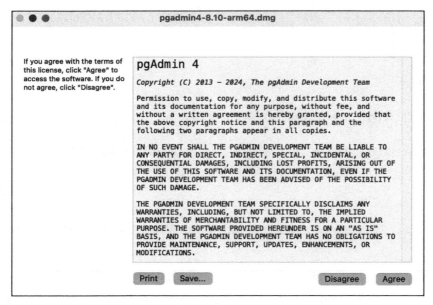

Figure 3.16 License Agreement for pgAdmin

Similar to what we've seen before, you'll be greeted by a window that indicates you should drag and drop the contained **pgAdmin 4**.app file to your **Applications** folder, as shown in Figure 3.17.

Figure 3.17 Drag and Drop Request for pgAdmin 4.App

Open the **Applications** folder and drag and drop **pgAdmin 4.app** there as requested. Once you're done, you should see **pgAdmin 4.app** among your other applications in this folder, as shown in Figure 3.18.

85

3 Setting Up the Environment

Figure 3.18 Applications Folder Containing pgAdmin 4.app

That concludes our installation! Now, we can move forward with the initial database setup.

Setup

Launch pgAdmin. The application will start with its initial window, as shown in Figure 3.19.

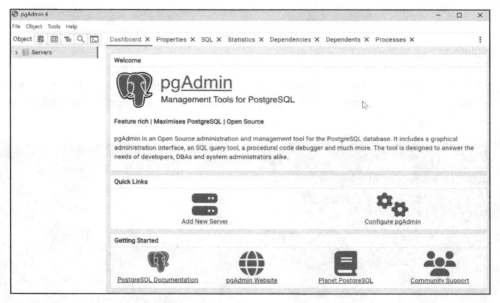

Figure 3.19 Initial pgAdmin Window

There are a lot of components and settings in this window, but you don't need to worry about them at this point. The defaults are more than able to run SQL statements.

The first thing you need to do is to connect to your local PostgreSQL instance. Click **Quick Links • Add New Server** or right-click the **Servers** element on the left and click **Add New Server**.

Mind you that this action is not creating a new PostgreSQL server. You're merely introducing an existing PostgreSQL server/engine into pgAdmin so that they can connect and communicate.

The window in Figure 3.20 should then show up. In the **General** tab, you can give your database a meaningful name, such as "local."

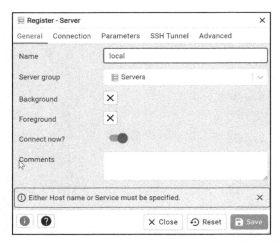

Figure 3.20 General Server Parameters

Then, move forward to Connection tab, as shown in Figure 3.21, and provide the parameters as outlined in Table 3.1.

Fields	Values	Defaults
Host name/address	The Network address of the target PostgreSQL server	localhost
Port	The Port number provided during installation.	5432
Maintenance database	The target default database.	postgres
Username	The administrator name provided during installation.	postgres
Password	The administrator password.	1234
Save password	If this is set, pgAdmin will store the password and won't ask again.	YES

Table 3.1 Connection Tab Parameters

Save the connection and close the window. If everything goes well, you should see the local PostgreSQL instance on the server list of pgAdmin, as demonstrated in Figure 3.22.

> **Shortcuts for pgAdmin**
>
> For convenience, you can create a shortcut for pgAdmin for easy access. Windows users can add it to the start menu, while Mac users can keep pgAdmin in the dock.

3 Setting Up the Environment

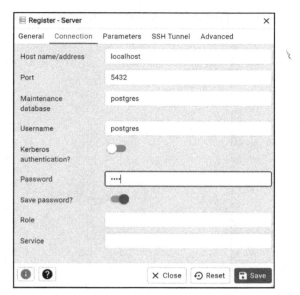

Figure 3.21 Connection Parameters

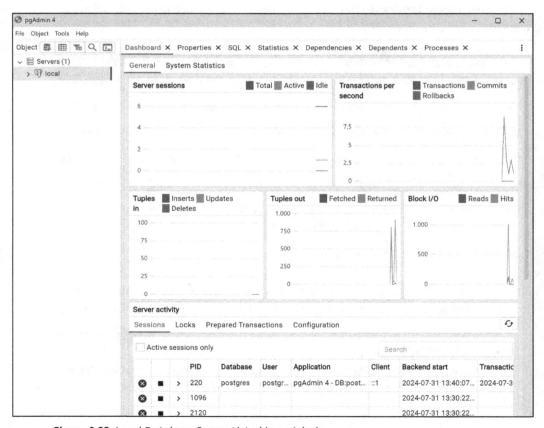

Figure 3.22 Local Database Server Listed in pgAdmin

Now that you've established the bridge between pgAdmin and the local database engine, you should be able to see the connection under the server list. In pgAdmin, unfold **Servers** as demonstrated in Figure 3.23 and ensure that you can see **local • Databases • postgres**.

Figure 3.23 Local Database Engine under pgAdmin Server List

Upon unfolding **Schemas**, you should also see the **public** schema underneath.

By default, we'll use the **postgres** database and the **public** schema in our examples. Since this is merely a playground, there's no harm in that, but you can use any other database or schema if you want to. This may be especially significant if you're sharing the database with others.

That's all there is to it! Now, you can connect to your local PostgreSQL instance using pgAdmin. The next step is to see how to write SQL code in pgAdmin.

3 Setting Up the Environment

SQL Test

Now, we come to a critical part: how can you write custom SQL code via pgAdmin? After all, that's what this section is all about: you should be able to try out the code samples for yourself.

Fortunately, this is very easy! Right-click the public schema (or your playground schema of choice) and select **Query Tool**, as shown in Figure 3.24.

Figure 3.24 Launching Query Tool in pgAdmin

This will open a code editor, where you can enter your SQL statement and execute. Easy peasy!

Listing 3.1 contains a SQL statement to create a table. Don't worry about understanding the SQL code at this point.

```
CREATE TABLE employee(
    id int PRIMARY KEY,
    first_name varchar(50),
    last_name varchar(50)
);
```

Listing 3.1 Sample SQL Statement to Create Table

Figure 3.25 demonstrates the execution of a SQL statement. After typing the statement in Listing 3.1 into the **Query** section, you should click the **Play** icon on the toolbar to execute.

As you can see, the database engine has happily processed your statement and created a new database table! Check **Schemas** • **public** • **Tables** • **employee**.

3.3 SQL IDE Setup

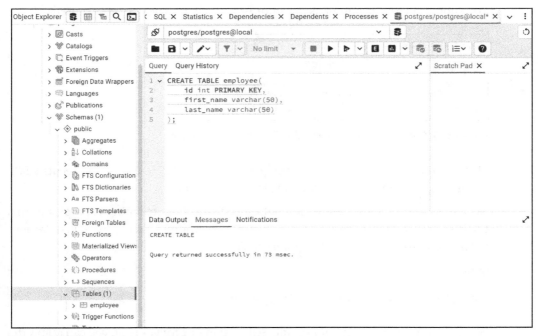

Figure 3.25 Executing Sample SQL Statement

Let's test another SQL statement! This time, you'll try to insert a new entry into your new table. Using the same steps, execute the SQL statement in Listing 3.2.

```
INSERT INTO
    employee (id, first_name, last_name)
VALUES
    (1, 'Kerem', 'Koseoglu');
```

Listing 3.2 Sample SQL Statement to Create Entry

This should create a new entry in the employee table. But how can you make sure?

Following the guidance in Figure 3.26, right-click on **employee** and follow the menu path **View/Edit Data • All Rows**. Note that you have the choice to view a limited number of rows as well, which is useful on very large tables.

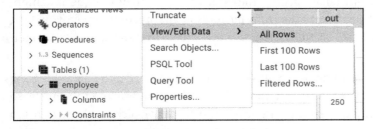

Figure 3.26 Displaying Table Contents in pgAdmin

91

You should get a table output as in Figure 3.27, which displays the table contents.

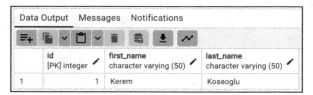

Figure 3.27 Contents of employee Table Displayed in pgAdmin

This functionality will be useful for the rest of this book! Whenever you execute a SQL statement, you can view table contents to see its effects.

Note that an actual employee table might be used in the upcoming examples in this book, so you don't want to keep this dummy table around. Execute the SQL statement in Listing 3.3 to get rid of this temporary table.

```
DROP TABLE employee;
```

Listing 3.3 SQL Statement to Delete employee Table

When the time comes to try our sample SQL statements for yourself, you can follow the steps described here and type in sample SQL statements.

3.3.2 Visual Studio Code

In this section, we'll cover VS Code installation on both Windows and macOS before moving on to the initial database setup and testing out SQL.

Installation

Since you're reading this tech book, you may have VS Code installed on your computer already. If not, you can download and install it from *https://code.visualstudio.com* as the first step. Installation should be very straightforward and intuitive; no step-by-step guidance is needed.

Setup

After you've completed installation, go to the **Extensions** section of VS Code as demonstrated in Figure 3.28. Search for the term **postgresql**, and unsurprisingly, you'll get many results! PostgreSQL is a popular database, and there are many extensions targeting it.

Let's simply pick the most popular extension for our purpose. On the date this book was written, **PostgreSQL Management Tool** by Chris Kolkman was the top choice, so we're going forward with this extension as an example. You can pick another extension if you want; the configuration steps should be similar to our steps in the following paragraphs.

Figure 3.28 PostgreSQL Extension Selection in VS Code

Simply click the **Install** button next to the extension and wait until the installation is complete. It should take a few seconds. Afterward, a new PostgreSQL icon will appear on the tool icon stack, as shown in Figure 3.29. Click to open this view.

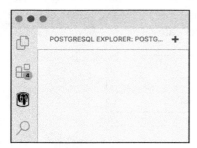

Figure 3.29 PostgreSQL Extension Icon in VS Code

Make sure that your PostgreSQL database engine is running, then click the **+** icon in the extension to create a connection to your playground database. You'll have to go through a series of mini popup prompts to complete the task.

The first popup shown in Figure 3.30 will ask for the hostname of the database. You can enter "localhost" for your local PostgreSQL instance, or you can enter the hostname of the remote database if that's your case.

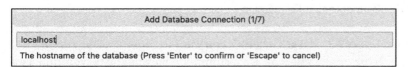

Figure 3.30 VS Code Prompt for Database Hostname

Next, the popup in Figure 3.31 will ask for your database user. You can enter "postgres" if you've followed our local installation steps, or you can enter another database user you have the credentials for.

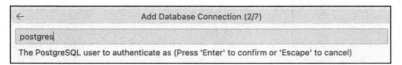

Figure 3.31 VS Code Prompt for Database User

Next, the popup in Figure 3.32 will ask for the password of the given database user. You can enter "1234" if you've followed our local installation steps, or you can enter the password of your user otherwise.

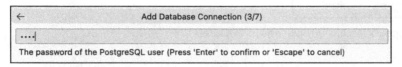

Figure 3.32 VS Code Prompt for Database Password

Next, the popup in Figure 3.33 will ask for the database port. You can enter the default port "5432" if you've followed our local installation steps, but if the target database works on a different port, you should enter the correct value.

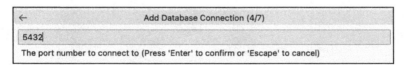

Figure 3.33 VS Code Prompt for Database Port

Next, the popup in Figure 3.34 will ask if you want a Secure Sockets Layer (SSL) connection or not. You'll most likely not require an SSL connection on a local installation, but if a remote database enforces SSL, you should select it.

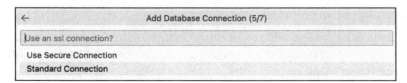

Figure 3.34 VS Code Prompt for SSL Connection

Next, the popup in Figure 3.35 will ask whether you want to show all databases or just a selected database. To be on the safe side, we recommend picking the playground database only—that will prevent you from mistakenly connecting to another database and manipulating data. But it's up to you! If you've followed our local installation guide, you can select **postgres** here. Otherwise, you can select your playground database of choice.

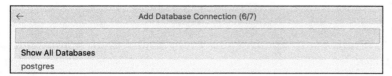

Figure 3.35 VS Code Prompt for Databases

Finally, the popup in Figure 3.36 will prompt an alias for this connection. You can simply call it "localhost" or pick any meaningful name. The name given here doesn't have any technical correspondence; it's just an alias.

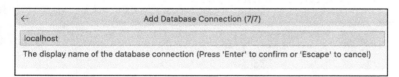

Figure 3.36 VS Code Prompt for Database Connection Display Name

If everything goes well, your playground database should appear in **PostgreSQL Explorer** as seen in Figure 3.37. Connection and database names may appear differently, depending on your choices in previous steps.

Figure 3.37 Playground Database Connection in VS Code

SQL Test

Now that the connection is ready, it's time to learn how to execute SQL code. After all, that's our main purpose!

As demonstrated in Figure 3.38, right-click the playground database and select **New Query**.

Figure 3.38 Creating New Query in VS Code

3   Setting Up the Environment

This should open a blank editor that's ready for your SQL input. Listing 3.4 contains a SQL statement to create a table. Don't worry about understanding the SQL code at this point.

```
CREATE TABLE employee(
    id int PRIMARY KEY,
    first_name varchar(50),
    last_name varchar(50)
);
```

Listing 3.4 Sample SQL Statement to Create Table

Put this SQL statement into the blank editor, as demonstrated in Figure 3.39. Once you complete your statement, you can execute it by pressing F5.

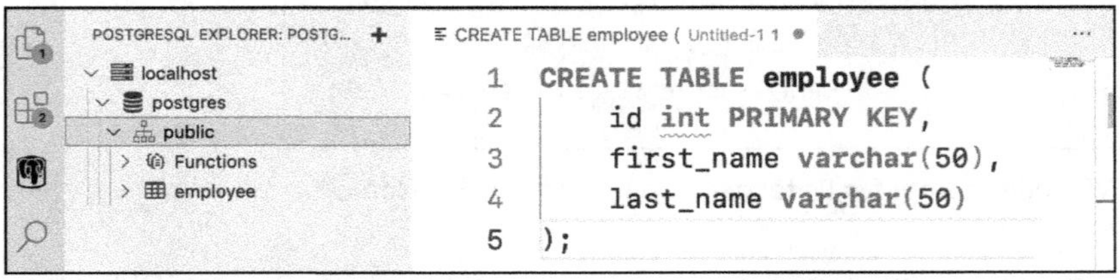

Figure 3.39 SQL Example in VS Code

In this example, we've created a table called employee by typing in the appropriate SQL statement and executing it. Check the left panel—a new table called employee really appeared there! If the table doesn't appear automatically after the execution, we can right-click the database name and select **Refresh Items** in the popup.

Let's test another SQL statement. This time, we'll try to insert a new entry into our new table. Using the same steps, execute the SQL statement in Listing 3.5.

```
INSERT INTO
    employee (id, first_name, last_name)
VALUES
    (1, 'Kerem', 'Koseoglu');
```

Listing 3.5 Sample SQL Statement to Create Entry

This should create a new entry in the employee table. But how can you make sure?

Following the guidance in Figure 3.40, right-click on **employee** and follow the **Select · Run Select Top 1000** menu. Note that there are other intuitive choices on the same popup menu that you can try for yourself. The option to limit the number of rows is useful in very large tables.

You should get a table output as in Figure 3.41, which displays the table contents.

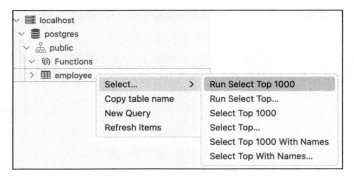

Figure 3.40 Displaying Table Contents in VS Code

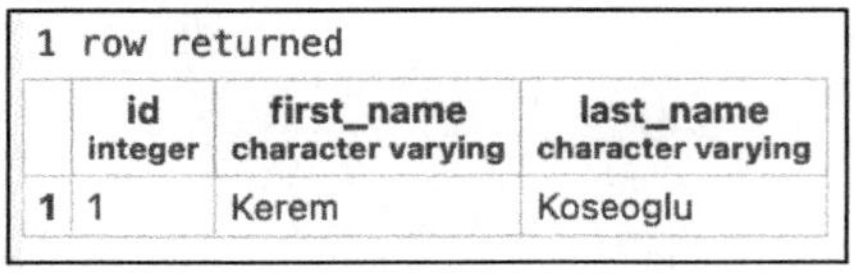

1 row returned		
id integer	first_name character varying	last_name character varying
1 1	Kerem	Koseoglu

Figure 3.41 Contents of employee Table Displayed in VS Code

This functionality will be useful in the rest of this book. Whenever you execute an SQL statement, you can view table contents to see the statement's effects.

Note that we may use an actual employee table in the upcoming examples in this book, so you don't want to keep this dummy table around. Execute the SQL statement in Listing 3.6 to get rid of this temporary table.

```
DROP TABLE employee;
```

Listing 3.6 SQL Statement to Delete employee Table

This concludes our guidance on manual SQL execution.

3.4 Summary

In this chapter, we went through the necessary steps to set up a playground database as well as an IDE to write and execute SQL code.

We evaluated the options for installing a local database instance or accessing an existing remote database. We also conducted the necessary steps for a local installation, in case you need one.

We also went over two alternative applications you can use to write and execute SQL code. The pgAdmin application is the official PostgreSQL GUI, while VS Code with an appropriate extension is another very popular choice. You can also use another application of your choice if you want to.

Finally, we went over a simple SQL demo to ensure that you know where to write and execute SQL code in your IDE of choice.

Now that we're geared up for our upcoming SQL adventures, we can proceed with our first SQL chapter and start writing hands-on SQL code!

Chapter 4
Data Definition Language

SQL has several sublanguages: data definition language (DDL), data manipulation language (DML), transaction control language (TCL), data query language (DQL), and data control language (DCL). Over the next chapters, the book will follow the logical sequence of these languages, starting with DDL. Before you can query data in a table, you must have a table, and before you can create a table, you must have a schema. You use the data definition language to create database objects like schemas and tables, and in this chapter, you'll learn how to create and alter database objects that will contain data in the future.

Welcome to the first chapter in which we officially get hands-on with SQL! As mentioned before, SQL has several sublanguages, and we're following a logical sequence among them.

In this debut chapter, we'll delve into DDL. We use this sublanguage to create fundamental database structures, such as schemas and tables. DDL is a significant topic because without having such containers for storing data, we simply can't store data. Remember that relational databases force us to define tables to store structured data. DDL is the sublanguage targeting that requirement. Therefore, it makes sense to begin our hands-on SQL journey with DDL. We ought to be able to create containers before we can write and read data through them.

DDL is not used to create structures only. Using DDL statements, we can also modify or even delete existing structures, such as tables. For instance, it's typical for software requirements to change over time, requiring the developer to add new fields to an existing table. In such cases, we can easily use DDL commands to complete the task at hand.

In the first section, we'll learn how to create, modify, and delete databases and schemas, as well as how to work under different databases and schemas simultaneously.

Once we're through with those fundamental components, we'll move on to table manipulation. This topic will be of interest for many, simply because tables are created and modified relatively often. We'll learn how to create and delete tables using SQL and modify them by adding, removing, and modifying columns and constraints.

4 Data Definition Language

And we haven't forgotten about views! We'll also cover view creation and deletion using SQL here.

At the end of the chapter, you'll be equipped with the know-how to create database artifacts for data containment.

4.1 Database Manipulation

In this section, we'll learn about SQL statements that are used to create, modify, and delete databases.

As we've learned already, a database product instance can contain multiple databases. Although it's generally possible to manipulate databases through the GUI application of the database product, it's also possible to do that using SQL.

Such operations are usually not part of daily database tasks. It's more common to create a database once and use it for a long time, but depending on the technical architecture of the project, you may need to dynamically and programmatically alter databases.

So, let's learn how!

> **Going Beyond the Playground**
>
> In the previous chapter, we decided to pick a single playground database and run all our examples there. However, we need to make an exception here. SQL allows us to create, modify, and even delete databases programmatically, and to demonstrate those commands, we need to briefly go beyond our regular playground and work in additional playground databases—simply because we don't want to destroy our regular playground. We're going to need it!

4.1.1 Database Creation

To understand this simple topic, we'll create a second (temporary) playground database. Listing 4.1 demonstrates the syntax for database creation.

```
CREATE DATABASE { database_name };
```

Listing 4.1 Syntax for Database Creation

The statement itself is very intuitive. The CREATE DATABASE command declares our intention to create a new database, and the statement concludes with the name of the new database. Listing 4.2 demonstrates this statement in action.

```
CREATE DATABASE playground2;
```

Listing 4.2 Creation of New Playground Database

Upon execution of this statement, a new database will be created under the database product instance. You can refresh the pgAdmin GUI and see it for yourself, as in Figure 4.1.

Figure 4.1 New Database Listed in pgAdmin

You may get an error message if your system already has a namesake database called playground2. Each database must have a unique name, so you can't have two databases with the same name. If you do, simply pick another name for your example.

Other than that, the statement itself is very simple, don't you think?

> **SQL Is English**
> Did you notice that the SQL statement is in almost pure English? That's the beauty of SQL: anyone with basic English skills and database knowledge can understand it easily! This feature will be a big advantage in the rest of your SQL journey.

This is the first time we've encountered the CREATE keyword, which is used to create other database components as well, such as schemas, tables, and views. Don't worry— we'll go over these later in Section 4.2.1, Section 4.3.1, and Section 4.4.1, respectively.

4.1.2 Database Modification

Creating a database was our initial step. However, we may need to make changes to the database after a while. In such cases, we can make use of database modification statements.

Most of the time, we'll use the ALTER DATABASE command to make changes on the database. ALTER is the common keyword to modify database structures, and by adding the DATABASE keyword afterward, we can build the prefix for database modification statements. Easy as English!

Further details are covered in the sections below.

Renaming a Database
Imagine that you provided an invalid name during the creation of the database. Alternatively, the software requirements may change over time, and you may need to rename an existing database. Listing 4.3 showcases the SQL syntax you should use in such cases.

4 Data Definition Language

```
ALTER DATABASE { existing_name } RENAME TO { new_name };
```
Listing 4.3 Syntax to Rename Existing Database

Once again, the intuitive syntax is almost pure English. `ALTER DATABASE` declares our intention to make a database-level change, and `RENAME TO` declares our intention to rename it. Listing 4.4 demonstrates the SQL statement in action, when we rename our new playground database.

```
ALTER DATABASE playground2 RENAME TO playground3;
```
Listing 4.4 Renaming Existing Playground Database

When you execute this statement, the existing `playground2` database will be renamed as `playground3`, as seen in Figure 4.2.

Figure 4.2 Renamed Database Listed in pgAdmin

As in the case of database creation, you may get an error message if your system already has a namesake database called `playground3`. Each database must have a unique name, you can't have two databases with the same name. If you do, then simply pick another name for your example.

We will discuss the risks involved in renaming a database in Section 4.5.

Changing the Owner of a Database

Each database has an owner. The owner of the database differs from regular database users by having special privileges; some of the significant ones are listed in Table 4.1.

Owner Privileges	Explanations
Full control over the database	The owner has unrestricted access to all database components, including tables and schemas.
Access control	The owner can grant authorization privileges to other users or revoke them.
Management	The owner can perform maintenance tasks like backups and configuration.

Table 4.1 Some Privileges of Database Owner

Due to such privileges, being the owner of the database can be a big responsibility—especially if sensitive data is stored in it. Typically, trusted system administrators become database owners—but the user who initially created the database becomes the database owner by default.

If we need to change the owner after creating the database, we can do that via a simple SQL statement. The syntax for this is in Listing 4.5.

```
ALTER DATABASE { database_name } OWNER TO { new_owner };
```

Listing 4.5 Syntax for Database Owner Change

Once again, the syntax is very intuitive. `ALTER DATABASE` declares our intention to make a database-level change, and `OWNER TO` declares a change of ownership. Let's see this command in action by changing the owner of `playground3`.

We're going to need a second user to hand the ownership to, so to quickly create a new user for this purpose, we execute statement in Listing 4.6.

```
CREATE USER keremk WITH PASSWORD '1234';
```

Listing 4.6 Creation of New Database User

User and authorization management is covered later on, in Chapter 8, so, don't worry about completely understanding the SQL statement in Listing 4.6. It's enough for you to know that we've created a new user called `keremk`.

Now that we have a second user, we can hand the ownership of `playground3` to them! Listing 4.7 contains the statement for handing over the ownership to user `keremk`.

```
ALTER DATABASE playground3 OWNER TO keremk;
```

Listing 4.7 Changing Owner of Temporary Playground Database

Once you've executed this statement, right-click **playground3** in pgAdmin and select **Properties**, as demonstrated in Figure 4.3.

If everything goes well, **keremk** should be displayed as the new database owner, as in Figure 4.4.

If you don't see the change immediately, you can refresh or restart pgAdmin and check again.

From now on, `keremk` will be assumed to be the database owner, and it will own all privileges that come with that title.

4   Data Definition Language

Figure 4.3 Selecting Properties of playground3 in pgAdmin

Figure 4.4 New Owner of playground3 in pgAdmin

Database Configuration Parameters

Like any other software applications, databases have configuration parameters, which you can basically imagine as its settings. If you right-click **playground3** in pgAdmin and select **Properties**, you can see some of these settings under **Definition**, as demonstrated in Figure 4.5.

Typically, we can change configuration parameters via the GUI application or the command line tools of the database product. However, we can change them programmatically via SQL as well, if the need arises.

> **Database Configuration**
> Configuration and maintenance of a relational database is a comprehensive subject all its own. It falls under the domain of system administration, and some people even base their entire careers on this subject. Since our focus is SQL, we won't delve into such details. Instead, we'll see how to change parameter values using SQL in a simple example.

104

4.1 Database Manipulation

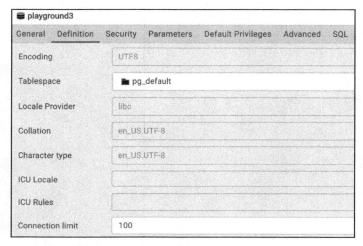

Figure 4.5 Definition of playground3 in pgAdmin

Let's get familiar with the syntax first. Take a look at Listing 4.8.

```
ALTER DATABASE { database_name } { parameter_name } { parameter_value };
```

Listing 4.8 Syntax for Database Parameter Change

Syntax elements are mostly self-explanatory. As usual, we start with the ALTER DATABASE command, declaring that we want to make a database-level modification. We continue with three arguments:

- The database_name argument declares the name of our target database.
- The parameter_name argument declares the name of the parameter.
- The parameter_value argument declares the new value of the parameter.

Let's see this in action to get a better understanding. Our purpose will be to change our parameters so that the database doesn't enable more than 200 simultaneous connections. PostgreSQL has a special parameter called CONNECTION LIMIT, which serves this exact purpose. With that information at hand, Listing 4.9 demonstrates our SQL statement.

```
ALTER DATABASE playground3 CONNECTION LIMIT 200;
```

Listing 4.9 Limiting Number of Connections

Once you execute this statement, it will set the value of the CONNECTION LIMIT database parameter to 200, just like we wanted! As shown in Figure 4.6, if you check the pgAdmin **Definition** of **playground3** again, you should see the new value. You may need a GUI refresh, though.

4 Data Definition Language

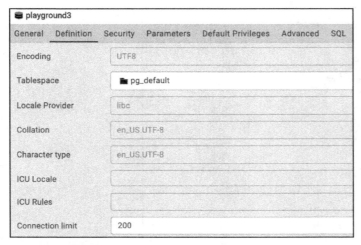

Figure 4.6 Connection Limit Changed to 200

Moving forward, you can change many other parameter values by using the same syntax. Be advised, though—in a production system, you shouldn't conduct such operations without the approval of the system administrator. Setting a parameter to an incorrect value can disrupt database operations.

> **Parameter Names**
> Each database product has its own set of parameter names, and new ones may be introduced in new versions. You may refer to the documentation of your database product to get a glimpse of parameters you're allowed to change via SQL.

4.1.3 Database Deletion

So far, we've gotten to know SQL statements that let us create and modify databases. Naturally, it's also possible to delete an existing database using SQL. The syntax in Listing 4.10 showcases how to do it.

```
DROP DATABASE { database_name };
```

Listing 4.10 Syntax for Deleting Database

DROP is the usual keyword declaring that we want to delete a database component, and we'll use this keyword for similar purposes in due course. DROP DATABASE is the command declaring that we want to delete an entire database, and we need to add the name of the target database as the suffix.

To see this in action, we can delete our temporary playground3 playground database. It has served its purpose, and we can bid it farewell by using the syntax in Listing 4.11 before returning to our original playground database for further exercises.

```
DROP DATABASE playground3;
```

Listing 4.11 Deletion of Temporary Playground Database

As shown in Figure 4.7, once you execute of this statement, playground3 should be destroyed and should disappear from the database list in pgAdmin. You might need to refresh the GUI, though.

Figure 4.7 Disappearance of playground3 from pgAdmin

We'll discuss the risks involved in deleting a database in Section 4.5.

Now that we're through with database manipulation, we can move one step further and see what we can do about schema manipulation.

4.2 Schema Manipulation

Schema manipulation follows a template similar to that of database manipulation. Statements and the overall syntax are nearly identical, with the obvious difference that we'll be targeting schemas instead of databases.

> **Going Beyond the Playground**
>
> In the previous chapter, we decided to pick a single playground schema and run all our examples there. However, we need to make an exception here—just like we did for database manipulation. SQL allows us to create, modify, and even delete schemas programmatically, and to demonstrate those commands, we need to briefly go beyond our regular playground and work on additional playground schemas—simply because we don't want to destroy our regular playground. We're going to need it!

4.2.1 Schema Creation

Let's start by creating a second (temporary) schema in our playground database. Listing 4.12 demonstrates the syntax for schema creation.

```
CREATE SCHEMA { schema_name };
```

Listing 4.12 Syntax for Schema Creation

4   Data Definition Language

The syntax is very intuitive and very similar to that for database creation. The CREATE SCHEMA command declares our intention to create a new schema, and it concludes with the name of the schema. Listing 4.13 demonstrates this statement in action.

```
CREATE SCHEMA public2;
```

Listing 4.13 Creation of New Schema

If you try to execute this statement, a new schema will be created in the database you're working on—which should be your playground database. Once you refresh the pgAdmin GUI, you should see the new schema under **Schemas**, as shown in Figure 4.8.

Figure 4.8 New Schema Listed in pgAdmin

Although this schema is empty at the moment, it can contain data structures, such as tables and views—just like any other schema!

Mind you that relational databases don't allow namesake objects—if you already have a schema called public2, you won't be able to create a second one. In such a case, you should pick a new name for your new schema or carefully rename the old one if you must—which is, coincidentally, the subject of our next topic!

4.2.2   Schema Modification

We're going to follow a path similar to database modification in this section. The main difference is that instead of using the ALTER DATABASE command, we'll use the ALTER SCHEMA command. Because we're targeting a schema, it's natural for the command to contain the SCHEMA keyword as well.

Mind you that like database modification, schema modification is not a common daily task. It occurs in relatively rare cases where a fundamental change is needed, such as migration, product retirement, and system redesign.

Renaming a Schema

We were recently talking about renaming schemas. Now is the time to learn the SQL syntax for that. Check Listing 4.14.

```
ALTER SCHEMA { existing_name } RENAME TO { new_name };
```

Listing 4.14 Syntax to Rename Existing Schema

The syntax should be obvious to someone who can speak English and has gone over SQL statements regarding database manipulation. It's nearly the same syntax, but we use the SCHEMA keyword instead of DATABASE.

Let's see it in action! Listing 4.15 demonstrates the SQL statement we use to rename our example schema.

```
ALTER SCHEMA public2 RENAME TO public3;
```

Listing 4.15 Renaming Example Schema

Once we execute this statement, the existing public2 schema will be renamed to **public3**, as shown in Figure 4.9.

Figure 4.9 Renamed Schema Listed in pgAdmin

Our aforementioned rule of namesake components is valid once again: the new name of the schema must be a unique name under the same database, and you can't have two namesake schemas. We'll discuss the risks involved in renaming a schema in Section 4.5.

Changing the Owner of a Schema

As with databases, each schema has an owner. The owner of the schema differs from other users by having special privileges; some of the significant ones are listed in Table 4.2.

4 Data Definition Language

Owner Privileges	Explanations
Full control over the schema	The owner has unrestricted access to all schema components, including tables and views.
Access control	The owner can grant authorization privileges to other users within the scope of the schema or revoke them.
Administration	The owner can change schema ownership and rename or delete the schema.

Table 4.2 Some Privileges of Schema Owner

Mind you that we have a similar list of privileges for database owners, listed earlier in Table 4.1. The natural difference is that while the privileges of the database owner are valid throughout the entire database, including all schemas within it, the privileges of the schema owner are valid within that particular schema only. Figure 4.10 contrasts this difference visually.

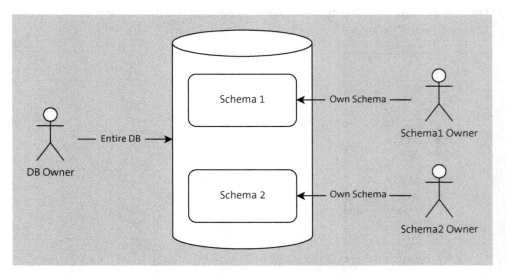

Figure 4.10 Comparison between Database and Schema Owners

Back to the topic at hand... To change the owner of an existing schema, we can do that with a simple SQL statement. The syntax can be seen in Listing 4.16.

ALTER SCHEMA { schema_name } OWNER TO { new_owner };

Listing 4.16 Syntax for Schema Owner Change

Evaluating the intuitive syntax; ALTER SCHEMA declares our intention to make a schema-level change, and OWNER TO declares a change of ownership. Let's see this command in action by changing the owner of the sample public3 schema.

You're going to need a second user to hand the ownership to, and to keep this section self-contained, you're going to create a new user for this purpose. Execute the statement in Listing 4.17, and don't worry about understanding the statement beyond the fact that it creates a new user called kerems.

```
CREATE USER kerems WITH PASSWORD '1234';
```
Listing 4.17 Creation of New Database User

Now that you have an alternative user, you need to hand the ownership of the schema public3 to them. Listing 4.18 contains the statement for doing just that.

```
ALTER SCHEMA public3 OWNER TO kerems;
```
Listing 4.18 Changing Owner of Sample Schema

After executing this statement, right-click **public3** in pgAdmin and select **Properties,** as demonstrated in Figure 4.11.

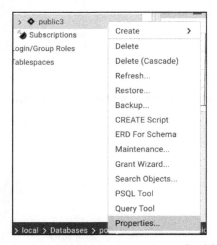

Figure 4.11 Selecting Properties of public3 in pgAdmin

If everything goes well, kerems should be displayed as the new database owner, as in Figure 4.12.

Figure 4.12 New Owner of public3 in pgAdmin

You might need to refresh pgAdmin to see the change. From now on, kerems will be assumed as the schema owner, and it will own all privileges that come with that title.

4.2.3 Schema Deletion

Straightforward logic tells us that if we can create or modify a schema, we should be able to delete it as well.

We'll discuss the risks of deleting a schema in Section 4.5. For our brave readers, Listing 4.19 showcases the syntax for that purpose.

```
DROP SCHEMA { schema_name } [ CASCADE | RESTRICT ];
```

Listing 4.19 Syntax to Delete Schema

A statement for deleting the schema would start with the command DROP SCHEMA, followed by the name of the schema. So far, so good! If we simply execute this statement for our sample public3 schema, we'll surely get rid of it. Listing 4.20 demonstrates the appropriate statement for that, which you can try for yourself.

```
DROP SCHEMA public3;
```

Listing 4.20 Deletion of Sample Schema

Once you execute this statement, the example schema will disappear from the schema list in pgAdmin, as demonstrated in Figure 4.13.

Figure 4.13 Disappearance of public3 from pgAdmin

Let's take a look a closer look at the syntax in the following sections.

Cascade

You may have noticed that the syntax in Listing 4.19 has an optional keyword: CASCADE. What is this mysterious keyword good for?

A relational database is a structure of interdependent components, and even in the most basic sense, tables refer to each other by using foreign keys. Ignoring recommendations and best practices, it's technically possible for tables from two different schemas to have a foreign key relationship.

Figure 4.14 contains an ERD with two distinct schemas: hr is the schema of the human resources department, and canteen is the schema of the company canteen.

4.2 Schema Manipulation

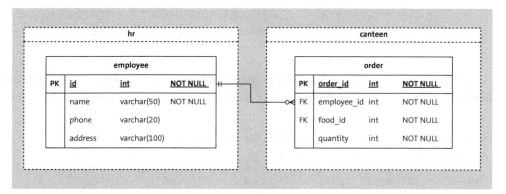

Figure 4.14 ERD with canteen.order referring to hr.employee

The hr.employee table contains employee master data, and the canteen.order table contains the order history of employees. Although they belong to different schemas, it's natural that canteen.order.employee_id refers to hr.employee.id as its foreign key.

> **Interschema Relationships**
> We don't intend to assert that having relationships between tables in different schemas is a good practice. It's merely a technical possibility, and in many cases, you may want to keep schemas completely isolated.

Now, let's assume that the HR department will start using another software system and we don't need the hr schema any longer. You've been instructed to delete this schema, so naturally, you'll apply the SQL commands you recently learned and execute the statement in Listing 4.21.

```
DROP SCHEMA hr;
```

Listing 4.21 SQL Statement to Delete hr Schema

And you'll be unsuccessful. The database will return an error message instead, indicating that the schema has dependencies and can't be deleted—and it'll be right! There's a dependency between hr.employee.id and canteen.order.employee_id, so if you simply delete the hr schema, this dependency will become inconsistent.

This may look like an obstacle to you, but actually, it's a beautiful security feature! Relational databases don't let us simply delete stuff at will if there are such dependencies. This reduces human mistakes and ensures database-wide consistency.

But is it impossible to delete the hr schema, then? Are we stuck with it forever? Of course not!

We have two alternatives for getting rid of hr. The first alternative is to follow a two-step plan:

1. Delete all dependencies regarding `hr`. In our case, we need to remove the foreign key relationship between `canteen.order.employee_id` and `hr.employee.id`.
2. Delete the `hr` schema.

This may seem simple in such a basic scenario, but imagine a schema with dozens of tables and relationships! Manual removal of all relationships would be a cumbersome task and take a long time.

Thus, we have the second alternative. We can simply delete the schema with the optional CASCADE keyword, as in Listing 4.22.

```
DROP SCHEMA hr CASCADE;
```

Listing 4.22 SQL Statement to Delete hr Schema and All Relationships

Having the CASCADE keyword in the statement tells the database to delete all dependencies automatically and then delete the schema as well. Practical, eh?

> **Orphan Data**
>
> No matter which deletion method you pick, you need to be mindful of orphan data. After you delete the `hr` schema, rows in `canteen.order` will become orphans because `canteen.order.employee_id` doesn't refer to a table any longer. Those are just numbers instead of meaningful employee IDs now.
>
> If this were a migration to a new schema, `canteen.order.employee_id` would have to point to the new `schema.table` at some point very soon.

Restrict

Our syntax in Listing 4.19 has a second optional keyword, which we ignored momentarily: RESTRICT. This keyword is actually the default behavior of the command. In other words, the statements in Listing 4.23 are identical and would execute in exactly the same way.

```
DROP SCHEMA hr;
DROP SCHEMA hr RESTRICT;
```

Listing 4.23 Using Optional RESTRICT Keyword

But if you're using another database product, the default behavior may be different. So, to be on the safe side and to express your intention more clearly, it's advisable to add the optional RESTRICT or CASCADE keyword explicitly when coding SQL in a production environment.

Wow! You're through with databases and schemas, and you're doing great. It's time to move forward to table manipulation, so take a break, get something to drink, and see you there!

4.3 Table Manipulation

Compared to database and schema manipulation, table manipulation is a requirement that pops up more often. Databases and schemas are subject to high-level organization of data structures and are relatively stable areas, while tables are subject to direct data containment and may need to be modified more often as software requirements change.

Since table structures directly correlate with the code accessing them, table manipulations are typically conducted by developers who maintain the application code. But this is not the rule by any means, and organizations may have different technical procedures.

In this section, we're going to cover the most common types of table manipulation and their corresponding SQL statements. Following our former approach, let's begin by creating a table and gradually going over modification and deletion operations.

4.3.1 Table Creation

In previous sections, we performed some "unofficial" operations of table creation. Now, we'll delve into this topic officially.

The things you should consider when creating a new table should be as follows:

- Naming the table
- Defining columns
- Defining constraints (such as primary and foreign keys)

> **Constraint Definitions**
>
> Although imposing constraint definitions is technically optional, it's such a common best practice that it should be considered as a rule. Even the simplest table should have at least a primary key, and further constraints ought to be present.

But let's not rush this! The following sections take you through this process step by step, starting with simple examples and then advancing in due course.

Columns Only

To see table creation in its simplest form, let's start with table creation without constraints. Check Listing 4.24 for the syntax.

4 Data Definition Language

```
CREATE TABLE { table_name } (
    { column_name } { column_type },
    [, ... ]
);
```

Listing 4.24 Syntax for Table Creation

This may look more complicated to you than it really is, so let's quickly jump to an actual SQL code to give you a better understanding. See Listing 4.25, where a table to store basic employee data is created.

```
CREATE TABLE employee (
    id INT,
    name VARCHAR(50),
    phone VARCHAR(20),
    address VARCHAR(100)
);
```

Listing 4.25 SQL Statement to Create Employee Table

Feels better, doesn't it? We're back to near-plain English, so let's execute this statement and see what it does before we delve into the details. Once execution is completed, you should see the employee table in pgAdmin under your playground database, as shown in Figure 4.15.

Figure 4.15 employee Table Listed in pgAdmin

If you want to see more details of your columns, you can right-click **employee** and select **Properties,** as demonstrated in Figure 4.16.

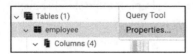

Figure 4.16 Calling employee Properties in pgAdmin

In the new window, you can click the **Columns** tab to see them, as in Figure 4.17.

The column list in pgAdmin naturally corresponds to the field list in our SQL statement in Listing 4.25. Now, we can break down the statement into its components.

4.3 Table Manipulation

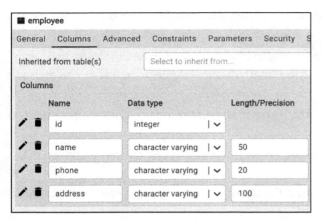

Figure 4.17 Column Details of employee Table in pgAdmin

Table creation statements begin with the CREATE TABLE command, which is very obvious and self-explanatory, right? We already know that the CREATE keyword is used to create new database components, and using it together with the TABLE suffix turns it into a command to create a new table.

The name of the table is given afterwards. In our case, we're creating a table to store employee data, so a simple and clear name like employee is appropriate. Mind you that namesake tables won't be allowed under the same schema, and each table must have a unique name.

Finally, we need to provide the list of columns. In each column entry, we need to provide the three basic parts listed in Table 4.3.

Parts	Examples	Explanations
Column name	id	This is the name of the column, which must be unique within the table.
Data type	INT	This is the data type of the column.
Nullability	NOT NULL	This is an optional declaration stating whether the column can have null values.

Table 4.3 Parts of Column Definition

The column name is the obvious part. Mind you that a table can't have namesake columns. Instead, each column of the table must have a unique name. Just like variables of a programming language, columns should have clear, unambiguous, and understandable names.

The data type column is where we define the type of values. In our example, employee.id would contain a number, while employee.name / employee.phone / employee.address would contain characters. We need to declare this during table creation—the database

117

engine simply needs to know what will be stored in each field. This is required for clean data and consistency.

We already mentioned basic data types in Chapter 2, so we won't list them here again. A point of interest is determining the length of character fields, which we can revisit in Listing 4.25:

- `name VARCHAR(50)` means that the name of an employee can have a maximum of 50 characters.
- `phone VARCHAR(20)` means that the phone number of an employee can have a maximum of 20 characters.
- `address VARCHAR(100)` means that the address of an employee can contain a maximum of 100 characters.

> **Picking Data Types**
>
> Picking the correct data type and length initially is very important! Although you can change them later, dependent applications may malfunction if you don't update them in parallel. It would be a good idea to keep some safety buffer on lengths, considering future implications.
>
> Integrations are another typical case to consider. When integrating two applications, one of the core questions is whether their data types and lengths match or not. If the source column is `VARCHAR(30)` and the target column is `VARCHAR(3)`, you can't directly pass the data without the risk of truncating 27 characters. If you know of possible integrations in advance, it may be a good idea to determine column types and lengths in harmony with partner systems whenever possible.

Easy, right? We've successfully created our first table! Now, we're ready for a slightly more advanced feature: constraints.

A *constraint* is a database rule or restriction that ensures the integrity and consistency of the data. Primary keys and foreign keys are some of the constraints we've seen before. During the creation of a table, we can declare some constraints and rules that will apply to all data entries into that table. The database will then reject future database statements, which would disrupt the constraint. Listing 4.26 demonstrates the overall syntax for creating tables with constraints.

```
CREATE TABLE { table_name } (
    { column_name } { column_type } [ column_constraint ],
    [, ... ],
    [ further_constraints ]
);
```

Listing 4.26 Syntax for Table Creation with Constraints

Don't worry, applying constraints is easy in practice! Let's go over some significant constraints.

Primary Key Constraints

We've already talked about primary keys and their purposes, and if you need a refresher, you can check Chapter 2. But before proceeding with the primary key, there might be a chore to do: if you've followed the example above, you can execute the statement in Listing 4.27 to delete the employee table and start anew.

```
DROP TABLE employee;
```

Listing 4.27 SQL Statement to Delete employee Table

You can take this step for other constraint types in the following sections as well, so we won't repeat this SQL statement in other topics.

Now, let's re-create the same table by providing the PRIMARY KEY constraint and making employee.id the primary key of the table by following Listing 4.28.

```
CREATE TABLE employee (
    id INT PRIMARY KEY,
    name VARCHAR(50),
    phone VARCHAR(20),
    address VARCHAR(100)
);
```

Listing 4.28 SQL Statement to Create Table with Primary Key

The only difference from the former statement occurs in the id column. We added the PRIMARY KEY constraint for this column, which made it the primary key of the table. Easy as English, as usual! Figure 4.18 showcases the result in pgAdmin.

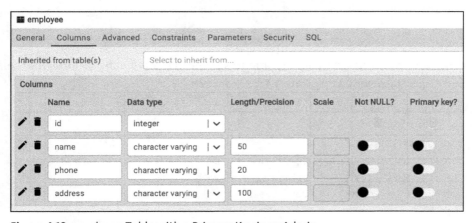

Figure 4.18 employee Table with a Primary Key in pgAdmin

4 Data Definition Language

Note that the **Primary key?** option is active for the **id** column, simply because it's the primary key!

> **Not Null**
>
> You may have noticed that **Not NULL?** is also active for the same column. We'll address this shortly, in the Null Constraints section. Before that, there's one more primary key feature to address.

In this example, we created a table in which a single primary key is present: employee.id. However, a table can also have multiple primary keys, and in that case, we need a slightly different syntax. Check employee_bonus in Figure 4.19.

employee				
PK	id	int	NOT NULL	
	name	varchar(50)	NOT NULL	
	phone	varchar(20)		
	address	varchar(100)		

employee_bonus			
PK,FK	employee_id	int	NOT NULL
PK	bonus_year	int	NOT NULL
	bonus_amount	numeric(12, 2)	NOT NULL
	currency	varchar(3)	NOT NULL

Figure 4.19 ERD for employee_bonus Table

In this table, we would store the annual bonus amounts of each employee. Each row represents a combination of an employee and a year, so two key fields—employee_id and bonus_year— ensure the uniqueness of each row. In other words, the primary key of the employee_bonus table is made up of two fields: employee_id and bonus_year.

> **Foreign Key Constraints**
>
> The employee_id field is displayed as a foreign key in Figure 4.19, and we have a special constraint for that! We'll learn about it shortly, but let's keep our focus on primary keys for now.

Now that the case study is clear, it's time to see the SQL statement that creates the employee_bonus table with two primary keys. See Listing 4.29.

```
CREATE TABLE employee_bonus (
    employee_id INT,
    bonus_year INT,
    bonus_amount NUMERIC(12, 2),
    currency VARCHAR(3),
    PRIMARY KEY (employee_id, bonus_year)
);
```

Listing 4.29 SQL Statement to Create Table with Two Primary Keys

Since we have two primary key fields, our syntax has deviated slightly. We added the
PRIMARY KEY keyword to the end of the SQL statement, followed by our employee_id and
bonus_year primary keys. Easy when you know how, right?

Once we've executed of this statement, we can check how the table looks in pgAdmin.
Take a look at Figure 4.20.

Figure 4.20 employee_bonus Table with Two Primary Keys in pgAdmin

As you can see, both the employee_id field and the bonus_year field are marked as primary keys, just as we intended!

We can use this syntax for tables with single primary keys as well. We could have created the employee table by using the statement in Listing 4.30.

```
CREATE TABLE employee (
    id INT,
    name VARCHAR(50),
    phone VARCHAR(20),
    address VARCHAR(100),
    PRIMARY KEY (id)
);
```

Listing 4.30 Alternative Primary Key Constraint for Tables with Single Keys

This is identical to Listing 4.28, in which we provided the PRIMARY KEY statement directly on the column line. You can use whichever format you like, but if you must memorize one, we recommend Listing 4.30 because it supports any number of primary key fields.

Primary keys are the most fundamental constraints, and nearly every relational database table should have at least one primary key. Moving forward, we can delve into the second fundamental constraint: foreign keys.

Foreign Key Constraints

Figure 4.19 showcased the foreign key relationship between employee_bonus and employee, and now, it's time to keep our promise and see how to declare such a constraint using SQL! Listing 4.31 demonstrates how to achieve that.

```
CREATE TABLE employee_bonus (
    employee_id INT,
    bonus_year INT,
    bonus_amount NUMERIC(12, 2),
    currency VARCHAR(3),
    PRIMARY KEY (employee_id, bonus_year),
    FOREIGN KEY (employee_id) REFERENCES employee(id)
);
```

Listing 4.31 Declaration of Foreign Key between employee_bonus and employee

Very intuitive as usual, don't you think? Following the FOREIGN KEY declaration, we provided three inputs:

- employee_id is the column in our current table.
- REFERENCES is a fixed keyword.
- employee(id) is the master data table and field – so this basically means employee.id or "id column in employee table."

Once we execute this statement, we can see the effect in pgAdmin if we check the properties of employee_bonus, as in Figure 4.21.

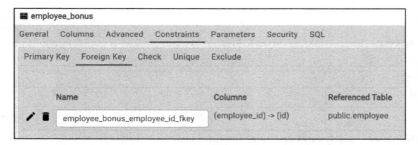

Figure 4.21 employee_bonus Foreign Key Shown in pgAdmin

This example covers a one-to-one foreign key relationship between tables. However, since it's possible to have composite foreign keys containing multiple fields, we ought to express that using SQL as well.

For this purpose, let's evaluate the case study in which employee bonuses are paid in installments. To track payment installments, we would need a new table: employee_bonus_payment. Figure 4.22 contains the ERD of this new table.

4.3 Table Manipulation

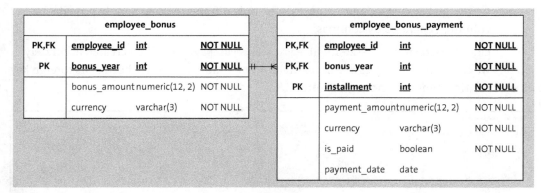

Figure 4.22 ERD for employee_bonus_payment Table

The logic of the table is very straightforward. For each employee_bonus row, we have multiple employee_bonus_payment rows, each corresponding to one planned payment installment.

Now, the foreign key relationship between employee_bonus_payment and employee_bonus is a composite key, consisting of the combination of two key fields: employee_id and bonus_year. When creating the employee_bonus_payment table, we need to provide the correct syntax for such a foreign key relationship. Listing 4.32 is what we want.

```
CREATE TABLE employee_bonus_payment (
    employee_id INT,
    bonus_year INT,
    installment INT,
    payment_amount NUMERIC(12, 2),
    currency VARCHAR(3),
    is_paid BOOLEAN,
    payment_date DATE,
    PRIMARY KEY (employee_id, bonus_year, installment),
    FOREIGN KEY (employee_id) REFERENCES employee(id),
    FOREIGN KEY (employee_id, bonus_year)
       REFERENCES employee_bonus(employee_id, bonus_year)
);
```

Listing 4.32 Declaring Composite Foreign Key in SQL

Wow, that was a mouthful! But actually, it's very simple; don't let the length of the statement scare you. Up until the last line, we don't have anything new – we've simply declared each column of employee_bonus_payment, as well as some constraints we've seen before already.

On the last line, we declare the composite foreign key relationship with employee_bonus – containing the ID of the employee and the bonus year. The syntax is almost identical

123

to foreign keys with single columns – the only difference is, we simply provide further columns separated by commas.

Once we execute this statement, `employee_bonus_payment` will be created accurately. If we check the properties of this new table in pgAdmin, we can see both of its foreign key relationships – as shown in Figure 4.23.

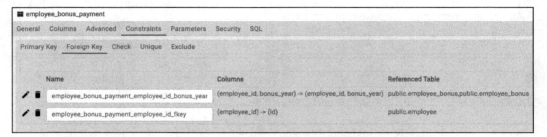

Figure 4.23 Foreign keys of employee_bonus_payment shown in pgAdmin

Now that we've covered the most fundamental constraint types, we can delve into nulls – which we encountered multiple times already.

Null Constraints

Before talking about the meaning of null, let's make a fast start by applying it first. Let's decorate our initial SQL statement with some null constraints. Check Listing 4.33.

```
CREATE TABLE employee (
    id INT PRIMARY KEY NOT NULL,
    name VARCHAR(50) NOT NULL,
    phone VARCHAR(20),
    address VARCHAR(100)
);
```

Listing 4.33 SQL Statement to Create Table with Null Constraints

When we execute of the statement, the `employee` table will be created once again—but this time, with null constraints. Figure 4.24 shows the table columns in pgAdmin; note that some have **Not NULL?** activated.

Now, null is a significant point of interest. In Listing 4.33, the `id` and `name` columns have the `NOT NULL` suffix, while others don't. *Null* means there's a missing value, but that's different from an empty value. It's important for a novice to understand the difference between a null value and an empty value because they're not the same thing.

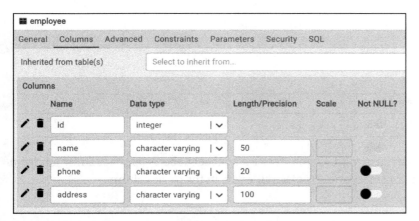

Figure 4.24 employee Table in pgAdmin with Null Constraints

Check Table 4.4 for a mock data snapshot of our employee table.

id	name	phone	address
1	Jessica Turner	(555) 123-4567	456 Elm Street, Apt 12B, Springfield, IL 62704
2	Michael Roberts		NULL
3	Emily Johnson	NULL	123 Maple Lane, Unit 5, Portland, OR 97209

Table 4.4 Sample employee Table Data

In the first row, all data is provided and present. Jessica Turner has values in all columns, so there's no case to differentiate between an empty value and a null value.

In the second row, Michael Roberts has an empty value in the phone column. This is an empty value, not a null value, the former of which might indicate that he doesn't have a land phone line at all. However, he has a null value in address, which means that his address is a missing value rather than an empty value. If address is null, we can assume that the address is not known yet and is simply missing, while if address had an empty value, we could imagine that Michael Roberts lives in a van and doesn't have a fixed address.

In the last row, Emily Johnson has a null value in phone. We all know what this means now: she might actually have a phone number, but this information is not provided yet and is missing.

Here's a fun sneak peek into a future topic: when we're querying database tables, null values and empty values are handled differently. For example, Listing 4.34 would return Emily Johnson (and not Michael Roberts) because she is the only one who has a null value (not an empty value) in the phone column.

```
SELECT
    *
FROM
    employee
WHERE
    phone IS NULL;
```

Listing 4.34 Query Returning Emily Johnson

On the other hand, Listing 4.35 would return Michael Roberts (and not Emily Johnson) because he has an empty value (not a null value) in the phone column.

```
SELECT
    *
FROM
    employee
WHERE
    phone = '';
```

Listing 4.35 Query Returning Michael Roberts

> **Null Values in Queries**
> Beyond the basic example above, null values will become much more interesting in due course, when we fetch data from multiple tables using JOIN commands. But let's not get ahead of ourselves.

Now that we understand the difference between a null value and empty value, the purpose of the NOT NULL suffix in table definition syntax should be obvious.

A column with the NOT NULL suffix must contain a value during row creation. In our example, we marked the name column as NOT NULL, simply because every employee must provide their name! If someone is attempting to insert an employee row without their name, it won't make sense and the database won't allow it.

On the other hand, the phone and address columns don't have the NOT NULL suffix. That means we're more flexible in those columns and accept the fact that not all employees might provide a phone number or an address initially. For example, a new employee may be immigrating from another country and may not have a local phone number or address yet. But they must have a name, right? That's why name is marked as NOT NULL.

Primary keys certainly can't be null! They're unique identifiers of table rows, and we simply can't have a row without a unique ID. That's why we don't need to explicitly add the NOT NULL suffix to primary key fields during table creation. Listing 4.36 would bear the same results as Listing 4.33—even if we don't add the NOT NULL constraint to the id column, the database engine is smart enough to do it automatically on our behalf.

```
CREATE TABLE employee (
    id INT PRIMARY KEY,
    name VARCHAR(50) NOT NULL,
    phone VARCHAR(20),
    address VARCHAR(100)
);
```

Listing 4.36 Creation of employee Table without Explicitly Adding NOT NULL to Primary Keys

Now that we understand the creation of primary keys and the specification of null constraints, we can get more adventurous and provide further constraints during table creation.

Unique Constraint

We can use the unique constraint to ensure that all values in a column (or a combination of columns) are unique across table rows. Duplicate values are naturally prevented.

Following our recent example, we can add this constraint to the phone column. Two employees are not supposed to share the same phone number, and we can enforce this constraint during table creation as demonstrated in Listing 4.37.

```
CREATE TABLE employee (
    id INT PRIMARY KEY,
    name VARCHAR(50) NOT NULL,
    phone VARCHAR(20) UNIQUE,
    address VARCHAR(100)
);
```

Listing 4.37 Enforcing Unique Values in phone Column

In the definition of the phone column, we've simply added the UNIQUE keyword to achieve our goal! If we check the properties of this table in pgAdmin now, we can see that this constraint is effective, as shown in Figure 4.25.

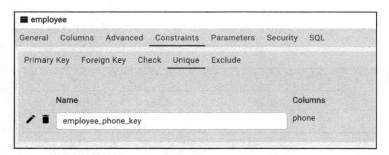

Figure 4.25 UNIQUE Constraint Displayed in pgAdmin

4   Data Definition Language

From now on, we can't insert two employee rows having the same phone value.

> **Unique Constraint and Nulls**
>
> In the example above, the database engine will prevent us from inserting rows that have duplicate phone values—even if the value is empty. However, it will allow rows that have *null* as the phone value.
>
> This should not be confusing. When phone has a null value, it means that the phone number is missing or unknown. We may have multiple employees with unknown phone values, so the UNIQUE constraint has tolerance for such cases.
>
> On the other hand, when phone has an empty value, the database engine assumes that the empty value is a valid phone number. Therefore, the UNIQUE constraint has no tolerance for duplicate employee entries with empty phone values.
>
> In summary, two rows where phone is null would be allowed, while two rows where phone is ' ' would not be allowed.

In some cases, we may want to enforce a combination of columns to be unique, instead of a single column. Imagine that we added a column called country_code to the employee table, as demonstrated in Figure 4.26.

```
                    employee
PK │ id            int          NOT NULL
   │ name          varchar(50)  NOT NULL
   │ country_code  varchar(3)
   │ phone         varchar(20)
   │ address       varchar(100)
```

Figure 4.26 Country Code Added to employee Table

In this state, phone doesn't contain the entire phone number. Instead, the combination of country_code and phone gives the entire phone number. Check Table 4.5 for a sample case.

id	name	country_code	phone	address
67	James Smith	+1	202-555-1234	1234 Market Street, Suite 567, San Francisco, CA 94103, USA
68	Elise Dubois	+33	202-555-1234	56 Rue de Rivoli, 75001 Paris, France

Table 4.5 Two Employee Rows with Identical Phone Numbers but Different Country Codes

Although the two rows have the same phone value, they have different country_code values because those people live in different countries. If we apply the UNIQUE constraint to phone alone, the database engine won't allow these rows to exist simultaneously. Instead, we need to apply the UNIQUE constraint to the combination of country code and phone. Listing 4.38 showcases the SQL statement we use to achieve this goal.

```
CREATE TABLE employee (
    id INT PRIMARY KEY,
    name VARCHAR(50) NOT NULL,
    country_code VARCHAR(3),
    phone VARCHAR(20),
    address VARCHAR(100),
    UNIQUE (country_code, phone)
);
```

Listing 4.38 SQL Statement to Apply UNIQUE Constraint to Combination of Columns

This is very similar to applying the PRIMARY KEY constraint to multiple rows, right? Once we execute this statement, we can check the properties of employee in pgAdmin to see the constraint visually, as in Figure 4.27.

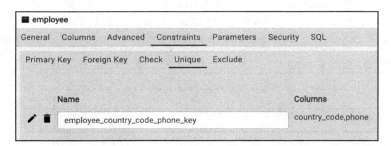

Figure 4.27 UNIQUE Constraint with Multiple Columns Shown in pgAdmin

Note that the constraint name was autogenerated on our behalf. Beautiful, isn't it?

Check Constraints

In a nutshell, CHECK constraints are used to validate the values of an incoming row.

For our first case study, we're going to use the employee_bonus table that we created already. Figure 4.28 will help refresh your memory of this.

Now, here's the requirement: bonus payments can be made in either the EUR currency or the USD currency. We want to ensure this validation on the database level, and Listing 4.39 is the solution!

```
CREATE TABLE employee_bonus (
    employee_id INT,
    bonus_year INT,
```

4 Data Definition Language

```
    bonus_amount NUMERIC(12, 2),
    currency VARCHAR(3),
    PRIMARY KEY (employee_id, bonus_year),
    FOREIGN KEY (employee_id) REFERENCES employee(id)
    CHECK (currency = 'USD' OR currency = 'EUR')
);
```

Listing 4.39 SQL Statement Containing CHECK Constraint

	employee_bonus		
PK,FK	employee_id	int	NOT NULL
PK	bonus_year	int	NOT NULL
	bonus_amount	numeric(12, 2)	NOT NULL
	currency	varchar(3)	NOT NULL

Figure 4.28 ERD for employee_bonus

If you check final part of the statement, you'll find the intuitive CHECK constraint, which will act like a gatekeeper and won't allow any value other than USD or EUR in the currency field. Figure 4.29 showcases this constraint in pgAdmin.

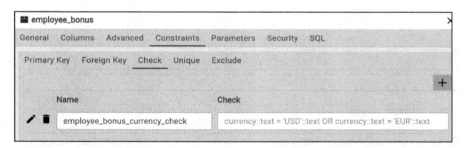

Figure 4.29 employee_bonus Check Constraint in pgAdmin

Admittedly, some basic programming knowledge is required to code the CHECK constraint condition between the parentheses, but anyone who's able to write conditions in Excel should be able to write CHECK conditions as well. To stay on our subject, we won't delve deeper into that.

However, it ought to be said that CHECK conditions can go beyond literals. You can also write CHECK conditions to compare different columns of an incoming row, as in Listing 4.40.

```
CREATE TABLE employee (
    id INT PRIMARY KEY,
    name VARCHAR(50) NOT NULL,
```

```
    country_code VARCHAR(3),
    phone VARCHAR(20),
    address VARCHAR(100),
    CHECK (phone <> address)
);
```

Listing 4.40 SQL Statement with Intercolumn CHECK Constraint

Here, we ensure that `phone` and `address` must have different values, which prevents some basic entry mistakes while an operator is quickly copy-pasting data. Figure 4.30 demonstrates how this constraint looks in pgAdmin.

Figure 4.30 employee Check Constraint in pgAdmin

> **Complex Check Constraints**
> Mind you that CHECK constraints are not easy to debug. Beyond some core checks, it would be advisable to leave complex data validations to the application layer instead of the database layer.
>
> An application supporting multiple database products may prohibit the usage of CHECK constraints altogether, consolidating data validations on the application layer completely. This prevents code duplication between different database products.

The CHECK constraint also supports some built-in functions. Take a look at Listing 4.41 to see an example in which we validate the length of a value.

```
CREATE TABLE employee (
    id INT PRIMARY KEY,
    name VARCHAR(50) NOT NULL,
    country_code VARCHAR(3),
    phone VARCHAR(20),
    address VARCHAR(100),
    CHECK (phone <> address),
    CHECK (LENGTH(address) >= 10)
);
```

Listing 4.41 Demonstration of LENGTH Function in CHECK Constraint

4   Data Definition Language

This check ensures that no one can insert or update a row with an address value of less than 10 characters.

LENGTH is one of many functions in CHECK constraints, and there are many other functions available. Some of them are listed in Table 4.6.

Functions	Purposes	Categories
LENGTH	Returns the length of a string	String
TRIM	Removes leading and trailing spaces from a string	String
UPPER	Converts a string to upper case	String
LOWER	Converts a string to lower case	String
ABS	Calculates the absolute value of a number	Math
ROUND	Rounds a number	Math
CEIL	Rounds a number up	Math
FLOOR	Rounds a number down	Math
CURRENT_DATE	Returns the current date	Temporal
CURRENT_TIMESTAMP	Returns the current timestamp	Temporal
DATEDIFF	Calculates the difference between two dates	Temporal
COALESCE	Returns the first non-null value in a list	Logical
CASE	Returns either true or false	Logical

Table 4.6 Some Built-In CHECK Constraint Functions

Most of these functions resemble spreadsheet formula functions, don't you think? They're intuitive and easy to use. Now that you've grasped the syntax of CHECK constraints, you can apply any function you need.

> **Check Constraint Functions**
>
> Different database products may support different CHECK constraint functions. Although Table 4.6 serves as a good starting point, you should consult the documentation of your database product of choice for a full list of functions and their exact syntax.
>
> Our purpose has been to help you learn about the syntax you'll use to apply functions to CHECK constraints, and we have! It's up to you to advance your knowledge about functions.

Default Constraint

OK, this is an easy one! We can apply the `DEFAULT` constraint to specify a default value for a column in case a value is not provided during insertion. Check Listing 4.42 to see it in use.

```
CREATE TABLE employee (
    id INT PRIMARY KEY,
    name VARCHAR(50) NOT NULL,
    country_code VARCHAR(3),
    phone VARCHAR(20),
    address VARCHAR(100) DEFAULT 'Not specified'
);
```

Listing 4.42 DEFAULT Constraint in Use

In this example, we used the `DEFAULT` constraint for the `address` column. If an address is not provided, the database engine will automatically set the `'Not specified'` literal as the `address` value.

Fun fact: the `DEFAULT` constraint supports most of the functions that the `CHECK` constraint supports as well! Listing 4.43 gives an example.

```
CREATE TABLE employee (
    id INT PRIMARY KEY,
    NAME VARCHAR(50) NOT NULL,
    country_code VARCHAR(3),
    phone VARCHAR(20),
    address VARCHAR(100)
      DEFAULT 'Not known as of ' || TO_CHAR(CURRENT_DATE, 'YYYY-MM-DD')
);
```

Listing 4.43 DEFAULT Constraint Used with Function

This time, we've provided a calculated default value for the `address` column. If an address is not provided during row creation, the database engine will concatenate the `'Not known as of'` literal with the current data and set it as the address. Table 4.7 demonstrates the result of such an operation.

id	name	country_code	phone	address
473	Emma Johnson	+33	1 45 67 89 01	Not known as of 2024-08-10

Table 4.7 Sample employee Row Inserted without Providing an Address

> **Defaults and Nulls**
>
> If the NULL value is explicitly inserted, the column value will be set to NULL rather than the default value. DEFAULT works in cases where no value is specified at all—not even NULL.

So far, we've covered SQL statements for table creation, and we've seen a lot! Now, we can move on to SQL statements regarding table modification purposes.

4.3.2 Table Modification

A software application is never "done." Every application goes through a lifecycle, in which it gets changed and modified over time and thus evolves into different versions. Being common data storage platforms, relational databases are no exception. As applications change, their corresponding database tables need to change as well.

In this section, we'll learn about SQL statements targeting changes in database tables.

> **Version Control**
>
> As database tables are often integral parts of their corresponding software applications, they might be subject to version control and documentation in many cases. You should comply with the development standards of your organization, and you should track and document table changes as needed.

Table modification statements mostly start with the ALTER TABLE prefix, which declares our intention to make a structural change to a database table. The following sections contain the details of the change we want to make.

Renaming a Table

Let's start with an easy one. Listing 4.44 contains the syntax for renaming a table.

```
ALTER TABLE { table_name } RENAME TO { new_table_name };
```

Listing 4.44 Syntax for Renaming Table

Very easy and self-explanatory, don't you think? Listing 4.45 demonstrates this syntax in a real SQL statement.

```
ALTER TABLE employee_bonus_payment RENAME TO employee_bonus_pay;
```

Listing 4.45 SQL Statement Renaming Sample Table

Once we execute this statement and refresh the table list in pgAdmin, we should see the table renamed as in Figure 4.31.

4.3 Table Manipulation

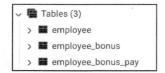

Figure 4.31 Table List in pgAdmin after Renaming Operation

Since a schema doesn't allow namesake tables, your new table name needs to be a unique name. That's the first consideration. We'll discuss further risks of renaming a table in Section 4.5.

Now that we've learned how to rename a table, let's move forward to changing the structure of a table.

Column Modifications

In this section, we'll learn about types of modifications that target the basic structure of a column. Listing 4.46 showcases the common syntax for such SQL statements.

```
ALTER TABLE { table_name }
{ operation } COLUMN { column_name }
{ parameters }
```

Listing 4.46 Common Syntax for Column Modifications

If the syntax looks a bit confusing to you, no worries! The actual statements are nearly plain English as usual and are easily understandable. For starters, check Listing 4.47 to see how to add a new column to an existing table.

```
ALTER TABLE employee ADD COLUMN birthday DATE NOT NULL;
```

Listing 4.47 SQL Statement to Add New Column to Table

We start with ALTER TABLE and the target table name, which is the usual prefix. ADD COLUMN is the obvious operator to add a new column, and we follow it with the column name date and the data type date. We can optionally add some single column constraints, such as NOT NULL, as the statement suffix.

Easy as promised, right? Once we've executed this statement, we'll be able to see the change in our table structure in pgAdmin, as demonstrated in Figure 4.32.

What if we want to rename our new column? That's even easier than creating it! Listing 4.48 renames birthday to birth_date.

```
ALTER TABLE employee
RENAME COLUMN birthday TO birth_date;
```

Listing 4.48 Example of SQL Statement for Renaming Column

4   Data Definition Language

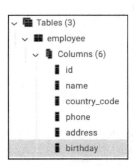

Figure 4.32 New employee.birthday Column Shown in pgAdmin

Once we execute this statement, we should see its effect in pgAdmin, as shown in Figure 4.33.

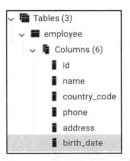

Figure 4.33 Renamed birth_date Column Shown in pgAdmin

If we want to get rid of this column completely, Listing 4.49 shows how it's done.

```
ALTER TABLE employee DROP COLUMN birth_date;
```

Listing 4.49 SQL Statement to Delete employee.birth_date Column

> **Data Loss upon Column Deletion**
>
> Once you delete a column, each row will irreversibly lose its value in that column as well. In the case above, you would lose the `birth_date` values of all employees.
>
> Therefore, you should only execute `DROP COLUMN` operations with the utmost caution. You may want to create a backup copy of those values before deleting the column, in case you ever want to reverse the operation.

Data Type Changes

Changing the data type of a column is also a common requirement. There may cases in which `employee.address` is not long enough anymore, so we'll need to execute a statement like the one in Listing 4.50 to change the data type to `varchar(110)`.

```
ALTER TABLE employee
ALTER COLUMN address
SET DATA TYPE VARCHAR(110);
```

Listing 4.50 SQL Statement Changing Data Type of employee.address

Once we execute of this command, we'll be able to see the new column type in pgAdmin, as shown in Figure 4.34.

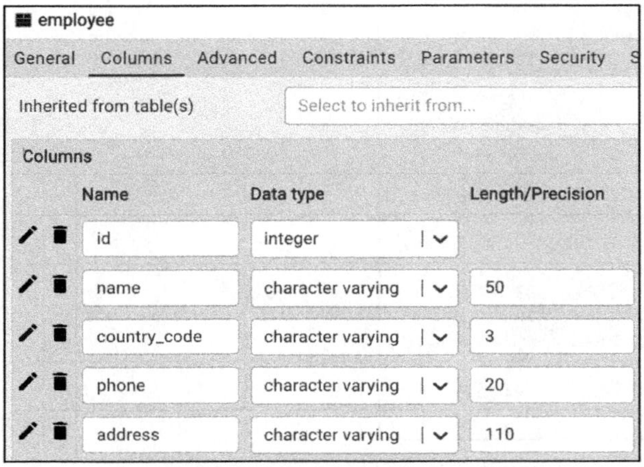

Figure 4.34 New employee.address Data Type in pgAdmin

Previous warnings about disrupting client applications are also valid for data type changes. You need to ensure that applications accessing the table won't fail due to the change at hand, so we recommend that you apply the changes on a test system and modify applications accordingly.

You also need to be mindful of data type changes if the table contains data already. If you change a column to a smaller data type, you may cause data loss in that column. For example, if you convert varchar(100) to varchar(10), you'll lose the characters after the tenth position in each row.

You also can't change the former data type to an uncorrelated data type. For instance, you can't simply change the employee.address type to date because the database engine can't convert text-based address values to dates.

You may encounter cases in which you want to convert a text column containing only numeric values to a numeric column. There's a common multistep approach you can use to achieve this goal.

To prepare your case and do some further exercises, add a new column to the employee table called child_count. Listing 4.51 deliberately defines it as a character-type column instead of a numeric column, to demonstrate the change later.

4   Data Definition Language

```sql
ALTER TABLE employee ADD COLUMN child_count VARCHAR(3);
```

Listing 4.51 Adding employee.child_count Column with Inaccurate Data Type

Once you execute this statement, you'll be able to see the new column in pgAdmin, as shown in Figure 4.35.

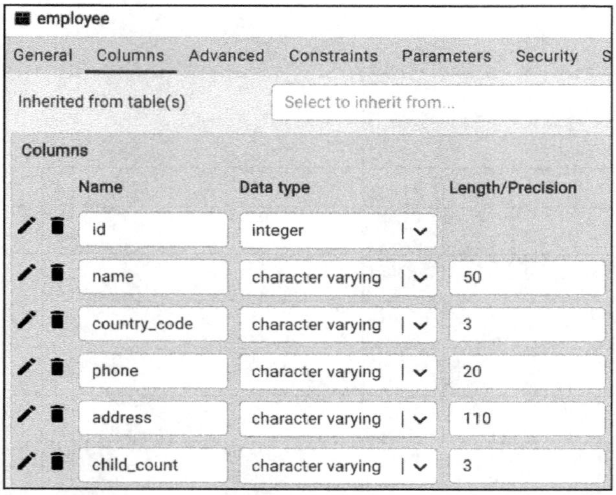

Figure 4.35 New Incorrect employee.child_count Column Shown in pgAdmin

After you insert some entries into this table, its contents may look like those shown in Table 4.8.

Id	name	child_count
1	Emily Turner	2
2	Liam Carter	3

Table 4.8 Sample Content of employee Table

At this point, Listing 4.52 will fail because the database engine can't automatically convert varchar(3) values to int values. Despite the fact that the values in child_count look like numbers to us humans, they're technically characters.

```sql
ALTER TABLE employee
ALTER COLUMN child_count
SET DATA TYPE INT;
```

Listing 4.52 SQL Statement to (Unsuccessfully) Change Type of employee.child_count

Now, let's go over our multistep plan. The first step is to create a new column with the correct data type, as demonstrated in Listing 4.53.

```
ALTER TABLE employee ADD COLUMN new_child_count INT;
```

Listing 4.53 Creating New employee.new_child_count Column

After you execute this statement, the table structure will look like Figure 4.36. Note that the child_count and new_child_count columns exist simultaneously—for now.

Figure 4.36 employee.new_child_count Column Created with Correct Data Type

The second step is to copy values from the old employee.child_count column to the new employee.new_child_count column, including a data type change, as demonstrated in Listing 4.54.

```
UPDATE employee SET new_child_count = CAST(child_count AS INT);
```

Listing 4.54 SQL Statement to Copy Values between Columns

> **UPDATE Keyword**
>
> The UPDATE keyword actually belongs to DML, which is the subject of Chapter 5. But since the syntax is intuitive and understandable, there's no harm in having a sneak peek! We'll cover this keyword comprehensively when the time comes.

Once you've executed this statement, the contents of the employee table will look like Table 4.9.

4 Data Definition Language

id	name	child_count	new_child_count
1	Emily Turner	2	2
2	Liam Carter	3	3

Table 4.9 Table Contents After Filling employee.new_child_count

Now, we've got all we need! All that's left to do is to delete the `child_count` column and rename `new_child_count` as `child_count`. Clever, eh? Let's do them both at once, as in Listing 4.55.

```
ALTER TABLE employee
DROP COLUMN child_count;

ALTER TABLE employee
RENAME COLUMN new_child_count TO child_count;
```

Listing 4.55 SQL Statements to Delete child_count and Rename new_child_count

Upon this change, the contents of the `employee` table will look like Table 4.10.

id	name	child_count
1	Emily Turner	2
2	Liam Carter	3

Table 4.10 Contents of employee Table after Data Type Change

Although the data in `child_count` looks the same, its type has changed. See Figure 4.37.

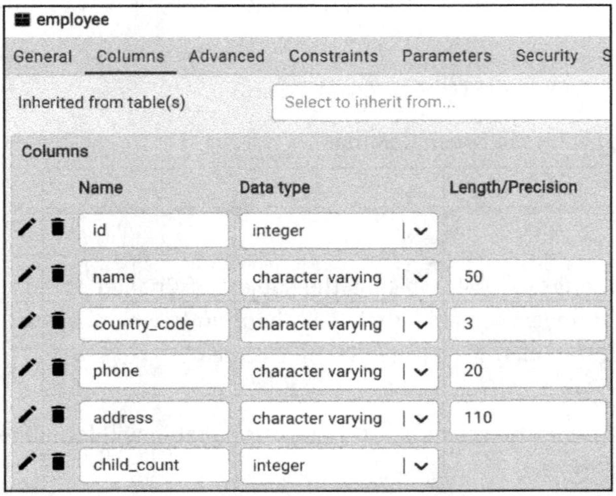

Figure 4.37 New Data Type of employee.child_count Shown in pgAdmin

140

We can also use this multistep approach between other data types, as long as they're logically convertible.

PostgreSQL has a clever shortcut that reduces this multistep approach to one step. By providing the USING keyword, we can define a conversion routine. Listing 4.56 showcases the entire statement we can use to replace our multistep approach.

```
ALTER TABLE employee
ALTER COLUMN child_count TYPE INT
USING child_count::INT;
```

Listing 4.56 Shortcut for Data Type Change

It's good to know both solutions, because you won't find this exact shortcut in other database products.

Constraint Modifications

Now that we can change columns and data types, we should be able to change constraints as well.

Let's start with the syntax for single column constraints, which is very similar to changing data types. Check Listing 4.57.

```
ALTER TABLE { table_name } ALTER COLUMN { column_name } SET { constraint };
```

Listing 4.57 Syntax to Add Single Column Constraint

We can use this syntax for DEFAULT and NOT NULL constraints. Listing 4.58 demonstrates both cases simultaneously, setting a default value and NOT NULL for the employee.child_count column.

```
ALTER TABLE employee ALTER COLUMN child_count SET DEFAULT 0;
ALTER TABLE employee ALTER COLUMN child_count SET NOT NULL;
```

Listing 4.58 SQL Statements to Add Two Constraints to employee.child_count

After we execute these SQL statements, the properties of employee.child_count should change as shown in Figure 4.38.

What if we want to get rid of an existing single column constraint? That's easy—we simply make use of the DROP keyword, as in Listing 4.59.

```
ALTER TABLE { table_name } ALTER COLUMN { column_name } DROP { constraint };
```

Listing 4.59 Syntax for Removing Single Column Constraint

4 Data Definition Language

Figure 4.38 employee Columns in pgAdmin after Constraint Change

Let's remove our recent constraints by using Listing 4.60.

```
ALTER TABLE employee ALTER COLUMN child_count DROP DEFAULT;
ALTER TABLE employee ALTER COLUMN child_count DROP NOT NULL;
```

Listing 4.60 SQL Statements to Remove Our Single Column Constraints

Once we execute these statements, the column properties of `employee.child_count` should change as in Figure 4.39.

Figure 4.39 employe.child_count in pgAdmin After Constraint Removal

Those were the constraints that are based on single columns. Now, we can move on to modifying constraints that may cover multiple columns, such as PRIMARY KEY, FOREIGN KEY, UNIQUE, and CHECK.

4.3 Table Manipulation

To have a self-contained example, we're going to make a fresh start in which we don't have any employee bonus tables yet. If you're following along with the examples, you can do this by executing the statements in Listing 4.61.

```
DROP TABLE employee_bonus_pay;
DROP TABLE employee_bonus;
```

Listing 4.61 SQL Statements to Delete Bonus Tables for Fresh Start

Now, using Listing 4.62, let's re-create employee_bonus without any constraints to make a fresh start.

```
CREATE TABLE employee_bonus (
    employee_id INT,
    bonus_year INT,
    bonus_amount NUMERIC(12, 2),
    currency VARCHAR(3)
);
```

Listing 4.62 SQL Statement to Create employee_bonus without Any Constraints

To add a new (potentially) multicolumn constraint, we ought to use a SQL statement that follows the syntax in Listing 4.63.

```
ALTER TABLE { table_name }
ADD CONSTRAINT { constraint_name }
{ constraint_parameters }
```

Listing 4.63 Syntax to Add Multicolumn Constraint to Existing Table

Let's make a demonstration to set the PRIMARY KEY of employee_bonus, which is the most fundamental constraint of them all. See Listing 4.64.

```
ALTER TABLE employee_bonus
ADD CONSTRAINT employee_bonus_pkey
PRIMARY KEY (employee_id, bonus_year);
```

Listing 4.64 SQL Statement to Set Primary Key of employee_bonus

That's very similar to providing the primary key during initial table creation, right? You can refer back to Section 4.3.1 if you need to refresh your memory. Note that we provided the employee_bonus_pkey constraint name explicitly—it could have been any meaningful name. This name will be important very soon, when we want to get rid of a constraint.

If we check the properties of employee_bonus in pgAdmin, we should see it as in Figure 4.40.

4 Data Definition Language

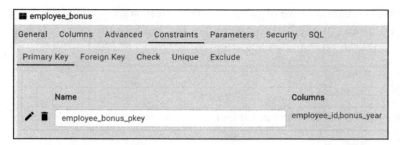

Figure 4.40 Primary Key Constraint of employee_bonus Shown in pgAdmin

Let's make another exercise—adding a foreign key this time! See Listing 4.65.

```
ALTER TABLE employee_bonus
ADD CONSTRAINT employee_bonus_fkey1
FOREIGN KEY (employee_id)
REFERENCES employee (id);
```

Listing 4.65 Adding FOREIGN KEY Constraint to Existing employee_bonus Table

This takes a very similar approach, like declaring a foreign key during the initial table creation. You can check Section 4.3.1 if you need to refresh your memory. Once you're on track, you should be able to follow Listing 4.66, where you'll add a CHECK constraint this time.

```
ALTER TABLE employee_bonus
ADD CONSTRAINT employee_bonus_chk1
CHECK (currency = 'USD' OR currency = 'EUR');
```

Listing 4.66 Adding CHECK Constraint to Existing employee_bonus Table

All our new constraints should appear in pgAdmin, and you can check the properties of the employee_bonus table as we did before.

Now, what if we want to get rid of an existing constraint? That has a very easy syntax that's showcased in Listing 4.67.

```
ALTER TABLE { table_name }
DROP CONSTRAINT { constraint_name };
```

Listing 4.67 Syntax to Remove Existing Constraint

That's why it's important to know the names of the constraints—we need to know their names in case we want to remove them.

As an exercise, let's remove our latest CHECK constraint. First, we need the name of the constraint. If we don't know it, we can check the table properties in pgAdmin. The constraint names are visible as shown in Figure 4.41.

Figure 4.41 Constraint Name Shown in pgAdmin

Once we have the name of the constraint (employee_bonus_chk1), we can remove it easily by using the statement in Listing 4.68.

```
ALTER TABLE employee_bonus
DROP CONSTRAINT employee_bonus_chk1;
```

Listing 4.68 SQL Statement to Remove CHECK Constraint from employee_bonus Table

The same syntax applies to other constraint types as well. As long as we provide the correct constraint name, we can remove it by using the exact same statement template.

> **Constraint Modification Risks**
>
> Adding and removing constraints is not something you'll do very often. Although you've learned how to conduct such operations using SQL, you should only execute them with management approval and utmost caution. For example, removing a constraint from a production table can cause data inconsistencies, while adding a constraint can cause unexpected application errors.
>
> You should always conduct such operations with the consent and approval of technical leaders, and you should modify client applications accordingly if needed.

This concludes our journey through table modification statements. Our next stop will be the potentially dangerous know-how on table deletion.

4.3.3 Table Deletion

We briefly touched on the subject of table deletion when we were learning about constraints in Section 4.3.1. Now is the time to learn about it officially. Despite its risks, which we'll discuss in Section 4.5, table deletion has a simple and straight-forward syntax, as shown in Listing 4.69.

```
DROP TABLE [ IF EXISTS ] { table_name } [ CASCADE | RESTRICT ];
```

Listing 4.69 Syntax to Delete Table

4   Data Definition Language

The most basic form of this syntax is demonstrated in Listing 4.70. This statement will delete the employee_bonus table if possible, including all of its rows. If the table doesn't exist or has relationships to other tables, you'll get an error message and the table won't be deleted.

DROP TABLE employee_bonus;

Listing 4.70 Basic SQL Statement to Delete Table

You can bypass these limitations by adding optional keywords, which we discuss in the following sections.

If Exists

Listing 4.71 demonstrates the addition of IF EXISTS. Once you execute this statement, the database engine will silently ignore the statement if the employee_bonus table doesn't exist—without generating any error messages.

DROP TABLE IF EXISTS employee_bonus;

Listing 4.71 SQL Statement to Delete Table If It Exists

This mechanism is particularly useful if you have an application targeting different environments. You can execute the same SQL statement in each environment, and only existing tables will be deleted.

Cascade

CASCADE is another useful keyword that we inspected for schemas in Section 4.2.3, which you can refer back to if you need a refresher. Following the same logic as in schema deletion, CASCADE will force-delete the table, even if it has relationships to other tables. All relationships will be deleted along with the table. Listing 4.72 demonstrates the usage of this keyword.

DROP TABLE employee_bonus CASCADE;

Listing 4.72 SQL Statement to Force-Delete Table and All Its Relationships

If the need arises, you can get creative and use both optional mechanisms together, as in Listing 4.73.

DROP TABLE IF EXISTS employee_bonus CASCADE;

Listing 4.73 Using All Optional Keywords Together

Restrict

Our syntax in Listing 4.69 had an optional keyword—RESTRICT—which we ignored momentarily. This keyword is actually the default behavior of the command, which means that the statements in Listing 4.74 are identical and will execute in exactly the same way.

```
DROP TABLE employee_bonus;
DROP TABLE employee_bonus RESTRICT;
```

Listing 4.74 Usage of RESTRICT Keyword

But if you're using another database product, the default behavior might be different. So, to be on the safe side and to express your intention more clearly, you should add the optional RESTRICT or CASCADE keyword explicitly when coding SQL in a production environment.

Truncate

So far, we've inspected the DROP TABLE command, which destroys the table with its rows. However, there's a second command that keeps the table but deletes all its rows. See Listing 4.75.

```
TRUNCATE TABLE { table_name };
```

Listing 4.75 Syntax to Delete All Rows in Table

To see TRUNCATE TABLE in action, check Listing 4.76.

```
TRUNCATE TABLE employee_bonus;
```

Listing 4.76 SQL Statement to Delete all rows in employee_bonus Table

Easy, right?

Look at that! We've concluded the entire chapter on table manipulation, and we're getting close to the end of DDL overall! We have only a few topics left, so take a break, get something fresh to drink, and let's continue with view manipulation.

4.4 View Manipulation

We talked about views in Chapter 2, and you can refer back to it if you need a memory refresher. Once you're clear about the purpose of views and their differences from tables, we can proceed to SQL statements regarding view manipulation.

To proceed with this topic, we need to know the very basics of data query language (DQL), simply because view manipulation statements must contain DQL code. We use DQL to query database tables and extract data from them, and although DQL is the subject of an upcoming chapter, we'll briefly touch here on the SELECT keyword, which is the entry point of DQL.

To showcase our example, Figure 4.42 contains the latest ERD of the employee table.

4 Data Definition Language

	employee		
PK	id	int	NOT NULL
	name	varchar(50)	NOT NULL
	country_code	varchar(3)	
	phone	varchar(20)	
	address	varchar(110)	
	child_count	int	

Figure 4.42 Latest ERD of employee Table

Table 4.11 contains some sample `employee` rows. (It's mock data, as usual.)

id	name	country_code	phone	address	child_count
344	Bonnie Perez	256	548-2515	1371 Fowler Plains, Kurtfort, NY 36886	1
345	Marcus Evans	344	109-1239	495 Haley Drive, Suite 472, Joneston, AZ 74718	3
346	Patricia Green	1	927-851-6000	129 Mallory Ville, Apt. 468, Colinburgh, SC 47331	4
347	Jonathan Williams	834	999-7626	3556 Griffin Springs, South Meredithport, NE 53745	0
348	Diane Becker	474	901-8125	2188 Molly Mount, Apt. 679, Port Shaunburgh, PA 81052	2

Table 4.11 Sample employee Table Data

If we need the IDs and names of employees who have at least three children, we can get that list by using Listing 4.77.

4.4 View Manipulation

```
SELECT
    id,
    name,
    child_count
FROM
    employee
WHERE
    child_count >= 3;
```
Listing 4.77 SQL Statement to Retrieve Employees with at Least Three Children

Since this is not the DQL chapter, we won't delve into the details of this statement. Besides, it's intuitive and self-explanatory. Once we execute this statement, the database will return a list like in Table 4.12.

id	name	child_count
345	Marcus Evans	3
346	Patricia Green	4

Table 4.12 Employees with at Least Three Children

Clear, right? Using this basic example, we can delve into view manipulation statements.

> **Views and Data Query Language**
>
> Although you'll use basic DQL statements for view manipulation, you can get as complex as you want! Once you finish the chapter on DQL, you can use the same view manipulation statements—but ones that contain much more comprehensive DQL code.

4.4.1 View Creation

Once you have DQL under your belt, writing syntax to create a new view is merely a matter of throwing in some additional keywords. See Listing 4.78.

```
CREATE VIEW { view_name } AS { dql_code };
```
Listing 4.78 Syntax for View Creation

Let's start by creating a view that will contain our basic SELECT statement in Listing 4.77 as the DQL code. See Listing 4.79 and see how similar it is to the SELECT statement itself.

```
CREATE VIEW
    employee_with_many_children AS
SELECT
    id,
    NAME,
    child_count
FROM
    employee
WHERE
    child_count >= 3;
```

Listing 4.79 SQL Statement to Create employee_with_many_children View

Once we execute this SQL statement, the view will be created and available in pgAdmin, as shown in Figure 4.43.

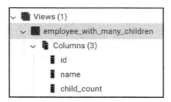

Figure 4.43 employee_with_many_children View Shown in pgAdmin

Now that we have this view available, we don't need to write the entire SQL statement in Listing 4.77 to get a list of employees with many children. Instead, we can simply use the statement in Listing 4.80.

```
SELECT
    *
FROM
    employee_with_many_children;
```

Listing 4.80 SQL Statement to Retrieve Data from Our New View

Executing this statement will return the same list as in Table 4.12. Neat, eh?

This highlights one of the advantages of views: even the most complex query can be packed into a view. Whenever we need to access this list again, we can simply view the contents of the view instead of re-writing the complex SQL statement all over again.

As with other database elements, you can't have namesake views under the same schema. Every view must have a unique name.

4.4.2 View Modification

As with table modifications, you should conduct view modifications with care because you may unintentionally disrupt client applications. The caveats for table modifications in Section 4.3.2 are all valid for view modifications as well. With that in mind, we may proceed!

Renaming a View

Renaming a view is very similar to renaming a table—we'll simply replace the TABLE keyword with the VIEW keyword. Check the syntax in Listing 4.81.

```
ALTER VIEW { view_name } RENAME TO { new_view_name };
```

Listing 4.81 Syntax for Renaming View

Let's see it in action in Listing 4.82 and rename our sample view.

```
ALTER VIEW employee_with_many_children
RENAME TO employees_with_many_children;
```

Listing 4.82 SQL Statement to Rename Our New View

Once we execute this statement, we should see the view with its new name in pgAdmin, as seen in Figure 4.44.

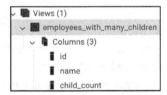

Figure 4.44 Renamed View in pgAdmin

Changing View Contents

Modifying the contents of a view is very similar to creating the view in the first place. Check Listing 4.83 and see for yourself!

```
CREATE OR REPLACE VIEW { view_name } AS { new_dql_code };
```

Listing 4.83 Syntax to Change View

As an example, we'll cover a scenario in which the employee_with_many_children view should return employees with at least four children (instead of three). Listing 4.84 contains the SQL statement that will make this change for us.

```
CREATE OR REPLACE VIEW
    employees_with_many_children AS
SELECT
    id,
    name,
    child_count
FROM
    employee
WHERE
    child_count >= 4;
```

Listing 4.84 Changing employee_with_many_children View

Once you execute this statement, the DQL part of the view will be replaced with the new content. Also, once you retrieve data from this new version of the view, the database engine will return only Patricia Green, as in Table 4.13—simply because she's the only one with at least four children.

id	name	child_count
346	Patricia Green	4

Table 4.13 Employees with at Least Four Children

Easy as creating the view in the first place, right?

This example showcases another advantage of views. Even though the definition of "employees with many children" changed by +1 child count, the name of the view didn't change at all—only the DQL body changed. Once this change is deployed, any client application accessing `employees_with_many_children` will start getting the list in Table 4.13 instead of the former list in Table 4.12. That way, the change of the definition could be applied to the entire system centrally, without touching a single line of client application code.

This statement is also particularly useful if you have an application targeting different environments. You can execute the same SQL statement in each environment and ensure that the target view is either created or updated—hence, the CREATE OR REPLACE prefix.

4.4.3 View Deletion

Deleting a view is very similar to deleting a table. The syntax is showcased in Listing 4.85.

```
DROP VIEW [ IF EXISTS ] { view_name } [ CASCADE | RESTRICT ];
```

Listing 4.85 Syntax for View Deletion

To see it in action, check Listing 4.86, which we can execute to get rid of our sample view.

```
DROP VIEW employees_with_many_children;
```

Listing 4.86 SQL Statement to Delete employees_with_many_children View

The uses of the optional parameters, as well as the caveats for deleting a database object, were all highlighted for tables in Section 4.3.3. All of that is also valid for views, so there's no need to repeat the same content here. Just replace the `TABLE` keyword with the `VIEW` keyword, and you're good to go!

The only difference? Views don't contain data; they're simply mirrors of data. Therefore, deleting a view won't cause data loss.

4.5 Common Pitfalls of Data Definition Language

In the previous sections, we mentioned multiple times that renaming or deleting existing database objects comes with certain risks. In this section, we'll highlight some of those risks.

4.5.1 Renaming Objects

You need to be careful when renaming objects. It's a relatively rare requirement to rename an existing data structure, but if such a need arises, we advise you to get approval from all stakeholders before proceeding. For example, if there's an application that accesses the `playground2` database, it will probably stop functioning after you rename the database as `playground3`. The application will keep trying to access `playground2`, which doesn't exist anymore.

The same logic applies to schemas, tables, etc.

4.5.2 Deleting Objects

As with renaming objects, it's a relatively rare requirement to delete an existing production object. Migrations, upgrades, space management, data consolidation, or software retirement might be some of the factors leading to such a decision.

In such a case, we advise you to get approval from all stakeholders before proceeding. Even if a database object won't be needed for live transactions any longer, some users might need to access it in the future, for reporting or legal purposes. So, creating a backup before deleting the object might be a good idea, just in case.

This logic also applies to databases, schemas, tables, columns, etc.

4.6 Summary

In this chapter, we learned about DDL and how to build and execute corresponding SQL statements.

At this point, we know how to create, modify, and delete databases, schemas, tables, constraints, and views. All of this should come in handy in your database adventures!

We've also discussed the risks of changing or deleting existing database components. Client applications relying on those components may fail if you don't proceed with caution.

Now that we can create database components, it's time to create table entries by using DML, which is the subject of our next chapter.

Chapter 5
Data Manipulation Language

With database objects in place, the next logical step is to put data into tables and learn to modify data when needed. In this chapter, you'll learn to insert, update, and delete data. (These are the second most common set of database operations—data querying being the first). You'll also see some automation options with triggers, which are set up to execute upon data insertion, modification, or deletion in a table and are used to automatically alter data in related tables. Stored procedures are similar mechanisms, but they aren't executed automatically—they need to be called manually.

So far, we've learned about SQL statements for data definition language (DDL), which we use to create database structures to hold data. Now, we're "officially" getting hands-on with actual data operations. Exciting, right?

So, welcome to the wonderful world of data manipulation language (DML)! In this chapter, we'll learn all about data manipulation in relational databases. Inserting new rows into tables and modifying and deleting existing rows is the main focus of this chapter. We'll cover SQL syntax and practical examples of such operations, and we'll also delve into automation options and learn about stored procedures and triggers. DML operations also have some common pitfalls, so we'll highlight and discuss some of them.

We're going to need a set of tables on which to run our examples, so we'll begin by building a network of tables to serve as our playground. Let's do it and start our DML journey!

> **Note**
>
> Every database product has a unique language for procedures, which means that developing stored procedures is a topic distinct from SQL and beyond the scope of this book. This chapter will only briefly explore the role of stored procedures in databases and show some basic examples.

5 Data Manipulation Language

5.1 Building a Data Manipulation Language Playground

To practice DML statements, we'll build a network of tables related to an imaginary concert venue called Harmony Garden. This venue has multiple theaters, in which concert events take place simultaneously. For each event, there are tickets of different categories that have varying prices. Online members of Harmony Garden can purchase tickets and return them if they change their minds.

Let's start by designing the structure of fundamental master data tables. See Figure 5.1.

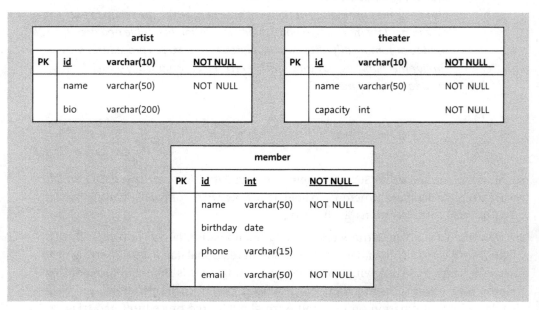

Figure 5.1 Fundamental Master Data Tables for Harmony Garden

The artist table will contain a list of artists or bands performing in the theaters of Harmony Garden. We need to store their names and biographies.

The theater table will contain a list of available theaters in Harmony Garden. We'll store the name and capacity of each theater.

The member table will contain a list of online members of Harmony Garden, who will be able to buy tickets and such. We'll store their basic master data and contact information.

Let's create those tables using DDL, which we learned in the previous chapter! For a good exercise, you can try creating them yourself now, without peeking at the example. Or you can simply use the code in Listing 5.1.

5.1 Building a Data Manipulation Language Playground

> **Schema Decision**
>
> In a real-world situation, it would make sense to create a new schema called harmony_garden and create all tables under that schema. That would ensure a logical and isolated collection of related tables. You can go that way if you like, or you can simply stick to our playground schema—it's up to you!
>
> We've already gone through how to create a new schema and work under it. If you need refresher, you can revisit Chapter 4. Code samples in this chapter stick to the playground schema.

```
CREATE TABLE
    artist (
        id VARCHAR(10) PRIMARY KEY,
        name VARCHAR(50) NOT NULL,
        bio VARCHAR(200)
    );

CREATE TABLE
    theater (
        id VARCHAR(10) PRIMARY KEY,
        name VARCHAR(50) NOT NULL,
        capacity INT NOT NULL
    );

CREATE TABLE
    member (
        id SERIAL PRIMARY KEY,
        name VARCHAR(50) NOT NULL,
        birthday DATE,
        phone VARCHAR(15),
        email VARCHAR(50) NOT NULL
    );
```

Listing 5.1 Creation of Fundamental Master Data Tables for Harmony Garden

Once you complete the statements, you should see those tables in pgAdmin, as in Figure 5.2 (although you might need to refresh the GUI).

Figure 5.2 Fundamental Master Data Tables in pgAdmin

157

5   Data Manipulation Language

> **SERIAL Data Type**
>
> The SERIAL data type is actually an INTEGER, which auto-increments every time a new row is inserted. For member rows, we won't have to explicitly provide an id value—the database engine will automatically gather the biggest member.id, increment it by 1, and use that value as the new member.id for the upcoming row.
>
> This is particularly useful for transactional tables with ever-increasing numbers of rows. It would be very difficult to keep track of keys otherwise.

Now, let's extend our structure with tables related to events and tickets. As you can see in Figure 5.3, we've added two new tables.

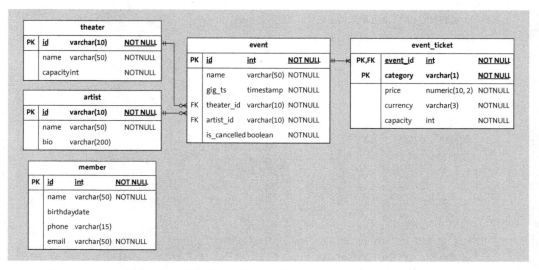

Figure 5.3 ERD Extended with Event-Related Tables

The event table will contain a new row for each event in Harmony Garden. The name, date, and time of each event is naturally stored, and beyond that, the table will store the ID of the theater in the theater_id column and the ID of the artist in the artist_id column as foreign keys. If the event ever gets cancelled, we'll set is_cancelled to true. All reasonable, right?

The event_ticket table will contain the list of ticket categories for each event. This table has a composite primary key of two columns: event_id (foreign key) and category (A, B, or C). This means that each event has tickets of different categories, with A being the most expensive, B being the middle tier, and C being the most affordable. We'll store the price, currency, and number of released tickets under their respective columns.

Listing 5.2 contains the SQL statements you use to create those tables. You can write the code yourself (without peeking at the example) as an exercise, or you can follow the provided statements if you want to.

5.1 Building a Data Manipulation Language Playground

```
CREATE TABLE
    event (
        id SERIAL PRIMARY KEY,
        name VARCHAR(50) NOT NULL,
        gig_ts timestamp NOT NULL,
        theater_id VARCHAR(10) NOT NULL,
        artist_id VARCHAR(10) NOT NULL,
        is_cancelled BOOLEAN NOT NULL DEFAULT FALSE,
        FOREIGN KEY (theater_id) REFERENCES theater (id),
        FOREIGN KEY (artist_id) REFERENCES artist (id)
    );

CREATE TABLE
    event_ticket (
        event_id INT NOT NULL,
        category VARCHAR(1) NOT NULL,
        price NUMERIC(10, 2) NOT NULL,
        currency VARCHAR(3) NOT NULL DEFAULT 'USD',
        capacity INT NOT NULL,
        PRIMARY KEY (event_id, category),
        FOREIGN KEY (event_id) REFERENCES EVENT (id)
    );
```

Listing 5.2 Creation of Event-Related Tables for Harmony Garden

Once you execute those statements, you should see your event tables in pgAdmin, as in Figure 5.4. You may need to refresh the GUI, though.

Figure 5.4 Event Tables in pgAdmin

Category and Currency

In a real-world scenario, it would make sense to declare event_ticket.category and event_ticket.currency as foreign keys, which refer to their distinct master data tables. However, we want to keep things simple and understandable because our main focus is on understanding DML statements. Drowning in an ocean of tables won't benefit us, so we'll keep the number of tables limited and follow a simplified path.

159

5 Data Manipulation Language

Now is the time to sell tickets! Figure 5.5 demonstrates the new ERD, to which we've added two sales-related tables.

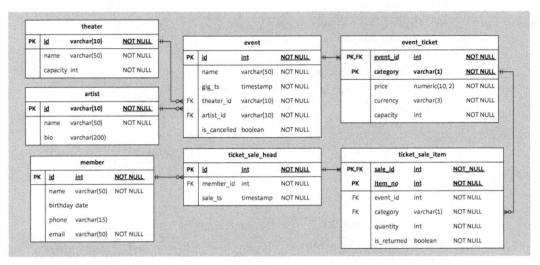

Figure 5.5 ERD Extended with Sales-Related Tables

In each online order, a member may purchase tickets to different events at the same time. Therefore, we need two distinct tables regarding ticket sales.

The `ticket_sale_head` table is the sales header table, and it will have a new row for each purchase made by a member. It contains a unique sales id, the corresponding member_id, and the purchase date and time—nothing out of ordinary.

The `ticket_sale_item` table is the sales item table, and it contains all tickets included in a single member purchase. This table has a composite primary key that's built by two columns: sale_id, which refers to `ticket_sale_head.id`, and item_no, which is an incremental number for each ticket in the purchase. The non-key fields are mostly intuitive: event_id and category refer to event_ticket, while quantity contains the number of tickets purchased. Finally, `ticket_sale_item.is_returned` would be set to true if the member returns the purchased tickets.

We encourage you to create these tables manually, as an exercise. You can follow through Listing 5.3 if you have difficulties.

```
CREATE TABLE
    ticket_sale_head (
        id SERIAL PRIMARY KEY,
        member_id INT NOT NULL,
        sale_ts TIMESTAMP NOT NULL,
        FOREIGN KEY (member_id) REFERENCES member (id)
    );
```

```
CREATE TABLE
    ticket_sale_item (
        sale_id INT NOT NULL,
        item_no INT NOT NULL,
        event_id INT NOT NULL,
        category VARCHAR(1) NOT NULL,
        quantity INT NOT NULL,
        is_returned BOOLEAN NOT NULL DEFAULT FALSE,
        PRIMARY KEY (sale_id, item_no),
        FOREIGN KEY (sale_id) REFERENCES ticket_sale_head (id),
        FOREIGN KEY (event_id) REFERENCES EVENT (id),
        FOREIGN KEY (event_id, category) REFERENCES event_ticket (event_id, category)
    );
```

Listing 5.3 Creation of Sales-Related Tables of Harmony Garden

Once you execute these statements, the new sales tables should appear in pgAdmin like in Figure 5.6, possibly after a GUI refresh.

Figure 5.6 Sales Tables in pgAdmin

> **Additional Constraints**
>
> These tables could use some check constraints! We recommend that you add the following constraints as a personal exercise by using the ALTER TABLE statements we learned in Chapter 4:
>
> - The theater.capacity constraint must be greater than zero.
> - The member.birthday constraint must be later than 1900.
> - The event_ticket.price and event_ticket.capacity constraints must be greater than zero.
> - The ticket_sale_item.quantity constraint must be greater than zero.

Looks great! Now, we have a basic business scenario and its corresponding set of tables on which to run our DML examples. Let's set sail to DML statements, then!

5.2 Data Manipulation Language Operations

In this section, we'll cover basic DML operations in the logical order of the data lifecycle. First, we'll create a new row using the INSERT keyword. Over time, we may modify the row by using the UPDATE keyword. And finally, when the row is no longer needed, we can destroy it by using the DELETE keyword. Keeping with our case study of Harmony Garden, we'll go over each operation and learn about its finer points.

5.2.1 Insert

This is the first step of the common data lifecycle. Inserting a new row into a database table is similar to typing a new row into a spreadsheet.

Creation of a new master data entry is a typical case in which row insertion is needed. In our case study, if an artist is to perform at Harmony Garden for the first time, we will create a new row in the artist table for them. Alternatively, if a new member signs up on the website, we will create a new row in the member table for them. You get the idea!

Recording transactions is another typical case. Whenever a ticket sale is completed on the website, we need to create new rows in the ticket_sale_head and ticket_sale_item tables to keep records of the tickets sold. These transactional rows will be useful for concert entries and building sales statistics later on.

In the following sections, we'll make use of INSERT commands to achieve these results.

Inserting a Single Row

Let's create some master data, then! Listing 5.4 showcases the basic syntax for inserting a new row into a database table.

```
INSERT INTO { table_name } ( [ column_names ] ) VALUES ( [ column_values ] );
```

Listing 5.4 Basic Syntax for Row Insertion

If that looks complicated to you, don't fret—it's not! The syntax may look more complicated than the actual statement, so let's quickly jump to creating a new artist row. See Listing 5.5.

```
INSERT INTO
    artist (id, name, bio)
VALUES
    (
        'LUNE',
        'Lunar Echoes',
        'An ambient duo known for ethereal soundscapes.'
    );
```

Listing 5.5 SQL Statement to Create New Artist Row

That's better, right? Very intuitive! We start with the command `INSERT INTO`, which declares our intention to create a new table row, followed by the name of the target table, `artist`. Next, we provide a list of columns we have values for: `id`, `name`, and `bio`. In the last part, we provide the `VALUES` keyword and provide our values following the same order of given column names.

Once we execute Listing 5.5, a new row is created in the `artist` table, as shown in Table 5.1. You can also check the contents of the `artist` table via pgAdmin.

id	name	bio
LUNE	Lunar Echoes	An ambient duo known for ethereal soundscapes

Table 5.1 New Entry in artist Table

Easy enough, right? Now, we encourage you to run through the exercise, in which you'll insert further rows into the `artist` table so that its contents look like Table 5.2. Make sure not to duplicate LUNE—the database engine will return an error if you attempt that.

id	name	bio
CRHR	Crimson Horizon	A rock band with powerful anthems
ECSR	Echo Serenade	An acoustic singer-songwriter with heartfelt ballads
JZWH	Jazz Whispers	A smooth-jazz trio with a hint of blues
LUNE	Lunar Echoes	An ambient duo known for ethereal soundscapes
NHMY	Neon Harmony	An indie pop group with a nostalgic 80s vibe
SFSN	Sapphire Sun	An experimental electronic producer
SLSR	The Silver Strum	A folk band blending traditional and modern melodies
SNTD	Sonic Tides	A surf rock band inspired by the coastlines
URPL	Urban Pulse	A hip-hop artist with socially conscious lyrics
VLRY	Velvet Rhythms	A funk band that brings the groove to life

Table 5.2 Final Form of artist Table

Inserting Multiple Rows at the Same Time

If you've followed through the exercise, you've had to write and execute ten distinct `INSERT` statements. But there's a shortcut syntax for bulk insertion.

To see this shortcut in action, we're going to fill in the `theater` table, which must contain a row for each theater in our venue of Harmony Garden. Listing 5.6 demonstrates how to achieve that goal with one single SQL statement.

5 Data Manipulation Language

```
INSERT INTO
    theater (id, name, capacity)
VALUES
    ('AURA', 'Aura Plaza', 750),
    ('VIBE', 'Vibe Lounge', 650),
    ('ECHO', 'Echo Hall', 900),
    ('ZENI', 'Zenith Arena', 850),
    ('PULS', 'Pulse Center', 950);
```

Listing 5.6 SQL Statement to Insert All Theater Rows at Same Time

This is very similar to inserting an individual row. The only difference is that we provide multiple entries after the VALUES keyword. Once you execute this statement, the theater table should look like Table 5.3.

id	name	capacity
AURA	Aura Plaza	750
ECHO	Echo Hall	900
PULS	Pulse Center	950
VIBE	Vibe Lounge	650
ZENI	Zenith Arena	850

Table 5.3 Final Form of theater Table

See, we're making progress already! We've got all our artists and theaters defined.

Serial Columns on Insertion

In our recent examples, we provided values for every column of our target table. But this doesn't have to be the case all the time.

Remember the columns of our member table. You can use Table 5.4 as a memory refresher.

Column	Data type	Can be null
id	serial	No
name	varchar(50)	No
birthday	date	Yes
phone	varchar(15)	Yes

Table 5.4 Columns of member Table

164

Column	Data type	Can be null
email	`varchar(50)`	No

Table 5.4 Columns of member Table (Cont.)

Let's focus first on the `id` column. It has the `serial` data type, which indicates an auto-increasing number for each new `member` row. Therefore, we don't have to provide a value for that column during row insertion. See Listing 5.7 for a demonstration.

```
INSERT INTO
    member (name, birthday, phone, email)
VALUES
    (
        'Alex Johnson',
        '1985-06-15',
        '555-1234',
        'alex.johnson@example.com'
    );
```

Listing 5.7 Inserting New member Row without Specifying ID

We didn't provide a value for `member.id` because we expect the database engine to autofill this column. Once we execute the statement, `member` table should look like Table 5.5.

id	name	birthday	phone	email
1	Alex Johnson	1985-06-15	555-1234	alex.johnson@example.com

Table 5.5 member Table after Insertion of Initial Row

To help us understand the mechanism a little better, let's also execute Listing 5.8, in which we insert another `member` row.

```
INSERT INTO
    member (name, birthday, phone, email)
VALUES
    (
        'Jordan Lee',
        '1990-11-22',
        '555-5678',
        'jordan.lee@example.com'
    );
```

Listing 5.8 Inserting Another member Row without Specifying ID

5   Data Manipulation Language

Once we execute the statement, the member table should look like Table 5.6.

id	name	birthday	phone	email
1	Alex Johnson	1985-06-15	555-1234	alex.johnson@example.com
2	Jordan Lee	1990-11-22	555-5678	jordan.lee@example.com

Table 5.6 member Table After Insertion of Second Row

As you can see, member.id becomes autogenerated sequential values, even though we didn't provide its value in our INSERT statements. Cool, eh?

Null Values on Insertion

Let's move on to another case. It's evident in Table 5.4 that member.birthday and member.phone may have null values. This means that we can build a SQL statement in which these columns are excluded, in case the member didn't provide this information. See Listing 5.9, in which a new member is created that way.

```
INSERT INTO
    member (name, email)
VALUES
    ('Morgan Taylor', 'morgan.taylor@example.com');
```

Listing 5.9 Inserting member Row with Missing Nullable Columns

Once we execute this statement, the member table should look like Table 5.7.

id	name	birthday	phone	email
1	Alex Johnson	1985-06-15	555-1234	alex.johnson@example.com
2	Jordan Lee	1990-11-22	555-5678	jordan.lee@example.com
3	Morgan Taylor	NULL	NULL	morgan.taylor@example.com

Table 5.7 member Table after Insertion of Third Row

In a bulk INSERT operation, you can still provide all column names but explicitly pass NULL for missing values. See Listing 5.10 for such a case.

```
INSERT INTO
    member (name, birthday, phone, email)
VALUES
    (
        'Samantha Brown',
        '1987-03-30',
```

```
        '555-8765',
        'samantha.brown@example.com'
    ),
    (
        'Chris Smith',
        NULL,
        '555-4321',
        'chris.smith@example.com'
    ),
    (
        'Taylor Wilson',
        '1992-08-17',
        NULL,
        'taylor.wilson@example.com'
    ),
    (
        'Jordan Davis',
        NULL,
        NULL,
        'jordan.davis@example.com'
    ),
    (
        'Riley Adams',
        '1984-12-05',
        '555-6789',
        'riley.adams@example.com'
    );
```

Listing 5.10 Inserting Further member Rows with Occasional Null Values

Although we provided all column names initially, we've simply used the NULL keyword in rows with missing values. Once we execute this statement, the member table should look like Table 5.8.

id	name	birthday	phone	email
1	Alex Johnson	1985-06-15	555-1234	alex.johnson@example.com
2	Jordan Lee	1990-11-22	555-5678	jordan.lee@example.com
3	Morgan Taylor	NULL	NULL	morgan.taylor@example.com
4	Samantha Brown	1987-03-30	555-8765	samantha.brown@example.com
5	Chris Smith	NULL	555-4321	chris.smith@example.com

Table 5.8 member Table after Insertion of Further Rows

5 Data Manipulation Language

id	name	birthday	phone	email
6	Taylor Wilson	1992-08-17	NULL	taylor.wilson@example.com
7	Jordan Davis	NULL	NULL	jordan.davis@example.com
8	Riley Adams	1984-12-05	555-6789	riley.adams@example.com

Table 5.8 member Table after Insertion of Further Rows (Cont.)

> **Not Null Columns on Insertion**
>
> If a column is marked as NOT NULL, you must provide a value for that column in each new row. Otherwise, the database engine will generate an error and cancel the insertion. In our example, we must provide values for member.name and member.email because they have the NOT NULL constraint.

Default Values on Insertion

Another case in which we don't need to specify values for all columns occurs when a column has a default value. We'll put our event tables under the magnifying glass for that. Table 5.9 is a memory refresher for event columns.

Column	Data type	Default value
id	serial	
name	varchar(50)	
gig_ts	timestamp	
theater_id	varchar(10)	
artist_id	varchar(10)	
is_cancelled	boolean	false

Table 5.9 Columns of event Table

Mind you that event.is_cancelled has a default value: false. This means that if we leave this column out of an INSERT statement, the value of this column for the new row will automatically be set to false instead of NULL. See Listing 5.11 for an example.

```
INSERT INTO
    event (name, gig_ts, theater_id, artist_id)
VALUES
    (
```

```
        'Lunar Echoes Single Debut',
        '2025-02-15 21:30:00',
        'AURA',
        'LUNE'
    );
```

Listing 5.11 Inserting New event Row without Specifying is_cancelled

Once we execute this statement, the contents of the event table should look like Table 5.10. Note that the value of event.is_cancelled being set to false by default.

id	name	gig_ts	theater_id	artist_id	is_cancelled
1	Lunar Echoes Single Debut	2025-02-15 21:30:00	AURA	LUNE	false

Table 5.10 event Table Contents after Initial INSERT Statement

Naturally, we can apply the same approach if we're inserting multiple rows at the same time, as demonstrated in Listing 5.12.

```
INSERT INTO
    event (name, gig_ts, theater_id, artist_id)
VALUES
    (
        'Summer Fest',
        '2024-09-01 20:00:00',
        'AURA',
        'LUNE'
    ),
    (
        'Night Beats',
        '2024-10-15 19:30:00',
        'VIBE',
        'ECSR'
    ),
    (
        'Rock Legends',
        '2024-11-05 21:00:00',
        'ECHO',
        'SLSR'
    ),
    (
        'Acoustic Vibes',
        '2024-12-20 18:00:00',
```

5 Data Manipulation Language

```
        'ZENI',
        'CRHR'
);
```

Listing 5.12 Inserting Multiple Rows at Same Time with Default Values

Once we execute this latest statement, we'll have a bunch of events! The contents of the event table should look like Table 5.11.

id	name	gig_ts	theater_id	artist_id	is_cancelled
1	Lunar Echoes Single Debut	2025-02-15 21:30:00	AURA	LUNE	false
2	Summer Fest	2024-09-01 20:00:00	AURA	LUNE	false
3	Night Beats	2024-10-15 19:30:00	VIBE	ECSR	false
4	Rock Legends	2024-11-05 21:00:00	ECHO	SLSR	false
5	Acoustic Vibes	2024-12-20 18:00:00	ZENI	CRHR	false

Table 5.11 event Table Contents after Bulk Insertion

Inserting Rows from Another Table

There's another method of inserting rows into a table: we can pick the values from a source table, modify them as needed, and insert them into the target table. The syntax of such an operation is shown in Listing 5.13, in which a data selection statement replaces individual values.

```
INSERT INTO { table_name } ( [ column_names ] ) { selection };
```

Listing 5.13 Syntax to Insert Rows from Another Table

Let's see this syntax in practice. Figure 5.7 provides a reminder of the relationship between the event table and the event_ticket table. For each event row, we ought to have multiple event_ticket rows, each of which corresponds to each ticket category of the event at hand. Here, we define the price of the ticket as well as the number of tickets issued.

In our case, we'll aim at creating event_ticket rows out of event rows automatically. For each event row, we want to have a corresponding event_ticket row, in which the ticket category is A, the price is 100 USD, and the ticket capacity is 30 people.

To keep the example simple, we're declaring a fixed price of 100 USD for category A tickets to each event. So, event tickets won't have varying prices. The same applies to capacities: we're selling 30 category A tickets to each event. Listing 5.14 contains the SQL statement we use to achieve this goal.

5.2 Data Manipulation Language Operations

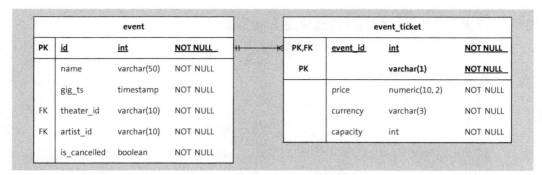

Figure 5.7 ERD Regarding event and event_ticket

```
INSERT INTO
    event_ticket (event_id, category, price, capacity)
SELECT
    id,
    'A',
    100,
    30
FROM
    event;
```

Listing 5.14 SQL Statement to Create event_ticket Rows of Category A

The top part of our statement is exactly like our regular INSERT statements. The difference is in the bottom part: instead of providing literal values, we've provided a SELECT statement to return values from the event table.

Let's break it down to make it more understandable. Try executing only the SELECT part of the statement, as shown in Listing 5.15.

```
SELECT
    id,
    'A',
    100,
    30
FROM
    event;
```

Listing 5.15 SELECT Part of Statement

The results of this statement are demonstrated in Table 5.12. Note that the id values came from the event table, while the rest of the values have been entered into the statement manually. In other words, for each row in the event table, an output row that includes our manual values is generated.

171

5 Data Manipulation Language

event.id	(category)	(price)	(capacity)
1	A	100	30
2	A	100	30
3	A	100	30
4	A	100	30
5	A	100	30

Table 5.12 Results of SELECT Statement

> **Data Query Language Content**
>
> Don't worry about the SELECT statement above too much—understanding the basics is enough at this point. SELECT statements belong to the realm of DQL, into which we'll dive deeply in Chapter 7.
>
> You can revisit this section after finishing our DQL chapter if you want. Most SELECT elements you'll learn there can be applied to INSERT statements, and as you get more adept at SELECT statements, your INSERT statements will be empowered accordingly.

By combining this SELECT substatement with the INSERT INTO command, we get to build Listing 5.14, where event_ticket table entries will be generated from event rows. Once you execute this statement, the event_ticket table should look like Table 5.13.

event_id	category	price	currency	capacity
1	A	100.00	USD	30
2	A	100.00	USD	30
3	A	100.00	USD	30
4	A	100.00	USD	30
5	A	100.00	USD	30

Table 5.13 event_ticket Filled with Category A Rows

Practical, eh?

However, from the business point of view, we've created rows for category A tickets only. Following the same method, let's create rows for other ticket categories too. Once again, we'll provide fixed prices and capacities for the sake of simplicity. For each event, we'll have 50 category B tickets for 80 USD and 100 category C tickets for 60 USD. Listing 5.16 contains the SQL statements we use to achieve this goal.

```
INSERT INTO
    event_ticket (event_id, category, price, capacity)
SELECT
    id,
    'B',
    80,
    50
FROM
    event;

INSERT INTO
    event_ticket (event_id, category, price, capacity)
SELECT
    id,
    'C',
    60,
    100
FROM
    event;
```

Listing 5.16 SQL Statements to Create event_ticket Rows for Further Ticket Categories

Once we execute these statements, the `event_ticket` table will contain entries for the remaining ticket categories and will assume its complete form, as shown in Table 5.14.

event_id	category	price	currency	capacity
1	A	100.00	USD	30
1	B	80.00	USD	50
1	C	60.00	USD	100
2	A	100.00	USD	30
2	B	80.00	USD	50
2	C	60.00	USD	100
3	A	100.00	USD	30
3	B	80.00	USD	50
3	C	60.00	USD	100
4	A	100.00	USD	30
4	B	80.00	USD	50

Table 5.14 event_ticket Table Filled with All Ticket Categories

5   Data Manipulation Language

event_id	category	price	currency	capacity
4	C	60.00	USD	100
5	A	100.00	USD	30
5	B	80.00	USD	50
5	C	60.00	USD	100

Table 5.14 event_ticket Table Filled with All Ticket Categories (Cont.)

That concludes our journey through row creation! Now, we'll move on to an equally important operation, in which we update the values of existing rows in database tables.

5.2.2   Update

In this section, we'll make use of the UPDATE keyword in its raw form and also supported by literals, calculations, subqueries, and conditions. UPDATE is the basic prefix for SQL statements, and it declares our intention to make changes to existing table rows.

Updating existing table rows is a very common task. Such a requirement may arise for many reasons, such as reflecting changes in the real world, correcting wrong data, and making value adjustments.

Since we already have some tables and rows at hand, we'll continue to use our example of Harmony Garden in this section.

> **Common Pitfalls**
>
> After we go through this topic, we strongly recommend that you go over the common DML pitfalls in Section 5.2.4 before applying your knowledge to databases.

Updating with Literals

Let's begin with a relatively light topic. Updating rows with manually provided literals is the most basic form of a value update, and it's arguably the most common one too. Listing 5.17 showcases the syntax for such operations.

```
UPDATE { table_name } SET { equations } [ WHERE { conditions } ];
```

Listing 5.17 Basic Syntax for Table Updates

As you can see, UPDATE statements have a straightforward syntax. To see it in action, we'll go over a case in which we need to change the ticket currency from USD to EUR for the Night Beats event. Let's locate it in the event table (see Table 5.15).

id	name	gig_ts	theater_id	artist_id	is_cancelled
3	Night Beats	2024-10-15 19:30:00	VIBE	ECSR	false

Table 5.15 Night Beats Event in event Table

Note that event.id has a value of 3, which is the primary key of the table. Now, we can find the ticket prices of this event in the event_ticket table, as shown in Table 5.16.

event_id	category	price	currency	capacity
3	A	100.00	USD	30
3	B	80.00	USD	50
3	C	60.00	USD	100

Table 5.16 Night Beats Ticket Prices in event_ticket Table

For these records, event_ticket.currency needs to be converted from USD to EUR. We'll achieve our goal with the simple UPDATE statement in Listing 5.18.

```
UPDATE event_ticket
SET
    currency = 'EUR'
WHERE
    event_id = 3;
```

Listing 5.18 SQL Statement to Set Night Beats Ticket Currency to EUR

A typical update statement would start with the UPDATE keyword, followed by the name of the table to be updated. The second part starts with the SET keyword, followed by the value change we want. The final (optional) WHERE part declares the criteria for rows to be updated. In other words, only the rows corresponding to our WHERE condition would be updated.

If you don't provide a WHERE condition, all rows in the table will be updated—which is not a common requirement. Most of the time, developers will provide a WHERE condition to pinpoint the scope of the UPDATE.

> **WHERE Condition**
>
> The WHERE condition of an UPDATE statement can be much more complex than in our humble example. We'll learn about WHERE conditions in greater detail in Chapter 7, where we'll discuss DQL. Once you finish that chapter, you can apply the WHERE logic to UPDATE statements easily.

5   Data Manipulation Language

Once you execute the statement in Listing 5.18, the event_ticket.currency values of our event will change to EUR—but the rows corresponding to other events won't change, thanks to our WHERE condition! Thus, the rows of the event_ticket table should look like Table 5.17.

event_id	category	price	currency	capacity
1	A	100.00	USD	30
1	B	80.00	USD	50
1	C	60.00	USD	100
2	A	100.00	USD	30
2	B	80.00	USD	50
2	C	60.00	USD	100
3	A	100.00	EUR	30
3	B	80.00	EUR	50
3	C	60.00	EUR	100
4	A	100.00	USD	30
4	B	80.00	USD	50
4	C	60.00	USD	100
5	A	100.00	USD	30
5	B	80.00	USD	50
5	C	60.00	USD	100

Table 5.17 event_ticket Rows after UPDATE Statement

In this example, we've modified the values in a single column: event_ticket.currency. However, it's also possible to modify the values in multiple columns at once. We'll learn about that through a new requirement, in which we should set the price of category A tickets to 120 USD and the capacity to 25 people for all events except Night Beats.

Does that sound complicated? Actually, it's an easy task! Let's build the UPDATE statement step by step. In the first part, we need to initialize the statement and declare the name of the table to be updated, as in Listing 5.19.

```
UPDATE event_ticket
```

Listing 5.19 First Part of Multicolumn UPDATE Statement

Then, we need to declare the list of value changes we want, as in Listing 5.20.

```
UPDATE event_ticket
SET
    price = 120,
    capacity = 25
```

Listing 5.20 First and Second Parts of Multicolumn UPDATE Statement

Finally, we need to provide a WHERE condition to define the rows to change. In our case, we need to conduct the update for all rows except event 3 (Night Beats), which are of category A. Thus, we arrive at the final statement in Listing 5.21.

```
UPDATE event_ticket
SET
    price = 120,
    capacity = 25
WHERE
    event_id <> 3
    AND category = 'A';
```

Listing 5.21 Final Form of Multicolumn UPDATE Statement

Once we execute of this statement, the rows of the event_tickets table should look like Table 5.18. Note that price and capacity have changed for all category A rows, except for event 3 (Night Beats).

event_id	category	price	currency	capacity
1	A	120.00	USD	25
1	B	80.00	USD	50
1	C	60.00	USD	100
2	A	120.00	USD	25
2	B	80.00	USD	50
2	C	60.00	USD	100
3	A	100.00	EUR	30
3	B	80.00	EUR	50
3	C	60.00	EUR	100
4	A	120.00	USD	25
4	B	80.00	USD	50

Table 5.18 event_ticket Rows after Multicolumn Update

event_id	category	price	currency	capacity
4	C	60.00	USD	100
5	A	120.00	USD	25
5	B	80.00	USD	50
5	C	60.00	USD	100

Table 5.18 event_ticket Rows after Multicolumn Update (Cont.)

Congratulations! Now, you know how to update table rows with literal values.

Updating with Calculations

It's also possible to build UPDATE statements containing calculations. Let's assume that we want to increase the prices of all category B and category C tickets by 10%. We can achieve this goal easily by using the SQL statement in Listing 5.22.

```
UPDATE event_ticket
SET
    price = price * 1.1
WHERE
    category = 'B'
    OR category = 'C';
```

Listing 5.22 UPDATE Statement with Calculation

The only significant change is in the SET part. Instead of providing a fixed new value, we've provided a formula to calculate the new value. After we execute this statement, the event_ticket.price values of all category B and category C tickets should increase by 10%. Our rows should look like Table 5.19.

event_id	category	price	currency	capacity
1	A	120.00	USD	25
1	B	88.00	USD	50
1	C	66.00	USD	100
2	A	120.00	USD	25
2	B	88.00	USD	50
2	C	66.00	USD	100
3	A	100.00	EUR	30

Table 5.19 event_ticket Rows after UPDATE Statement with Calculation

event_id	category	price	currency	capacity
3	B	88.00	EUR	50
3	C	66.00	EUR	100
4	A	120.00	USD	25
4	B	88.00	USD	50
4	C	66.00	USD	100
5	A	120.00	USD	25
5	B	88.00	USD	50
5	C	66.00	USD	100

Table 5.19 event_ticket Rows after UPDATE Statement with Calculation (Cont.)

The formula can also contain values from other columns if we want it to. Listing 5.23 demonstrates this possibility, in which we calculate the values in the price column based on the values in the capacity column.

```
UPDATE event_ticket
SET
    price = 1000 / capacity
WHERE
    event_id = 5;
```

Listing 5.23 SQL Statement with Intercolumn Calculation

The results of this statement for event 5 can be seen in Table 5.20.

event_id	category	price	currency	capacity
1	A	120.00	USD	25
1	B	88.00	USD	50
1	C	66.00	USD	100
2	A	120.00	USD	25
2	B	88.00	USD	50
2	C	66.00	USD	100
3	A	100.00	EUR	30
3	B	88.00	EUR	50

Table 5.20 event_ticket Rows for Event 5 after Intercolumn Calculation

5 Data Manipulation Language

event_id	category	price	currency	capacity
3	C	66.00	EUR	100
4	A	120.00	USD	25
4	B	88.00	USD	50
4	C	66.00	USD	100
5	A	40.00	USD	25
5	B	20.00	USD	50
5	C	10.00	USD	100

Table 5.20 event_ticket Rows for Event 5 after Intercolumn Calculation (Cont.)

Neat, eh? Using the same technique, you can get more creative and use more complex calculations if the need arises. Your SQL syntax will remain the same!

Updating with Subqueries

This section is going to use an approach that's similar to inserting new data with subqueries, which we've seen and executed before.

In our example statement for this topic, we'll have the following requirement: for event 4, the ticket price of category C should be the minimum USD ticket price in the entire ticket range for all events. If we eyeball the latest values in Table 5.20, we find out that the lowest value is 10 and that it belongs to event 5.

That was easy to spot, but what if we had a million records in the event_ticket table? It would be nearly impossible to do this task with the human eye, but luckily, we're about to learn how to do it with SQL! Let's see the statement first and evaluate it later. See Listing 5.24.

```
UPDATE event_ticket
SET
    price = (
        SELECT
            MIN(price)
        FROM
            event_ticket
        WHERE
            category = 'C'
            AND currency = 'USD'
    )
```

```
WHERE
    event_id = 4
    AND category = 'C';
```

Listing 5.24 SQL Statement to Set Low Price for Event 4 Category C

Although our UPDATE … SET … WHERE syntax is the same, we have something little different in the SET part: a subquery!

The database engine will execute the SELECT statement first, to fetch the lowest category C price in USD from the event_ticket table. You can execute the subquery in Listing 5.25 in isolation and see that the value of 10 is returned.

```
SELECT
    MIN(price)
FROM
    event_ticket
WHERE
    category = 'C'
    AND currency = 'USD'
```

Listing 5.25 SQL Statement to Fetch Lowest Category C Price in USD

Once we merge this SELECT statement into our parent UPDATE statement as in Listing 5.24, the database engine will use the resulting value of 10 to update our target category C price from event 4. As a result, our event_ticket table should look like Table 5.21. Check our target row.

event_id	category	price	currency	capacity
1	A	120.00	USD	25
1	B	88.00	USD	50
1	C	66.00	USD	100
2	A	120.00	USD	25
2	B	88.00	USD	50
2	C	66.00	USD	100
3	A	100.00	EUR	30
3	B	88.00	EUR	50
3	C	66.00	EUR	100
4	A	120.00	USD	25

Table 5.21 Updated Price of Event 4 Category C after SQL Statement

5   Data Manipulation Language

event_id	category	price	currency	capacity
4	B	88.00	USD	50
4	C	10.00	USD	100
5	A	40.00	USD	25
5	B	20.00	USD	50
5	C	10.00	USD	100

Table 5.21 Updated Price of Event 4 Category C after SQL Statement (Cont.)

> **Data Query Language Content**
>
> As mentioned in Section 5.2.1, SELECT statements belong to the realm of DQL, which we'll dive deeper into in Chapter 7.
>
> You can revisit this section after finishing our DQL chapter, if you want to. Most SELECT elements you'll learn there can be applied to UPDATE statements. As you get more adept at SELECT statements, your UPDATE statements will be empowered accordingly.

Updating with Conditions

In this topic, we're going to learn how to do conditional updates. Let's jump directly to the statement and evaluate it afterward. See Listing 5.26.

```
UPDATE event_ticket
SET
    price = CASE
        WHEN category = 'A' THEN price + 20
        WHEN category = 'B' THEN price + 10
        WHEN category = 'C' THEN price + 5
    END
WHERE
    currency = 'USD';
```

Listing 5.26 SQL Statement Containing Conditional Update

It's evident that we're updating USD ticket prices once more. The new and exciting part is the CASE keyword and the following conditions. Using this functionality, we can determine a new ticket price based on the ticket category in that row:

- If the ticket category is A, we're raising the price by $20.00.
- If the ticket category is B, we're raising the price by $10.00.
- If the ticket category is C, we're raising the price by $5.00.

The database engine will process through CASE conditions sequentially and execute updates in the first matching condition. So, although our example is a simple one, the order of the conditions is important because it signifies their execution priority.

After executing the statement in Listing 5.26, the event_ticket rows should look like Table 5.22. Note that only USD rows were updated, due to our WHERE condition.

event_id	category	price	currency	capacity
1	A	140.00	USD	25
1	B	98.00	USD	50
1	C	71.00	USD	100
2	A	140.00	USD	25
2	B	98.00	USD	50
2	C	71.00	USD	100
3	A	100.00	EUR	30
3	B	88.00	EUR	50
3	C	66.00	EUR	100
4	A	140.00	USD	25
4	B	98.00	USD	50
4	C	15.00	USD	100
5	A	60.00	USD	25
5	B	30.00	USD	50
5	C	15.00	USD	100

Table 5.22 event_ticket Rows after Conditional Update

Following the same syntax, you can get creative and write more complex CASE conditions if the need arises. See Listing 5.27 for such an example.

```
UPDATE event_ticket
SET
    capacity = CASE
        WHEN category = 'A' AND currency = 'EUR' THEN 50
        WHEN category = 'B' THEN 42
        ELSE capacity
```

```
        END
WHERE
        event_id <> 1;
```

Listing 5.27 Relatively Complex SQL Statement for Conditional Update

In this example, we're aiming at changing the values of the `capacity` column. The capacity for category A tickets bought with the EUR currency will become 50, while the capacity for category B tickets will become 42. Our WHERE statement ensures that event 1 is excluded from the update—just because!

The `capacity` values of the rows, which don't correspond to the CASE conditions, become the values specified through the ELSE keyword at the end of the conditions. In our example, we set the `capacity` value itself—indicating that we don't want a change. If we don't exclusively specify an ELSE part, rows not corresponding to any condition will get a NULL value. If that's your intention, fine, but that will be a rare case. As a best practice, we recommend that you include ELSE keywords in conditional updates, even if you're setting it to NULL.

Once we execute the statement in Listing 5.27, the `event_ticket` rows should look like Table 5.23. Note how rows corresponding to our conditions have changed while others have remained untouched, just as we intended.

event_id	category	price	currency	capacity
1	A	140.00	USD	25
1	B	98.00	USD	50
1	C	71.00	USD	100
2	A	140.00	USD	25
2	B	98.00	USD	42
2	C	71.00	USD	100
3	A	100.00	EUR	50
3	B	88.00	EUR	42
3	C	66.00	EUR	100
4	A	140.00	USD	25
4	B	98.00	USD	42
4	C	15.00	USD	100
5	A	60.00	USD	25

Table 5.23 event_ticket Rows after Complex Conditional Update

event_id	category	price	currency	capacity
5	B	30.00	USD	42
5	C	15.00	USD	100

Table 5.23 event_ticket Rows after Complex Conditional Update (Cont.)

That concludes our journey through row updates. Now, we're approaching a far more dangerous topic: deletion of table rows!

5.2.3 Delete

Deletion is a dangerous but sometimes necessary operation. The danger lies in the fact that you're deleting rows and that it may be nearly impossible to call back those rows, so you need to handle such operations with the utmost care. Some cases where data deletion is necessary are removing outdated records, clearing temporary data, and removing mistakenly posted rows.

Some software systems, such as SAP S/4 HANA, have a general tendency to not delete data in general. Instead of data deletion, they use other techniques, like the following:

- Limiting validity of rows by date intervals
- Adding a deleted column (boolean) to the table and marking obsolete rows as true instead of deleting them
- Recording new reverse-post entries in financial tables with mirroring negative amounts, so that the original or reversal records add up to zero, negating any financial effect
- Archiving old data

This ensures that even old or invalid data remains in the system and can be reported for controlling purposes if necessary.

That being said, there's no harm in learning how to delete rows, as long as you use that knowledge with common sense and good evaluation of the situation. So, let's move forward to the corresponding SQL capabilities.

> **Common Pitfalls**
>
> After you go through this topic, we strongly recommend that you go over common DML pitfalls in Section 5.2.4 before applying your knowledge to databases.

Setting Up Sample Data

As we progress through this section, we're going to need to delete data—obviously! We'll create a short SQL script to insert mock data into the ticket_sale_head and ticket_sale_item tables. Every time you need a fresh start, you can re-execute this script to rebuild those tables with fresh data. Neat, eh? But just a small reminder: these are the tables related to online ticket sales. Whenever a member buys tickets for a show, we store the sold tickets in those tables. You can refer back to Section 5.1 if you need more details.

Listing 5.28 contains the SQL code to reset and refill these tables.

```
DELETE FROM ticket_sale_item CASCADE;
DELETE FROM ticket_sale_head CASCADE;
ALTER SEQUENCE ticket_sale_head_id_seq RESTART WITH 1;

INSERT INTO ticket_sale_head (member_id, sale_ts)
SELECT id, CURRENT_TIMESTAMP AS sales_ts
FROM member
ORDER BY NAME LIMIT 3;

WITH
    ranked_events AS (
        SELECT id AS event_id,
        ROW_NUMBER() OVER (ORDER BY id) AS rn
        FROM event ),
    expanded_sales AS (
        SELECT id AS sale_id,
        ROW_NUMBER() OVER (ORDER BY id) * 2 - 1 AS rn1,
        ROW_NUMBER() OVER (ORDER BY id) * 2 AS rn2
        FROM ticket_sale_head)
INSERT INTO ticket_sale_item (sale_id, item_no, event_id, category, quantity)
    SELECT es.sale_id, 1, re1.event_id, 'B', 1
    FROM expanded_sales es JOIN ranked_events re1 ON es.rn1 = re1.rn
    UNION ALL
    SELECT es.sale_id, 2, re2.event_id, 'C', 3
    FROM expanded_sales es JOIN ranked_events re2 ON es.rn2 = re2.rn;
```

Listing 5.28 SQL Script to Build Ticket Sales Tables with Mock Data

Admittedly, this SQL script is a bit advanced for our current level because it contains window functions. But don't worry about it at this point; we're advancing step-by-step! At this point, you can think of it as a magic spell that refills your sample tables every time you execute it. But if you're feeling curious and adventurous, you're more than welcome to slice and dice the statement and study its individual parts.

> **Delete Statements in Magic Formula**
> Careful readers may have already noticed the fun fact that Listing 5.28 starts with DELETE keywords, which corresponds to our topic at hand!

Whenever we execute Listing 5.28, the ticket_sale_head table will look like Table 5.24.

id	member_id	sale_ts
1	1	(current date and time)
2	5	(current date and time)
3	7	(current date and time)

Table 5.24 Mock Data in ticket_sale_head Table

Here, we see three ticket orders that have been placed by members 1, 5, and 7. As an optional exercise, you can check the identities of these members on the member table by using a SELECT statement.

Our corresponding item table, ticket_sale_item, will look like Table 5.25.

sale_id	item_no	event_id	category	quantity	is_returned
1	1	1	B	1	false
1	2	2	C	3	false
2	1	3	B	1	false
2	2	4	C	3	false
3	1	5	B	1	false

Table 5.25 Mock Data in ticket_sale_item Table

As an optional exercise, you can check the names of these events on the event table by using another SELECT statement.

If we do a combined reading of those tables, we find out the following:

- In ticket sale #1, member 1 (Alex Johnson) purchased the following:
  - A category B ticket for event 1 (Lunar Echoes Single Debut)
  - Three category C tickets for event 2 (Summer Fest)
- In ticket sale #2, member 5 (Chris Smith) purchased the following:
  - A category B ticket for event 3 (Night Beats)
  - Three category C tickets for event 4 (Rock Legends)
- In ticket sale #3, member 7 (Jordan Davis) purchased a category B ticket for event 5 (Acoustic Vibes)

Cool? Understandable? Good, then we can proceed!

5   Data Manipulation Language

Deleting Some Rows

Start this section by executing Listing 5.28. We need fresh mock data for examples.

Deleting select rows is arguably the most common type of deletion operation. See the syntax for this in Listing 5.29.

```
DELETE FROM { table_name } [ WHERE { conditions } ];
```
Listing 5.29   Basic Syntax for Row Deletion

Once again, we have intuitive, straightforward syntax. To see it in action, we'll delete entries from the `ticket_sale_item` table that belong to category C. The syntax in Listing 5.30 achieves just that.

```
DELETE FROM ticket_sale_item WHERE category = 'C';
```
Listing 5.30   Sample SQL Statement for Literal Based Row Deletion

Our statement starts with the `DELETE FROM` command, which declares our intention to delete rows, followed by the name of the table in which the deletion will occur. Finally, we provide the values of rows to be deleted. In our case, we intend to delete rows containing `WHERE category = 'C'`.

Once the statement is executed, the `ticket_sale_item` table will look like Table 5.26 and be free from category C tickets!

sale_id	item_no	event_id	category	quantity	is_returned
1	1	1	B	1	false
2	1	3	B	1	false
3	1	5	B	1	false

Table 5.26   ticket_sale_item after Row Deletion

> **WHERE Condition**
>
> The `WHERE` condition of a `DELETE` statement can be much more complex than in our humble example. We'll learn about `WHERE` conditions in greater detail in Chapter 7, where we'll cover DQL. Once you finish that chapter, you'll be able to easily apply the `WHERE` logic to `DELETE` statements.

Deleting All Rows

There may be some cases where we'll want to purge a database table completely. There are two basic and simple ways to do this.

5.2 Data Manipulation Language Operations

The first way is to simply leave the WHERE condition out. If you execute a DELETE statement without a WHERE condition, it will simply delete all rows. To see this in action, execute Listing 5.28 and refill our sample tables first. Then, execute Listing 5.31.

```
DELETE FROM ticket_sale_item;
```

Listing 5.31 Deletion Statement without WHERE Condition

If you check `ticket_sale_item` now, you should see that it's completely empty. Just like we intended.

The second method is to use the TRUNCATE TABLE command – which we've seen on the previous chapter as well. To see this in action, execute Listing 5.28 and refill our sample tables first. Then, execute Listing 5.32.

```
TRUNCATE TABLE ticket_sale_item;
```

Listing 5.32 Deleting All Rows Using TRUNCATE TABLE Command

If you check the `ticket_sale_item` table afterward, you should see that it's completely empty.

So, what is the difference between those methods? If both end up deleting table contents completely, can we just flip a coin and pick the winning method?

Well, that might be the case in simple playgrounds—but in a production database, they have different use cases, as summarized in Table 5.27.

Feature	Deletion	Truncation
Performance	It's slow.	It's fast.
Logs	It generates large volumes of logs on big tables.	It generates a minimum volume of logs.
Transaction	It can be rolled back (undone) during a transaction, about which we'll learn in due course.	It can't be rolled back (undone) during a transaction.
SERIAL columns	It doesn't reset serial columns, and new entries continue from the last known number.	It resets serial columns, and new entries start from a fresh counter.
Indexes	It requires manual index updates on most database products.	It resets indexes automatically on most database products.

Table 5.27 Feature Comparison of Deletion Methods

So, which method is preferable? It depends! If you want to maintain the ability to roll back and/or trigger ON DELETE actions, DELETE would be the preferable method. If you need to quickly remove all rows and don't need rollbacks or triggers, TRUNCATE would be the preferable method.

That concludes our content on row deletion. Now is the right time to talk about common pitfalls to avoid during DML operations, as we've mentioned multiple times.

5.2.4 Common Pitfalls of Data Manipulation Language Operations

In some cases, updating or deleting existing database records may turn out to be a risky operation. In this section, we'll go over some obvious dangers to increase your awareness of the issue.

First and foremost, in a typical multiuser database environment, users may attempt to modify the same set of rows simultaneously—which may lead to data inconsistencies or even data loss. To prevent such cases, we advise you to take advantage of Transaction Control Language (TCL) and lock the rows before applying any modifications. TCL is the subject of our next chapter, so stay tuned! In most cases, you should use DML modification commands in conjunction with the TCL mechanism. Executing UPDATE or DELETE statements without a WHERE condition will change or delete all entries in the target table—which is not we want, in most cases! Although WHERE conditions are technically optional, they will be present in most statements. So, never forget them—and if you intend to execute such a statement, think twice and peek at table entries to ensure that your intention is accurate.

When you add a WHERE condition, it's not the end of the story—there are further points to consider. The performance of the operation may suffer if the table is very large and your WHERE condition contains nonkey or nonindexed fields. You may be able to ignore this runtime cost during a one-time execution, but it may be disruptive if your statement is part of common algorithms.

You should also consider the differentiation of empty or null values on WHERE conditions. In Listing 5.33, each statement will behave completely differently!

```
DELETE FROM member WHERE phone = '';
DELETE FROM member WHERE phone IS NULL;
DELETE FROM member WHERE phone = '' OR phone IS NULL;
```

Listing 5.33 DELETE Statements with Null Conditions

When we compare these statements, we learn the following:
- The first statement will delete members with empty phone values but keep members with null phone values.
- The second statement will delete members with null phone values but keep members with empty phone values.
- The third statement will delete both groups of members.

This example demonstrates the importance of empty/null differentiation. You should always be mindful about that in WHERE conditions.

Speaking of data deletions, we should mention that you must consider logical data relations when deleting rows. Although the database will refuse to execute update or delete operations that cause constraint inconsistencies, it's the programmer's responsibility to keep track of logical consistency.

In our example, `ticket_sale_header` and `ticket_sale_item` are related tables. You can't delete a `ticket_sale_header` row if it has corresponding rows in `ticket_sale_item` because the database engine will refuse that due to the foreign key relationship. However, if you delete all rows in the `ticket_sale_item` table, the engine will allow it—but the rows in the `ticket_sale_header` table will become logically pointless, so you should delete them too.

This also demonstrates the correct order in which to delete data. You should delete child records before parent records, lest you anger the database engine due to its constraints!

Finally, as in any software development field, testing your code in test environments before executing it on production databases is strongly recommended. In risky bulk operations, you may even consider backing up the production tables and/or disabling transactions before the execution, so you can revert to the previous state if anything goes wrong.

If your risky operation involves data in multiple tables, we strongly recommend that you execute those SQL statements via TCL, which is the subject of Chapter 6.

Before we get into that subject, our current chapter has one final topic to cover: DML automation.

5.3 Data Manipulation Language Automation

In a production database environment, task automation is an essential tool in our toolbox. In this section, we'll explore two powerful tools for automation: stored procedures and triggers.

Stored procedures allow us to create SQL-based subroutines in the database that we can then execute either manually or on a schedule to complete specific tasks. Triggers, on the other hand, are also SQL based subroutines, but they get executed by the database engine upon a change in a table.

This difference highlights the use cases of those mechanisms. Stored procedures preferably contain SQL code to be executed occasionally, while triggers preferably contain SQL code to be executed automatically (upon an INSERT, UPDATE, DELETE operation).

Now that we've highlighted the differences between stored procedures and triggers, let's explore these mechanisms and see how they help us.

5   Data Manipulation Language

> **Database Dependency**
>
> Unlike other database components (such as schemas, tables, etc.), stored procedures and triggers are highly dependent on the specific database product. If your application logic relies on these mechanisms, it means that your application is tightly coupled to the underlying database product. Applications that support multiple databases often avoid or minimize DML automation technologies for that reason. Instead, they implement similar logic within the application itself, enhancing the application's portability and reducing database dependency.
>
> This doesn't mean that you should avoid DML automation altogether. Rather, it's a consideration to keep in mind when designing a system.

5.3.1   Stored Procedures

Stored procedures are basically subroutines of databases. You can compare them to functions, methods, forms, and procedures, but your favorite programming language names subroutines! Stored procedures can be defined as reusable sets of SQL statements that are stored in the database and that can be invoked with a single call.

A typical use case for stored procedures is to keep a chain of SQL statements together. Whenever we want to execute the chain, we can simply call the procedure instead of copying and pasting the statements from somewhere. Neat, right?

Some other use cases of stored procedures are as follows:

- Data validation before inserting or updating data in a table
- Running automated maintenance tasks
- Database-level application programming interfaces (APIs) for application integration

As we go over some examples in the following sections, these use cases will make more sense.

> **Scope of Stored Procedures**
>
> The stored procedure mechanisms of database products are comprehensive programming platforms. Each database product has an original language for developing stored procedures, and any of these languages can easily become the subject of another standalone book.
>
> To draw an even more accurate scope, it ought to be said that some database products even support multiple languages for stored procedure development.
>
> Since our main focus is SQL, we'll merely go over some basic PostgreSQL procedures to understand their structure and draw up a general framework. Once you understand

how they work, you can dive deeper into stored procedure development with your language of choice if you need to.

Procedures without Parameters

The most basic form of a stored procedure is a procedure without parameters. You can simply execute the procedure by its name and let it run to fulfill its task.

Remember Listing 5.28, which we used to fill our ticket tables with mock data? Every time we needed fresh mock data, we had to copy and paste and execute this code. That use case is an ideal candidate for a stored procedure—we can simply declare those statements as a stored procedure and call it whenever we want! All we need to do is to frame our set of SQL statements with some additional commands. Listing 5.34 demonstrates the syntax for that.

```
CREATE OR REPLACE PROCEDURE { procedure_name }([ parameters ])
LANGUAGE plpgsql AS $$
BEGIN
{ sql statements }
END; $$
```

Listing 5.34 Syntax to Create (or Replace) Stored Procedure

As you see, we merely have three prefix lines and one suffix line. We're free to put nearly any chain of SQL statements in between them. Creating a stored procedure is that simple. Now, check Listing 5.35 to see how we can create a stored procedure called create_mock_ticket_data, which will obviously create mock ticket data using our previous statements in Listing 5.28.

```
CREATE OR REPLACE PROCEDURE create_mock_ticket_data()
LANGUAGE plpgsql AS $$
BEGIN
    DELETE FROM ticket_sale_item CASCADE;
    DELETE FROM ticket_sale_head CASCADE;
    ALTER SEQUENCE ticket_sale_head_id_seq RESTART WITH 1;

    INSERT INTO ticket_sale_head (member_id, sale_ts)
    SELECT id, CURRENT_TIMESTAMP AS sales_ts
    FROM member
    ORDER BY NAME LIMIT 3;

    WITH
        ranked_events AS (
            SELECT id AS event_id,
```

```
                ROW_NUMBER() OVER (ORDER BY id) AS rn
                FROM event ),
        expanded_sales AS (
            SELECT id AS sale_id,
            ROW_NUMBER() OVER (ORDER BY id) * 2 - 1 AS rn1,
            ROW_NUMBER() OVER (ORDER BY id) * 2 AS rn2
            FROM ticket_sale_head)
    INSERT INTO ticket_sale_item (sale_id, item_no, event_id, category,
quantity)
        SELECT es.sale_id, 1, re1.event_id, 'B', 1
        FROM expanded_sales es JOIN ranked_events re1 ON es.rn1 = re1.rn
        UNION ALL
        SELECT es.sale_id, 2, re2.event_id, 'C', 3
        FROM expanded_sales es JOIN ranked_events re2 ON es.rn2 = re2.rn;
END; $$
```

Listing 5.35 Stored Procedure without Parameters

See? Except for the first three lines and the last line, nothing changed! Still, we'd better go over the syntax once to get a better understanding.

We start the statement with the CREATE OR REPLACE PROCEDURE command, which declares our intentions regarding the procedure. Clearly, we can use the same command to create a new procedure or replace an existing procedure with the newly provided code. This command is followed by the name of the procedure, which is create_mock_ticket_data in our case.

On the second line, we declare the language of the procedure. PostgreSQL supports multiple languages, such as PL/pgSQL, PL/Tcl, PL/Perl, and PL/Python. We need to declare which language we're using so the database engine can interpret our code correctly. In our case, we've picked PL/pgSQL because it's the most SQL-like language of them all.

After this declaration, we simply put our code between BEGIN and END keywords. Straightforward, right?

Once you execute Listing 5.35, you'll have a stored procedure in the database, waiting to be executed. You can also see it in pgAdmin, as shown in Figure 5.8.

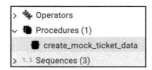

Figure 5.8 create_mock_ticket_data Procedure in pgAdmin

Once you have a stored procedure in place, executing it is very easy! You'll simply use the CALL keyword, followed by the name of the procedure.

Once you execute `create_mock_ticket_data` as in Listing 5.36, it'll remove all entries from your ticket tables and put fresh data in the ticket, fulfilling its task.

```
CALL create_mock_ticket_data();
```

Listing 5.36 Executing Stored Procedure

Congratulations! You now know the basics of creating and executing a stored procedure.

Procedures with Parameters

Some procedures, such as the one in Listing 5.35, can work just fine with fixed values in them. However, more often than not, stored procedures may need to import parameters to use them in SQL statements. This is like any other subroutine in any other programming language, really—nothing's different.

Let's assume a case where we want to create a stored procedure to insert a new theater table entry. As a reminder, Figure 5.9 contains the structure of the theater table.

		theater	
PK	id	varchar(10)	NOT NULL
	name	varchar(50)	NOT NULL
	capacity	int	NOT NULL

Figure 5.9 Structure of theater Table

To insert a new theater table row, we need three values: the id, name, and capacity of the new theater. In more technical terms, our stored procedure needs to import these three values so it can create a new theater table row.

The syntax for a new stored procedure was highlighted earlier in Listing 5.34. We'll use the same syntax, but this time, we'll make use of (optional) parameters. See Listing 5.37 for the finished procedure.

```
CREATE OR REPLACE PROCEDURE add_theater (
    theater_id VARCHAR(10),
    theater_name VARCHAR(50),
    theater_capacity INTEGER
) LANGUAGE plpgsql AS $$
BEGIN

    INSERT INTO theater(id, name, capacity)
```

```
        VALUES (theater_id, theater_name, theater_capacity);

END; $$
```

Listing 5.37 Stored Procedure to Create New Theater Row

Our new procedure is called `add_theater`, which makes its purpose obvious. Just as intended, it imports three parameters and uses them in a familiar INSERT statement. Clear, right?

Now, once you execute Listing 5.37 and create the stored procedure, you can execute it as in Listing 5.38. Note that values are passed in the same order as the parameters of the procedure.

```
CALL add_theater('LUNA', 'Luna Vista', 500);
```

Listing 5.38 Calling Our New Stored Procedure

Once you execute the procedure, you should see a new entry in the theater table, as in Table 5.28.

id	name	capacity
AURA	Aura Plaza	750
ECHO	Echo Hall	900
LUNA	Luna Vista	500
PULS	Pulse Center	950
VIBE	Vibe Lounge	650
ZENI	Zenith Arena	850

Table 5.28 Contents of theater Table after Executing Procedure

Error Handling

Although it's not the number-one priority in playground development, defensive programming is one of the crucial aspects in real-world development. A professional developer is expected to implement mechanisms in their code for error handling. Stored procedure languages usually empower us with the necessary tools for defensive programming.

In our recent `add_theater` stored procedure, we don't have a mechanism to defend us in a case where a user attempts to insert duplicate records. Try executing the code in Listing 5.38 multiple times and see what happens! You should get an exception like **ERROR: duplicate key**. If you call the procedure from an application, you'll get such an exception as well.

But what if we simply want to ignore and bypass that error if a theater is a duplicate? Easy! See Listing 5.39.

```
CREATE OR REPLACE PROCEDURE add_theater (
    theater_id VARCHAR(10),
    theater_name VARCHAR(50),
    theater_capacity INTEGER
) LANGUAGE plpgsql AS $$
BEGIN

    INSERT INTO theater(id, name, capacity)
    VALUES (theater_id, theater_name, theater_capacity);

EXCEPTION
    WHEN unique_violation
    THEN RAISE NOTICE 'Theater already exists';

END; $$
```

Listing 5.39 add_theater Extended with Exception Handling

Did you notice the new EXCEPTION part of the procedure? Here, we declare to the database engine that in case there's a unique_violation error (meaning that the record is a duplicate), we simply want to produce a console message and silently end the procedure without any exceptions.

Whether or not this is a good idea depends on the scenario, but technically, you can execute Listing 5.38 multiple times now, and you won't get any exceptions due to duplicate keys!

Obviously, the code under WHEN unique_violation could contain a much more comprehensive error handling logic if needed, but this is enough for our simple case.

> **Exception Types**
>
> PostgreSQL provides many further exception types, such as foreign_key_violation, not_null_violation, division_by_zero, and data_exception. You can explore them using the official PostgreSQL documentation if you want to go deeper into stored procedures.

The previous example was about catching a standard PostgreSQL exception and handling it, but there may also be also cases in which we want to intentionally raise a custom exception in odd situations. See Listing 5.40.

```
CREATE OR REPLACE PROCEDURE add_theater (
    theater_id VARCHAR(10),
    theater_name VARCHAR(50),
```

```
    theater_capacity INTEGER
) LANGUAGE plpgsql AS $$
BEGIN

    IF length( theater_name ) < 5 THEN
        RAISE EXCEPTION 'Theater name too short';
    END IF;

    INSERT INTO theater(id, name, capacity)
    VALUES (theater_id, theater_name, theater_capacity);

EXCEPTION
    WHEN unique_violation
    THEN RAISE NOTICE 'Theater already exists';

END; $$
```

Listing 5.40 Stored Procedure with Custom Exception

In this version of add_theater, we're checking the length of the name of the new theater entry. If it's shorter than 5 characters, we raise a custom exception that contains a message of choice.

Once you update add_theater, you can try to execute Listing 5.41.

```
CALL add_theater('MINI', 'Mini', 100);
```

Listing 5.41 Command to Fail due to Insufficient Name Length

Because the Mini value is shorter than five characters, you're sure to get an exception that will tell you that the theater name is too short. Just as we intended!

Deleting Stored Procedures

Finally, we'll learn how to delete a stored procedure in case you don't need it any longer. The syntax can be seen in Listing 5.42, which is very similar to the DDL deletion commands we learned in the previous chapter.

```
DROP PROCEDURE [ IF EXISTS ] { procedure_name };
```

Listing 5.42 Syntax for Procedure Deletion

To see this simple syntax in action, you can check and execute the statements in Listing 5.43.

```
DROP PROCEDURE add_theater;
DROP PROCEDURE IF EXISTS add_theater;
```

Listing 5.43 Two Examples of How to Delete Procedure

The first statement will delete the add_theater procedure but generate an error if there's no such procedure.

The second statement will delete the procedure, too, but will silently bypass the statement if there's no such procedure. This mechanism is particularly useful if you have an application targeting different environments. You can execute the same SQL statement in each environment, and only existing procedures will be deleted.

> **Deleting Procedures**
>
> Like any other program, deleting a stored procedure is a risky operation and can be very expensive—quite literally! Deleting a mission-critical procedure may stop applications from functioning altogether, and you may not be able to rewrite the procedure in many cases.
>
> Some procedures may include meticulous code honed by dozens of tests and years of real-world use, so even if you intend to delete a procedure and you have managerial approval to do it, it's wise to at least back up the source code somewhere. Just in case!

That concludes our overview of stored procedures. Now, we'll learn about triggers to advance further into automation.

5.3.2 Triggers

A *trigger* is a mechanism that automatically initiates actions in response to changes in a database table. You can imagine it as a stored procedure that is executed whenever a row is inserted, updated, or deleted in a certain table. In this section, we'll take a closer look at how triggers work and then get into using triggers.

How Triggers Work Logically

As a very basic example, we can imagine a regular database table to which the following two preprogrammed triggers are assigned:

- BEFORE INSERT contains the code to be executed right before a row is inserted.
- AFTER INSERT contains the code to be executed right after a row is inserted.

A corresponding sketch can be seen in Figure 5.10.

In this case, when we execute an INSERT INTO statement against this table, we're executing more than the statement itself. As demonstrated in Figure 5.11, the following order is applied:

1. BEFORE INSERT code is executed.
2. INSERT INTO statement itself is executed.
3. AFTER INSERT code is executed.

5 Data Manipulation Language

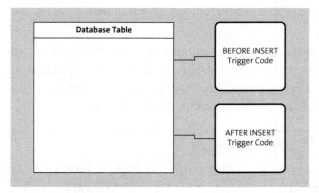

Figure 5.10 Database Table with Triggers

Figure 5.11 Code Execution Order on Table with Triggers

Cool, right? We could, for example, code extra data consistency checks into the BEFORE INSERT trigger and prevent the insertion if anything is wrong. Likewise, we could code satellite table updates into the AFTER INSERT trigger, and those triggers would be executed by the database engine for each new incoming row.

> **Trigger Language**
>
> In most database products, the language used for triggers is the same language used for stored procedures. As you learn this language, you'll be advancing in both directions.

Obviously, data insertion is not the only event we'd put a trigger into. We can assign triggers to other SQL commands as well. Table 5.29 showcases a matrix of trigger time and event combinations.

Trigger Times	Trigger Events	Explanations	Sample Use Cases
BEFORE	INSERT	The code is executed right before a row is inserted into the table.	Validation of values in a fresh row, preventing insertion of an error
BEFORE	UPDATE	The code is executed right before an existing row is updated.	Validation of values of the updated row, preventing updates of an error
BEFORE	DELETE	The code is executed right before an existing row is deleted.	Checking whether the row is logically deletable, preventing deletion of an error
AFTER	INSERT	The code is executed right after a row is inserted into the table.	Inserting additional rows into satellite tables
AFTER	UPDATE	The code is executed right after an existing row is updated.	Modifying additional rows in satellite tables
AFTER	DELETE	The code is executed right after an existing row is deleted.	Deleting additional rows in satellite tables
INSTEAD OF	INSERT	A SQL statement to insert a row through a view is replaced with the trigger code.	Data insertion into tables behind a view

Table 5.29 Trigger Time and Event Matrix

5   Data Manipulation Language

Trigger Times	Trigger Events	Explanations	Sample Use Cases
INSTEAD OF	UPDATE	A SQL statement to update a row through a view is replaced with the trigger code.	Data updates in tables behind a view
INSTEAD OF	DELETE	A SQL statement to delete a row through a view is replaced with the trigger code.	Data deletion in tables behind a view

Table 5.29 Trigger Time and Event Matrix (Cont.)

> **INSTEAD OF Triggers**
>
> For now, you can mentally set aside INSTEAD OF triggers. Instead, focus on BEFORE and AFTER triggers to get a better understanding. We'll address INSTEAD OF triggers after them.

If you study the matrix in Table 5.29, the purposes of triggers should become evident: automating tasks, enforcing business rules, maintaining data integrity, automatically filling missing fields, logging changes, maintaining related data, and much more. The strength of triggers lies in the fact that they are automatically executed, without manual interference.

The overall syntaxes of triggers and corresponding time and event combinations are similar. We'll continue with our overview of the general syntax and follow it up with select examples featuring various combinations.

> **Triggers and Performance**
>
> Mind you that triggers cost runtime! Since they get executed before and/or after each corresponding statement, they add unavoidable delays to transactions and workload to the server. Extra runtime cost may be trivial in inactive tables but may become a critical factor in busy tables.
>
> Recursive triggers are another type of danger. If two separate tables have triggers firing each other, a seemingly harmless SQL statement may cause an infinite loop of death between those tables.
>
> Last but not least, we advise you to keep trigger code simple and clean. If the trigger is getting out of hand, you may consider implementing its logic in the application back-end language instead.

Trigger Syntax

A trigger is made of the following two parts:

- **The trigger function**
  This is basically a stored procedure. The only difference is in the prefix, where we declare the code to be a trigger function instead of a procedure.
- **The trigger link**
  In this step, we bind the table, trigger time, and event to the trigger function at hand.

If this sounds confusing, Figure 5.12 should make it crystal clear.

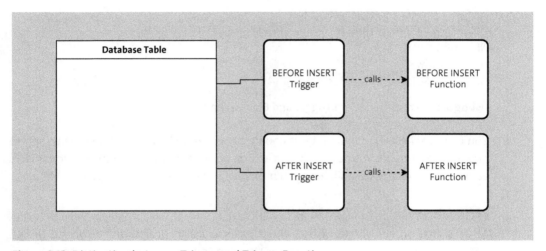

Figure 5.12 Distinction between Trigger and Trigger Function

So the actual code resides within the function, and the link between the function and the table is made through the trigger. Simple, right?

> **Separation of the Function**
>
> Having the trigger and the function be separate gives you an advantage: you can bind the function to multiple triggers if you have to. That way, you can share and reuse the same chunk of code, thus preventing code duplication.

To declare the function, we would use the template in Listing 5.44. As you can see, it's very similar to the stored procedure declaration syntax we went through in Section 5.3.1, so we won't go over its individual syntax elements redundantly.

```
CREATE OR REPLACE FUNCTION { function_name } () RETURNS TRIGGER AS $$
BEGIN
    { function code }
END;
$$ LANGUAGE plpgsql;
```

Listing 5.44 Syntax to Declare Trigger Function

Once we have the function in hand, we must bind it to our database table as a trigger. Listing 5.45 demonstrates this syntax.

```
CREATE TRIGGER { trigger_name }
[ BEFORE | AFTER | INSTEAD OF ] [ INSERT | UPDATE | DELETE ]
ON { table_name }
FOR EACH ROW
EXECUTE FUNCTION { function_name } ();
```

Listing 5.45 Syntax to Declare Trigger and Bind to Function

You can use these syntax listings as cookie cutter templates and fill them with appropriate code to create your own triggers, which we cover in the following sections! We'll go over some examples and declare our own triggers using these templates.

BEFORE Triggers

As we stated previously, we use BEFORE triggers as early checkpoints *before* an INSERT, UPDATE, or DELETE statement is executed. We can implement our custom code to run custom operations *before* the actual statement.

As a case study, we'll implement a custom check regarding ticket returns. Assume that management has made a decision that customers can no longer return category C tickets that they've bought. We must now implement a corresponding mechanism in the database that will prevent such operations.

As a reminder, Figure 5.13 showcases database tables related to ticket sales. Whenever a ticket is returned, ticket_sale_item.is_returned would be set to true.

To implement the managerial decision, we're going to create a trigger for ticket_sale_item that will execute before an update operation. We'll check the row to be updated, and if we find that category = 'C' AND is_returned = true, we'll raise an exception that will disrupt the update. Because returning category C tickets is simply not allowed, our trigger will reflect just that!

Figure 5.14 contains a diagram of our ultimate purpose. We're aiming at creating a trigger called ticket_return_category_c, which will run before each update statement. It will call the function check_category_c_return, which will conduct the aforementioned value check.

5.3 Data Manipulation Language Automation

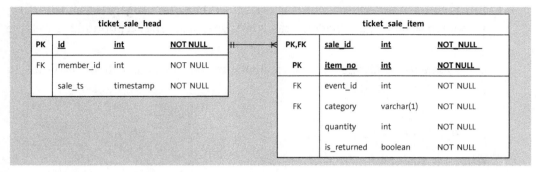

Figure 5.13 Database Tables Related to Ticket Sales

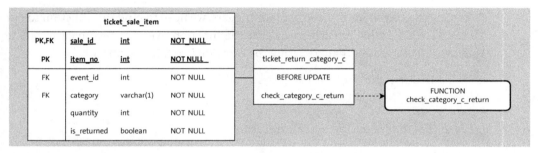

Figure 5.14 Overview of Trigger Plan

Following the common two-step plan for triggers, we'll start by declaring a function. See Listing 5.46.

```
CREATE OR REPLACE FUNCTION check_category_c_return () RETURNS TRIGGER AS $$
BEGIN
    IF NEW.category = 'C' AND NEW.is_returned = TRUE THEN
        RAISE EXCEPTION 'Cannot return a ticket with category C';
    END IF;

    RETURN NEW;
END;
$$ LANGUAGE plpgsql;
```

Listing 5.46 Trigger Function to Prevent Category C Ticket Returns

We've given the function the name check_category_c_return, which corresponds to its purpose. The code between BEGIN and END declares what the trigger function does.

The NEW keyword symbolizes the incoming new row. We can access the columns of this row by using the dotted syntax, as seen in NEW.category and NEW.is_returned. If needed, we can also access the former version of the row (before the update) by using the OLD keyword, but our example doesn't contain that.

Just as we intended, the function checks whether the ticket category is C and the ticket is about to be returned. If that's the case, the trigger raises an exception and cancels the operation.

Once you execute Listing 5.46 and create the trigger function, it should be visible in pgAdmin as seen in Figure 5.15.

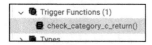

Figure 5.15 Trigger Function Shown in pgAdmin

So far, so good! Our first step is complete.

Following the common two-step plan for triggers, we need to bind this function to our `ticket_sale_item` table in such a way that the function executes before each update statement. That's easier than declaring the function itself. See Listing 5.47.

```
CREATE TRIGGER ticket_return_category_c
BEFORE UPDATE ON ticket_sale_item
FOR EACH ROW
EXECUTE FUNCTION check_category_c_return ();
```

Listing 5.47 Trigger to Bind Table to Function

We've named our trigger `ticket_return_category_c` and declared that it must be executed before each `UPDATE` statement in the `ticket_sale_item` table. In the final line, we bind it to the `check_category_c_return` function, which was created in the first step.

Once you execute Listing 5.47, you should see the trigger binding in pgAdmin as shown in Figure 5.16.

Figure 5.16 Trigger Binding Shown in pgAdmin

That's it! We have the trigger in place, and now, it's time to test it.

Let's start by ensuring that we have fresh mock data in our tables. In Section 5.3.1, you created a stored procedure for that, and you can simply reuse it. Execute the code in Listing 5.36 to refill our tables. After you complete the operation, `ticket_sale_item` should look like Table 5.30.

sale_id	item_no	event_id	category	quantity	is_returned
1	1	1	B	1	false
1	2	2	C	3	false
2	1	3	B	1	false
2	2	4	C	3	false
3	1	5	B	1	false

Table 5.30 Mock Data in ticket_sale_item Table

According to our new trigger, we shouldn't be able to set is_returned = true in a row where category = 'C', right? Let's put it to the test! Listing 5.48 targets a row of category C and attempts to set true to is_returned.

```
UPDATE ticket_sale_item
SET
    is_returned = TRUE
WHERE
    sale_id = 1
    AND item_no = 2;
```

Listing 5.48 SQL Statement Attempting to Make Invalid Update against Trigger Function

If you try to execute this statement, you should get an error message from the database engine, saying **Cannot return a ticket with category C**. Just as we intended! This means that the trigger has functioned properly.

To ensure that the trigger doesn't affect other categories, try executing Listing 5.49, which targets a row where the ticket category is B.

```
UPDATE ticket_sale_item
SET
    is_returned = TRUE
WHERE
    sale_id = 1
    AND item_no = 1;
```

Listing 5.49 SQL Statement Attempting to Make Valid Update

This statement should run successfully, and the ticket_sale_item table should look like Table 5.31 afterward.

sale_id	item_no	event_id	category	quantity	is_returned
1	1	1	B	1	true
1	2	2	C	3	false
2	1	3	B	1	false
2	2	4	C	3	false
3	1	5	B	1	false

Table 5.31 ticket_sale_item Rows after Successful Update

Cool, right? We've gone through the creation of a custom trigger via the BEFORE topic, so now, AFTER should feel like an afterparty—easier and more chill!

AFTER Triggers

Let's continue with another example, this time demonstrating an AFTER trigger. Our case will be about a special requirement: if an event gets cancelled, all sold tickets (except category C) should automatically be marked as "returned."

As a reminder, Figure 5.17 showcases the tables involved in our case and excludes other tables that are not.

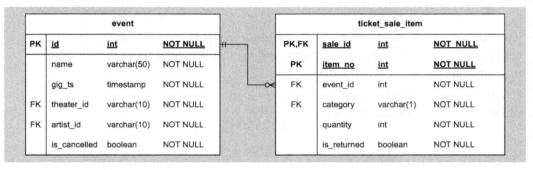

Figure 5.17 Tables Involved in Our Case

Technically speaking, if an event row is updated as is_cancelled = true, we want to automatically update the corresponding ticket_sale_item rows as is_returned = true (except where category = 'C').

We can clearly achieve this goal with the help of a trigger. Figure 5.18 contains an extended ERD that includes the upcoming trigger development. We're aiming at creating a trigger called event_cancel_ticket_return, which will run after each update statement. It will call the return_cancelled_tickets function, which will update the necessary ticket_sale_item rows in case the event is cancelled.

5.3 Data Manipulation Language Automation

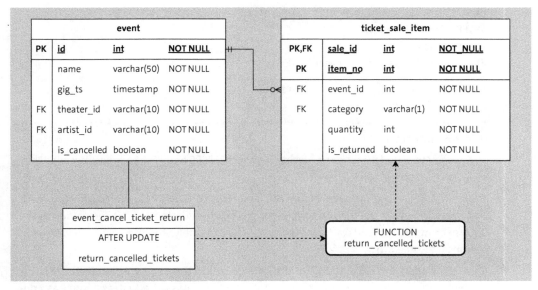

Figure 5.18 Overview of Trigger Plan

The first step is to declare our function. See Listing 5.50.

```
CREATE OR REPLACE FUNCTION return_cancelled_tickets () RETURNS TRIGGER AS $$
BEGIN
    IF NEW.is_cancelled = TRUE THEN
        UPDATE ticket_sale_item
        SET is_returned = TRUE
        WHERE event_id = NEW.event_id
          AND category <> 'C';
    END IF;

    RETURN NEW;
END;
$$ LANGUAGE plpgsql;
```

Listing 5.50 Trigger Function to Update ticket_sale_item if Necessary

Let's focus on the code between the BEGIN and END keywords. Here, the NEW keyword symbolizes the updated row of the event table. If the updated row has the value is_cancelled = true, then the function will update some ticket_sale_item rows of that event as necessary, setting them as is_returned = true.

Now that we have the function in place, we can define the trigger. See Listing 5.51—it's very similar to the trigger code in our former example, so there's nothing fancy to discuss. The only thing to note is that we're declaring an AFTER trigger that will fire after the UPDATE operation.

```
CREATE TRIGGER event_cancel_ticket_return
AFTER UPDATE ON event
FOR EACH ROW
EXECUTE FUNCTION return_cancelled_tickets ();
```

Listing 5.51 Trigger to Bind Table to Function

> **Before or After?**
>
> You may be wondering how to decide between BEFORE and AFTER triggers because they seem to be very similar.
>
> BEFORE triggers are executed *before* the incoming INSERT, UPDATE, or DELETE statement is executed. It's a good place to implement extra validations or change values in the target row, symbolized by the keyword NEW. We can safely stop the operation via exceptions if we need to.
>
> AFTER triggers are executed *after* the change in the target row is conducted. At this point, we're sure that the incoming statement has passed all checks (such as constraints and other triggers) and executed successfully, bringing the row to the intended state. It's a good place to make for extra updates in secondary satellite tables because we're sure that the initial operation has completed successfully.

After executing the statements, we should see the trigger and function in pgAdmin, as in Figure 5.19.

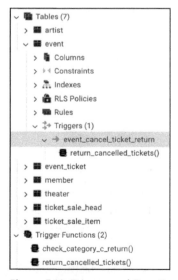

Figure 5.19 Trigger and Function in pgAdmin

Now that we have everything in place, it's time for a test! Let's start by ensuring that we have fresh mock data in our tables. In Section 5.3.1, you created a stored procedure for that, and you can simply reuse it! Execute the code in Listing 5.36 to refill our tables.

In our current state, the contents of the event table should look like Table 5.32.

id	name	gig_ts	theater_id	artist_id	is_cancelled
1	Lunar Echoes Single Debut	2025-02-15 21:30:00	AURA	LUNE	false
2	Summer Fest	2024-09-01 20:00:00	AURA	LUNE	false
3	Night Beats	2024-10-15 19:30:00	VIBE	ECSR	false
4	Rock Legends	2024-11-05 21:00:00	ECHO	SLSR	false
5	Acoustic Vibes	2024-12-20 18:00:00	ZENI	CRHR	false

Table 5.32 Initial Contents of event Table

At the other end, the contents of the ticket_sale_item table should look like Table 5.33.

sale_id	item_no	event_id	category	quantity	is_returned
1	1	1	B	1	false
1	2	2	C	3	false
2	1	3	B	1	false
2	2	4	C	3	false
3	1	5	B	1	false

Table 5.33 Initial Contents of ticket_sale_item Table

To test our recent trigger, let's cancel an event. Picking the example of Acoustic Vibes, execute the statement in Listing 5.52.

```
UPDATE event
SET is_cancelled = TRUE
WHERE id = 5;
```

Listing 5.52 SQL Statement to Cancel Acoustic Vibes Event

The initial expectation is the obvious update to the event table. After the statement, it should look like Table 5.34, in which Acoustic Vibes seems to be cancelled.

5 Data Manipulation Language

Id	name	gig_ts	theater_id	artist_id	is_cancelled
1	Lunar Echoes Single Debut	2025-02-15 21:30:00	AURA	LUNE	false
2	Summer Fest	2024-09-01 20:00:00	AURA	LUNE	false
3	Night Beats	2024-10-15 19:30:00	VIBE	ECSR	false
4	Rock Legends	2024-11-05 21:00:00	ECHO	SLSR	false
5	Acoustic Vibes	2024-12-20 18:00:00	ZENI	CRHR	true

Table 5.34 Contents of event Table After Statement

But did the trigger work? To verify that, we need to investigate the `ticket_sale_item` table. Check Table 5.35.

sale_id	item_no	event_id	category	quantity	is_returned
1	1	1	B	1	false
1	2	2	C	3	false
2	1	3	B	1	false
2	2	4	C	3	false
3	1	5	B	1	true

Table 5.35 Contents of ticket_sale_item Table after Statement and Trigger

Indeed, it worked! If we check the last row, where `event_id` is 5 (Acoustic Vibes), we see that `is_returned` is automatically set to `true` by the trigger. Voila!

That concludes our example regarding AFTER triggers.

INSTEAD OF Triggers

In this section, we'll be focusing on views. As we discussed before, views are merely mirrors of database tables. They don't hold data; they simply reflect data from other tables.

As a memory refresher and a case study for our triggers, we're going to create a view called `event_theater`, which will combine columns of the `event` and `theater` tables. The ERD for this plan can be seen in Figure 5.20, which makes the source of each column evident.

Let's create this view. Listing 5.53 contains the SQL statement to create the `event_theater` view, and you can execute it on your playground database.

```
CREATE VIEW
    event_theater AS
```

5.3 Data Manipulation Language Automation

```
SELECT
    event.id AS event_id,
    event.name AS event_name,
    event.gig_ts,
    event.theater_id,
    event.artist_id,
    event.is_cancelled,
    theater.name AS theater_name,
    theater.capacity AS theater_capacity
FROM
    event
    INNER JOIN theater ON theater.id = event.theater_id;
```

Listing 5.53 SQL Statement to Create event_theater View

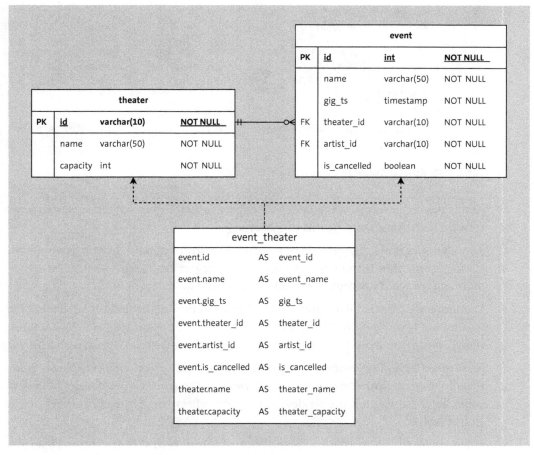

Figure 5.20 ERD for event_theater View

> **View Creation Statement**
> Although we've gone over the topic of view creation before, the statement in Listing 5.53 contains keywords that are unfamiliar to some, such as INNER JOIN. Don't fret—we'll cover these subjects in the chapter on DQL. For now, it's enough to know that this keyword is used to pull together data from related tables.

Once the view is ready, we can check its contents. Initially, they should look like Table 5.36.

event_id	event_name	gig_ts	theater_id	artist_id	is_cancelled	theater_name	theater_capacity
1	Lunar Echoes Single Debut	2025-02-15 21:30:00	AURA	LUNE	false	Aura Plaza	750
2	Summer Fest	2024-09-01 20:00:00	AURA	LUNE	false	Aura Plaza	750
3	Night Beats	2024-10-15 19:30:00	VIBE	ECSR	false	Vibe Lounge	650
4	Rock Legends	2024-11-05 21:00:00	ECHO	SLSR	false	Echo Hall	900
5	Acoustic Vibes	2024-12-20 18:00:00	ZENI	CRHR	true	Zenith Arena	850

Table 5.36 Rows Returned by event_theater View

At this point, our setup for the INSTEAD OF trigger case study is ready. Now, we can move forward with understanding this trigger type.

As we've mentioned before, views are merely mirrors of data. In our example, the event_theater view is a mirror of the event and theater tables. The event_theater view pulls and reflects data from those tables but doesn't hold data of its own.

Therefore, we can read data from event_theater (reflecting its underlying tables), but we shouldn't be able to conduct INSERT, UPDATE, or DELETE operations there. Makes sense, right? Trying to delete data from a view is like trying to wipe our reflection off a mirror.

Now, this is technically true—but in practice, many database products enable programmers to execute DML statements against views. Although the view doesn't hold data, some database engines are flexible enough to reflect these operations back at the source tables.

That's where INSTEAD OF triggers shine. We can hook up INSTEAD OF triggers to views (not tables), which are called when a DML statement is executed against the view. Table 5.37 showcases such trigger types and their effects.

5.3 Data Manipulation Language Automation

Triggers	Effects
INSTEAD OF INSERT	The trigger code is called when an INSERT statement is executed against the view.
INSTEAD OF UPDATE	The trigger code is called when an UPDATE statement is executed against the view.
INSTEAD OF DELETE	The trigger code is called when a DELETE statement is executed against the view.

Table 5.37 INSTEAD OF Triggers and Their Effects

Now, let's create an INSTEAD OF INSERT trigger for our event_theater view. This trigger will be called when someone executes an INSERT INTO event_theater statement. Our purposes are as follows:

- If this is a new theater, insert theater data into the theater table.
- Insert event data into the event table.

If you want to see a bird's-eye view of the trigger, you can check Figure 5.21.

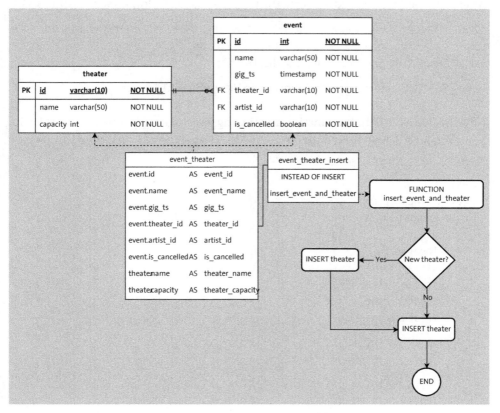

Figure 5.21 Visual Overview of Upcoming INSTEAD OF INSERT Trigger

215

5   Data Manipulation Language

As with other trigger types, we have a two-step plan: creating the function and creating the trigger. Listing 5.54 contains the SQL statement to declare the function.

```
CREATE OR REPLACE FUNCTION insert_event_and_theater () RETURNS TRIGGER AS $$
BEGIN
    IF NOT EXISTS ( SELECT id FROM theater WHERE id = NEW.theater_id ) THEN
        INSERT INTO theater(id, name, capacity)
        VALUES (NEW.theater_id, NEW.theater_name, NEW.theater_capacity);
    END IF;

    INSERT INTO event(name, gig_ts, theater_id, artist_id, is_cancelled)
    VALUES (NEW.event_name, NEW.gig_ts, NEW.theater_id,
            NEW.artist_id, NEW.is_cancelled);

    RETURN NEW;
END;
$$ LANGUAGE plpgsql;
```

Listing 5.54 Declaration of insert_event_and_theater Trigger Function

After the function, we need to create the trigger as usual. Follow up with Listing 5.55.

```
CREATE TRIGGER event_theater_insert INSTEAD OF INSERT ON event_theater FOR EACH ROW
EXECUTE FUNCTION insert_event_and_theater ();
```

Listing 5.55 SQL Statement to Bind Function to View as INSERT Trigger

Now that we have both the function and the trigger in place, it's time for a test! Listing 5.56 contains a SQL statement that runs an INSERT operation against the event_theater view.

```
INSERT INTO
    event_theater (
        event_name,
        gig_ts,
        theater_id,
        artist_id,
        is_cancelled,
        theater_name,
        theater_capacity
    )
VALUES
    (
        'Afro Party',
        '2025-02-02 20:00:00',
        'CUBA',
```

```
            'URPL',
            FALSE,
            'Cuban Street',
            200
    );
```

Listing 5.56 SQL Statement to Insert Rows through event_theater View

These values contain a fresh event (Afro Party), as well as a fresh venue (CUBA/Cuban Street). Following our recent trigger, we expect this statement to insert rows into the theater and event tables simultaneously.

And it does! If we check the theater table now, it should look like Table 5.38 and contain the new theater: CUBA/Cuban Street.

id	name	capacity
AURA	Aura Plaza	750
CUBA	Cuban Street	200
ECHO	Echo Hall	900
LUNA	Luna Vista	500
PULS	Pulse Center	950
VIBE	Vibe Lounge	650
ZENI	Zenith Arena	850

Table 5.38 Contents of theater Table after INSERT Statement and Underlying Trigger

If we check the event table now, it should look like Table 5.39. It'll contain the new Afro Party event, which will take place in the CUBA/Cuban Street theater.

id	name	gig_ts	theater_id	artist_id	is_cancelled
1	Lunar Echoes Single Debut	2025-02-15 21:30:00	AURA	LUNE	false
2	Summer Fest	2024-09-01 20:00:00	AURA	LUNE	false
3	Night Beats	2024-10-15 19:30:00	VIBE	ECSR	false
4	Rock Legends	2024-11-05 21:00:00	ECHO	SLSR	false
5	Acoustic Vibes	2024-12-20 18:00:00	ZENI	CRHR	false
6	Afro Party	2025-02-02 20:00:00	CUBA	URPL	false

Table 5.39 Contents of event Table after INSERT Statement and Underlying Trigger

Cool, right? Using this mechanism, you can let your clients execute DML statements against your views and keep control of how exactly the DML behaves. For instance, you can make an `INSTEAD OF DELETE` trigger behave in such a way that the event is deleted but the theater is not. Likewise, with an `INSTEAD OF UPDATE` trigger, you can make the database update the theater's name but not its capacity. You get the idea: you have total control over what to modify.

That concludes our content on the creation of triggers. We'll finish up this section with knowledge about disabling and deleting triggers.

Disabling Triggers

Disabling and enabling triggers are very easy tasks and have straightforward syntaxes, so we can jump directly to code samples. Listing 5.57 showcases a statement to disable an existing trigger.

```
ALTER TABLE event DISABLE TRIGGER event_cancel_ticket_return;
```

Listing 5.57 SQL Statement to Disable Existing Trigger

Once you execute this statement, pgAdmin will display this trigger as disabled. Can you spot the X in Figure 5.22?

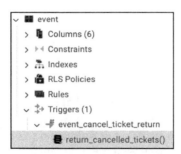

Figure 5.22 Disabled Trigger in pgAdmin

At this state, the trigger will stay in place but won't react to DML statements—because, well, it's disabled! This is a good alternative to deleting a trigger if you just want to stop the trigger temporarily.

To reenable the trigger, you can use the statement in Listing 5.58.

```
ALTER TABLE event ENABLE TRIGGER event_cancel_ticket_return;
```

Listing 5.58 SQL Statement to Enable Existing Trigger

Simple, right?

Deleting Triggers

We know by now that a trigger declaration is made of two parts: the trigger itself and the underlying function. When the time comes to delete a trigger, we should decide if we want to delete the trigger only or the function as well. If we're still using the function behind other triggers, or if we might have a use for it in the future, then it would be a good idea to keep it.

To complete our learning journey, though, we'll demonstrate how to delete both.

Listing 5.59 showcases the syntax to delete a trigger.

```
DROP TRIGGER [ IF EXISTS ] { trigger_name } ON { table_name } [ CASCADE | RESTRICT ];
```

Listing 5.59 Syntax to Delete Trigger

Thanks to our experience in deleting other database components, the syntax should be intuitive. We start with the DROP TRIGGER command, declaring our core intention. The optional addition IF EXISTS would tell the database engine to ignore the statement if the trigger doesn't exist at all. We continue with the trigger and table names, and we conclude with the optional CASCADE or RESTRICT suffix.

These suffixes behave exactly like our earlier DROP statements: CASCADE automatically drops objects that depend on the trigger, while RESTRICT makes the database engine refuse the deletion if any objects depend on it. In PostgreSQL, RESTRICT is the default behavior.

Listing 5.60 is a sample implementation of this syntax that deletes an event trigger.

```
DROP TRIGGER event_cancel_ticket_return ON event;
```

Listing 5.60 SQL Statement to Delete Trigger

In case we decide to delete the underlying function as well, we can use the syntax in Listing 5.61.

```
DROP FUNCTION [ IF EXISTS ] { function_name } [ CASCADE | RESTRICT ];
```

Listing 5.61 Syntax to Delete Function

The optional IF EXISTS, CASCADE, and RESTRICT keywords behave exactly as above, so we won't go over them redundantly. Listing 5.62 demonstrates this syntax in action.

```
DROP FUNCTION return_cancelled_tickets;
```

Listing 5.62 SQL Statement to Delete Function

5.4 Summary

In this chapter, we went through the DML sublanguage. After creating a network of playground tables, we learned about INSERT, UPDATE, and DELETE statements—which are frequently addressed in the life of a developer. We also learned about DML automation options through stored procedures and triggers.

DML statements are staples of SQL, but they are not always sufficient. Sometimes, we have a stored procedure in which we run DML operations on multiple tables. In such cases, we usually want either all the statements to execute successfully or no statement to be executed in case one of them would cause an error.

SQL has a special sublanguage exactly for this purpose, and it's called TCL. We'll learn about it in the next chapter.

Chapter 6
Transaction Control Language

We use data manipulation language (DML) to modify data on a single table, but sometimes, we need to modify multiple tables and either save the modifications together or not save them at all. If we need to update ten tables and the system shows an error after we update the first six tables, the resulting data inconsistency will probably cause application errors. Transaction control language (TCL) helps eliminate those risks. In TCL, mass modifications are either completely executed or cancelled altogether when errors occur. In this chapter, you'll learn how TCL works and walk through code examples to help you understand how to take advantage of TCL mechanisms.

In the previous chapter, we learned about DML, which we use to manipulate table rows. We can insert, update, or delete rows in a table or use stored procedures or triggers to automate those operations.

This chapter is about TCL, which is a critical follow-up to DML.

If we're doing simple data manipulations targeting single noncritical tables, we can use DML directly. However, in many cases, we need additional mechanisms on a busy production database to ensure data integrity and consistency—especially if we need to execute a chain of DML operations on multiple tables. TCL mechanisms help us ensure that such operations are either fully completed or fully cancelled. TCL also provides further useful features, such as preventing concurrent updates and providing consistent datasets to clients.

While DML frames the core part of data manipulation operations, TCL acts as a data consistency checkpoint mechanism. In many cases, you should use DML and TCL together.

We'll start by building a network of tables as our TCL playground, followed by a short discussion about the necessity of TCL. Then, we'll delve into TCL concepts like commits, rollbacks, save points, locks, and concurrency. Finally, we'll discuss some common pitfalls of TCL.

Let's start building a playground!

6 Transaction Control Language

6.1 Building a Transaction Control Language Playground

To ensure that this is a self-contained chapter, we'll build a network of tables and fill them with some mock data, just like we did in the previous chapter on DML. Our case study will be an imaginary bank called Daisy Bank. We'll simplify the data structure as usual—our goal is to learn about TCL, not to build a realistic bank database.

First and foremost, we need a table in which to store customer master data. Figure 6.1 showcases the ERD for such a table: bank_customer. All columns are intuitive, right?

	bank_customer		
PK	id	int	NOT NULL
	name	varchar(50)	NOT NULL
	phone	varchar(20)	NOT NULL
	email	varchar(50)	

Figure 6.1 ERD for bank_customer Table

Naturally, bank customers have bank accounts. Some customers may have a single account, while others may have multiple accounts. Therefore, we need to store those accounts in a separate table. Figure 6.2 showcases the addition of the customer_acc table, where account master data is stored.

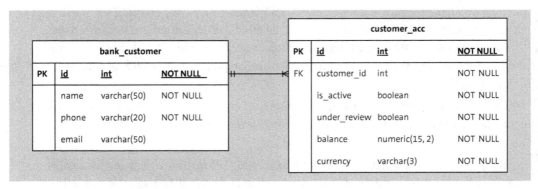

Figure 6.2 ERD for customer_acc Table

This table naturally stores the IDs of the customer, account balance, and currency. Additionally, we have two further boolean fields: is_active denotes whether the account is active or not, while under_review denotes whether the account is under review or not.

6.1 Building a Transaction Control Language Playground

A bank customer may also have credit cards. Some customers may have no cards at all, some could have only one card, and some could have multiple cards. As demonstrated in Figure 6.3, we'll use the `credit_card` table for this purpose.

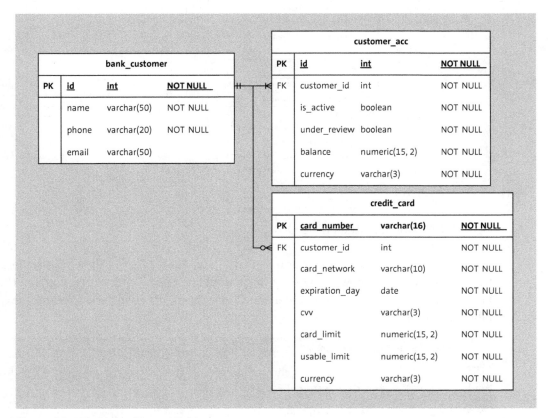

Figure 6.3 ERD for credit_card Table

> **Storing Sensitive Data**
>
> In a real-world application, it would be a very bad idea to store sensitive information (such as credit card numbers) openly in a database table like this. There are more secure ways of doing that, but this is simply a playground and we won't store real card numbers here. There's no harm in playing around.

A bank surely needs to keep track of customer transaction histories, and Figure 6.4 adds the `transaction` table to the picture to take care of that.

6 Transaction Control Language

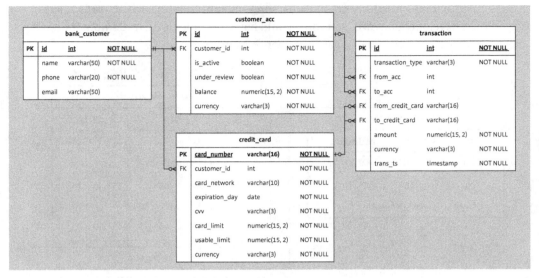

Figure 6.4 ERD for transaction Table

Following the simplified rules of our imaginary Daisy Bank, Table 6.1 showcases some transaction types and how foreign-key fields would be filled. Don't worry, you don't have to memorize any of that to understand TCL—this is just giving you a feel for the table's purpose.

Transaction Types	Descriptions	Foreign Keys
DEP	A cash deposit, either via an ATM or a branch	to_acc: target account
WIT	A cash withdrawal, either via an ATM or a branch	from_acc: source account
TRA	A money transfer	from_acc: source account to_acc: target account
CRP	A payment with a credit card	from_credit_card: source card
CRD	A credit card debt payment	from_acc: source account to_credit_card: target card
FEE	An annual maintenance fee	from_acc: deductible account

Table 6.1 Some Bank Transaction Types

And finally, Daisy Bank runs a daily consolidation job that summarizes daily amounts in the bank_day_sum table, as shown in Figure 6.5.

224

6.1 Building a Transaction Control Language Playground

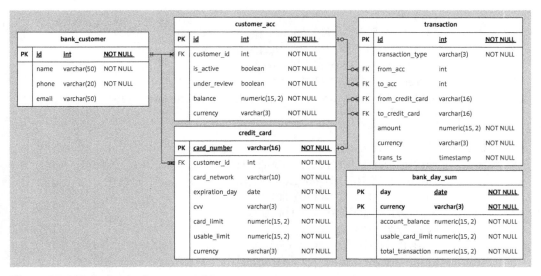

Figure 6.5 ERD for bank_day_sum Table

This table becomes a new row every day for each currency (primary keys), and the columns are filled as in Table 6.2.

Columns	Contents
account_balance	Sum of customer_acc.balance
usable_card_limit	Sum of credit_card.usable_limit where expiration_day > today
total_transaction	Sum of transaction.amount

Table 6.2 Value Columns of bank_day_sum Table

Now that our ERD is ready, we can create these tables in our playground schema. If you feel like creating a new schema for this chapter, feel free to do so. You can also turn this into a DDL exercise and create these tables on your own. Otherwise, you can simply execute the SQL statements in Listing 6.1 to create them.

```
CREATE TABLE bank_customer (
        id SERIAL PRIMARY KEY,
        name VARCHAR(50) NOT NULL,
        phone VARCHAR(20) NOT NULL,
        email VARCHAR(50)
    );

CREATE TABLE customer_acc (
        id SERIAL PRIMARY KEY,
```

225

6   Transaction Control Language

```sql
        customer_id INT NOT NULL,
        is_active BOOLEAN NOT NULL,
        under_review BOOLEAN NOT NULL,
        balance NUMERIC(15, 2) NOT NULL,
        currency VARCHAR(3) NOT NULL,
        FOREIGN KEY (customer_id) REFERENCES bank_customer (id)
);

CREATE TABLE credit_card (
        card_number VARCHAR(16) PRIMARY KEY,
        customer_id INT NOT NULL,
        card_network VARCHAR(10) NOT NULL,
        expiration_day DATE NOT NULL,
        cvv VARCHAR(3) NOT NULL,
        card_limit NUMERIC(15, 2) NOT NULL,
        usable_limit NUMERIC(15, 2) NOT NULL,
        currency VARCHAR(3) NOT NULL,
        FOREIGN KEY (customer_id) REFERENCES bank_customer (id)
);

CREATE TABLE transaction (
        id SERIAL PRIMARY KEY,
        transaction_type VARCHAR(3) NOT NULL,
        from_acc INT,
        to_acc INT,
        from_credit_card VARCHAR(16),
        to_credit_card VARCHAR(16),
        amount NUMERIC(15, 2) NOT NULL,
        currency VARCHAR(3) NOT NULL,
        trans_ts TIMESTAMP NOT NULL,
        FOREIGN KEY (from_acc) REFERENCES customer_acc (id),
        FOREIGN KEY (to_acc) REFERENCES customer_acc (id),
        FOREIGN KEY (from_credit_card) REFERENCES credit_card (card_number),
        FOREIGN KEY (to_credit_card) REFERENCES credit_card (card_number)
);

CREATE TABLE bank_day_sum (
        day DATE NOT NULL,
        currency VARCHAR(3) NOT NULL,
        account_balance NUMERIC(15, 2) NOT NULL,
        usable_card_limit NUMERIC(15, 2) NOT NULL,
        total_transaction NUMERIC(15, 2) NOT NULL,
        PRIMARY KEY (DAY, currency)
);
```

Listing 6.1 Creation of Daisy Bank Tables

Finally, we need some mock data. Luckily, the chapter on DML is behind us and we can use that knowledge to create such a stored procedure. Every time we execute this stored procedure, all the rows of the mock tables will be removed and the tables will be filled with fresh mock data. Once again, you can write such a procedure yourself as an exercise—but feel free to refer to Listing 6.2 if you want to.

```
CREATE OR REPLACE PROCEDURE reset_and_populate_bank_data ()
LANGUAGE plpgsql AS $$
BEGIN
    -- Truncate tables and reset serials
    TRUNCATE TABLE transaction, credit_card, customer_acc, bank_customer,
bank_day_sum
    RESTART IDENTITY CASCADE;

    -- Insert mock data into bank_customer
    INSERT INTO bank_customer (name, phone, email) VALUES
    ('John Doe', '123-456-7890', 'john.doe@example.com'),
    ('Jane Smith', '234-567-8901', 'jane.smith@example.com'),
    ('Alice Johnson', '345-678-9012', 'alice.johnson@example.com');

    -- Insert mock data into customer_acc
    INSERT INTO customer_acc (customer_id, is_active, under_review, balance,
currency)
    VALUES
    (1, TRUE, FALSE, 10000.00, 'USD'),
    (2, TRUE, TRUE, 5000.00, 'USD'),
    (3, FALSE, FALSE, 7500.00, 'EUR');

    -- Insert mock data into credit_card
    INSERT INTO credit_card (card_number, customer_id, card_network,
expiration_day, cvv, card_limit, usable_limit, currency)
    VALUES
    ('1234567812345678', 1, 'VISA', '2026-01-01', '123', 5000.00, 4500.00,
'USD'),
    ('2345678923456789', 2, 'MASTER', '2025-12-01', '456', 3000.00, 2800.00,
'USD'),
    ('3456789034567890', 3, 'AMEX', '2027-03-15', '789', 7000.00, 7000.00,
'EUR');

    -- Insert mock data into transaction
    INSERT INTO transaction (transaction_type, from_acc, to_acc,
from_credit_card, to_credit_card, amount, currency, trans_ts)
```

```
    VALUES
    ('TRA', 1, 2, NULL, NULL, 1500.00, 'USD', '2024-09-02 16:30:00'),
    ('CRD', 2, NULL, NULL, '2345678923456789', 5.00, 'USD', '2024-09-03 10:00:00'),
    ('TRA', 3, 1, NULL, NULL, 300.00, 'EUR', '2024-09-04 14:14:00');

    -- Insert mock data into bank_day_sum
    INSERT INTO bank_day_sum (day, currency, account_balance, usable_card_limit, total_transaction)
    VALUES
    ('2024-01-01', 'USD', 15000.00, 7300.00, 2000.00),
    ('2024-01-01', 'EUR', 7500.00, 7000.00, 300.00);

END;
$$;
```

Listing 6.2 Stored Procedure to Reset and Refill Playground Tables

Once you have the procedure in the system, you can call it as in Listing 6.3 every time you need a reset. After executing the stored procedure, you can browse the contents of our mock tables and see the populated data in place.

```
CALL reset_and_populate_bank_data();
```

Listing 6.3 Calling Stored Procedure

That concludes our playground preparation. Using these data structures for Daisy Bank, we can go over TCL concepts now and see how they help with data consistency in critical applications.

6.2 Why Is Transaction Control Language Necessary?

As stated earlier, TCL stands for *transaction control language*. To understand the necessity of TCL, we need to understand the core term *transaction* first.

A *transaction* is a sequence of SQL operations (such as INSERT, UPDATE, and/or DELETE) that make up a single unit. This unit is treated as an atomic operation, meaning that all operations in the sequence must either succeed or cancel altogether if any operation fails.

Rollbacks (undoing) are one of the significant benefits of TCL. As a tangible example from our Daisy Bank playground, imagine a stored procedure that conducts a money transfer between two accounts. That procedure needs to conduct a transaction made up of three operations:

- Creating a new row in the `transaction` table that contains the details of the transfer
- Decreasing the `customer_acc.balance` of the sender
- Increasing the `customer_acc.balance` of the receiver

Now, assume that the first two operations have finished successfully but that the third operation has failed due to unforeseeable circumstances, leaving the balance of the receiver without an increase. That would be a bummer, right? Although the sender has spent their money, the receiver hasn't gained any—so the money has disappeared into thin air.

We can prevent that with the help of TCL. If we implement the necessary TCL mechanism in the stored money transfer procedure, the database engine will undo all the operations if the third operation fails, keeping the involved records with their previous values.

This example alone should be enough to highlight the importance of TCL, but there's more.

Another significant benefit of TCL is concurrency management. Imagine a customer has a balance of $1,000 and has a corresponding entry in `customer_acc`.

If this customer receives three distinct payments of $50, $200, and $140 at different hours of the day, we'll rightfully expect to see `customer_acc.balance` increase to $1,000 + $50 + $200 + $140 = $1,390.

But what if the customer receives three distinct payments at the same moment? The following will occur:

- The first transaction will try to increase the balance to $1,050.
- The second transaction will try to increase the balance to $1,200.
- The third transaction will try to increase the balance to $1,140.

Depending on the database engine, one of those updates may succeed and others may not, which would lead to a data error. You wouldn't want to be the one getting the phone call from that angry client because they have missing funds in their account.

TCL empowers us with the necessary tools to handle such concurrent transactions as well. When you use them correctly, you can make a queue out of such concurrent transactions to ensure that they get executed sequentially.

These cases made it clear why you should often use multistep transactions together with TCL. There's more to come, though—let's move forward and learn how to apply TCL in our custom transactions.

6 Transaction Control Language

> **Atomicity, Consistency, Isolation, and Durability Compliance**
>
> Using TCL ensures that our transactions are ACID compliant. We discussed ACID in Chapter 1, but here's a reminder: ACID principles require a database product to ensure that each transaction fulfills the following properties:
>
> - **Atomicity**
>   All operations of a transaction should either succeed completely or be cancelled completely, preventing partial data modifications.
> - **Consistency**
>   Any transaction should bring the database from one valid state to another, maintaining all constraints.
> - **Isolation**
>   Any transaction must be isolated from all others, and its effects should be invisible until committed.
> - **Durability**
>   Once committed, changes asserted by a transaction must be permanent.

6.3 COMMIT and ROLLBACK

Now that we understand the necessity and overall logic of transactions, let's advance with the fundamentals of coding a transaction with SQL. A simple template for a transaction is provided in Listing 6.4.

```
BEGIN;
{ sql_code }
[ COMMIT; ]    -- Commit changes
[ ROLLBACK; ]  -- Undo changes
```

Listing 6.4 Template for Simple Transaction

There are three fundamental keywords to be aware of.

BEGIN declares the starting point of a transaction. Once the database engine sees this keyword, it understands that whatever is coded underneath this keyword belongs to a transaction—until the engine encounters a concluding keyword.

COMMIT is one of the possible concluding keywords. It means that all statements since BEGIN have executed successfully and can cumulatively be committed. Once COMMIT is executed, the transaction is finished, and all changes to database tables have been realized.

ROLLBACK is another possible concluding keyword. It means that something went wrong after BEGIN, and all pending changes should be cumulatively undone. Once ROLLBACK is executed, the transaction is finished without any changes to database tables.

Logically speaking, we start a transaction with BEGIN and end it with COMMIT under normal circumstances. We should use ROLLBACK in exceptional cases when an error has been detected, which we'll do now!

We'll start by resetting our bank mock data by executing Listing 6.5.

`CALL reset_and_populate_bank_data();`

Listing 6.5 Resetting Mock Data

We're aiming at writing a stored procedure to execute money transfers. For example, if we're making a money transfer of $100 between accounts 1 and 2, the stored procedure must do the following:

- Decrease the account 1 balance by $100.
- Increase the account 2 balance by $100.
- Create a new transaction entry.

But we need an extra control: both the source account and the target account must have the transfer currency. Otherwise, the operation should not complete. Figure 6.6 showcases our flowchart.

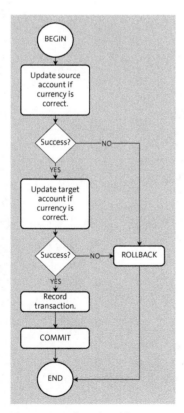

Figure 6.6 Flowchart for Money Transfer

As you can see, we're doing a ROLLBACK as soon as an unexpected situation is detected—such as the existence of an inappropriate currency in the source or target account. This enables us to undo the entire operation, no matter how far the procedure has advanced.

Listing 6.6 contains the stored procedure of this flowchart, which takes advantage of TCL to ensure a money transfer with increased security.

```
CREATE OR REPLACE PROCEDURE do_money_transfer (
    source_acc INT,
    target_acc INT,
    trn_amount NUMERIC(15, 2),
    trn_currency VARCHAR(3),
    time_stamp TIMESTAMP
) LANGUAGE plpgsql AS $$
DECLARE updated_row_count INTEGER;
BEGIN
    -- Update source account
    UPDATE customer_acc SET balance = balance - trn_amount
    WHERE id = source_acc AND currency = trn_currency;

    GET DIAGNOSTICS updated_row_count = ROW_COUNT;

    IF updated_row_count < 1 THEN
        ROLLBACK;
        RAISE EXCEPTION 'Invalid source account';
    END IF;

    -- Update target account
    UPDATE customer_acc SET balance = balance + trn_amount
    WHERE id = target_acc AND currency = trn_currency;

    GET DIAGNOSTICS updated_row_count = ROW_COUNT;

    IF updated_row_count < 1 THEN
        ROLLBACK;
        RAISE EXCEPTION 'Invalid target account';
    END IF;

    -- Record transaction
    INSERT INTO transaction(transaction_type, from_acc, to_acc,
                            amount, currency, trans_ts)
    VALUES ('TRA', source_acc, target_acc, trn_amount, trn_currency,
time_stamp);
```

```
    -- Finish transaction
    COMMIT;
END; $$
```

Listing 6.6 Stored Procedure for Money Transfer

In Listing 6.6, we sneaked in a new PostgreSQL stored procedure command: GET DIAGNOSTICS, which we can use to fetch the affected row count right after a DML operation. If no rows were updated, ROW_COUNT would return zero. If one or more rows were updated, ROW_COUNT would return the number of those rows.

Using this knowledge, you can follow through the code much easier. After every UPDATE operation, you can check the affected row count to see if you were able to update the source or target account—ensuring that they had the correct currency. If the operation failed, you would execute a ROLLBACK, undoing the entire block.

In case we need to do a ROLLBACK, we're also raising an exception. This is useful for notifying client applications about the fact that something went wrong. If we silently do a ROLLBACK but don't raise an exception, client applications will assume that everything went well.

Before we start the operation, customer_acc has the set of rows shown in Table 6.3.

id	customer_id	is_active	under_review	balance	currency
1	1	true	false	10,000	USD
2	2	true	true	5,000	USD
3	3	false	false	7,500	EUR

Table 6.3 Initial State of customer_acc Table

And transaction has the set of rows shown in Table 6.4.

id	transaction_type	from_acc	to_acc	from_credit_card	to_credit_card	amount	currency
1	TRA	1	2	null	null	1,500	USD
2	CRD	2	null	null	2345678923456789	5	USD
3	TRA	3	1	null	null	300	EUR

Table 6.4 Initial State of transaction Table

6   Transaction Control Language

In this example, we should be able to do USD transfers between accounts 1 and 2, but not EUR transfers—because both accounts are in currency USD.

To put our procedure to the test, try an invalid transaction. Try to execute Listing 6.7, which intentionally attempts to do a EUR money transfer between USD accounts.

```
CALL do_money_transfer(1, 2, 100, 'EUR', '2024-09-03 19:58:00');
```

Listing 6.7 Calling Stored Procedure with Incorrect Values

The database engine will raise our custom exception and return our own error message as **ERROR: Invalid source account**. That's great—it means the transaction executed the appropriate `ROLLBACK` (undo). If you check the `customer_acc` and `transaction` tables, you'll find that nothing has changed and they're in the exact same state as before.

Now, do a correct money transfer with USD currency. Execute Listing 6.8.

```
CALL do_money_transfer(1, 2, 100, 'USD', '2024-09-03 19:58:00');
```

Listing 6.8 Calling Stored Procedure with Correct Values

This time, the transaction should succeed! Because the provided data is correct, the database engine will follow through our code and `COMMIT` everything at the end.

After the execution, the `customer_acc` table should look like Table 6.5. Note that the balance of account 1 has decreased while the balance of account 2 has increased—hence, the $100 transfer.

id	customer_id	is_active	under_review	balance	currency
1	1	true	false	9,900	USD
2	2	true	true	5,100	USD
3	3	false	false	7,500	EUR

Table 6.5 State of customer_acc after Transfer

Also, `transaction` should become a new row regarding the money transfer, and its final state should look like it does in Table 6.6.

id	transaction_type	from_acc	to_acc	from_credit_card	to_credit_card	amount	currency
1	TRA	1	2	null	null	1,500	USD

Table 6.6 State of transaction after Transfer

id	transaction_type	from_acc	to_acc	from_credit_card	to_credit_card	amount	currency
2	CRD	2	null	null	2345678923456789	5	USD
3	TRA	3	1	null	null	300	EUR
4	TRA	1	2	null	null	100	USD

Table 6.6 State of transaction after Transfer (Cont.)

You can use this mechanism in any case where a ROLLBACK (undo) could be necessary. Some such cases are highlighted in Table 6.7.

Cases	Descriptions
Multiple dependent operations	Just as in our case above, if one of the chain-statements encounters an error, you can do a ROLLBACK.
Data validations	If you detect invalid data in the middle of the transaction, you can do a ROLLBACK.
Timeout	In a batch process procedure, you can keep track of the time, and if the completion takes too long, you can do a ROLLBACK.

Table 6.7 Some Typical Cases for ROLLBACK

Now that we've seen the basics of a database transaction, we can enhance our new knowledge with the concept of save points.

6.4 Save Points

Most gamers probably understand the concept of this topic already: *save points* are optional (but welcome) landmarks to which a transaction can be rolled back. For the rest of us, a detailed explanation follows.

In the previous example, we saw that a ROLLBACK can undo an entire transaction. In some cases, this is exactly what we want, but in other cases, we might want to partially undo the transaction. That's where save points come into play.

This easy mechanism will become clear when we go through an example. Table 6.8 shows the initial rows of the bank_customer table.

6 Transaction Control Language

id	name	phone	Email
1	John Doe	123-456-7890	john.doe@example.com
2	Jane Smith	234-567-8901	jane.smith@example.com
3	Alice Johnson	345-678-9012	alice.johnson@example.com

Table 6.8 Initial State of bank_customer Table

As a warmup, we'll start with a three-step transaction sketched in Figure 6.7. Nothing fancy at this point, just building a framework.

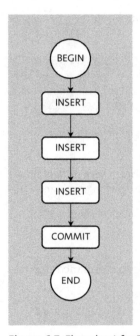

Figure 6.7 Flowchart for Three-Step Transaction

Now, inspect the corresponding code in Listing 6.9. Here, we start a transaction with BEGIN, insert three fresh rows into the bank_customer table, and complete the transaction with COMMIT. This simple structure will be the framework of our case study, which also demonstrates the possibility of using transactions outside of stored procedures.

```
BEGIN;

INSERT INTO bank_customer (name, phone)
VALUES ('Sarah Livingston', '+1-555-897-2341');

INSERT INTO bank_customer (name, phone)
VALUES ('Michael Thompson', '+1-555-762-1943');
```

```
INSERT INTO bank_customer (name,phone)
VALUES ('Emma Reynolds', '+1-555-348-7265');

COMMIT;
```

Listing 6.9 SQL Statement to Insert New bank_customer Table Rows

After we execute this statement, the `bank_customer` table will become three new rows and look like Table 6.9.

id	name	phone	email
1	John Doe	123-456-7890	john.doe@example.com
2	Jane Smith	234-567-8901	jane.smith@example.com
3	Alice Johnson	345-678-9012	alice.johnson@example.com
4	Sarah Livingston	+1-555-897-2341	null
5	Michael Thompson	+1-555-762-1943	null
6	Emma Reynolds	+1-555-348-7265	null

Table 6.9 bank_customer Table with Three New Rows

So far, so good! We've mostly made use of DML elements and made three new entries appear in the table.

In the previous chapter, we learned that `ROLLBACK` creates an undo operation on the entire transaction. To see this in action once again, execute the code in Listing 6.10. Note that the code begins by calling `reset_and_populate_bank_data` to ensure that the `bank_customer` table returns to its initial state shown earlier in Table 6.8.

```
CALL reset_and_populate_bank_data ();
BEGIN;

INSERT INTO bank_customer (name,phone)
VALUES ('Sarah Livingston', '+1-555-897-2341');

INSERT INTO bank_customer (name,phone)
VALUES ('Michael Thompson', '+1-555-762-1943');

INSERT INTO bank_customer (name,phone)
VALUES ('Emma Reynolds', '+1-555-348-7265');

ROLLBACK;
```

Listing 6.10 Rolling Back Entire Transaction

Despite having executed three INSERT statements, we finish the transaction with a ROLLBACK—undoing all three! Due to the ROLLBACK, all operations are cancelled altogether, and the bank_customer table remains in its initial state shown in Table 6.8, without any new rows.

So far, we've gone over our existing knowledge once again and set the stage for save points. Now, we'll add the SAVEPOINT keyword to the equation. After each INSERT statement, we'll plant a SAVEPOINT to be used in the very near future. Figure 6.8 showcases this logic.

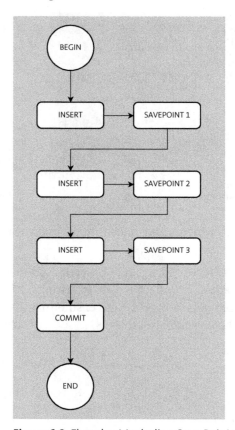

Figure 6.8 Flowchart Including Save Points

The SQL implementation of this logic can be seen in Listing 6.11.

```
CALL reset_and_populate_bank_data ();
BEGIN;

-- Customer 1
INSERT INTO bank_customer (NAME,phone)
VALUES ('Sarah Livingston', '+1-555-897-2341');
```

```
SAVEPOINT first_customer;

-- Customer 2
INSERT INTO bank_customer (NAME,phone)
VALUES ('Michael Thompson', '+1-555-762-1943');

SAVEPOINT second_customer;

-- Customer 3
INSERT INTO bank_customer (NAME,phone)
VALUES ('Emma Reynolds', '+1-555-348-7265');

SAVEPOINT third_customer;

-- Finish
COMMIT;
```

Listing 6.11 Transaction Involving SAVEPOINT

After inserting the first customer, we declared a SAVEPOINT called first_customer. This serves as a landmark, where our changes so far are temporarily saved in the memory. If we ROLLBACK to first_customer, the database engine will forget and undo all changes after first_customer—keeping only the insertion of the first customer in the queue. This is sketched in Figure 6.9.

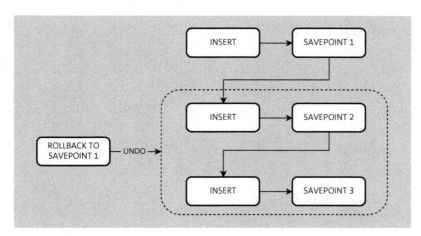

Figure 6.9 Rolling Back to First Save Point

After inserting the second customer, we declared a SAVEPOINT called second_customer. This serves as another landmark, where our changes so far (the insertion of two new customers) are temporarily saved in the memory. If we ROLLBACK to second_customer, the database engine will forget and undo all changes after second_customer—keeping only the insertion of the first and second customer in the queue. This is sketched in Figure 6.10.

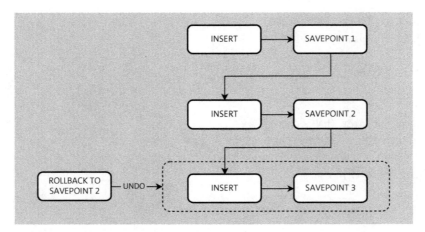

Figure 6.10 Rolling Back to Second Save Point

You get the idea—you can follow through the same logical chain for further save points.

Now, let's put it to the test! Listing 6.11 didn't include a ROLLBACK, so let's set one. Listing 6.12 provides the exact same code but finalizes the transaction with ROLLBACK TO second_customer, which will undo all operations after SAVEPOINT second_customer—ignoring the insertion of the third customer.

```
CALL reset_and_populate_bank_data ();
BEGIN;

-- Customer 1
INSERT INTO bank_customer (name,phone)
VALUES ('Sarah Livingston', '+1-555-897-2341');

SAVEPOINT first_customer;

-- Customer 2
INSERT INTO bank_customer (name,phone)
VALUES ('Michael Thompson', '+1-555-762-1943');

SAVEPOINT second_customer;

-- Customer 3
INSERT INTO bank_customer (name,phone)
VALUES ('Emma Reynolds', '+1-555-348-7265');
```

```
SAVEPOINT third_customer;

-- Finish
ROLLBACK TO second_customer;
COMMIT;
```

Listing 6.12 Rolling Back to second_customer

Once we execute this transaction, the `bank_customer` table should look like Table 6.10.

id	name	phone	email
1	John Doe	123-456-7890	john.doe@example.com
2	Jane Smith	234-567-8901	jane.smith@example.com
3	Alice Johnson	345-678-9012	alice.johnson@example.com
4	Sarah Livingston	+1-555-897-2341	null
5	Michael Thompson	+1-555-762-1943	null

Table 6.10 Rows of bank_customer Table after Save Point Rollback

Voila! The execution of `ROLLBACK TO second_customer` worked just as intended—the `INSERT` statement after `SAVEPOINT second_customer` was rolled back, but statements before that were realized and ended up creating two fresh rows in the `bank_customer` table. Neat, right?

As an exercise, you can repeat the execution of Listing 6.12 by rolling back to a different `SAVEPOINT` each time and seeing how the `bank_customer` table changes.

Save points are particularly useful in scenarios where partial rollbacks are needed. This mechanism gives you fine-grained control over the transaction, preventing complete transaction failure while preserving successful operations.

Mind you that different database products may have different approaches to save points. Some may allow save point usage freely, while others may limit it due to its reliance on automatic transaction handling mechanisms. You can check the documentation of your database product for more information.

Now that you understand optional save points, we can move on to a critical subject: handling transaction concurrency.

6.5 Locks and Concurrency

Transaction control is relatively easy when you're the only one working on the database. You can freely read or write rows without worrying about anyone else. However, things take a different turn when you have multiple users working on the same database.

What if two people attempt to update the same row(s) at the exact same time? How would the database engine handle those records—toss a coin and apply the lucky one?

What if user A reads data from multiple related tables while user B runs a deletion of them? It's possible for A to find a row but not find the corresponding foreign key row because the entries were being deleted at that time.

Luckily, SQL empowers us with mechanisms for dealing with such risks. In this section, we'll learn about preventing such unfortunate scenarios.

6.5.1 Locks

The database term *lock* correlates very well with its usual meaning. Locks allow us to lock rows before we make changes to them.

In our TCL examples so far, we executed DML statements directly. We started the transactions, ran DML statements, and concluded everything with a COMMIT (or ROLLBACK, if we need to undo). This basic flow can be seen in Figure 6.11.

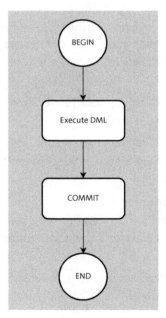

Figure 6.11 Basic TCL Flow without Locks Involved

However, when locks are involved, we get an extra step in our TCL structures. Instead of executing UPDATE or DELETE statements directly, we start by locking the rows in advance. Once the lock is successful, we can be sure that no one else can modify those rows until our transaction is complete. We can safely execute our DML statements, and once we

COMMIT, the database engine releases the locks automatically. This extended flow can be seen in Figure 6.12.

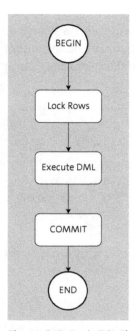

Figure 6.12 Basic TCL Flow with Locks Involved

While user A has an active lock on some rows, lock requests or DML statements (such as UPDATE) on the same rows from user B won't be executed by the database engine. Instead, user B's statements will wait until user A's operation is completed. Then, the engine will take user B's statements into consideration and process through them.

Figure 6.13 demonstrates this process on a timeline.

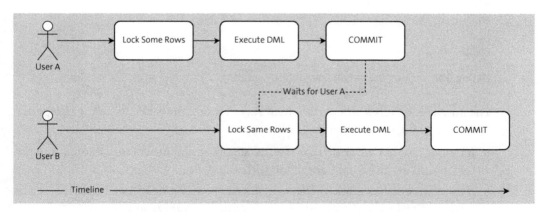

Figure 6.13 Basic Lock Logic on Timeline

6 Transaction Control Language

This mechanism prevents concurrent modifications neatly and in a standardized way. We don't have to worry about the sequence of client users either because the database engine will handle such tasks.

If you're executing DML statements against rows, where concurrent access is a possibility, we strongly advise you to take advantage of the lock mechanism and lock those entries before making any changes. Otherwise, concurrent modifications may cause data inconsistencies or even data loss in some cases.

> **Deadlocks**
> The term *deadlock* identifies a situation where two transactions set competing locks in such a way that they both wait for each other forever. Many database products have internal deadlock prevention mechanisms—they simply pick a deadlock transaction and roll it back, returning an error to the client application. Still, it's best to design the system in such a way that deadlock risks are prevented or at least minimized.

Now that we've grasped the purpose of locks, we can get hands-on with them. Locks come in two flavors: row-level locks and table-level locks.

Row-Level Locks

SQL gives us the opportunity to lock select rows before modifying them. Listing 6.13 demonstrates such an example.

```
BEGIN;

SELECT * FROM bank_customer WHERE id = 1 FOR UPDATE;

UPDATE bank_customer
SET phone = '+1-555-849-6237'
WHERE id = 1;

COMMIT;
```

Listing 6.13 Locking Individual Row Before Updating

The initial SELECT ... FOR UPDATE statement sets a lock on the bank_customer row where id = 1. At this point, one of two things will happen:

- If no one else has a lock on that row, the database engine will lock it for us and protect it until we finish the transaction with a COMMIT or a ROLLBACK.
- If someone else has a lock on that row, the database engine will wait until their transaction is finished, and only then will it resume our transaction.

In either case, concurrent modifications will be prevented.

> **SELECT statement**
>
> The SELECT statement belongs to the realm of DQL, which is covered next in Chapter 7. Although we mostly use it to read data from database tables, we can also use it to lock rows when we use it with the FOR UPDATE suffix.

In our former example, we've locked a single row in the bank_customer table because we've provided its primary key value as WHERE id = 1. However, it's also possible to lock multiple rows by extending the WHERE condition. See Listing 6.14 for such an example.

```
BEGIN;

SELECT * FROM credit_card WHERE customer_id = 1 FOR UPDATE;

UPDATE credit_card
SET usable_limit = usable_limit * 1.25
WHERE customer_id = 1;

COMMIT;
```

Listing 6.14 Locking Individual Rows before Updating

In this example, we've listed all of customer 1's credit card entries. If they have multiple credit cards, all of them will be locked in the credit_card table. Once the lock is in place, we extend usable limits of those cards by 25% and finish the operation with COMMIT.

While this transaction is running, no one else will be able to modify customer 1's credit card entries.

Locks can (and should) be used for entry deletions as well! Listing 6.15 showcases a sample code where rows are locked before deletion.

```
BEGIN;

SELECT * FROM bank_day_sum
WHERE
    day = CURRENT_DATE
    AND currency = 'EUR'
FOR UPDATE;

DELETE FROM bank_day_sum
WHERE
    day = CURRENT_DATE
```

```
    AND currency = 'EUR';

COMMIT;
```

Listing 6.15 Locking Rows before Deleting Them

> **Deletion Locks**
> Note that our SELECT statement still ended as FOR UPDATE, despite our intention to delete rows. The UPDATE keyword in FOR UPDATE shouldn't be confused with the UPDATE DML keyword. The FOR UPDATE prefix declares our intention to modify these rows, either by UPDATE or by DELETE, covering both cases.

Row-level locks provide a practical concurrency solution for cases in which we have a specific subset of rows to modify. But if we find ourselves in a situation where we'd rather lock an entire table, we can achieve that via special SQL commands without addressing individual rows. How? Read on!

Table-Level Locks

Most database products let us lock an entire table instead of individual rows. Table-level locks function nearly the same way as row-level locks, with the obvious difference that we don't have to identify individual rows to lock. Instead, we provide the table's name, and that's it!

Listing 6.16 demonstrates a table-level lock in exclusive mode. When it's locked in exclusive mode, other clients may neither read nor modify the rows of the table until the transaction is finished. Such requests will wait until the table lock is lifted, just like with row-level locks.

```
BEGIN;
LOCK TABLE customer_acc IN EXCLUSIVE MODE;
-- Further SQL statements
COMMIT;
```

Listing 6.16 Locking Entire Table in Exclusive Mode

Exclusive mode is especially useful in some cases. For instance, if you're about to execute DDL statements to alter columns, it's a good idea to lock the table in exclusive mode first to ensure that no other transactions touch the table until you're finished.

Listing 6.17 showcases such an example, in which we lock the credit_card table exclusively before adding a new column. This could prevent potential DML or DQL errors from being executed simultaneously.

```
BEGIN;
LOCK TABLE credit_card IN EXCLUSIVE MODE;
ALTER TABLE credit_card ADD COLUMN is_active BOOLEAN;
COMMIT;
```

Listing 6.17 Exclusive Lock before DDL Operation

Bulk data operation is another typical case for this. Before doing a bulk insertion, update, or deletion, you may want to lock target tables in exclusive mode to pause other transactions until you're finished. Otherwise, they may read incomplete or inconsistent data due to the unfinished task.

Another type of table lock is share mode, which is demonstrated in Listing 6.18. When a table is locked in share mode, other clients may read rows of the table but may not modify them until the transaction is finished.

```
BEGIN;
LOCK TABLE customer_acc IN SHARE MODE;
-- Further SQL statements
COMMIT;
```

Listing 6.18 Locking Entire Table in Shared Mode

Share mode is useful in some other cases. If you're about to run multiple queries for audit purposes to build aggregate data, you must ensure that you should freeze the tables before reading. Otherwise, ongoing transactions may cause inconsistent results for you. You can easily freeze your tables by using the share mode, which can pause data modification transactions but won't stop harmless data reading transactions.

Listing 6.19 showcases such an example. We set a share lock on the bank_customer and customer_acc tables before calculating the average number of accounts per customer. This temporarily prevents data flow into those tables, allowing us to make a consistent calculation over a frozen dataset.

```
BEGIN;

LOCK TABLE bank_customer IN SHARE MODE;
LOCK TABLE customer_acc IN SHARE MODE;

SELECT
    (COUNT(*) / (SELECT COUNT(*) FROM bank_customer)) AS
avg_account_per_customer
FROM customer_acc;

COMMIT;
```

Listing 6.19 Share Lock before DQL Operation

6 Transaction Control Language

Running consistency checks across tables is another example. If your read operation tangles with other write operations, you may experience fake data inconsistencies merely due to a data race. It's best to freeze modification operations using shared mode, run your queries, and finish the transaction.

> **Table-Level Locks**
>
> No matter what kind of table-level lock you choose, it will inevitably have an effect on other transactions—you'll be pausing them until your task is done. To prevent performance bottlenecks, we advise you to finish your tasks and release the lock as quick as possible.
>
> If you foresee long execution times, you may schedule your task at a point in time when transaction intensity is at a minimum. In extreme cases, you can even consider locking client applications "due to system maintenance" for a scheduled time span and run your lock-related transactions at that time.

This concludes our content on locks. Now, we can move on to the topic of transaction isolation, which is equally useful in many cases.

6.5.2 Transaction Isolation

At this point, we're well aware that production databases are expected to run multiple parallel transactions simultaneously. As we attempt to read data from tables, there may be countless parallel transactions modifying data on the same tables. Some changes may be committed, while some others may be uncommitted.

The transaction isolation mechanism enables us to instruct the database engine about the data state we're interested in. What do we mean by *data state*? Let's directly answer that question by using the practical examples in the following sections!

READ UNCOMMITTED Mode

In Listing 6.20, we begin our transaction with a SET TRANSACTION statement.

```
BEGIN;
    SET TRANSACTION ISOLATION LEVEL READ UNCOMMITTED;
    SELECT * FROM bank_customer;
END;
```

Listing 6.20 Reading Uncommitted Rows as Well as Committed Rows

The statement on the second line tells the database engine explicitly that we want to read uncommitted rows as well as committed rows. As we know, the default behavior of database engines is to read committed rows only. Uncommitted rows are invisible to us because they might be rolled back eventually. But in special cases, we have the power to override this default behavior and gain the ability to read uncommitted entries as well, if the need arises. Using Listing 6.20, we can read both committed and uncommitted rows in the bank_customer table. Cool, right? Although this won't be required very often, it's nice to have the flexibility.

This approach is sometimes called a *dirty read*, and you may use it when performance is more important that perfect data consistency, such as in data analysis queries targeting generic overviews. Since the database engine won't have to deal with parallel transactions, it can read all entries in the table directly—even if some may be rolled back soon.

Reading historical data is a natural match to this approach. If the data in question won't be modified any longer, you can read it directly without worrying about commits and rollbacks.

> **SET TRANSACTION ISOLATION LEVEL Statement**
> It's enough to use the SET TRANSACTION ISOLATION LEVEL statement once at the beginning of the transaction. All subsequent queries will run according to the mentioned isolation level.

READ COMMITTED Mode

Although it's the default behavior anyway, Listing 6.21 demonstrates how to instruct the database engine to read committed rows only and ignore uncommitted rows. In this transaction, we'll fetch committed bank_customer table rows only.

```
BEGIN;
    SET TRANSACTION ISOLATION LEVEL READ COMMITTED;
    SELECT * FROM bank_customer;
END;
```

Listing 6.21 Reading Committed Rows Only

SERIALIZABLE Mode

Another cool mode is SERIALIZABLE. In this mode, no other parallel transactions can modify data that has been read by our current transaction—until it completes. Parallel transactions can't insert new rows that correspond to the key values of our current transaction either. In other words, SERIALIZABLE ensures that no rows can be added or deleted in a way that affects our transaction's outcome. Listing 6.22 shows this mode in action.

```
BEGIN;
    SET TRANSACTION ISOLATION LEVEL SERIALIZABLE;
    SELECT * FROM bank_customer;
END;
```

Listing 6.22 Making Engine Wait for Uncommitted Changes

Legal reports and audits are perfect examples of cases in which SERIALIZABLE is useful, due to their criticality. We can ensure that our target dataset remains unchanged during the reporting process, ensuring a stable output. But it also means that we're choosing to endure the performance cost and that parallel transactions will be paused until we're done. Therefore, we advise that you to use SERIALIZABLE only when absolutely necessary. Otherwise, you should use alternative modes.

REPEATABLE READ Mode

Finally, we've got REPEATABLE READ. In this mode, the database engine ensures that all queries address the initial state of the table, even if parallel commits were applied to the accessed table.

In Listing 6.23, each SELECT statement will return the same bank_customer entries. Even if someone else inserts and commits a new row into the bank_customer table after the first SELECT statement, the database engine will ignore it on the second and third SELECT statements.

```
BEGIN;
    SET TRANSACTION ISOLATION LEVEL REPEATABLE READ;

    SELECT * FROM bank_customer;
    SELECT * FROM bank_customer;
    SELECT * FROM bank_customer;
END;
```

Listing 6.23 Repeatable Read Example

From that point of view, SERIALIZABLE and REPEATABLE READ are similar in a way: both can ensure that we get the same results on multiple queries. The differences are that SERIALIZABLE will realize this goal by pausing parallel transactions, while REPEATABLE READ will realize it by ignoring parallel transactions.

REPEATABLE READ doesn't prevent other DML statements, so it's the lenient option. It's the ideal choice for less critical reports, in which you need to access the same tables multiple times to build the output. REPEATABLE READ ensures that DML transactions between your queries don't affect your results.

6.6 Common Pitfalls of Transaction Control Language

Before we conclude this chapter, it's useful to highlight some pitfalls of TCL that you should avoid as much as possible.

Ignoring and avoiding TCL is an obvious pitfall. Some sample cases are as follows:

- Not using COMMIT or ROLLBACK despite modifying rows of multiple related tables
- Ignoring ROLLBACK on errors
- Not locking rows or tables before applying changes
- Not using transaction isolation in critical queries

However, abusing TCL to a point where other transactions are affected is another pitfall. Some sample cases are as follows:

- Locking more rows than necessary
- Keeping locks active for too long
- Using unnecessarily restrictive or too flexible transaction isolation modes

You should use TCL with common sense and keep it as simple as possible. You don't want to overengineer things, and complex TCL mechanisms may lead to unforeseeable complications, such as deadlocks. Even when the code is as simple as possible, you should test it in a playground or test datasets before using it in a production database.

6.7 Summary

In this chapter, we've learned about TCL and how it helps with data consistency in database environments with an unforeseeable number of parallel transactions.

The COMMIT and ROLLBACK mechanisms help us with multitable changes by either applying them all together or cancelling them altogether.

The lock mechanism helps us protect our target rows from other transactions until our DML statements are completed, preventing simultaneous write access.

The transaction isolation mechanism helps us read stable datasets matching our intent, by either allowing or parallel transactions or preventing them from interfering with our queries.

We've also briefly discussed some potential pitfalls of TCL.

That concludes our discussion of content related to data manipulation and transactions. Now that we know how to set data to database tables, it's time to learn how to query tables to transform data to information and knowledge. Our next chapter is on DQL, which is arguably the most used SQL sublanguage. Take a break, get some fresh air, and see you there!

Chapter 7
Data Query Language

Data query language (DQL) is arguably the most common database feature. We use it to query data from database tables. You'll learn about data queries from single tables and combined sets of tables, and you'll also learn about data filters, string and math operations, date- and time-based calculations, and advanced ranking functionalities (window functions). You'll be able to use this knowledge to query data in your own production databases to generate knowledge.

We've finally arrived at the long-awaited chapter on queries! You may presumably be more interested in this chapter than the ones on other SQL sublanguages because data entries are created once, modified when necessary, but queried all the time.

To make a formal introduction, DQL is the SQL sublanguage we use to read data from database tables programmatically. It empowers developers with wonderful tools to query database tables, converting data to information and knowledge.

Using DQL, we can go way beyond previewing data in single tables, which is possible via database applications like VS Code and pgAdmin anyway. Some functionalities in our upcoming toolbox are as follows:

- Running advanced queries with column selection, filters, aggregation, and sorting
- Querying multiple tables via foreign keys at the same time to produce nested results sets
- Processing values via string, math, and date/time operations
- Advanced ranking via window functions

Once you learn how to query tables via DQL, you can either use it directly in the console of your favorite database application or execute it programmatically through your custom application to retrieve results.

> **DQL versus SQL**
>
> Many people use the term *SQL* as a synonym for *DQL*. When they say, "SQL statement," they may actually mean "DQL statement" if they solely read data from tables. Although terminologically wrong, this tendency is an indicator of DQL's popularity.

DQL is a subject with a relatively wide set of audiences, some of which are listed in Table 7.1.

Audiences	Interests
Data analysts	Retrieving transformed data for analysis
Business intelligence specialists	Querying large datasets to generate reports
Data scientists	Retrieving historical data for training machine learning models
Software developers	Providing data for custom applications
Auditors	Retrieving data for compliance checks and audits
Data governance members	Monitoring and assessing data quality
Business professionals	Analyzing data for decision-making and reporting

Table 7.1 Some Parties Relying on DQL

Now that we're acquainted with DQL, let's start building our playground for the upcoming chapters.

7.1 Building a Data Query Language Playground

To keep this chapter self-contained, we'll start with a fresh case study and create database tables accordingly. These tables will be our basis for executing and learning DQL statements.

Our case study will be about an imaginary online apparel store called Retro Loom, which sells original boutique pieces unlike others on the market. Our database structure will feature a simplified yet realistic set of tables for an entire sales, distribution, and invoicing mechanism. That will enable us to demonstrate even the most advanced DQL commands within a real-world context.

> **SAP ERP**
>
> The table structure we're about to create is loosely based on the sales and distribution module of SAP ERP. Although the structure is simplified for our DQL purposes, it reflects some real-world best practices.

7.1.1 Master Data Tables

First, we need to determine what kind of product we're going to sell. We know that Retro Loom is an online apparel store, but we can't simply list all products on a huge web page! Instead, it's a better practice to group products under categories.

For that purpose, we'll have a product_cat table in which categories like Tops, Bottoms, and Accessories will be distinguished from each other. Figure 7.1 showcases the simple structure of that table.

	product_cat		
PK	id	varchar(10)	NOT NULL
	name	varchar(50)	NOT NULL

Figure 7.1 ERD for product_cat Table

To create this table in the database, you can execute Listing 7.1.

```
CREATE TABLE
    product_cat (
        id VARCHAR(10) PRIMARY KEY,
        name VARCHAR(50) NOT NULL
    );
```

Listing 7.1 Creation of Product Category Table

> **Data Definition Language Commands**
>
> In this section, we'll create database tables using DDL commands as in Listing 7.1. If you're only interested in DQL and don't want to learn about DDL, you can copy and paste these DDL statements without understanding them in depth. You won't need any DDL knowledge once our playground dataset is finished; we'll jump into DQL right away.
>
> If you want to learn more about DDL, though, you can refer to Chapter 4.

Now that our categories are ready, we can determine what products are going to be sold. For that purpose, we need a product table that will store master data for our goods. Figure 7.2 showcases our ERD extended with a product table.

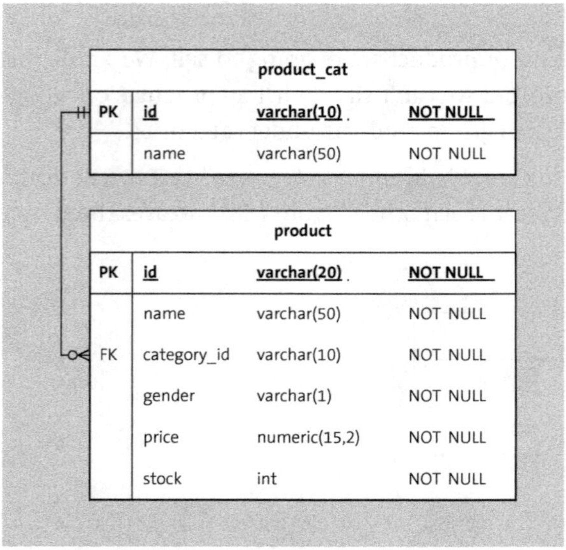

7   Data Query Language

Figure 7.2 ERD Extended with product Table

The columns of the product table are described in Table 7.2. We're ignoring apparel sizes intentionally for simplicity, and for the same reason, we're assuming that a single currency key applies to all prices.

Columns	Descriptions
id	Unique ID
name	Product description
category_id	Category ID (references product_cat.id)
gender	Target gender (male, female, or unisex)
price	Current unit price
stock	Number of items in stock

Table 7.2 Columns of product

Nothing out of the ordinary, right? Let's create this table using Listing 7.2.

```
CREATE TABLE
    product (
        id VARCHAR(20) PRIMARY KEY,
        name VARCHAR(50) NOT NULL,
        category_id VARCHAR(10) NOT NULL REFERENCES product_cat (id),
        gender CHAR(1) NOT NULL,
        price NUMERIC(15, 2) NOT NULL,
```

        stock INT NOT NULL
);

Listing 7.2 Creation of product Table

Now, where would an online store be without any customers? We naturally need a table to store our customer master data, and we'll simply call it customer. Figure 7.3 showcases our ERD extended with that table.

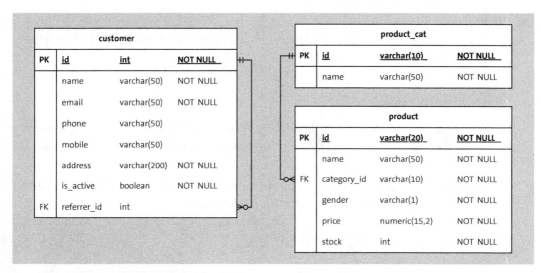

Figure 7.3 ERD Extended with customer Table

Most of the customer columns are intuitive and self-explanatory by name. The only interesting column is referrer_id, which stores the ID of the referring customer if they became a member by reference. To make this more obvious, Table 7.3 demonstrates a case in which Alice Smith referred Charlie Brown and Diana Prince as new members.

id	name	referrer_id
1	Alice Smith	null
3	Charlie Brown	1
4	Diana Prince	1

Table 7.3 Sample customer Rows Demonstrating Referrers

All clear? Good! Let's create the table, then. You can execute Listing 7.3 for that.

```
CREATE TABLE
    customer (
        id SERIAL PRIMARY KEY,
        name VARCHAR(50) NOT NULL,
```

```
        email VARCHAR(50) NOT NULL,
        phone VARCHAR(50),
        mobile VARCHAR(50),
        address VARCHAR(200) NOT NULL,
        is_active BOOLEAN NOT NULL,
        referrer_id INT REFERENCES customer (id)
);
```

Listing 7.3 Creation of customer Table

This concludes the creation of our master data tables. We'll continue with some transactional tables now.

7.1.2 Order Tables

Now that we have our master data tables at hand, let's continue following the logical order of events. Our sales and distribution scenario would start with an order placed by a customer.

Retro Loom gives its customers options to mark an order as a gift, enter a custom note or greeting, and request a special delivery date instead of ASAP. Therefore, our `customer_order` table should have columns corresponding to those options. Check Figure 7.4 to see the structure of this table.

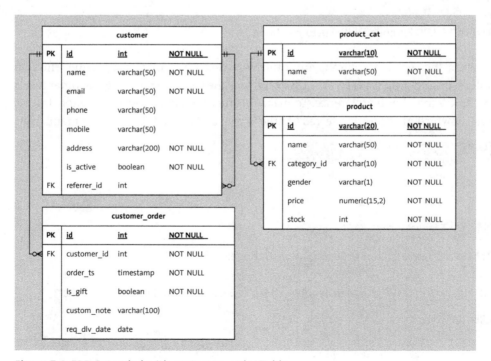

Figure 7.4 ERD Extended with customer_order Table

7.1 Building a Data Query Language Playground

The columns of the `customer_order` table are intuitive and self-explanatory, right? Now that we have the order table in place, we need an additional table to store purchased products for each order. Let's call this table `order_item` and inspect its structure in Figure 7.5.

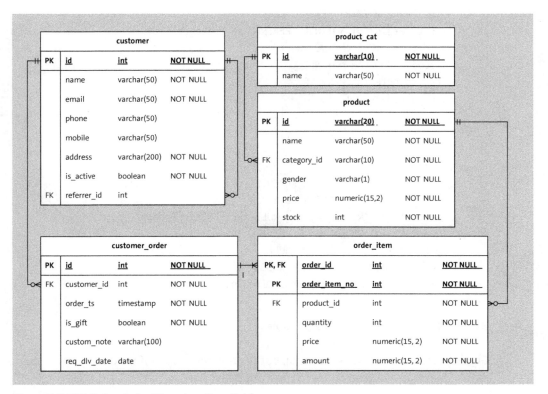

Figure 7.5 ERD Extended with order_item Table

It might be a good idea to go over the `order_item` table's columns once, to cleanse our minds of any doubts. Check Table 7.4.

Columns	Descriptions
order_id	Order ID (references `customer_order.id`)
order_item_no	Sequential number, starting from 1 for each order
product_id	ID of purchased product (references `product.id`)
quantity	Purchase quantity
price	Unit price of the product, which was valid on the date of the purchase and might differ from the current `product.price`
amount	Total cost of the item, calculated as quantity × price

Table 7.4 Columns of order_item Table

7 Data Query Language

Now that we've designed the structure of our order-related tables, it's time for you to create them! Execute Listing 7.4.

```
CREATE TABLE
    customer_order (
        id SERIAL PRIMARY KEY,
        customer_id INT NOT NULL REFERENCES customer (id),
        order_ts TIMESTAMP NOT NULL,
        is_gift BOOLEAN NOT NULL,
        custom_note VARCHAR(100),
        req_dlv_date DATE
    );

CREATE TABLE
    order_item (
        order_id INT NOT NULL REFERENCES customer_order (id),
        order_item_no INT NOT NULL,
        product_id VARCHAR(20) NOT NULL REFERENCES product (id),
        quantity INT NOT NULL,
        price NUMERIC(15, 2) NOT NULL,
        amount NUMERIC(15, 2) NOT NULL,
        PRIMARY KEY (order_id, order_item_no)
    );
```

Listing 7.4 Creation of Order-Related Tables

Getting customer orders is essential, but it's not very useful if we don't deliver them, right? Therefore, we need tables to track our deliveries.

7.1.3 Delivery Tables

Let's start with the easy part. Just like we have separate header and item tables for orders, we're going to follow the same approach for deliveries. The `delivery_header` table will contain common fields like date, customer ID, and tracking URL, while the `delivery_item` table will contain a list of products shipped with that delivery.

Adding the `delivery_header` table to the picture, our ERD extends as in Figure 7.6. All columns are intuitive and self-explanatory.

Let's think about delivery items now.

It would be an easy approach to send each order as a single delivery, once all order items are in stock and ready, right? We would simply copy `order_item` table entries into our upcoming `delivery_item` table and be done with it.

7.1 Building a Data Query Language Playground

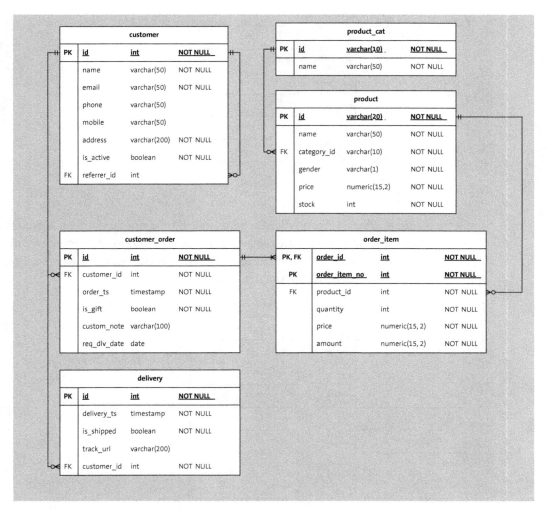

Figure 7.6 ERD Extended with delivery_header Table

But this would mean longer wait times for the customer. Even if one of the products in the order is not in stock yet, the customer would have to wait for it to receive the entire order, despite some products being available immediately.

Retro Loom goes the extra mile to increase customer satisfaction. If only some products in an order are available, the store will deliver what it can and ship the rest once the missing products are in stock again. Figure 7.7 demonstrates this policy visually, in a case where an order has been split into two deliveries.

Makes sense, right? Customers would surely prefer to receive a fast partial delivery (Delivery 1) containing whatever is available.

261

7 Data Query Language

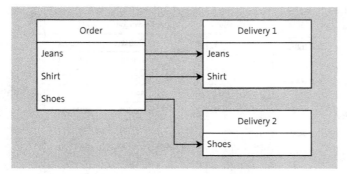

Figure 7.7 Order Split Example

But Retro Loom must consider shipment costs as well. If the same customer has multiple orders within the same time frame, it would be more economical to merge them into a single delivery. Figure 7.8 demonstrates this policy visually, in a case where a second order was partially merged with the first one.

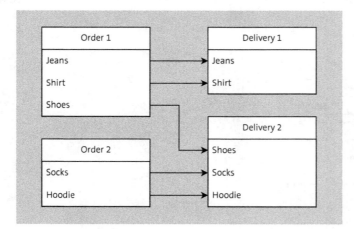

Figure 7.8 Order Merge Example

If we had to write down these references as a matrix, we would come up with Table 7.5.

Deliveries	Delivery Items	Reference Orders	Reference Order Items
301	1 (jeans)	101	1 (jeans)
301	2 (shirt)	101	2 (shirt)
302	1 (shoes)	101	3 (shoes)
302	2 (socks)	102	1 (socks)
302	3 (hoodie)	102	2 (hoodie)

Table 7.5 Delivery Item/Order Item Matrix

And surprise—this correlates with what our delivery table structure must look like! Each delivery item should refer to an order item, and multiple order items can be consolidated under a delivery—just as demonstrated above.

Following our logic, we can extend our ERD with the `delivery_item` table as in Figure 7.9. Note that each `delivery_item` table entry refers to an `order_item` table entry, which corresponds to the order merge logic explained above.

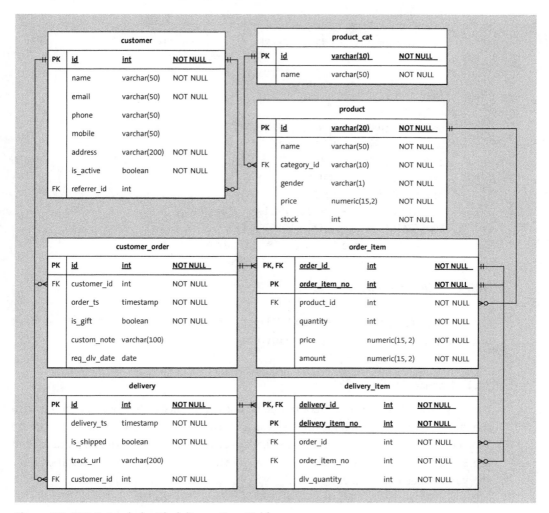

Figure 7.9 ERD Extended with delivery_item Table

Wow, the ERD sure is growing as we think about it! But since it grows step by step with logical explanations, it shouldn't be scary at all. We merely have a handful of tables and will add just a couple more soon—nothing is out of control.

7 Data Query Language

Now that we've the extended ERD in place, it's time for you to create our delivery tables. Execute the code in Listing 7.5.

```
CREATE TABLE
    delivery (
        id SERIAL PRIMARY KEY,
        delivery_ts TIMESTAMP NOT NULL,
        is_shipped BOOLEAN NOT NULL,
        track_url VARCHAR(200),
        customer_id INT NOT NULL REFERENCES customer (id)
    );

CREATE TABLE
    delivery_item (
        delivery_id INT NOT NULL REFERENCES delivery (id),
        delivery_item_no INT NOT NULL,
        order_id INT NOT NULL,
        order_item_no INT NOT NULL,
        dlv_quantity INT NOT NULL,
        PRIMARY KEY (delivery_id, delivery_item_no),
        CONSTRAINT fk_order_item FOREIGN KEY (order_id, order_item_no)
            REFERENCES order_item (order_id, order_item_no)
    );
```

Listing 7.5 Creation of Delivery Tables

This should create the `delivery` and `delivery_item` tables as intended. Now, we have one final missing piece of the puzzle: invoices.

7.1.4 Invoice Tables

Like any other business, Retro Loom needs to issue invoices. Since we're familiar with the sales and distribution logic now, we can go forward with the idea of having separate `invoice_header` and `invoice_item` tables. Let's get the obvious out of the way and extend our ERD with our `invoice_header` table, which includes nothing more than self-explanatory fields. See Figure 7.10.

7.1 Building a Data Query Language Playground

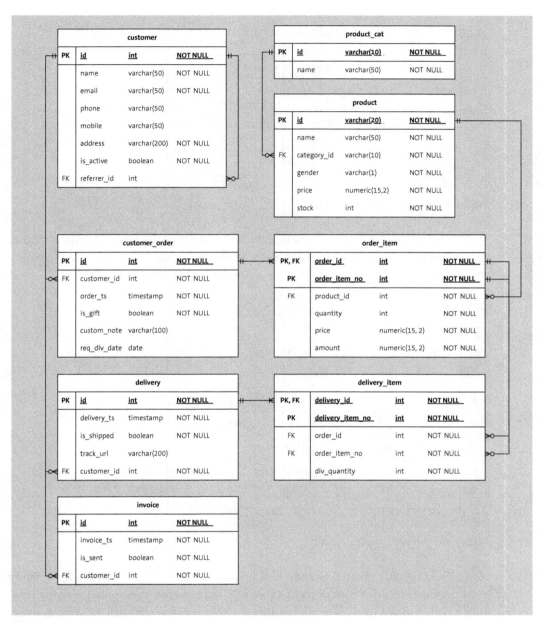

Figure 7.10 ERD Extended with invoice_header Table

According to the business rules of Retro Loom, we should only invoice products we can deliver; therefore, invoices should reference deliveries. But there's a catch: the accounting department wants some flexibility in terms of invoicing. If the total amount on the invoice is too big, accounting may decide to split a delivery into multiple invoices, as demonstrated in Figure 7.11.

7 Data Query Language

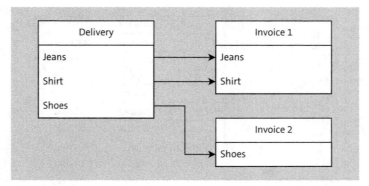

Figure 7.11 Delivery Split Example

On the other hand, if the invoice amount doesn't exceed the limit and the customer has multiple deliveries within the same time frame, accounting may decide to merge multiple deliveries into a single invoice, as demonstrated in Figure 7.12.

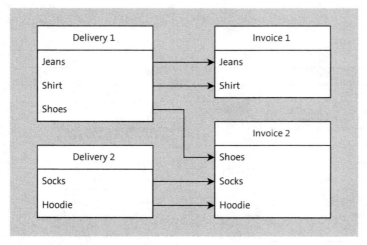

Figure 7.12 Delivery Merge Example

As you've probably noticed already, this follows the same logic as the order-delivery relationship that's demonstrated in Table 7.5. Therefore, we can apply the same solution to our invoice table, where each invoice item will reference an existing delivery item. This will give maximum flexibility to accounting—it can split or merge deliveries into invoices as desired.

Following this approach, we can extend our ERD with the invoice_item table as in Figure 7.13. Note that each invoice_item table entry refers to a delivery_item table entry, which covers the logic explained above.

7.1 Building a Data Query Language Playground

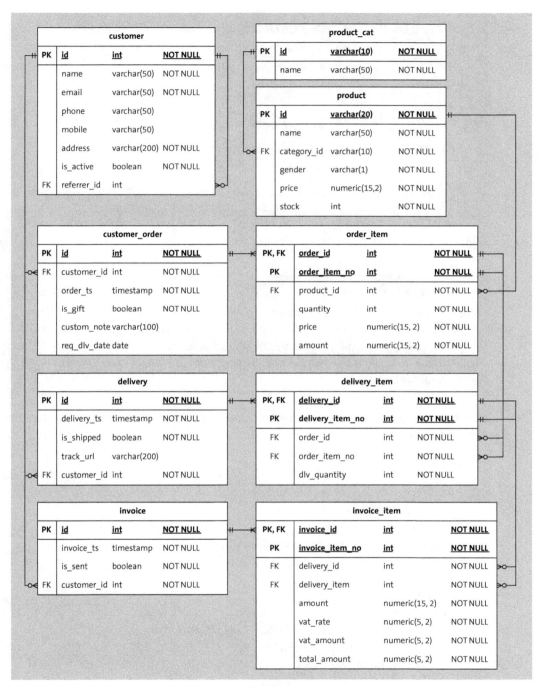

Figure 7.13 ERD Extended with invoice_item Table

Note that for each `invoice_item` table row, we have various value columns. Table 7.6 contains an explanation of these columns.

7   Data Query Language

Columns	Descriptions	Sample values
amount	Raw amount, calculated as follows: delivery_item.dlv_quantity × order_item.price	105
vat_rate	Value-added tax (VAT) percentage	20
vat_amount	VAT amount, calculated as follows: amount × vat_rate / 100	21 105 × 20 / 100
total_amount	Total item amount, calculated as follows: amount + vat_amount	126 105 + 21

Table 7.6 Explanation of invoice_item Value Columns

> **Basic Accounting Knowledge**
>
> Most of our readers will have the basic accounting knowledge they need to understand the concepts of raw amount, VAT, and total amounts on invoices. If you lack this knowledge, don't worry! You can consider these columns as random numeric columns for DQL examples and ignore the logic and math behind them. You won't need any tax experience to follow through.

Now that the design of our invoice tables is ready, it's time to create them! Execute the code in Listing 7.6.

```
CREATE TABLE
    invoice (
        id SERIAL PRIMARY KEY,
        invoice_ts TIMESTAMP NOT NULL,
        is_sent BOOLEAN NOT NULL,
        customer_id INT NOT NULL REFERENCES customer (id)
    );

CREATE TABLE
    invoice_item (
        invoice_id INT NOT NULL REFERENCES invoice (id),
        invoice_item_no INT NOT NULL,
        delivery_id INT NOT NULL,
        delivery_item_no INT NOT NULL,
        amount NUMERIC(15, 2) NOT NULL,
        vat_rate NUMERIC(5, 2) NOT NULL,
        vat_amount NUMERIC(5, 2) NOT NULL,
        total_amount NUMERIC(5, 2) NOT NULL,
        PRIMARY KEY (invoice_id, invoice_item_no),
```

```
    CONSTRAINT fk_delivery_item FOREIGN KEY (delivery_id, delivery_item_no)
       REFERENCES delivery_item (delivery_id, delivery_item_no)
);
```
Listing 7.6 Creation of Invoice Tables

7.1.5 Complaint Tables

Like any business, Retro Loom may receive complaints from customers. Some complaints may be related to a certain order, while others might be generic and independent of any order. For that reason, we must create a complaint table that may or may not be related to orders.

Figure 7.14 contains our ERD extended with the `complaint` table. All fields are intuitive and self-explanatory.

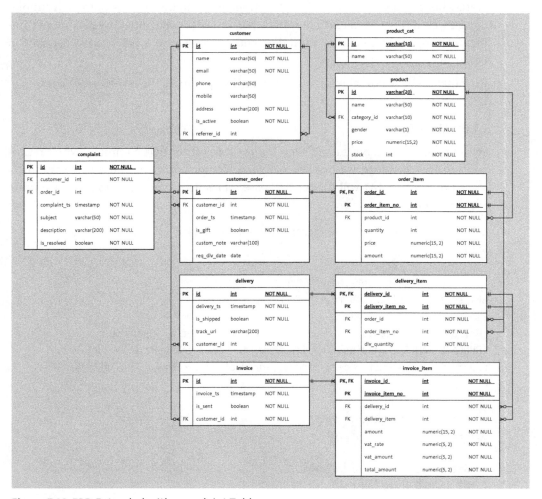

Figure 7.14 ERD Extended with complaint Table

To create the table, you can execute Listing 7.7.

```
CREATE TABLE complaint (
    id SERIAL NOT NULL PRIMARY KEY,
    customer_id INTEGER NOT NULL REFERENCES customer (id),
    order_id INTEGER REFERENCES customer_order (id),
    complaint_ts TIMESTAMP NOT NULL,
    subject CHARACTER VARYING(50),
    description CHARACTER VARYING(200),
    is_resolved BOOLEAN NOT NULL
);
```

Listing 7.7 Creation of Complaint Table

And that concludes our set of tables! You can rest assured that this case study was deliberately built to cover the entire DQL functionality contained in this chapter. A simpler design would force us to exclude some advanced DQL capabilities, while a more complex design would be harder to understand—so we've hit a balanced sweet spot in between.

Now that we have our tables in place, the final step is to fill them with mock data.

7.1.6 Mock Data

Without any data in our tables, even the most beautiful DQL command won't return any results. Therefore, we need to put some content in them. Listing 7.8 contains a stored procedure that will fill our database tables with mock data for our upcoming DQL examples.

```
CREATE OR REPLACE PROCEDURE generate_retro_loom_data () language plpgsql AS $$
BEGIN

-- Disable foreign key checks
SET session_replication_role = 'replica';

-- Truncate all tables to delete data and reset serial sequences
TRUNCATE TABLE complaint, invoice_item, invoice, delivery_item, delivery,
order_item, customer_order, product, product_cat, customer RESTART IDENTITY
CASCADE;

-- Re-enable foreign key checks
SET session_replication_role = 'origin';

-- Set up sequences for readability
ALTER SEQUENCE customer_id_seq RESTART WITH 71;
ALTER SEQUENCE customer_order_id_seq RESTART WITH 101;
```

```sql
ALTER SEQUENCE delivery_id_seq RESTART WITH 301;
ALTER SEQUENCE invoice_id_seq RESTART WITH 501;
ALTER SEQUENCE complaint_id_seq RESTART WITH 901;

-- Insert product categories
INSERT INTO product_cat (id, name) VALUES
('TOP', 'Tops'),
('BOT', 'Bottoms'),
('ACC', 'Accessories');

-- Insert apparel products
INSERT INTO product (id, name, category_id, gender, price, stock) VALUES
('TEE', 'T-Shirt', 'TOP', 'U', 19.99, 100),   -- Same price for rank demonstration
('SHIR', 'Shirt', 'TOP', 'M', 35.00, 50),
('BLZ', 'Blazer', 'TOP', 'M', 100.00, 25),
('JKT', 'Jacket', 'TOP', 'U', 100.00, 30),   -- Same price for rank demonstration
('PNT', 'Pants', 'BOT', 'M', 50.00, 60),
('SKT', 'Skirt', 'BOT', 'F', 45.00, 40),
('BAG', 'Bag', 'ACC', 'U', 60.00, 70),
('BELT', 'Belt', 'ACC', 'U', 25.00, 120);

-- Insert customers
INSERT INTO customer (name, email, phone, mobile, address, is_active, referrer_id) VALUES
('Alice Smith', 'alice@example.com', NULL, '555-1234', '123 Main St', TRUE, NULL),
('Bob Johnson', 'bob@example.com', '555-5678', NULL, '456 Elm St', TRUE, NULL),
('Charlie Brown', 'charlie@example.com', NULL, '555-4321', '789 Oak St', TRUE, 71),
('Diana Prince', 'diana@example.com', '555-8765', NULL, '246 Pine St', TRUE, 71),
('Eve Adams', 'eve@example.com', '555-9876', NULL, '135 Maple St', TRUE, NULL);

-- Insert customer orders
INSERT INTO customer_order (customer_id, order_ts, is_gift, custom_note, req_dlv_date) VALUES
(71, NOW(), FALSE, ' Special gift for friend', NULL),
(72, NOW(), TRUE, 'Urgent order', '2024-10-01'),
(73, NOW(), FALSE, ' Thanks for your business', '2024-10-05'),
(74, NOW(), FALSE, 'Order for special event', NULL),   -- NULL req_dlv_date
(75, NOW(), TRUE, ' Gift for a birthday', '2024-09-20');   -- Another order
```

7 Data Query Language

```sql
-- Insert order items
INSERT INTO order_item (order_id, order_item_no, product_id, quantity, price, amount) VALUES
(101, 1, 'TEE', 2, 18.99, 37.98),   -- Price less than product price
(101, 2, 'PNT', 1, 50.00, 50.00),   -- Price equal to product price
(102, 1, 'BLZ', 1, 105.00, 105.00), -- Price greater than product price
(102, 2, 'BELT', 2, 25.00, 50.00),  -- Price equal to product price
(103, 1, 'SHIR', 3, 35.00, 105.00), -- Price equal to product price
(103, 2, 'SKT', 1, 40.00, 40.00),   -- Price less than product price
(104, 1, 'BAG', 1, 60.00, 60.00),   -- Price equal to product price
(105, 1, 'JKT', 1, 100.00, 100.00); -- Price equal to product price

-- Insert deliveries
INSERT INTO delivery (delivery_ts, is_shipped, track_url, customer_id) VALUES
(NOW(), FALSE, 'http://trackurl.com/1', 71),  -- Pending delivery
(NOW(), TRUE,  'http://trackurl.com/2', 72),  -- Completed delivery
(NOW(), FALSE, 'http://trackurl.com/3', 73),  -- Pending delivery
(NOW(), TRUE,  'http://trackurl.com/4', 74),  -- Completed delivery
(NOW(), TRUE,  'http://trackurl.com/5', 72);  -- Another delivery for order 2

-- Insert delivery items
INSERT INTO delivery_item (delivery_id, delivery_item_no, order_id, order_item_no, dlv_quantity) VALUES
(301, 1, 101, 1, 1),  -- Partial delivery for order 101, item 1
(302, 1, 102, 1, 1),  -- Full delivery for order 102, item 1
(302, 2, 102, 2, 2),  -- Full delivery for order 102, item 2
(303, 1, 103, 1, 3),  -- Full delivery for order 103, item 1
(304, 1, 103, 2, 1),  -- Full delivery for order 103, item 2
(305, 1, 102, 1, 1),  -- Additional delivery for order 102, item 1
(305, 2, 104, 1, 1);  -- Delivery including item from order 104

-- Insert invoices
INSERT INTO invoice (invoice_ts, is_sent, customer_id) VALUES
(NOW(), FALSE, 71),  -- Pending invoice for customer 1
(NOW(), TRUE,  72),  -- Completed invoice for customer 2
(NOW(), FALSE, 73),  -- Pending invoice for customer 3
(NOW(), TRUE,  74);  -- Completed invoice for customer 4

-- Insert invoice items
INSERT INTO invoice_item (invoice_id, invoice_item_no, delivery_id, delivery_item_no, amount, vat_rate, vat_amount, total_amount) VALUES
(501, 1, 301, 1, 18.99, 20.00, 3.80, 22.79),  -- Partial invoice for dlv 301, item 1
```

```
(502, 1, 302, 1, 105.00, 20.00, 21.00, 126.00),  -- Full invoice for dlv 302, item 1
(502, 2, 302, 2, 50.00, 20.00, 10.00, 60.00),    -- Full invoice for dlv 302, item 2
(503, 1, 303, 1, 105.00, 20.00, 21.00, 126.00),  -- Full invoice for dlv 303, item 1
(504, 1, 304, 1, 40.00, 20.00, 8.00, 48.00);     -- Full invoice for dlv 304, item 2

-- Insert complaints
INSERT INTO complaint(customer_id, order_id, complaint_ts, subject, description, is_resolved) VALUES
(71, 101, NOW(), 'Website slow', 'I had to wait at submit', false), -- Order complaint
(75, null, NOW(), 'No gift card', 'We want gift card option', false); -- Generic complaint

END; $$
```

Listing 7.8 Stored Procedure to Create Mock Dataset

Once you create the stored procedure on your database, you can execute it as Listing 7.9 to reset and refill our tables.

```
CALL generate_retro_loom_data();
```

Listing 7.9 Executing Stored Procedure to Generate Mock Data

Great! We have everything we need to study DQL now! Before going forward with the following sections, you may want to browse through our tables using your database tool of choice and view their contents to get familiar with them. Once you're done, we can start writing DQL code together!

7.2 Single Table Queries

DQL statements can be as simple or complex as you want them to be. To warm up gradually, we'll start with the simplest examples and gradually move toward more advanced statements. Upon reaching the end of this chapter, we'll have you empowered to tackle all kinds of data selection requirements.

The most basic form of DQL is intended to read data from a single table, so that will be our starting point. We'll cover it in the following sections.

7.2.1 Selecting All Columns

If you want to read all rows and all columns of a database table, you'll need to write one of the simplest DQL statements possible! Check Listing 7.10 to see the syntax for that.

```
SELECT
    *
FROM
    { table_name };
```

Listing 7.10 DQL Syntax to Read All Rows and All Columns

SELECT is the most fundamental keyword of DQL, and it declares our intention to read data from tables. Most SQL statements will start with a SELECT keyword that's followed by a * sign, which declares that we need the values in all columns. This is a shortcut—instead of providing all column names one by one, we can type the * sign instead. If new columns will be added in the future, their values will be returned as well, with no need to modify the statement.

Finally, we need to provide the FROM keyword, followed by the name of our source table. That's it!

To see this command in action, execute Listing 7.11.

```
SELECT
    *
FROM
    customer;
```

Listing 7.11 Reading All Rows and Columns in customer Table

Once you execute the statement, you should receive the results set in Table 7.7.

id	name	email	phone	mobile	address	is_active	referrer_id
71	Alice Smith	alice@example.com		555-1234	123 Main St.	true	
72	Bob Johnson	bob@example.com	555-5678		456 Elm St.	true	
73	Charlie Brown	charlie@example.com		555-4321	789 Oak St.	true	71
74	Diana Prince	diana@example.com	555-8765		246 Pine St.	true	71
75	Eve Adams	eve@example.com	555-9876		135 Maple St.	true	

Table 7.7 All Rows and Columns in customer Table

If you check the contents of the `customer` table in your database administration app, you should see the same results.

To showcase another example, let's read all rows and columns in the `product` table this time. Execute Listing 7.12.

```
SELECT
    *
FROM
    product;
```

Listing 7.12 Reading All Rows and Columns in product Table

The statement should return the results set in Table 7.8.

id	name	category_id	gender	price	stock
TEE	T-shirt	TOP	U	19.99	100
SHIR	Shirt	TOP	M	35.00	50
BLZ	Blazer	TOP	M	100.00	25
JKT	Jacket	TOP	U	100.00	30
PNT	Pants	BOT	M	50.00	60
SKT	Skirt	BOT	F	45.00	40
BAG	Bag	ACC	U	60.00	70
BELT	Belt	ACC	U	25.00	120

Table 7.8 All Rows and Columns in product Table

Looking good! We can congratulate ourselves on running our first DQL statements successfully! Although SQL can get as complex as we want, its core structure will be based on the syntax in Listing 7.10.

> **Data Query Language Performance**
>
> Some beginners may find it tempting to select all rows and columns (as in Listing 7.10) whenever data is required and filter those results after the selection. Although it may be relatively harmless in small tables, you should avoid this approach as much as possible.
>
> Reading unnecessary data will result in unnecessarily increased performance and network loads, which is not what you want. Especially in frequently executed queries, you may be unintentionally causing energy wastage and increasing your carbon footprint! Even database administration tools typically limit the number of selected rows in data previews—and now you know why.

> Therefore, you should always aim at limiting the scope of your rows and columns as much as possible. We'll see how to do it in the upcoming topics.

7.2.2 Selecting Some Columns

Now that we're aware of potential performance costs and our carbon footprint, we should be motivated to read only the columns we need. Luckily, this is a very simple and straightforward operation in DQL! Check the syntax in Listing 7.13.

```
SELECT
    { column_names }
FROM
    { table_name };
```

Listing 7.13 DQL Syntax to Read Only Some Columns

See? It's almost the same syntax as the previous one, and the only difference lies between the SELECT and FROM keywords. Instead of providing a * sign, we're going to mention the names of the columns we need. Let's take a closer look at this in the following sections.

Selecting Columns by Original Name

To select columns keeping their original names, you can use Listing 7.14 as a template. Here, we're selecting merely three columns from the customer table, instead of all columns.

```
SELECT
    id,
    name,
    email
FROM
    customer;
```

Listing 7.14 Selecting All Rows but Only Some Columns From customer Table

Executing this statement should result in Table 7.9.

id	name	email
71	Alice Smith	alice@example.com
72	Bob Johnson	bob@example.com
73	Charlie Brown	charlie@example.com

Table 7.9 All Rows but Only Some Columns of customer Table

id	name	email
74	Diana Prince	diana@example.com
75	Eve Adams	eve@example.com

Table 7.9 All Rows but Only Some Columns of customer Table (Cont.)

Because we left unnecessary columns out, the query should run a little faster and data should be transported a little quicker. You may not see the difference in such a little dataset and a local database, but it may be significant on larger tables and remote databases.

Selecting Columns by Renaming

It's also possible to rename the columns of the results set! Although our sample columns were originally named name and email, we have no obligation to use the same names in our results set. We can, for example, name our output columns full_name and email_address instead.

To achieve that, we'll use the AS keyword in our query. Check Listing 7.15 to see it in action.

```
SELECT
    id,
    name AS full_name,
    email AS email_address
FROM
    customer;
```

Listing 7.15 Renaming Columns during Selection

Once we execute this query, we'll receive the exact same rows, but the column names will be different—as in Table 7.10.

id	full_name	email_address
71	Alice Smith	alice@example.com
72	Bob Johnson	bob@example.com
73	Charlie Brown	charlie@example.com
74	Diana Prince	diana@example.com
75	Eve Adams	eve@example.com

Table 7.10 Results Set with Renamed Columns

Mind you that the AS keyword renames the columns of our results set only! It won't rename original columns in the original customer table, and if you check the customer table you'll, see that those columns are still called name and email.

You may be wondering why we would need to rename results set columns at all. Table 7.11 showcases some typical reasons why a renaming operation can come in handy.

Reasons	Descriptions
Readability	If original column names are unclear or in another language, renaming results set columns may improve readability.
Name conflicts	When reading data from multiple tables, namesake columns between tables may cause conflicts. Renaming namesake columns helps distinguish them.
Aggregation	When summing values, it can make sense to pick a name that reflects the logic—like total_amount instead of amount.
Regulation	Some legal or audit reports may require us to provide predetermined column names that may be different from those of our original columns. Renaming column names is a simple way to comply.
Application compatibility	Likewise, some client applications may require us to provide predetermined column names that may be different from those of our original columns. Renaming them may be the solution.

Table 7.11 Some Reasons to Rename Columns

> **Upcoming Operations**
>
> Some operations in Table 7.11 will be covered in upcoming sections. These include reading data from multiple tables in Section 7.3 and aggregation in Section 7.2.8.

You're doing great! You can already select rows, cherry-pick columns, and even rename them. Now's the time to learn how to declare filters for row selection.

7.2.3 Filtering Rows with WHERE Conditions

Due to the performance reasons mentioned in Section 7.2.1, it's not advisable to read all rows in all cases. Instead, we should filter rows as much as possible and receive only the dataset we need. It makes much more sense to receive the three rows we need than 3,000 rows we don't need, right?

The syntax to filter rows is based on our regular DQL syntax, and we'll simply extend it with a WHERE condition as in Listing 7.16.

```
SELECT
    { column_names }
FROM
    { table_name }
WHERE
    { filter_conditions };
```
Listing 7.16 Syntax for Filtering Rows

Now that we have the basic syntax in place, let's put it into use in the following sections using sample DQL statements.

Operators

The simplest WHERE condition would be the case where we provide an exact column value. Listing 7.17 showcases such a query, in which we select product table rows of the 'TOP' category only.

```
SELECT
    *
FROM
    product
WHERE
    category_id = 'TOP';
```
Listing 7.17 Selecting product Table Rows of 'TOP' Category

The results of that query can be seen in Table 7.12. Note that in contrast to Table 7.8, we received rows corresponding to our WHERE condition only—which means that our filter is running correctly!

id	name	category_id	gender	price	stock
TEE	T-shirt	TOP	U	19.99	100
SHIR	Shirt	TOP	M	35.00	50
BLZ	Blazer	TOP	M	100.00	25
JKT	Jacket	TOP	U	100.00	30

Table 7.12 Products of 'TOP' Category

You're more than welcome to cherry-pick columns and provide a WHERE condition in the same query, as demonstrated in Listing 7.18.

```
SELECT
    id,
```

```
        name,
        stock
FROM
        product
WHERE
        category_id = 'TOP';
```

Listing 7.18 Providing Column Names and Row Filter in Same Query

This will return the same rows but only a handful of columns, as shown in Table 7.13.

id	name	stock
TEE	T-shirt	100
SHIR	Shirt	50
BLZ	Blazer	25
JKT	Jacket	30

Table 7.13 Products of 'TOP' Category with Some Columns

Although we've used the = operator in our WHERE condition, we can use further operators as well. The query in Listing 7.19 makes use of the < operator to get a list of products, which have a stock quantity less than 50.

```
SELECT
        id,
        name,
        stock
FROM
        product
WHERE
        stock < 50;
```

Listing 7.19 Selecting Products with Reduced Stock

The results of that query can be seen in Table 7.14. Note that all products have a stock quantity of less than 50.

id	name	stock
BLZ	Blazer	25
JKT	Jacket	30
SKT	Skirt	40

Table 7.14 Products with Less than 50 Stock

Thus, we've seen the = and < operators in action. Table 7.15 contains a list of common operators you can use. Now that you've grasped the basic logic of WHERE conditions, you can use these operators whenever necessary.

Operators	Descriptions
=	Equal to
<>	Doesn't equal
<	Less than
<=	Less than or equal to
>	Greater than
>=	Greater than or equal to

Table 7.15 Common Operators in WHERE Conditions

Logic

In our queries so far, we've used single WHERE conditions. However, it's also possible to provide multiple conditions merged with the logical keywords AND and OR.

Check the WHERE condition in Listing 7.20.

```
SELECT
    id,
    category_id,
    name,
    stock
FROM
    product
WHERE
    category_id = 'TOP'
    AND stock >= 50;
```

Listing 7.20 Selecting 'TOP' Products with Good Stock Quantities

In this query, we have two distinct conditions:

- category_id must be 'TOP'.
- stock must be at least 50.

When we bind these conditions with the AND keyword, the database engine will return rows that fulfill *both* conditions. We'll receive products of the TOP category that have at least 50 pieces in stock. The results set should be as Table 7.16.

7 Data Query Language

id	category_id	name	stock
TEE	TOP	T-shirt	100
SHIR	TOP	Shirt	50

Table 7.16 TOP Products with at Least 50 Pieces in Stock

> **String Literals in Data Query Language**
>
> Note that we had to put the 'TOP' value in quotes in our WHERE condition. That's due to the syntax rules of DQL. If the column has a numeric type (like 50), we can use it without quotes—but we must use quotes for string literals.
>
> In our upcoming examples throughout the rest of this chapter, you'll see many queries for both cases.

Another logic keyword is OR, which we use in cases where we want to see rows fulfilling any of the given criteria. Listing 7.21 contains such a query, which returns products having either a F (female) or a U (unisex) property.

```
SELECT
    id,
    name,
    price
FROM
    product
WHERE
    gender = 'F'
    OR gender = 'U';
```

Listing 7.21 Reading Products in Either Female (F) or Unisex (U) Category

The results of this query would look like Table 7.17, which provides a list of all products targeting female customers. Note that some rows have the F property, while others have the U property. Our query returns both.

id	gender	price
TEE	U	19.99
JKT	U	100.00
SKT	F	45.00

Table 7.17 All Products Targeting Female Customers

id	gender	price
BAG	U	60.00
BELT	U	25.00

Table 7.17 All Products Targeting Female Customers (Cont.)

We're allowed to chain more than two conditions as well. Check Listing 7.22, in which we provide three conditions with the AND keyword.

```
SELECT
    id,
    name,
    stock
FROM
    product
WHERE
    category_id = 'TOP'
    AND gender = 'M'
    AND stock <= 50;
```

Listing 7.22 Query with Multiple Conditions

This query will return products that fulfill all the provided conditions. The results set should look like Table 7.18.

id	name	stock
SHIR	Shirt	50
BLZ	Blazer	25

Table 7.18 Results of Query with Multiple Conditions

Parentheses

For complex logical conditions, we can also make use of parentheses. See the query in Listing 7.23.

```
SELECT
    id,
    name,
    category_id,
    stock
FROM
    product
```

7 Data Query Language

```
WHERE
    (
        category_id = 'TOP'
        AND stock > 50
    )
    OR (
        category_id = 'ACC'
        AND stock > 70
    );
```
Listing 7.23 Use of Parentheses in DQL

Let's translate this into plain English: I want a list of products that should have one of the following two things:

- The TOP category and more than 50 units in stock
- The ACC category and more than 70 units in stock

It's clearer that way, right? You can easily map the bullets above to the DQL statement in Listing 7.23. Using parenthesis enabled us to write two distinct sets of conditions and bind them with the main OR keyword.

The results of this query should be as Table 7.19.

id	name	category_id	stock
TEE	T-shirt	TOP	100
BELT	Belt	ACC	120

Table 7.19 Results Set of DQL with Parenthesis

Nested Parenthesis

Note that parenthesis can get as complex as necessary. You may have nested sets of parentheses that contain multiple combinations of AND / OR conditions.

There's a catch, though.

As your code grows in complexity, it may be harder to read and interpret and may therefore lead future developers into misunderstandings and ultimately application errors.

Computers have limitations as well. Some database engines may have a hard time determining the best execution strategy for complex queries and may fail to execute it quickly, leading to longer execution times and possible performance bottlenecks.

Therefore, we advise you to not overengineer queries and keep them as simple as possible.

NOT

NOT is a naturally expected logic keyword that negates any given condition. For starters, see Listing 7.24. It's nothing out of ordinary, just a logical query.

```
SELECT
    id,
    name,
    price,
    stock
FROM
    product
WHERE
    price > 50
    AND stock <= 40;
```

Listing 7.24 Regular Query with Positive Condition

This simple query will return products that have a price greater than $50 and units in stock less than or equal to 40. Plain English! Upon the execution of this query, we should get a results set like Table 7.20.

id	name	price	stock
BLZ	Blazer	100.00	25
JKT	Jacket	100.00	30

Table 7.20 Results of Positive Query

So far, so good. The database engine has returned all rows we've included with our query conditions.

Now, what if we need to exclude those rows and get all remaining rows as a result? That's very easy to do by using the NOT keyword. See Listing 7.25.

```
SELECT
    id,
    name,
    price,
    stock
FROM
    product
WHERE
    NOT (
```

```
        price > 50
        AND stock <= 40
);
```

Listing 7.25 Using NOT Keyword to Exclude Rows

Adding the NOT keyword to a condition ensures that the corresponding rows are excluded from the results set instead of being included. Check our result in Table 7.21 and note that the rows of the positive query are excluded and all other rows are included.

id	name	price	stock
TEE	T-shirt	19.99	100
SHIR	Shirt	35.00	50
PNT	Pants	50.00	60
SKT	Skirt	45.00	40
BAG	Bag	60.00	70
BELT	Belt	25.00	120

Table 7.21 Results of Negative Query

We can use positive and negative conditions together as well. Listing 7.26 demonstrates such an example.

```
SELECT
    id,
    name,
    category_id,
    gender,
    stock
FROM
    product
WHERE
    category_id = 'ACC'
    OR (
        NOT (
            gender = 'U'
            AND stock > 20
        )
    );
```

Listing 7.26 Positive and Negative Conditions Used Together

If we check the WHERE condition, it's evident that we want rows that either have the ACC category (accessories) or don't fulfill the condition (of being unisex and having more than 20 items in stock) simultaneously.

The results set of this composite query can be seen in Table 7.22. Note that each row either fulfills the positive condition or doesn't fulfill the negative condition.

id	name	category_id	gender	stock
SHIR	Shirt	TOP	M	50
BLZ	Blazer	TOP	M	25
PNT	Pants	BOT	M	60
SKT	Skirt	BOT	F	40
BAG	Bag	ACC	U	70
BELT	Belt	ACC	U	120

Table 7.22 Results of Composite Query

> **Using Parentheses Effectively**
>
> Although there's a natural priority among logical conditions like AND, OR, and NOT, we advise you to ignore that and rely on parentheses, just as in Listing 7.26. You can put parentheses everywhere a potential ambiguity is possible—for you, the database engine, or the next programmer who must understand your code.
>
> A priority error in a complex WHERE condition can have negative consequences, but it's easily avoidable with the help of parentheses—so, use them!

BETWEEN

A cool and commonly used DQL keyword is BETWEEN. It empowers us with the ability to query tables with number ranges. Listing 7.27 demonstrates the usage of BETWEEN in a query that selects products with a price between $35.00 and $55.00.

```
SELECT
    id,
    name,
    price
FROM
    product
WHERE
    price BETWEEN 35 AND 55;
```

Listing 7.27 Query Demonstrating BETWEEN Keyword

The result of this query should be like in Table 7.23.

id	name	price
SHIR	Shirt	35.00
PNT	Pants	50.00
SKT	Skirt	45.00

Table 7.23 Products with Prices Between 35 and 55 Dollars

If you take a closer look at the first result, you'll notice that the price is exactly $35.00. This means that BETWEEN stands for >= OR <= in terms of operators. To make it clearer, we could have expressed the same query as Listing 7.28.

```
SELECT
    id,
    name,
    price
FROM
    product
WHERE
    price >= 35
    AND price <= 55;
```

Listing 7.28 Same Query, Avoiding BETWEEN Keyword

Although the WHERE condition would bring the exact same results, preferring the BETWEEN keyword makes the code easier to read and understand. Don't you think?

As with any logical condition, BETWEEN can be negated with the NOT prefix. Check Listing 7.29—it excludes the rows from the previous statement by using this method.

```
SELECT
    id,
    name,
    price
FROM
    product
WHERE
    NOT (price BETWEEN 35 AND 55);
```

Listing 7.29 Negating BETWEEN Condition

The results of this query can be seen in Table 7.24. Note that it excludes all products within the price range of $35.00 to $5500, as we intended it to!

id	name	price
TEE	T-shirt	19.99
BLZ	Blazer	100.00
JKT	Jacket	100.00
BAG	Bag	60.00
BELT	Belt	25.00

Table 7.24 Results of NOT BETWEEN Query

IN

Just like BETWEEN, our new IN keyword can improve the readability of your code drastically by replacing multiple OR conditions. Check Listing 7.30 to see this easy keyword in action.

```
SELECT
    id,
    name,
    category_id
FROM
    product
WHERE
    category_id IN ('TOP', 'BOT');
```

Listing 7.30 Usage of IN Keyword

This intuitive query will read products that belong to either the TOP or the BOT category. Naturally, an IN condition can contain more than two values as well. The results can be seen in Table 7.25. Note that only the requested categories are present.

id	name	category_id
TEE	T-shirt	TOP
SHIR	Shirt	TOP
BLZ	Blazer	TOP
JKT	Jacket	TOP
PNT	Pants	BOT
SKT	Skirt	BOT

Table 7.25 Results of IN Query

Theoretically, we can ignore the IN keyword and express the same query as Listing 7.31.

```
SELECT
    id,
    name,
    category_id
FROM
    product
WHERE
    category_id = 'TOP'
    OR category_id = 'BOT';
```

Listing 7.31 Same Query without IN Keyword

Obviously, the query including the IN keyword is much more readable. As the number of potential values increases, the readability gap increases as well.

Like any logical condition, IN can be negated with the NOT prefix. See Listing 7.32 for the negated version of our last query.

```
SELECT
    id,
    name,
    category_id
FROM
    product
WHERE
    NOT (category_id IN ('TOP', 'BOT'));
```

Listing 7.32 Negating IN Condition

The output of this query can be seen in Table 7.26. Note that it's the "evil twin" of Table 7.25—what the one lacks, the other has.

id	name	category_id
BAG	Bag	ACC
BELT	Belt	ACC

Table 7.26 Results of NOT IN Query

LIKE

We sometimes need to use wildcards in queries. Although using regular expressions is possible (and upcoming), wildcards provide a more readable alternative for simpler cases.

7.2 Single Table Queries

To put this concept into practice, we'll search for products that start with the letter *S* and end with the letters *rt*. See the query in Listing 7.33.

```
SELECT
    id,
    name,
    category_id
FROM
    product
WHERE
    name LIKE 'S%rt';
```

Listing 7.33 Basic Query Demonstrating LIKE Keyword

In this query, you should notice two significant points:

- The keyword `LIKE` was used to express our intention to search with a wildcard.
- The % character was used as a wildcard.

In plain English, our `WHERE` condition means we want products that have names that match the pattern S%rt. They must start with the letter *S* and end with the letters *rt*. See the results set in Table 7.27.

id	name	category_id
SHIR	Shirt	TOP
SKT	Skirt	BOT

Table 7.27 Results of Wildcard Query

If we check the results set, we can see that each row corresponds to our wildcard pattern.

- *Shirt* really starts with *S* and ends with *rt*.
- *Skirt* also starts with *S* and ends with *rt*.
- Irrelevant rows are excluded.

Cool, right? What's even cooler is that you can place the wildcard anywhere you want in the pattern and even use multiple wildcards. See Listing 7.34.

```
SELECT
    id,
    name,
    category_id
FROM
    product
```

7   Data Query Language

```
WHERE
    name LIKE '%ir%';
```

Listing 7.34 Alternative Wildcard Usage

In this query, we want all rows that have the substring *ir* within the body of their name. Table 7.28 shows the corresponding results.

id	name	category_id
TEE	T-shirt	TOP
SHIR	Shirt	TOP
SKT	Skirt	BOT

Table 7.28 Results of Alternative Wildcard Query

Like any logical condition, `LIKE` can be negated with the `NOT` prefix. Check Listing 7.35 to see the negated version of our last query.

```
SELECT
    id,
    name,
    category_id
FROM
    product
WHERE
    NOT (name LIKE '%ir%');
```

Listing 7.35 Negating LIKE Condition

Naturally, the results set will include all rows that were excluded in the last results set, as shown in Table 7.29.

id	name	category_id
BLZ	Blazer	TOP
JKT	Jacket	TOP
PNT	Pants	BOT
BAG	Bag	ACC
BELT	Belt	ACC

Table 7.29 Results of Negated Wildcard Query

That concludes our section on filters. Now, we'll review our options for sorting results sets.

7.2.4 Ordering Results

You'll be pleased to know that we can sort DQL results sets by any column(s) we want, just like sorting a spreadsheet table by columns. The main command for this purpose will be ORDER BY, which we add after the WHERE conditions. Listing 7.36 showcases the syntax for that.

```
SELECT
    { column_names }
FROM
    { table_name }
WHERE
    { filter_conditions }
ORDER BY
    { order_conditions };
```

Listing 7.36 Syntax for Ordering Results

In the following sections, we'll discuss ascending, descending, and composite ordering results.

Ascending Order

If our purpose is to sort results from the smallest to the largest column value, we're talking about sorting them in ascending order. Listing 7.37 is a sample query in which all products will be listed and sorted by their price, with the cheapest coming first and the most expensive coming last.

```
SELECT
    id,
    name,
    price
FROM
    product
ORDER BY
    price ASC;
```

Listing 7.37 Query to Select Products by Price in Ascending Order

The final ASC keyword declares our intention to execute an ascending sort operation, from the smallest to the largest value. The results set of this query can be seen in Table 7.30. Note how they are sorted by their price, just as we intended.

7   Data Query Language

id	name	price
TEE	T-shirt	19.99
BELT	Belt	25.00
SHIR	Shirt	35.00
SKT	Skirt	45.00
PNT	Pants	50.00
BAG	Bag	60.00
BLZ	Blazer	100.00
JKT	Jacket	100.00

Table 7.30 Products Sorted by Their Price

> **The ASC Suffix Is the Default**
>
> If you finalize the query as ORDER BY price without adding the ASC suffix, most database engines will sort the result set in ascending order. In other words, ASC is the default behavior for ordering rows. We also have other options like DESC (descending), which we'll cover very soon. Still, it could be nice to add the ASC keyword anyway—it would make your intention to other developers clear. No one will assume that you forgot to provide the sort order.

Naturally, ORDER BY can be combined with WHERE conditions as well, as demonstrated in Listing 7.38.

```
SELECT
    id,
    name,
    category_id,
    price
FROM
    product
WHERE
    category_id = 'ACC'
ORDER BY
    price ASC;
```

Listing 7.38 Using WHERE and ORDER BY Together

The results of this query are shown in Table 7.31. Note that both WHERE and ORDER BY were executed successfully. We see only ACC-type products, and they are sorted by their price.

id	name	category_id	price
BELT	Belt	ACC	25.00
BAG	Bag	ACC	60.00

Table 7.31 ACC Products, Sorted by Their Price

So far, we've sorted results by a single column only, but it's possible to sort them by multiple columns as well. This approach is demonstrated in Listing 7.39. The results will be sorted by price initially, but if two products have the same price value, then they will be sorted by stock.

```
SELECT
    id,
    name,
    price,
    stock
FROM
    product
ORDER BY
    price ASC,
    stock ASC;
```

Listing 7.39 Sorting Results by Multiple Columns

The results set of this query will be as in Table 7.32. Although all products were sorted by their price, the products in the last two rows have the same price. In this case, the database engine used our secondary sort criterion, which is their stock value.

Id	name	price	stock
TEE	T-shirt	19.99	100
BELT	Belt	25.00	120
SHIR	Shirt	35.00	50
SKT	Skirt	45.00	40
PNT	Pants	50.00	60
BAG	Bag	60.00	70

Table 7.32 Products Sorted by Their Price and Stock Value

7   Data Query Language

Id	name	price	stock
BLZ	Blazer	100.00	25
JKT	Jacket	100.00	30

Table 7.32 Products Sorted by Their Price and Stock Value (Cont.)

Descending Order

ASC lets us sort by values in ascending order, from the smallest to the largest—and DESC lets us sort by values in descending order, from the largest to the smallest.

To see this in action, let's simply modify one of our former queries by replacing ASC with DESC and see its effect. Check Listing 7.40, where the results are sorted by their price in descending order.

```
SELECT
    id,
    name,
    category_id,
    price
FROM
    product
WHERE
    category_id = 'ACC'
ORDER BY
    price DESC;
```

Listing 7.40 Sorting Results in Descending Order

The results set can be seen in Table 7.33. Note that the expensive product is listed first and the cheaper product is listed second, just as we intended.

id	name	category_id	price
BAG	Bag	ACC	60.00
BELT	Belt	ACC	25.00

Table 7.33 Products Sorted by Their Price in Descending Order

Composite

Naturally, we can combine ascending and descending orders in the same query! Let's modify one of our former queries to demonstrate this feature as in Listing 7.41.

```
SELECT
    id,
```

```
    name,
    price,
    stock
FROM
    product
ORDER BY
    price DESC,
    stock ASC;
```

Listing 7.41 Combination of Ascending and Descending Orders

Following our query, the database engine will first attempt to sort products by their prices in descending order. If two products have the same price, the engine will resort to the secondary rule and sort them by their stock value in ascending order.

The results set of this query will be as in Table 7.34. If you check the first two rows, you'll see that they follow our composite rule. Other rows have different prices, so they were sorted by their price alone—the database engine didn't need to resort to sorting by prices for them.

id	name	price	stock
BLZ	Blazer	100.00	25
JKT	Jacket	100.00	30
BAG	Bag	60.00	70
PNT	Pants	50.00	60
SKT	Skirt	45.00	40
SHIR	Shirt	35.00	50
BELT	Belt	25.00	120
TEE	T-shirt	19.99	100

Table 7.34 Results Set Following Composite Sorting Rule

This concludes our section on sorting results. Now, we'll investigate how we can limit the number of rows in results sets.

7.2.5 Partial Selection

In some cases, we won't require all rows corresponding to our query; we'll need the first few rows instead. A typical case would be to detect the three most expensive products in our catalog. Listing 7.42 is the query we need for this.

```
SELECT
    id,
    name,
    price
FROM
    product
ORDER BY
    price DESC
LIMIT
    3;
```

Listing 7.42 Limiting Number of Results

We concluded the query as LIMIT 3. This declares our intention to limit the number of returning rows to three, after the WHERE and ORDER BY conditions are handled. In our case, we sorted products by their prices in descending order and limited the result size to three rows. Therefore, we'll get the three most expensive products as an output, as shown in Table 7.35.

id	Name	price
JKT	Jacket	100.00
BLZ	Blazer	100.00
BAG	Bag	60.00

Table 7.35 Three Most Expensive Products

Let's run one more example, this time including a WHERE condition too. We want to see the 2 BOT products that have the least quantity in stock. Listing 7.43 contains the query to achieve this result.

```
SELECT
    id,
    name,
    category_id,
    stock
FROM
    product
WHERE
    category_id = 'BOT'
ORDER BY
    stock ASC
LIMIT
    2;
```

Listing 7.43 Limiting Number of Results with WHERE Condition

Note that we used a WHERE condition to select BOT products only. Then, we sorted the results by their stocks in ascending order, ensuring that the least stock will appear first. Finally, we limited the results to two rows, ignoring the rows after that. The results can be seen in Table 7.36.

id	name	category_id	stock
SKT	Skirt	BOT	40
PNT	Pants	BOT	60

Table 7.36 Two BOT Products with Least Stock

Neat, eh? There's no need to take up memory and cause network traffic for rows we don't want.

7.2.6 Unique Selection

DQL empowers us with a feature to eliminate duplicate entries in results sets. We can use this feature with the DISTINCT keyword.

We'll go over a case in which we need a list of product categories for which unisex items are offered. Initially, we can read all unisex products by using Listing 7.44.

```
SELECT
    id,
    name,
    category_id,
    gender
FROM
    product
WHERE
    gender = 'U';
```

Listing 7.44 Reading Unisex Products

Our initial query should result in Table 7.37.

id	name	category_id	gender
TEE	T-shirt	TOP	U
JKT	Jacket	TOP	U
BAG	Bag	ACC	U
BELT	Belt	ACC	U

Table 7.37 Unisex Products

7 Data Query Language

So far, so good. But remember our initial requirement: we're interested in categories only, not product details. Therefore, we can modify our query as in Listing 7.45, reading solely the category_id column.

```
SELECT
    category_id
FROM
    product
WHERE
    gender = 'U';
```

Listing 7.45 Reading Product Categories with Unisex Products

This will return the same results set but only the category_id column, as seen in Table 7.38.

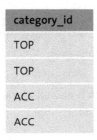

Table 7.38 Categories with Unisex Products

We're almost there! Now, all we need to do is eliminate duplicate categories from the list. We'll achieve this with the aforementioned DISTINCT keyword. Let's modify the query as in Listing 7.46.

```
SELECT DISTINCT
    category_id
FROM
    product
WHERE
    gender = 'U';
```

Listing 7.46 Reading Unique Product Categories with Unisex Products

This query will eliminate duplicates in the results set, leaving unique categories as in Table 7.39. Voila!

Table 7.39 Unique Categories with Unisex Products

We can apply unique selections in multiple columns as well. See Listing 7.47, where we build a unique list of categories and genders. Any duplicate category_id + gender combination will be eliminated, leaving only unique combinations.

```
SELECT DISTINCT
    category_id,
    gender
FROM
    product
ORDER BY
    category_id ASC;
```

Listing 7.47 DISTINCT in Multiple Columns

The results set of this query can be seen in Table 7.40. Note that there are no duplicates.

category_id	gender
ACC	U
BOT	F
BOT	M
TOP	U
TOP	M

Table 7.40 Unique Category + Gender Combinations

7.2.7 Null Values

In Chapter 4, we discussed the meaning of null values and how they differ from empty values. Now, we'll learn how to refer to null values in queries. Luckily, it's very easy to do!

To build our case, let's take a look at our customers with the query in Listing 7.48.

```
SELECT
    id,
    name,
```

301

```
        mobile
FROM
        customer;
```

Listing 7.48 Query for Customers

The output of this query can be seen in Table 7.41. Note that some customers have null values as their mobile numbers.

id	name	mobile
71	Alice Smith	555-1234
72	Bob Johnson	NULL
73	Charlie Brown	555-4321
74	Diana Prince	NULL
75	Eve Adams	NULL

Table 7.41 List of Customers

Our purpose will be to build a list of customers that have null values for mobile numbers. To achieve that, we'll modify our initial query as in Listing 7.49.

```
SELECT
        id,
        name,
        mobile
FROM
        customer
WHERE
        mobile IS NULL;
```

Listing 7.49 Query for Customers with Null Phone Numbers

Take a look at our WHERE condition. IS NULL is where the magic happens! By using that keyword, we can use null values as a condition. The results set in Table 7.42 is what we intuitively expect.

id	name	mobile
72	Bob Johnson	NULL
74	Diana Prince	NULL
75	Eve Adams	NULL

Table 7.42 Customers with Null Phone Numbers

7.2.8 Aggregate Functions

As their name suggests, aggregate functions are used to perform math calculations on a set of rows. They empower us developers to calculate sums, averages, minimum and maximum values, or even entry counts among table rows.

Aggregate functions are used extensively, which makes them important for us to understand and use efficiently.

The DQL template for aggregate functions is not too different, but we'll introduce a few new keywords. The overall syntax can be seen in Listing 7.50.

```
SELECT { columns | aggregations }
FROM { tables }
[ GROUP BY { group_columns } ]
[ HAVING { calculated_filters } ]
```

Listing 7.50 Syntax for Aggregate Functions

To put our syntax into practice, we'll start with sums and move on to other functions.

> **Aggregation Features**
>
> Aggregate functions have common features. Instead of overloading each function with all possible features, we're going to inspect different features under different functions. You'll be notified that each feature can be used with other aggregate functions as well.

SUM

Let's start with the simplest function possible. Listing 7.51 will calculate the total quantity of all products in stock.

```
SELECT
    SUM(stock)
FROM
    product;
```

Listing 7.51 Calculation of Total Items in Stock

If we inspect the query closer, the SELECT ... FROM table template did not change at all. What did change, though, is the column part. SUM(stock) declares our intention to summarize the values in the stock column for all rows in the product table.

To understand this visually, see the contents of the product table in Table 7.43.

7 Data Query Language

id	category_id	name	stock
TEE	TOP	T-shirt	100
SHIR	TOP	Shirt	50
BLZ	TOP	Blazer	25
JKT	TOP	Jacket	30
PNT	BOT	Pants	60
SKT	BOT	Skirt	40
BAG	ACC	Bag	70
BELT	ACC	Belt	120

Table 7.43 All Stock Values in product Table

Once you execute Listing 7.51, the database engine will calculate the sum of all stock values, which is 100 + 50 + 25 + 30 + 60 + 40 + 70 + 120. It will return the value 495.

Simple and intuitive, right?

What if we had to calculate the stock sum of each product category? In that case, we'd need to change our query slightly, as in Listing 7.52.

```
SELECT
    category_id,
    SUM(stock) AS total_stock
FROM
    product
GROUP BY
    category_id;
```

Listing 7.52 Calculation of Stock Sum by Category

Before diving into the query elements, let's see the output in Table 7.44. This will help us understand the commands within.

category_id	total_stock
TOP	205
ACC	190
BOT	100

Table 7.44 Total Items in Stock, Summed by Category

As you see, we have the total items in stock for each product category now. Here's what we did differently to achieve that:

- In the column selection, we naturally had to include `category_id`, simply because we want that column in our output! Remember the requirement—we're going to list categories with their stock sums.
- As a suffix, we added the declaration `GROUP BY category_id`. This should also make sense because we're grouping `SUM(stock)` values by category.

> **GROUP BY**
>
> GROUP BY is a natural part of all aggregate functions in most cases. In this part, we need to declare columns that will act as keys for aggregation. In the example above, we used `category_id` as the aggregation key.

Naturally, we can use all aggregate functions with WHERE conditions, as demonstrated in Listing 7.53.

```
SELECT
    category_id,
    SUM(stock) AS total_stock
FROM
    product
WHERE
    category_id <> 'ACC'
GROUP BY
    category_id;
```

Listing 7.53 Using Aggregate Functions with WHERE Conditions

The results set of this query will look like Table 7.45, which naturally excludes the ACC category.

category_id	total_stock
TOP	205
BOT	100

Table 7.45 Total Items in Stock, Summed by Category and Excluding ACC Category

AVG

Calculating average values is not too different from calculating sums. All we need to do is replace the SUM keyword with AVG, and we're good to go! Listing 7.54 showcases an intuitive query following our former example.

```
SELECT
    category_id,
    AVG(stock) AS average_stock
FROM
    product
GROUP BY
    category_id;
```

Listing 7.54 Calculation of Average Stock by Category

The results of this query can be seen in Table 7.46.

category_id	average_stock
TOP	51.25
ACC	95.00
BOT	50.00

Table 7.46 Average Stock by Category

We can calculate multiple aggregations in the same query, as in Listing 7.55.

```
SELECT
    category_id,
    SUM(stock) AS total_stock,
    AVG(stock) AS average_stock
FROM
    product
GROUP BY
    category_id;
```

Listing 7.55 Calculating Multiple Aggregations in Same Query

The database engine will happily calculate both aggregations and produce a single output, as in Table 7.47.

category_id	total_stock	average_stock
TOP	205	51.25
ACC	190	95.00
BOT	100	50.00

Table 7.47 Total and Average Stock by Category

MIN

Once you understand the logic, you'll see that most aggregate functions follow the same pattern. To calculate the minimum value in a column, you'll use the `MIN` keyword, as in Listing 7.56.

```
SELECT
    category_id,
    MIN(price) AS minimum_price
FROM
    product
GROUP BY
    category_id;
```

Listing 7.56 Calculation of Minimum Price per Category

The results set can be seen in Table 7.48.

category_id	minimum_price
TOP	19.99
ACC	25.00
BOT	45.00

Table 7.48 Minimum Price by Category

All aggregate functions give us the option to filter aggregated results by using the `HAVING` keyword, which is similar to a `WHERE` condition. Let's extend our query as shown in Listing 7.57.

```
SELECT
    category_id,
    MIN(price) AS minimum_price
FROM
    product
GROUP BY
    category_id
HAVING
    MIN(price) > 20;
```

Listing 7.57 Using HAVING Keyword to Filter Aggregation Results

The `HAVING` suffix tells the database engine to filter entries from the results set and leave in only those that fulfill the `MIN(price) > 20` condition. Check the new results set in Table 7.49 and note that the first row (TOP) is missing now because its `minimum_price` is less than 20.

category_id	minimum_price
ACC	25.00
BOT	45.00

Table 7.49 Results Filtered by HAVING Condition

To understand the difference between the WHERE and HAVING keywords, you can check Figure 7.15. WHERE conditions are used initially to read and filter database tables, while HAVING conditions are used to make a second filter for aggregated columns, such as minimum_price.

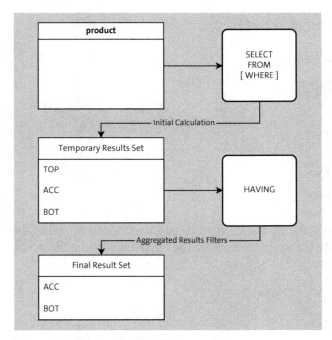

Figure 7.15 Effects of HAVING Keyword

MAX

Knowing that we can calculate minimum values, it's natural and right to assume that we can calculate maximum values as well. Let's simply replace the MIN keyword with MAX as in Listing 7.58 and see what happens.

```
SELECT
    category_id,
    MAX(price) AS maximum_price
FROM
    product
```

```
GROUP BY
    category_id;
```

Listing 7.58 Querying Maximum Price of Each Category

The results set of this query will be as in Table 7.50.

category_id	maximum_price
TOP	100.00
ACC	60.00
BOT	50.00

Table 7.50 Maximum Price by Category

So far, we've calculated aggregations in a single key column. However, all aggregate functions enable us to do calculations in multiple columns as well. Listing 7.59 demonstrates this case, in which we calculate the maximum price by category and gender.

```
SELECT
    category_id,
    gender,
    MAX(price) AS maximum_price
FROM
    product
GROUP BY
    category_id,
    gender
ORDER BY
    category_id,
    gender;
```

Listing 7.59 Query for Maximum Price by Category and Gender

Note that we had to mention both columns in the GROUP BY part because both are aggregation keys. Mentioning them in an ORDER BY part is optional.

The results set of this query will be as in Table 7.51. Note that the maximum price is calculated by category and gender now, so we have two aggregation keys.

category_id	gender	maximum_price
ACC	U	60.00
BOT	F	45.00

Table 7.51 Maximum Price by Category and Gender

category_id	gender	maximum_price
BOT	M	50.00
TOP	M	100.00
TOP	U	100.00

Table 7.51 Maximum Price by Category and Gender (Cont.)

COUNT

Finally, we'll learn how to count rows! Let's find out how many unique products we have under each category by using Listing 7.60.

```
SELECT
    category_id,
    COUNT(*) AS product_count
FROM
    product
GROUP BY
    category_id;
```

Listing 7.60 Counting Number of Products for Each Category

The effects of COUNT(*) should be intuitive—it's the keyword we use to count the number of rows. The results set will be as expected. See Table 7.52.

category_id	product_count
TOP	4
ACC	2
BOT	2

Table 7.52 Product Count by Category

> **To Count Nulls or Not?**
>
> When you use the COUNT(*) keyword, you'll be counting all rows, regardless of their content. If you use the COUNT(column_name) keyword, you'll be counting only those rows in which the column_name is not null.
>
> You can pick the appropriate approach depending on your requirements.

In aggregate functions, we can use WHERE and HAVING conditions simultaneously. To see this in action, let's add a WHERE condition to our former query, as shown in Listing 7.61.

```
SELECT
    category_id,
    COUNT(*) AS product_count
FROM
    product
WHERE
    (
        gender = 'F'
        OR gender = 'U'
    )
GROUP BY
    category_id;
```
Listing 7.61 Throwing in WHERE Condition

This way, we ensure that only unisex or female products are selected in our aggregation—which outputs the results set in Table 7.53.

category_id	product_count
ACC	2
BOT	1
TOP	2

Table 7.53 Female and Unisex Product Counts by Category

Now, let's extend the query with a HAVING condition and filter out rows where the product count is less than 2.

Remember Figure 7.15? The WHERE condition is applied during the initial selection, but the HAVING condition is applied after the aggregation, to aggregated fields. Following that logic, the database engine will build Table 7.53 first and then filter it by the HAVING condition and produce the final output as Table 7.54.

category_id	product_count
ACC	2
TOP	2

Table 7.54 Female and Unisex Product Count by Category HAVING Product Count Greater than 1

```
SELECT
    category_id,
    COUNT(*) AS product_count
```

```
FROM
    product
WHERE
    (
        gender = 'F'
        OR gender = 'U'
    )
GROUP BY
    category_id
HAVING
    COUNT(*) > 1;
```

Listing 7.62 Throwing in HAVING Condition

Wow, look at Listing 7.62! We've come a long way from zero to such complex aggregations! This query might look a bit scary at first glance, but DQL is not that hard once you understand the logic. Like other sublanguages of SQL, DQL is close to plain English, which makes it intuitive.

This concludes our section on single table queries. Now, we'll venture into an even more exciting section, where multiple tables will be queried simultaneously. Take a well-earned break, and then, let's go!

7.3 Multitable Queries

In this section, we'll learn how to query data from multiple tables simultaneously, which is a significant and commonly used DQL feature.

> **Table Relationships**
>
> In Chapter 2, we learned about relationships between tables via primary and foreign keys. You can go back and review that chapter if you need to because it's a prerequisite for our current topic.
>
> That being said, we've included a short memory refresher below as well.

7.3.1 Refresher on Relationships between Tables

As we know by now, intertable relationships are defined by foreign keys, in which a column of a table refers to a column of another table as the source of the value. In the case of Retro Loom, we can take the relationship between the order_item table and the product table as an example, as demonstrated in Figure 7.16.

7.3 Multitable Queries

The order_item.product_id condition refers to product.id, which is the master data table for products. For each item row in order_item, we should find a corresponding product row in product.

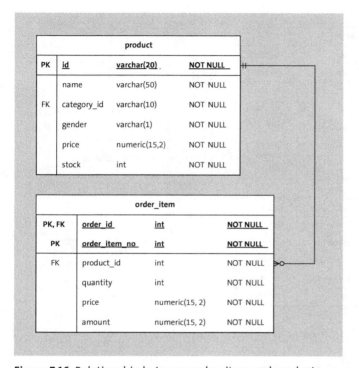

Figure 7.16 Relationship between order_item and product

To help you visualize this concept better, check Table 7.55, which contains two order_item rows. You can see the TEE and PNT product IDs there.

order_id	order_item_no	product_id	quantity	price	amount
101	1	TEE	2	18.99	37.98
101	2	PNT	1	50.00	50.00

Table 7.55 Sample order_item Rows

If we query product with those IDs, we'll see the corresponding values in Table 7.56.

id	Name	category_id	gender	price	stock
TEE	T-shirt	TOP	U	19.99	100
PNT	Pants	BOT	M	50.00	60

Table 7.56 Sample product Rows

313

7 Data Query Language

Following that relationship, we can join an `order_item` row with its corresponding `product` row via their common product ID fields, listing their values together as if they were a single row, as visualized in Figure 7.17.

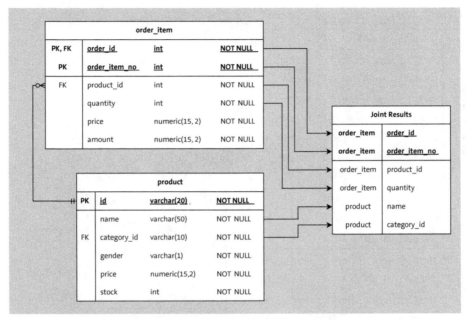

Figure 7.17 Joint Result Plan from order_item and product Tables

See Table 7.57 for a sample joint results set.

order_id	order_item_no	product_id	quantity	name	category_id
101	1	TEE	2	T-shirt	TOP
101	2	PNT	1	Pants	BOT

Table 7.57 Joint Results Set from order_item and product Tables

Note that first four columns came from the `order_item` table, while the two rows came from the corresponding rows in the `product` table. Cool, right? This clarifies the main purpose of multitable queries, but the question is, how can we build such joint results sets using DQL? We'll find the answer in the following sections.

> **Multitable Techniques**
> Nearly all techniques we learned for single table queries can be applied to multitable queries as well, so once you learn how to join tables, you can use filters, orders, and aggregations for joined tables. We'll use some of them in the examples in this chapter. Feel free to apply the rest yourself!

7.3.2 INNER JOIN

The most basic and straightforward form of joining tables is an INNER JOIN. Before discussing the details, let's jump right in and write a query to join the order_item and product tables, as we just discussed. Once we understand the syntax, the rest will follow easily.

Inner Join Syntax

To join order items with products, we'll use Listing 7.63.

```
SELECT
    order_item.order_id,
    order_item.order_item_no,
    order_item.product_id,
    order_item.quantity,
    product.name,
    product.category_id
FROM
    order_item
    INNER JOIN product ON product.id = order_item.product_id
LIMIT
    2;
```

Listing 7.63 Reading Joint Data with INNER JOIN

This query will produce the output in Table 7.58. For each order_item row, the database engine happily finds the corresponding product row and joins values from both rows to produce an output entry.

order_id	order_item_no	product_id	quantity	name	category_id
101	1	TEE	2	T-shirt	TOP
101	2	PNT	1	Pants	BOT

Table 7.58 Result of INNER JOIN Query

Now, let's put the query under the magnifying glass.

In the SELECT part, we declared a list of columns we want. There's nothing out of ordinary here—we want four order_item columns and two product columns.

The FROM part is where the magic happens. We mentioned our main order_item table name as usual, and then, we gave the INNER JOIN command, followed by the secondary product table name. This tells the database engine that we want to access corresponding product table columns too. Finally, the ON product.id = order_item.product_id condition declares how those tables are related, and that relationship is used to find a corresponding product table row.

What we gave as the ON condition is nothing more than the foreign key relationship. Simple, right?

> **Joins and Foreign Keys**
> Although it's a common practice to join tables via foreign keys, you can also join them via fields that don't reference each other—if you're sure that the correspondence is valid.

INNER JOIN Behavior

What makes an INNER JOIN special among other JOIN types is the fact that it asserts the existence of a corresponding row.

If there were an order_item row with an empty product_id, that row would be excluded from the results set—simply because there would be no correspondence in the product table. Therefore, you should use INNER JOIN in cases where you want to include rows that have correspondence in the joined table and you want to exclude rows that don't.

To clarify this logic in a realistic example, we'll look at the relationship between the order_item and delivery_item tables now. Check Figure 7.18.

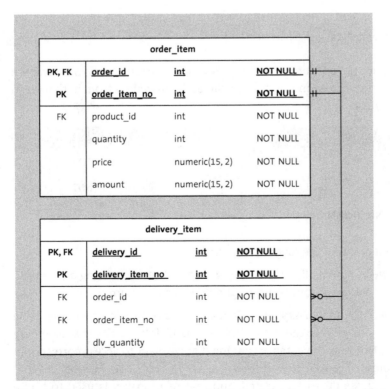

Figure 7.18 Relationship between order_item and delivery_item Tables

7.3 Multitable Queries

For each `order_item` entry, we may or may not have corresponding `delivery_item` entries. That makes sense—there's a time lag between placing an order and sending it out for delivery. Orders waiting to be sent out for delivery won't have any corresponding deliveries yet.

If we were to use INNER JOIN on our `order_item` and `delivery_item` tables, we would only get those `order_item` rows for which a `delivery_item` row exists. Other `order_item` rows (without deliveries) would be excluded, and that's a useful feature if you want to list only delivered orders!

> **Other Join Types**
>
> There are other join types that are more inclusive than INNER JOIN. We'll see those in due course, but let's keep our focus on INNER JOIN for now.

Another behavior of INNER JOIN is row duplication as necessary. An `order_item` table row may have multiple corresponding `delivery_item` table rows if it's been delivered as multiple packages. In such a case, our results set will have that `order_item` table row duplicated as many times as it has corresponding `delivery_item` table rows.

Before things get too complicated, take a look at Table 7.59, which summarizes INNER JOIN behavior in various cases.

Main Table	Secondary Table	Found Rows	Behavior
MT	ST	1 MT row and 0 ST rows	The MT row is excluded.
MT	ST	1 MT row and 1 ST row	A single MT row and a single ST row are merged into a single row.
MT	ST	1 MT row and 2 ST rows	An MT row is duplicated, and each MT row is merged with a different ST row.

Table 7.59 INNER JOIN Behavior, Depending on Row Correspondence

Let's jump to an example that will help us clearly see these features. To understand the behavior of INNER JOIN in action, we'll start by checking rows in the `order_item` table via Listing 7.64.

```
SELECT
    order_id,
    order_item_no,
    product_id
```

```
FROM
    order_item;
```

Listing 7.64 Query to Read All Order Items

The results of this query will be as in Table 7.60. Nothing fancy so far.

order_id	order_item_no	product_id
101	1	TEE
101	2	PNT
102	1	BLZ
102	2	BELT
103	1	SHIR
103	2	SKT
104	1	BAG
105	1	JKT

Table 7.60 All Order Items

Now, let's take a look at deliveries via Listing 7.65.

```
SELECT
    *
FROM
    delivery_item;
```

Listing 7.65 Query to Read All Delivery Items

The results of this query will be as in Table 7.61. Still, nothing fancy. We have delivery items corresponding to various order items.

delivery_id	delivery_item_no	order_id	order_item_no	dlv_quantity
301	1	101	1	1
302	1	102	1	1
302	2	102	2	2
303	1	103	1	3
304	1	103	2	1

Table 7.61 All Delivery Items

delivery_id	delivery_item_no	order_id	order_item_no	dlv_quantity
305	1	102	1	1
305	2	104	1	1

Table 7.61 All Delivery Items (Cont.)

Two points are worth noting, though:

- Order 105 has no delivery correspondence here, simply because it hasn't been delivered yet.
- Order 102, item 1, has multiple delivery correspondences here because it's been delivered as multiple packages on different dates.

Keeping those points in mind, we'll join those tables by using an INNER JOIN query to see a list of order items with their corresponding delivery items. Figure 7.19 showcases our planed output.

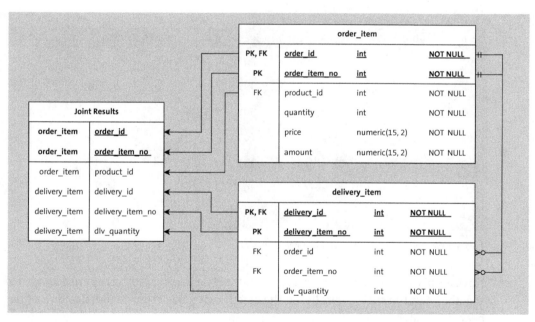

Figure 7.19 Joint Result Plan from order_item and delivery_item Tables

We can achieve this result with Listing 7.66.

```
SELECT
    order_item.order_id,
    order_item.order_item_no,
    order_item.product_id,
    delivery_item.delivery_id,
```

```
        delivery_item.delivery_item_no,
        delivery_item.dlv_quantity
FROM
        order_item
        INNER JOIN delivery_item ON delivery_item.order_id = order_item.order_id
        AND delivery_item.order_item_no = order_item.order_item_no
ORDER BY
        order_item.order_id,
        order_item.order_item_no,
        delivery_item.delivery_id,
        delivery_item.delivery_item_no;
```

Listing 7.66 Query to Read Order Items with Deliveries

Overall, the INNER JOIN template is the same as in the previous example. Because the `delivery_item` table references the `order_item` table via two foreign keys, we had to provide both as our INNER JOIN condition. Plus, we sorted the results to improve readability. The results set can be seen in Table 7.62.

order_id	order_item_no	product_id	delivery_id	delivery_item_no	dlv_quantity
101	1	TEE	301	1	1
102	1	BLZ	302	1	1
102	1	BLZ	305	1	1
102	2	BELT	302	2	2
103	1	SHIR	303	1	3
103	2	SKT	304	1	1
104	1	BAG	305	2	1

Table 7.62 Joint Results of INNER JOIN Query

Now, it's plain to see that the `order_item` and `delivery_item` rows were joined and listed together. But the critical part lies in the details: what has been excluded and what has been duplicated?

First, let's put order 105 under the magnifying glass. If you check Table 7.61, you'll see that there's no delivery (yet) for this order. Therefore, when we did an INNER JOIN for orders with deliveries, order 105 was excluded from the results set. Only entries with corresponding deliveries were included.

Now, let's inspect order 102, item 1. If you check Table 7.61 once again, you'll see that this order has been shipped via multiple deliveries. Since we used JOIN, the database engine has duplicated the `order_item` row for each corresponding `delivery_item` row.

Why? Because it must list `order_item` and `delivery_item` columns next to each other! If the order 2, item 1 row weren't duplicated, we could display only one of the delivery items—but we have two, so we must duplicate the order item rows accordingly.

Joining Multiple Tables

There's no rule that says joint queries are limited to two tables! See Listing 7.67, in which we join `order_item` with two secondary tables: `product` and `delivery_item`.

```
SELECT
    order_item.order_id,
    order_item.order_item_no,
    order_item.product_id,
    product.name,
    delivery_item.dlv_quantity
FROM
    order_item
    INNER JOIN product ON product.id = order_item.product_id
    INNER JOIN delivery_item ON delivery_item.order_id = order_item.order_id
    AND delivery_item.order_item_no = order_item.order_item_no
WHERE
    order_item.quantity > 1
ORDER BY
    order_item.order_id,
    order_item.order_item_no,
    delivery_item.delivery_id,
    delivery_item.delivery_item_no;
```

Listing 7.67 Joint Query from Three Tables

Our results set will be as in Table 7.63. Note that it contains columns from all source tables.

order_id	order_item_no	product_id	name	dlv_quantity
101	1	TEE	T-shirt	1
102	2	BELT	Belt	2
103	1	SHIR	Shirt	3

Table 7.63 Results Set of Joint Query

INNER JOIN and Aggregation

Although it's not an exclusive feature of JOIN queries, it's a common practice to combine JOIN with aggregate functions. If we were to build a list of products with their total delivered quantities, we could do it by using Listing 7.68.

```
SELECT
    order_item.product_id,
    SUM(delivery_item.dlv_quantity) AS delivered_quantity
FROM
    order_item
    INNER JOIN delivery_item ON delivery_item.order_id = order_item.order_id
    AND delivery_item.order_item_no = order_item.order_item_no
GROUP BY
    order_item.order_id,
    order_item.order_item_no
ORDER BY
    order_item.product_id;
```

Listing 7.68 Aggregate Function with JOIN

As you see, the query template is a hybrid of aggregation and joint selection. In the column list, we include a SUM as well as its corresponding GROUP BY condition. In the table list, we include our base order_item table, which has been INNER JOIN-ed with delivery_item as usual.

Once tables are joined, we can aggregate over any column of any table! We've gathered rows and columns from multiple related tables and summed the delivery quantities by product, and we can see the results set in Table 7.64.

product_id	delivered_quantity
BAG	1
BELT	2
BLZ	2
SHIR	3
SKT	1
TEE	1

Table 7.64 Delivered Quantities by Product

Now, you may have noticed that long table names may dominate queries, making them hard to read. That problem has a solution, which we'll cover in the next section.

7.3.3 Using Aliases

DQL gives us the option to use aliases for both database tables and their columns. We'll evaluate both options now.

Table Aliases

As the number of joined tables grows, DQL code becomes harder and harder to read. Case in point: Listing 7.68 contains long table names, increasing the time to read and understand the code.

You could consider using abbreviations for table names, but many would argue that it makes the database structure difficult to understand. Besides, you may be dealing with legacy tables, which can't be renamed easily due to their high usage rate.

Instead of renaming original table names, we have the option to use aliases instead of real table names in DQL statements. That's very easy to do—all we have to do is to make use of the AS keyword. Listing 7.69 demonstrates our former query transformed with aliases.

```
SELECT
    o.product_id,
    SUM(d.dlv_quantity) AS delivered_quantity
FROM
    order_item AS o
    INNER JOIN delivery_item AS d ON d.order_id = o.order_id
    AND d.order_item_no = o.order_item_no
GROUP BY
    o.order_id,
    o.order_item_no
ORDER BY
    o.product_id;
```

Listing 7.69 Using Aliases for Table Names

See? Now that the code is shorter, it's easier to follow through and understand it. Aliases can be used on single table queries as well, but they shine in multitable queries.

> **Naming Aliases**
>
> Although there's no strict rule for naming aliases in SQL, you should use common sense when naming them. The alias name should be meaningful and understandable throughout the entire query, and the resulting statement should be cleaner and more understandable than its version without aliases.
>
> If you're writing multiple subsequent queries, we advise you to use the same alias for the same table throughout the entire chain.
>
> You should avoid aliases that resemble SQL keywords, and snake-case (like `prod_cat`) aliases are preferable due to their readability.

Column Aliases

Naturally, we can use aliases for column names as well—using the same AS keyword. Beyond clarity, a typical reason for column aliases is compatibility. If a client system requires your query to return data with predefined column names, you can simply use aliases for your columns and use the exact naming as requested.

For example, if you're required to return product IDs and their delivered quantities under the p_id and d_quan column names, you can modify the query as in Listing 7.70.

```
SELECT
    o.product_id AS p_id,
    SUM(d.dlv_quantity) AS d_quan
FROM
    order_item AS o
    INNER JOIN delivery_item AS d ON d.order_id = o.order_id
    AND d.order_item_no = o.order_item_no
GROUP BY
    o.order_id,
    o.order_item_no
ORDER BY
    o.product_id;
```

Listing 7.70 Renaming Columns with Aliases

Although the query logic is exactly the same, we've merely renamed the column names of our results set by using column aliases, which can be seen in Table 7.65.

p_id	d_quan
BAG	1
BELT	2
BLZ	2
SHIR	3
SKT	1
TEE	1

Table 7.65 Results Set with Column Aliases

Now that we're familiar with aliases, we can use them comfortably through the rest of the chapter as needed.

7.3.4 OUTER JOIN

First, the good news: now that the topic of INNER JOIN is behind us, the road ahead is much easier. We covered the features of table joins in the section on INNER JOIN, and for other join types, all we need to learn is how their behavior differs from INNER JOIN, and we can use the same features right after. We're starting with OUTER JOIN.

Basically, OUTER JOIN is a more permissive version of INNER JOIN. As you'll remember, INNER JOIN only brings rows for which a correspondence exists in both main and secondary tables. On the other hand, OUTER JOIN brings rows from the main table, even if a correspondence doesn't exist with the secondary table, leaving secondary columns null.

The behavior of OUTER JOIN can be seen in Table 7.66. Note that only the first case is different from INNER JOIN—the rest are same.

Main Table	Secondary Table	Found Rows	Behavior
MT	ST	1 MT row and 0 ST rows	The MT row is included, and the ST columns are left as null.
MT	ST	1 MT row and 1 ST row	A single MT row and a single ST row are merged into a single row.
MT	ST	1 MT row and 2 ST rows	An MT row is duplicated, and each MT row is merged with a different ST row.

Table 7.66 OUTER JOIN Behavior, Depending on Row Correspondence

For a clearer understanding, Table 7.67 contrasts the different behaviors next to each other.

Tables	Found Rows	Inner Join Behavior	Outer Join Behavior
MT and ST	1 MT row and 0 ST rows	An MT row is excluded.	An MT row is included, and the ST columns are left as null.
MT and ST	1 MT row and 1 ST row	A single MT row and a single ST row are merged into a single row.	Same as INNER JOIN.
MT and ST	1 MT row and 2 ST rows	An MT row is duplicated, and each MT row is merged with a different ST row.	Same as INNER JOIN.

Table 7.67 INNER JOIN versus OUTER JOIN Behavior

7 Data Query Language

We'll discover the different syntactical approaches of OUTER JOIN now, and we'll provide sample queries and results sets for them to give you a better understanding.

Left Outer Join

Now that you're experienced in table joins, you should be able to easily gain an understanding this syntactical approach via an example. See Listing 7.71.

```
SELECT
    o.order_id,
    o.order_item_no,
    o.product_id,
    d.delivery_id,
    d.delivery_item_no,
    d.dlv_quantity
FROM
    order_item AS o
    LEFT OUTER JOIN delivery_item AS d ON d.order_id = o.order_id
    AND d.order_item_no = o.order_item_no
ORDER BY
    o.order_id,
    o.order_item_no,
    d.delivery_id,
    d.delivery_item_no;
```

Listing 7.71 LEFT OUTER JOIN Example

As you may have noticed, this is nearly the same "order/delivery" based query from our INNER JOIN section. There's one obvious difference, though: instead of an INNER JOIN, we've a LEFT OUTER JOIN here.

LEFT OUTER JOIN means that we want to receive all rows from the *left table* (the main table specified before the JOIN) and matched rows *optionally* from the *right table* (the table specified within the JOIN). If no match is found in the right table, the rows from the left table are still returned, but null values are filled in in the columns from the right table.

For a better understanding, check the query results set in Table 7.68.

order_id	order_item_no	product_id	delivery_id	delivery_item_no	dlv_quantity
101	1	TEE	301	1	1
101	2	PNT	null	null	null

Table 7.68 Results Set of LEFT OUTER JOIN Query

order_id	order_item_no	product_id	delivery_id	delivery_item_no	dlv_quantity
102	1	BLZ	302	1	1
102	1	BLZ	305	1	1
102	2	BELT	302	2	2
103	1	SHIR	303	1	3
103	2	SKT	304	1	1
104	1	BAG	305	2	1
105	1	JKT	null	null	null

Table 7.68 Results Set of LEFT OUTER JOIN Query (Cont.)

Now, pay close attention to order 101, item 2. This order item doesn't have any deliveries yet, but it's still included in our result set, filling delivery columns with null values. That's the exact behavior difference from an INNER JOIN: this row would be excluded if we had an INNER JOIN to deliveries.

Order 105, item 1 is the exact same case, and you may remember it from the INNER JOIN section.

Now, pay attention to order 102, item 1. It has been shipped as multiple deliveries and has multiple corresponding `delivery_item` rows. Therefore, the `order_item` row has been duplicated as many times as it has corresponding `delivery_item` rows. This is the exact same behavior as in INNER JOIN, for the same reasons explained under that topic.

Both behaviors match with Table 7.66.

DQL enables us to use INNER JOIN and OUTER JOIN in the same query as well. See Listing 7.72, where we throw an INNER JOIN into `product` and we also throw in a WHERE condition for fun. Note that the WHERE condition is set to the secondary table.

```
SELECT
    o.order_id,
    o.order_item_no,
    p.name AS prod_name,
    d.delivery_id,
    d.delivery_item_no,
    d.dlv_quantity
FROM
    order_item AS o
    INNER JOIN product AS p ON p.id = o.product_id
    LEFT OUTER JOIN delivery_item AS d ON d.order_id = o.order_id
    AND d.order_item_no = o.order_item_no
```

```
WHERE
    p.name LIKE '%a%e%'
ORDER BY
    o.order_id,
    o.order_item_no,
    d.delivery_id,
    d.delivery_item_no;
```

Listing 7.72 INNER JOIN and OUTER JOIN Used Together

The results set of that query can be seen in Table 7.69. Note that INNER JOIN and OUTER JOIN didn't affect each other's behavior.

order_id	order_item_no	prod_name	delivery_id	delivery_item_no	dlv_quantity
102	1	Blazer	302	1	1
102	1	Blazer	305	1	1
105	1	Jacket	null	null	null

Table 7.69 Results Set of Multijoin Query

Now, how would the null values of an OUTER JOIN affect an aggregation? Take another look at Table 7.69, where you'll see we have null values in some rows. What happens if we try to SUM(dlv_quantity)? Will we get an error, or will the database simply ignore the null values?

Only one way to find out! Let's take this query, turn it into an aggregation as in Listing 7.73 and see what the database engine does.

```
SELECT
    SUM(d.dlv_quantity) AS dlv_sum
FROM
    order_item AS o
    INNER JOIN product AS p ON p.id = o.product_id
    LEFT OUTER JOIN delivery_item AS d ON d.order_id = o.order_id
    AND d.order_item_no = o.order_item_no
WHERE
    p.name LIKE '%a%e%';
```

Listing 7.73 Aggregate Calculation of Null Values

The result of this query will be 2, as in Table 7.70. Now we know that null values are ignored when summing with non-null values.

Table 7.70 Calculated Sum, Including Null Values

Now, let's execute Listing 7.74. This is the same base query with one difference: instead of calculating an overall delivery sum, we're calculating delivery sums by product name.

```
SELECT
    p.name AS prod_name,
    SUM(d.dlv_quantity) AS dlv_sum
FROM
    order_item AS o
    INNER JOIN product AS p ON p.id = o.product_id
    LEFT OUTER JOIN delivery_item AS d ON d.order_id = o.order_id
    AND d.order_item_no = o.order_item_no
WHERE
    p.name LIKE '%a%e%'
GROUP BY
    p.name
ORDER BY
    p.name;
```

Listing 7.74 Query for Delivery Sum by Product

The results set of this query can be seen in Table 7.71.

prod_name	dlv_sum
Blazer	2
Jacket	null

Table 7.71 Delivery Sum by Product

This time, the delivery sum of Jacket was returned as null. That's natural—the database engine didn't have any other value to aggregate because there's only one Jacket entry in Table 7.69.

Using LEFT OUTER JOIN examples, we've grasped the functionality and behavior of outer joins. Now, let's move on to other OUTER JOIN types and see how they differ from LEFT OUTER JOIN queries.

7 Data Query Language

Right Outer Join

RIGHT OUTER JOIN is the mirrored twin of LEFT OUTER JOIN.

RIGHT OUTER JOIN means that we want to receive all rows from the right table (specified within the JOIN) and matched rows *optionally* from the left table (the main table, specified before the JOIN).

If no match is found in the left table, rows from the right table are still returned, but null values are filled into the columns from the left table.

So, by switching the order of the table names, you can express the exact same query as either a LEFT OUTER JOIN or a RIGHT OUTER JOIN.

In our previous query, we LEFT OUTER JOIN-ed order_item with delivery_item as in Listing 7.75.

```
FROM
    order_item AS o
    LEFT OUTER JOIN delivery_item AS d ON d.order_id = o.order_id
    AND d.order_item_no = o.order_item_no
```

Listing 7.75 order_item Left Outer Joined to delivery_item

We can assert the exact same behavior by switching the table order via a RIGHT OUTER JOIN as in Listing 7.76.

```
FROM
    delivery_item AS d
    RIGHT OUTER JOIN order_item AS o ON d.order_id = o.order_id
    AND d.order_item_no = o.order_item_no
```

Listing 7.76 delivery_item Right Outer Joined to order_item

It's that easy! Listing 7.75 and Listing 7.76 will behave identically. To have a complete example at hand, we can complete the query as in Listing 7.77.

```
SELECT
    o.order_id,
    o.order_item_no,
    o.product_id,
    d.delivery_id,
    d.delivery_item_no,
    d.dlv_quantity
FROM
    delivery_item AS d
    RIGHT OUTER JOIN order_item AS o ON d.order_id = o.order_id
    AND d.order_item_no = o.order_item_no
```

```
ORDER BY
    o.order_id,
    o.order_item_no,
    d.delivery_id,
    d.delivery_item_no;
```

Listing 7.77 Complete RIGHT OUTER JOIN Example

The output of this query can be seen in Table 7.72, which is identical to our previous LEFT OUTER JOIN output in Table 7.68.

order_id	order_item_no	product_id	delivery_id	delivery_item_no	dlv_quantity
101	1	TEE	301	1	1
101	2	PNT	null	null	null
102	1	BLZ	302	1	1
102	1	BLZ	305	1	1
102	2	BELT	302	2	2
103	1	SHIR	303	1	3
103	2	SKT	304	1	1
104	1	BAG	305	2	1
105	1	JKT	null	null	null

Table 7.72 Results Set of RIGHT OUTER JOIN Query

Why Both?

If we can use LEFT JOIN and RIGHT JOIN to produce identical outputs simply by switching the order of the tables, why does DQL support both?

The main reasons are query readability and flexibility. Depending on the context of the entire query, we can use either one to achieve an optional join between two tables.

When thinking about preserving rows from the left table, it's more intuitive to use LEFT JOIN. On the other hand, when thinking about preserving rows from the right table, RIGHT JOIN can be clearer.

Besides, rearranging tables to switch from LEFT JOIN to RIGHT JOIN (or vice versa) can complicate some queries—especially when multiple joins are present. Having both options allows more flexibility in terms of simplification.

7   Data Query Language

Full Outer Join

So far, we've learned that INNER JOIN is the strictest join type because it excludes rows without correspondence. LEFT OUTER JOIN and RIGHT OUTER JOIN are more inclusive because they include all rows from *one of the tables*—even the ones without correspondence.

FULL OUTER JOIN is the most inclusive type of join. It includes all rows from *both tables*—even rows without correspondence.

To understand this concept, we'll run a query to list complaints and orders together, on the same row if possible. Figure 7.20 contains a memory refresher regarding the complaint table.

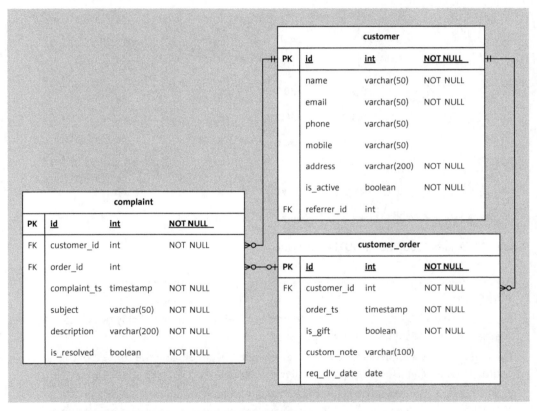

Figure 7.20 ERD for complaint and Related Tables

As you can see, complaint.order_id refers to customer_order.id but may be null as well. This means that a complaint may be related to an order, but it may also be unrelated to any order and contain generic feedback. This means the following:

- For a complaint, there may be a corresponding order (or not).
- For an order, there may be corresponding complaints (or not).

To gain a better understanding, check the `complaint` entries in Table 7.73. Complaint 901 is related to order 101, whereas complaint 902 is generic and not related to any order.

id	customer_id	order_id	complaint_ts	subject	description	is_resolved
901	71	101	2024-09-23 15:47:22	Website slow	I had to wait at submit.	false
902	75		2024-09-23 15:47:22	No gift card	We want a gift card option.	false

Table 7.73 Entries in complaint Table

In this light, our purpose will be to generate a data set in which complaints and orders are listed together. But if a complaint and an order are related, they need to be on the same row.

This is a typical requirement for FULL OUTER JOIN! Check the query in Listing 7.78.

```
SELECT
    c.id,
    c.customer_id AS c_customer,
    c.order_id AS c_order_id,
    c.subject,
    o.id AS o_order_id,
    o.customer_id AS o_customer,
    date (o.order_ts) AS o_date
FROM
    complaint AS c
    FULL OUTER JOIN customer_order AS o ON o.id = c.order_id;
```

Listing 7.78 Query Containing FULL OUTER JOIN

We have `complaint` on one side of FULL OUTER JOIN and `customer_order` on the other. In this situation, FULL OUTER JOIN will ensure that rows of both tables are included in the results set, whether they're related or not. But related entries will be merged in the same row.

The results set of this query can be seen in Table 7.74.

id	c_customer	c_order_id	subject	o_order_id	o_customer	o_date
901	71	101	Website slow	101	71	2024-09-23
null	null	null	null	102	72	2024-09-23

Table 7.74 Result Set for FULL OUTER JOIN

id	c_customer	c_order_id	subject	o_order_id	o_customer	o_date
null	null	null	null	103	73	2024-09-23
null	null	null	null	104	74	2024-09-23
null	null	null	null	105	75	2024-09-23
902	75	null	No gift card	**null**	null	null

Table 7.74 Result Set for FULL OUTER JOIN (Cont.)

In the first row, we have complaint 901, which is referencing order 101. For that complaint, the corresponding order is merged and displayed as a single row.

In the following four rows, we have orders without complaints. In those rows, the order columns are filled in but the complaint columns are left as null.

In the last row, we have complaint 902, which is generic and doesn't reference any order. In that row, the complaint columns are filled in but the order columns are left as null.

Just as we intended!

> **The Most Inclusive Join**
>
> This example makes it clear that FULL OUTER JOIN is the most inclusive type of join. All rows from any side of the join will definitely be included—as long as they match other conditions of the query (if there's any). Table relationships are merely used to decide if rows need to be merged or not.

This concludes our content on outer joins. Now, we'll move on to other methods of querying multiple tables at the same time.

7.3.5 Self-Join

Self-join is not an actual DQL command. Rather, it's a common technique for accessing table rows recursively.

Let's remember the customer table. As shown in Figure 7.21, we have a column called referrer_id, which is filled in if a customer becomes a member via a reference from another customer.

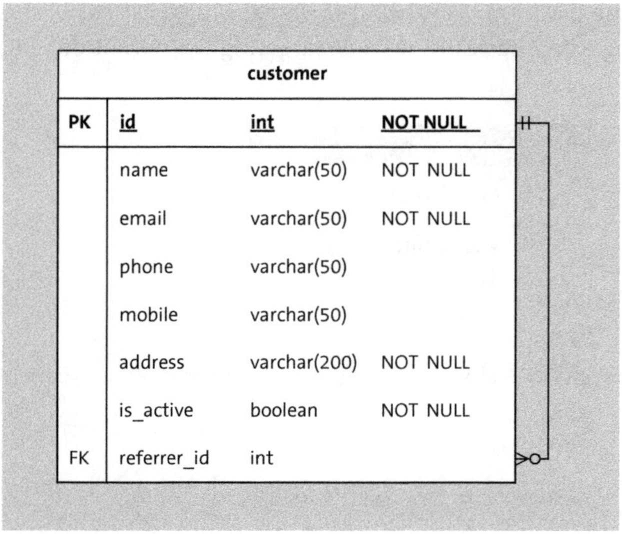

7.3 Multitable Queries

Figure 7.21 ERD for customer Table

We can list customers and referrers by using Listing 7.79.

```
SELECT
    id,
    name,
    referrer_id
FROM
    customer;
```

Listing 7.79 Query to Map Referrers

The results of this query will be as in Table 7.75. Apparently, Alice Smith was the referrer for Charlie Brown and Diana Prince.

id	name	referrer_id
71	Alice Smith	null
72	Bob Johnson	null
73	Charlie Brown	71
74	Diana Prince	71
75	Eve Adams	null

Table 7.75 Referral Map

7 Data Query Language

So far, so good—we've built the platform. Now, what if we needed to list customers next to their referrers, in a single list? Basically, we'd be targeting the output of Table 7.76.

id	name	referrer_id	referrer_name
73	Charlie Brown	71	Alice Smith
74	Diana Prince	71	Alice Smith

Table 7.76 Target Output with Self-Join

The first three columns are easy, right? A simple query like Listing 7.80 will take care of that.

```
SELECT
    c1.id,
    c1.name,
    c1.referrer_id
FROM
    customer AS c1;
```

Listing 7.80 Query to Fill First Three Columns

Now, how can we bring `referrer_name` into the output?

If referrers were stored in a secondary table, we could simply INNER JOIN from the `customer` table to that secondary table, just as we did many times before. But the referrers reside in the same table, so we need to INNER JOIN from `customer.referred_id` to `customer.id` recursively—which is exactly what a self-join is! Check the enhanced query in Listing 7.81, which will produce our target output.

```
SELECT
    c1.id,
    c1.name,
    c1.referrer_id,
    c2.name AS referrer_name
FROM
    customer AS c1
    INNER JOIN customer AS c2 ON c2.id = c1.referrer_id;
```

Listing 7.81 Self-Join Query

In this query, we're accessing the `customer` table twice:

- First, we access it as a main table and call it c1.
- Then, we access it via the join as a secondary table and call it c2.

7.3 Multitable Queries

And voila! A recursive self-join has saved the day!

The typical use case for a self-join is browsing parent-child relationships in the customer table. Other samples could be employee-manager relationships in an organizational hierarchy or product-component relationships in bills of materials.

You can use other types of joins as self-joins too and use multilevel recursions in the same query if needed.

> **Aliases in Self-Join**
>
> Aliases play a critical role in self-joins. In the example above, we gave the new aliases c1 and c2 to each level of the recursion. That enabled us to differentiate the target fields as c1.referrer_id and c2.name.
>
> Otherwise, if we used the customer name on each level, the database engine couldn't tell them apart. An expression like customer.name would be ambiguous, and the engine wouldn't understand whether we meant the name of the main customer or the referrer.

7.3.6 Subqueries

So far, we've gone through DQL examples in which a single SELECT statement gets the job done. That's fine for many requirements, but in more complex cases, DQL empowers us with a mechanism in which we can nest one or more SELECT statements.

Figure 7.22 represents this approach visually. We can inject secondary SELECT statements into the main SELECT statement, and the secondary statements will interact with the main DQL commands to build the desired results set.

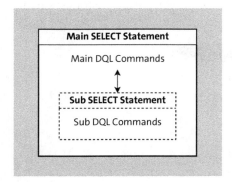

Figure 7.22 Visual Representation of Subqueries

There are multiple spots where a secondary query can be injected. As we go through them in the following sections, the purpose and power of this mechanism will become evident.

FROM

One possibility for subqueries is to inject a SELECT statement instead of a table name into the FROM section of a query. That way, we can join a concrete table in the database with a dynamic table created by the provided subquery. See Listing 7.82 for an example.

```
SELECT
    c.name AS customer_name,
    c.email AS customer_email,
    o.total_orders
FROM
    customer AS c
    INNER JOIN (
        SELECT
            customer_id,
            COUNT(*) AS total_orders
        FROM
            customer_order
        GROUP BY
            customer_id
    ) AS o ON o.customer_id = c.id;
```

Listing 7.82 Simple Join between Table and Subquery

We have customer as our main table of the query—that's nothing new. But following the INNER JOIN, instead of providing a secondary concrete table, we've provided a secondary DQL statement. The results of this statement will be evaluated like a database table and joined with the main customer table, just as visualized in Figure 7.22.

The results of this query can be seen in Table 7.77, in which each customer's name, email, and total number of orders are listed.

customer_name	customer_email	total_orders
Alice Smith	alice@example.com	1
Charlie Brown	charlie@example.com	1
Bob Johnson	bob@example.com	1
Diana Prince	diana@example.com	1
Eve Adams	eve@example.com	1

Table 7.77 List of Customer Names, Emails, and Total Orders

If we didn't use a subquery, we'd have to execute the inner query first and use its results to manually build the outer query with crowded WHERE conditions. Subqueries simplify this task and the code by letting us merge those queries.

Our previous example demonstrated this case, in which we used INNER JOIN between the main table and the subquery. This will return only those customers who have placed at least one order.

In other cases, we can use different join types. In Listing 7.83, LEFT JOIN was used to connect the main table with the subquery. In the inner query, we're selecting customer orders within the last month, while the outer/main query LEFT OUTER JOIN-s customer data with inner order results. This ensures that all customer rows will definitely be listed. For customers who have placed orders within the last month, the dates of those orders will also be listed.

```
SELECT
    c.name AS customer_name,
    recent_orders.order_ts
FROM
    customer AS c
    LEFT OUTER JOIN (
        SELECT
            customer_id,
            CAST(order_ts AS date)
        FROM
            customer_order
        WHERE
            order_ts >= NOW() - INTERVAL '1 month'
    ) AS recent_orders ON c.id = recent_orders.customer_id;
```

Listing 7.83 Query to Fetch Customers and Their Recent Order Dates

---

Subqueries and Performance

Subqueries in the FROM clause can impact performance, especially in complex queries of large datasets.

In many cases, the database engine has to execute the inner query first, materialize its results, and join those results with other tables after. If the results set of the inner query is too large, it may lead to performance problems, and if multiple subqueries are used simultaneously, it may lead to complex execution plans with poor optimization.

If you're unsure of what to do, you can use the EXPLAIN ANALYZE PostgreSQL command to analyze your query and see if there are bottlenecks.

WHERE IN and WHERE EXISTS

Another spot into which to inject subqueries is the WHERE clause. So far, we've used equations as WHERE conditions, which is fine in most cases. But if you have a more complex

7 Data Query Language

condition that involves querying a secondary table, you can do that with a `WHERE` subquery.

See the example in Listing 7.84. The inner query returns a list of customers with unresolved complaints from the `complaint` table. Let's call this LIST1, temporarily. Following that, the outer query returns master data for `customer` rows that have correspondence to LIST1.

```
SELECT
    c.id,
    c.name
FROM
    customer AS c
WHERE
    id IN (
        SELECT
            customer_id
        FROM
            complaint
        WHERE
            is_resolved = FALSE
    );
```

Listing 7.84 WHERE IN Subquery Example

The execution logic of `WHERE` subqueries is visualized in Figure 7.23.

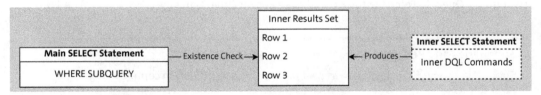

Figure 7.23 Execution Logic of WHERE Subqueries

The results set of this query can be seen in Table 7.78. Those are the customers with unresolved complaints.

id	name
71	Alice Smith
75	Eve Adams

Table 7.78 Customers with Unresolved Complaints

WHERE IN differs from joins on multiple points:

- Joins duplicate rows where multiple correspondence exists, and WHERE IN doesn't.
- You can include values from both tables in a join. WHERE IN is just a check and doesn't return values.

An alternative approach is to use a WHERE EXISTS clause. This clause is the sibling of WHERE IN because their functionalities overlap greatly. To demonstrate the similarity, Listing 7.85 demonstrates the same query refactored as WHERE EXISTS.

```
SELECT
    c.id,
    c.name
FROM
    customer AS c
WHERE
    EXISTS (
        SELECT
            customer_id
        FROM
            complaint
        WHERE
            customer_id = c.id
            AND is_resolved = FALSE
    );
```

Listing 7.85 WHERE EXISTS Subquery Example

The output of this query will be the same as that of our previous WHERE IN query. See Table 7.78. In the two cases, we build a list of customers having at least one unresolved complaint, but we do it in different ways.

If we use the WHERE IN clause, the database engine will execute the inner SQL, build the inner results set completely, and filter customers having correspondence in the inner result set.

If we use the WHERE EXISTS clause, the database engine won't build the inner results set immediately. Instead, it will scan through the results of the inner SQL and stop as soon as it finds a corresponding customer entry.

So, where's the difference if those clauses exchangeable?

The difference lies in performance.

If you expect a small inner result set, you may prefer WHERE IN. You'll let the database materialize and index the inner results set only once and compare outer values quickly via that.

On the other hand, if you expect a large inner results set, you may prefer WHERE EXISTS. You'll prevent memory and performance problems because the database engine won't try to build the huge inner results set in advance. Instead, it will evaluate row by row and stop the process as soon it finds matches.

A summary comparison can be seen in Table 7.79.

Clauses	Behaviors	Preferable Cases
WHERE IN	The database engine prebuilds the inner results set completely and then compares outer values.	A small inner result set
WHERE EXISTS	The database engine evaluates the inner results set row by row and stops when it finds matches.	A large inner result set

Table 7.79 Comparison of IN and EXISTS Clauses

CROSSTAB

CROSSTAB is a clause type that you use to build pivot tables and in which vertical values are transposed into horizontal columns. Most readers will be familiar with this concept from spreadsheets.

Pivot tables are best understood in two steps:

1. Understanding the purpose
2. Understanding the syntax

As the first step, we need to understand what pivot tables are used for. Let's start by inspecting Listing 7.86, which contains a query to calculate the sum of amounts by order and product gender.

```
SELECT
    cg.id,
    cg.gender,
    SUM(oi.amount) AS amount_sum
FROM
    (
        SELECT
            customer_order.id,
            g.gender
        FROM
            customer_order
            CROSS JOIN (
                SELECT DISTINCT
                    gender
```

```
                FROM
                    product
            ) AS g
    ) AS cg
    INNER JOIN product AS p ON p.gender = cg.gender
    LEFT OUTER JOIN order_item AS oi ON oi.order_id = cg.id
    AND oi.product_id = p.id
GROUP BY
    cg.id,
    cg.gender;
```

Listing 7.86 Query for Amount Sums by Order and Product Gender

The results of this query will be as in Table 7.80. We'll obtain the order amount sum for each order ID and product gender combination. Note that all genders are included for each order ID, even if the order doesn't contain corresponding products of that gender. In those rows, the amount_sum is calculated as 0. That way, we prevent value gaps—for each order, we definitely have the same F, M, and U values in the same order.

id	gender	amount_sum
101	F	0
101	M	50.00
101	U	37.98
102	F	0
102	M	105.00
102	U	50.00
103	F	40.00
103	M	105.00
103	U	0
104	F	0
104	M	0
104	U	60.00
105	F	0
105	M	0
105	U	100.00

Table 7.80 Order Amount Sum by Order ID and Gender

7   Data Query Language

Now, what if we wanted to turn this results set into a pivot table like Table 7.81? Note that we have a distinct order ID in each row and that gender values are distributed as columns, transposing the amount sums into a more readable format.

id	f_sum	m_sum	u_sum
101	0.00	50.00	37.98
102	0.00	105.00	50.00
103	40.00	105.00	0.00
104	0.00	0.00	60.00
105	0.00	0.00	100.00

Table 7.81 Target Pivot Table

That's the exact purpose of a typical pivot table!

Now that we understand our purpose, we can move to step 2 and learn how to achieve our goal. Building pivot tables is possible by using CROSSTAB statements. To enable CROSSTAB in your database system, you may have to execute Listing 7.87 once.

```
CREATE EXTENSION tablefunc;
```

Listing 7.87 Enabling tablefunc Extension

Listing 7.88 showcases the DQL statement you use to produce the output in Table 7.81.

```
SELECT
    *
FROM
    CROSSTAB (
$$
    SELECT
        cg.id,
        cg.gender,
        COALESCE(SUM(oi.amount), 0) AS amount_sum
    FROM
        (
            SELECT
                customer_order.id,
                g.gender
            FROM
                customer_order
                CROSS JOIN (
                    SELECT DISTINCT
                        gender
```

```
                    FROM
                            product
                ) AS g
            ) AS cg
            INNER JOIN product AS p ON p.gender = cg.gender
            LEFT OUTER JOIN order_item AS oi ON oi.order_id = cg.id
            AND oi.product_id = p.id
    GROUP BY
        cg.id,
        cg.gender
    ORDER BY
        cg.id,
        cg.gender
$$
    ) AS ct (
        id INTEGER,
        f_sum NUMERIC(15, 2),
        m_sum NUMERIC(15, 2),
        u_sum NUMERIC(15, 2)
    );
```

Listing 7.88 Building Pivot Table by Using CROSSTAB

Wow, that's a big statement for sure! But if you take a closer look, you'll see that it's not that complex at all.

The first thing to notice is that CROSSTAB statements have an outer query and an inner query. In our case, the inner query is the exact same query as in Listing 7.86.

Taking that into consideration, we can temporarily express the long query as a pseudo-coded query to understand it better. See Listing 7.89, where the inner query has been temporarily replaced with { inner_query } to make the statement more understandable.

```
SELECT
    *
FROM
    CROSSTAB ( { inner_query } ) AS ct (
        id INTEGER,
        f_sum NUMERIC(15, 2),
        m_sum NUMERIC(15, 2),
        u_sum NUMERIC(15, 2)
    );
```

Listing 7.89 Pseudo-Coded Query

7   Data Query Language

That feels better, doesn't it? Now, we have a better overview of the structure of a CROSSTAB statement.

The inner query must return exactly three columns (described in Table 7.82), without any value gaps. Also, the results need to be sorted by row and column keys.

Column Numbers	Descriptions	Our Examples	Sample Values
1	Pivot row key	Order ID	101
2	Pivot column key	Gender	M
3	Values	Order amount sum	50

Table 7.82 Columns of Inner Query

Our inner query was expressed in Listing 7.86, and it matches this requirement perfectly—we're returning precisely three columns (without any value gaps), and they're to be used as row keys, column keys, and values. They're also sorted correctly.

Once we establish the inner query, the outer query almost shapes itself. Following the inner query, we defined a series of pivot columns: id, f_sum, m_sum, and u_sum. We started with the row key and followed it up with each column key.

Thus, our final CROSSTAB query produces the output in Table 7.81.

Join Lateral

Suppose you want to find the most expensive item in each order. In such a case, JOIN LATERAL is useful because it allows the subquery to reference columns from the preceding table. Check Listing 7.90 to see it in action.

```
SELECT
    customer_order.id AS order_id,
    expensive_item.product_id,
    expensive_item.amount
FROM
    customer_order
    INNER JOIN LATERAL (
        SELECT
            product_id,
            amount
        FROM
            order_item
        WHERE
            order_id = customer_order.id
        ORDER BY
            amount DESC
```

```
       LIMIT
          1
) AS expensive_item ON TRUE;
```

Listing 7.90 Finding Most Expensive Item in Each Order

Before evaluating the query, let's quickly look at its results set in Table 7.83.

order_id	product_id	amount
101	PNT	50.00
102	BLZ	105.00
103	SHIR	105.00
104	BAG	60.00
105	JKT	100.00

Table 7.83 Most Expensive Item in Each Order

The outer query doesn't offer anything new—it's just a usual query with field selection. The inner query following JOIN LATERAL is where the magic happens. There, we provide an independent subquery targeting order_item, which refers to customer_order.id for each order row at hand.

Here's how we make this more obvious:

- The subquery runs for order 101, and its most expensive order_item row (PNT – 50) is fetched.
- The subquery runs for order 102, and its most expensive order_item row (BLZ – 105) is fetched.
- The subquery runs for order 103, and its most expensive order_item row (SHIR – 105) is fetched.
- The subquery runs for order 104, and its most expensive order_item row (BAG – 60) is fetched.
- The subquery runs for order 105, and its most expensive order_item row (JKT – 100) is fetched.

Although the actual database execution plan may be different, the symbolic sequence highlights the logic of JOIN LITERAL understandably.

> **Other Join Types**
>
> Although we used an INNER JOIN LATERAL in this case, you can use other join types with LATERAL as well.

7   Data Query Language

If we were asked for the most expensive pair of items in each order, we could easily determine it by changing the LIMIT 1 expression to LIMIT 2. The results set would look like Table 7.84, in which we get two results for each order or one result if the order has a single item.

order_id	product_id	amount
101	PNT	50.00
101	TEE	37.98
102	BLZ	105.00
102	BELT	50.00
103	SHIR	105.00
103	SKT	40.00
104	BAG	60.00
105	JKT	100.00

Table 7.84 Most Expensive Pair of Items in Each Order

In these examples, we've seen the typical use case of JOIN LITERAL queries. When you need to compute aggregate values for each row from the outer table, JOIN LATERAL can often be your ticket to that results set.

Another use case is filtering based on aggregates. Suppose we need a list in which we highlight order items with amounts less than the average amount of all order items. We can handle this request using Listing 7.91.

```
SELECT
    customer_order.id AS order_id,
    below_avg_item.product_id,
    below_avg_item.amount
FROM
    customer_order
    INNER JOIN LATERAL (
        SELECT
            product_id,
            amount
        FROM
            order_item
        WHERE
            order_id = customer_order.id
            AND amount < (
```

```
                SELECT
                    AVG(amount)
                FROM
                    order_item AS oi2
            )
        ORDER BY
            amount DESC
    ) AS below_avg_item ON TRUE;
```

Listing 7.91 Aggregation-based Filtering with JOIN LATERAL

This time, we have a filter in the subquery. For each order, the corresponding `order_item` rows having an amount greater than the average amount of all order items are filtered out, and the rows with amounts below average are kept in the results set. That complex filter can be handled by JOIN LATERAL, and the results set can be seen in Table 7.85.

order_id	product_id	amount
101	PNT	50.00
101	TEE	37.98
102	BELT	50.00
103	SKT	40.00
104	BAG	60.00

Table 7.85 Order Products with Amounts below Average

> **Advanced Features**
>
> The last two topics—crosstabs and join laterals—were relatively advanced; don't feel unmotivated if you found them a bit hard. For a beginner, it's enough to understand that such features are present. In the future, when you face a corresponding software requirement, you'll remember that you have a tool in your toolbox with which to tackle it and apply the correct DQL syntax—with a little trial and error, perhaps?

Now that we've concluded the topic of subqueries, we'll continue with the more straightforward topic of set operations.

7.3.7 Set Operations

Set operations in DQL treat results sets of queries as mathematical sets, allowing you to perform operations like union, intersection, and difference. In other words, the typical set operations you learned in school are applicable to DQL as well. In this section, we'll learn about different set types in DQL and how to build them.

UNION

UNION is the set operation in which we merge two datasets into a single dataset, as sketched in Figure 7.24.

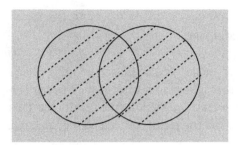

Figure 7.24 Union Logic

Once you see these math sets, the syntax becomes easy to understand. The left set symbolizes one query, the right set symbolizes another query, and we merge the two results sets by using the UNION keyword, building one joint result set.

As an example, we could be looking for a list of customers who either have an unshipped delivery or an unsent invoice. We can easily detect customers with unshipped deliveries by using Listing 7.92, which is the left math set.

```
SELECT
    customer.id,
    customer.name
FROM
    customer
WHERE
    EXISTS (
        SELECT
            id
        FROM
            delivery
        WHERE
            customer_id = customer.id
            AND is_shipped = FALSE
    );
```

Listing 7.92 Query to Find Customers with Unshipped Deliveries

Following up on the case study, we can easily detect customers with unsent invoices by using Listing 7.93, which is the right math set.

```
SELECT
    customer.id,
    customer.name
FROM
    customer
WHERE
    EXISTS (
        SELECT
            id
        FROM
            invoice
        WHERE
            customer_id = customer.id
            AND is_sent = FALSE
    );
```

Listing 7.93 Query to Find Customers with Unsent Invoices

To combine both results sets into a single results set, we'll simply put those queries together, binding them with the UNION keyword as in Listing 7.94.

```
SELECT
    customer.id,
    customer.name
FROM
    customer
WHERE
    EXISTS (
        SELECT
            id
        FROM
            delivery
        WHERE
            customer_id = customer.id
            AND is_shipped = FALSE
    )
UNION DISTINCT
SELECT
    customer.id,
    customer.name
FROM
    customer
WHERE
    EXISTS (
```

```
            SELECT
                id
            FROM
                invoice
            WHERE
                customer_id = customer.id
                AND is_sent = FALSE
    )
```

Listing 7.94 Query to Merge Results Sets

The results of this query will be as in Table 7.86.

id	name
71	Alice Smith
73	Charlie Brown

Table 7.86 Results of UNION DISTINCT Query

To make UNION work, both queries need to return the same number of columns having the same name and type. Plus, you can bind more than two queries with UNION if you want to.

Now, if you look at Listing 7.94 more closely, you'll see that we used the expression UNION DISTINCT, which ensures that any duplicate rows in the results set will be eliminated. If you want to preserve duplicates, you can use the UNION ALL expression instead, as in Listing 7.95.

```
SELECT
    customer.id,
    customer.name
FROM
    customer
WHERE
    EXISTS (
        SELECT
            id
        FROM
            delivery
        WHERE
            customer_id = customer.id
            AND is_shipped = FALSE
    )
UNION ALL
```

```
SELECT
    customer.id,
    customer.name
FROM
    customer
WHERE
    EXISTS (
        SELECT
            id
        FROM
            invoice
        WHERE
            customer_id = customer.id
            AND is_sent = FALSE
    )
```

Listing 7.95 Same Query with UNION ALL

The results of this query can be seen in Table 7.87. Apparently, Alice and Charlie lack at least one delivery and invoice each.

id	name
71	Alice Smith
73	Charlie Brown
71	Alice Smith
73	Charlie Brown

Table 7.87 Results of UNION ALL Query

INTERSECT

This is another fun set command. This time, we'll be looking for rows, which exist in results sets of all provided queries, as sketched in Figure 7.25.

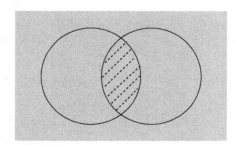

Figure 7.25 INTERSECT Logic

7 Data Query Language

We'll follow the same approach and rules as with UNION. The only difference is, we use the INTERSECT keyword instead.

As an example, we'll build a list of customers who have at least one shipped delivery *and* at least one sent invoice.

We can find customers with at least one shipped delivery by using Listing 7.96, which is the left math set.

```
SELECT
    customer.id,
    customer.name
FROM
    customer
WHERE
    EXISTS (
        SELECT
            id
        FROM
            delivery
        WHERE
            customer_id = customer.id
            AND is_shipped = TRUE
    );
```

Listing 7.96 Query to Find Customers with at Least One Shipped Delivery

We can find customers with at least one sent invoice by using Listing 7.97, which is the right math set.

```
SELECT
    customer.id,
    customer.name
FROM
    customer
WHERE
    EXISTS (
        SELECT
            id
        FROM
            invoice
        WHERE
            customer_id = customer.id
            AND is_sent = TRUE
    );
```

Listing 7.97 Query to Find Customers with at Least One Sent Invoice

To find the intersection of these results sets, we'll bind both queries with INTERSECT as in Listing 7.98.

```
SELECT
    customer.id,
    customer.name
FROM
    customer
WHERE
    EXISTS (
        SELECT
            id
        FROM
            delivery
        WHERE
            customer_id = customer.id
            AND is_shipped = TRUE
    )
INTERSECT
SELECT
    customer.id,
    customer.name
FROM
    customer
WHERE
    EXISTS (
        SELECT
            id
        FROM
            invoice
        WHERE
            customer_id = customer.id
            AND is_sent = TRUE
    )
```

Listing 7.98 Query to Intersect Result Sets

The results set of the final query will be as in Table 7.88. Apparently, Bob and Diana have had deliveries shipped and invoices sent to them simultaneously.

Id	name
72	Bob Johnson
74	Diana Prince

Table 7.88 Results of INTERSECT Query

7 Data Query Language

EXCEPT

Now that we understand the general logic of set operations, we can easily understand the behavior of EXCEPT in Figure 7.26.

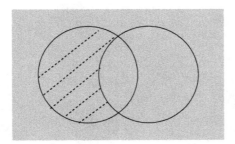

Figure 7.26 EXCEPT Logic

In this operation, we have a main query (the left set) and a reference query (the right set). Results from the reference query are excluded from the main results set, and remaining rows are returned as the final result.

In our case study, we'll build a list of customers who have at least one order (the main query, in the left set) but don't have any complaints (the reference query, in the right set).

The main query will be as in Listing 7.99.

```
SELECT
    customer.id,
    customer.name
FROM
    customer
WHERE
    EXISTS (
        SELECT
            id
        FROM
            customer_order
        WHERE
            customer_id = customer.id
    );
```

Listing 7.99 Query for Customers with at Least One Order

Now, we need the reference query, which we'll use to exclude results from the main query. This would be as in Listing 7.100.

```
SELECT
    customer.id,
    customer.name
FROM
    customer
WHERE
    EXISTS (
        SELECT
            id
        FROM
            complaint
        WHERE
            customer_id = customer.id
    );
```

Listing 7.100 Query for Customers with at Least One Complaint

Finally, we need to deduct the results set of the reference query from the results set of the main query, using the EXCEPT keyword. Listing 7.101 will take care of this.

```
SELECT
    customer.id,
    customer.name
FROM
    customer
WHERE
    EXISTS (
        SELECT
            id
        FROM
            customer_order
        WHERE
            customer_id = customer.id
    )
EXCEPT
SELECT
    customer.id,
    customer.name
FROM
    customer
WHERE
    EXISTS (
        SELECT
            id
```

```
    FROM
        complaint
    WHERE
        customer_id = customer.id
)
```
Listing 7.101 Query to Exclude Results Sets

The results set of the final query will be as in Table 7.89. Apparently, Charlie, Bob, and Diana have placed orders but made no complaints so far.

id	name
73	Charlie Brown
72	Bob Johnson
74	Diana Prince

Table 7.89 Results of EXCEPT Query

That concludes our section on set operations and multitable queries. This has been an exhaustive topic, but it's just as important as the others in this chapter. We all have earned a good break now, and afterwards, we'll follow up with a set of lighter topics: string, math, and temporal functions. You'll be able to merge these functions into any query you need!

7.4 String Functions

OK, this is going to be an easy and lightweight section. If you're familiar with any programming language or at least with spreadsheet formulas, then you know that string operations are an integral part of data processing. We can merge, split, slice, and dice text values as needed, and naturally, DQL supports such operations.

We'll go over significant string functions in the following sections and inspect the examples together.

7.4.1 Concatenation

In DQL, we concatenate strings by putting the || operator between them. For instance, the expression `'Hello'` || `'World'` would give out the value *HelloWorld*. You can put in as many strings as needed.

Let's see this in action via an example. As preparation, we'll pull the list of our customers by using Listing 7.102.

```
SELECT
    id,
    name,
    address,
    phone
FROM
    customer;
```

Listing 7.102 Query for List of Customers

As a result, our list of customers looks like Table 7.90. Note that some customers have null values for phone numbers—this will become relevant shortly.

id	name	address	phone
71	Alice Smith	123 Main St	null
72	Bob Johnson	456 Elm St	555-5678
73	Charlie Brown	789 Oak St	null
74	Diana Prince	246 Pine St	555-8765
75	Eve Adams	135 Maple St	555-9876

Table 7.90 List of All Customers

Our purpose is to build a list of full customer addresses in which address and phone number are joined together. We'll take care of this requirement by using the || operator, as in Listing 7.103.

```
SELECT
    id,
    name,
    address || ' (' || phone || ')' AS full_address
FROM
    customer;
```

Listing 7.103 Query for Full Address List

The resulting list can be seen in Table 7.91—but there seems to be a slight problem, right? Even though customers 71 and 73 have valid address values, their full_address was built as null.

id	name	full_address
71	Alice Smith	null
72	Bob Johnson	456 Elm St (555-5678)
73	Charlie Brown	null
74	Diana Prince	246 Pine St (555-8765)
75	Eve Adams	135 Maple St (555-9876)

Table 7.91 Full Address List with Null Values

The reason for the null anomaly is that both customers have null values in the phone column. PostgreSQL's behavior outputs a null value if one of the concatenated strings is null.

To tackle this problem and build the `full_address` with whatever string we have at hand, we can throw in the COALESCE keyword. Although this keyword will be covered later on in Section 7.8.4, there's no harm in mentioning here that it's used to pick the first nonnull value from a chain of possible values.

In light of this information, we can modify our query as in Listing 7.104. The database engine will use the address or phone value if it exists or simply use an empty value if both of them are null.

```
SELECT
    id,
    name,
    COALESCE(address, '') || ' (' || COALESCE(phone, '') || ')' AS full_address
FROM
    customer;
```

Listing 7.104 Query for Full Address List with COALESCE Support

The results set of this enhanced query will be as in Table 7.92. See how COALESCE did its work and prevented null values from eating up entire `full_address` values?

id	name	full_address
71	Alice Smith	123 Main St ()
72	Bob Johnson	456 Elm St (555-5678)
73	Charlie Brown	789 Oak St ()
74	Diana Prince	246 Pine St (555-8765)
75	Eve Adams	135 Maple St (555-9876)

Table 7.92 Full Address List without Null Values

7.4 String Functions

It's possible to beautify our results set even further, but it's enough to understand how to concatenate strings. Section 7.8 will empower you more for that purpose.

7.4.2 LEFT and RIGHT

These keywords are useful for extracting either the first few characters or the last few characters from a string.

Our example will revolve around custom notes in orders, so let's start by fetching them with Listing 7.105.

```
SELECT
    id,
    custom_note
FROM
    customer_order;
```

Listing 7.105 Query to List Custom Order Notes

The results of this query can be seen in Table 7.93. Note that some notes have leading spaces; that's intentional for use in our upcoming examples.

id	custom_note
101	Special gift for friend.
102	Urgent order.
103	Thanks for your business.
104	Order for special event.
105	Gift for a birthday.

Table 7.93 Custom Notes in Orders

Now, let's extract some texts! See how the LEFT and RIGHT keywords were used in Listing 7.106. LEFT will extract the first five characters from each note, whereas RIGHT will extract the last five characters.

```
SELECT
    id,
    LEFT(custom_note, 5) AS first_5,
    RIGHT(custom_note, 5) AS last_5
FROM
    customer_order;
```

Listing 7.106 Extracting Substrings from Custom Notes

The results of this query can be seen in Table 7.94. If you compare it with Table 7.93, you'll see how our string functions have run as intended.

id	first_5	last_5
101	Spec	riend
102	Urgen	order
103	Tha	iness
104	Order	event
105	Gift	thday

Table 7.94 Extracted Substrings from Custom Notes

> **Leading Spaces**
>
> If the leading spaces bother you, no worries—we'll take care of them later in Section 7.4.5.

Here's a fun fact: you can combine string functions, as in Listing 7.107. Here, we used a combination of LEFT, RIGHT, and || to build shortened versions of custom notes.

```
SELECT
    id,
    LEFT(custom_note, 5) || '...' || RIGHT(custom_note, 5) AS short_note
FROM
    customer_order;
```

Listing 7.107 Combining String Functions

The results of the query can be seen in Table 7.95. Note that the first and last few characters of each custom note have been concatenated with three dots in between. Cool, right?

id	short_note
101	Spec...riend
102	Urgen...order
103	Tha...iness
104	Order...event
105	Gift...thday

Table 7.95 Shortened Custom Notes

7.4 String Functions

> **Combining String Functions**
>
> Many string functions can be nested, as in the example above. This is also valid for our upcoming string functions. In this book, we won't showcase each and every possible combination of all functions—that would be impossible. Using common sense, you can combine them as needed.

Another fun fact: you can use string functions in WHERE conditions as well, as in Listing 7.108.

```
SELECT
    id,
    name
FROM
    customer
WHERE
    LEFT(name, 3) = 'Ali';
```

Listing 7.108 Using String Functions as Conditions

The results of this query will be as shown in Table 7.96.

id	name
71	Alice Smith

Table 7.96 Users Whose Name Starts with Ali

> **String Functions in WHERE Conditions**
>
> You can use many string functions as conditions, but you should be aware of the performance cost. In the example above, the database engine must compute the substring for each row in the table and can't leverage indexes efficiently, leading to a slow full table scan.
>
> If you expect such read operations to occur frequently, you may consider precalculating the query value (like 'Ali') in a trigger and storing it in a separate indexed column. That enables you to query the table via this new column, which will be much faster—especially as the table grows.

7.4.3 Length

We use this simple keyword to determine the length of a given string. Listing 7.109 demonstrates the basic usage of LENGTH as a calculated column.

```
SELECT
    id,
    name,
    LENGTH(name) AS name_length
FROM
    customer;
```

Listing 7.109 Usage of LENGTH as Calculated Column

The results set of this query can be seen in Table 7.97, in which the length (in letters) of each customer's name has been calculated.

id	name	name_length
71	Alice Smith	11
72	Bob Johnson	11
73	Charlie Brown	13
74	Diana Prince	12
75	Eve Adams	9

Table 7.97 Customer Names and Name Lengths

Like many DQL functions, you can use the LENGTH function as a WHERE condition as well—as demonstrated in Listing 7.110, in which only customers with long names are selected.

```
SELECT
    id,
    name
FROM
    customer
WHERE
    LENGTH(name) > 11;
```

Listing 7.110 Usage of LENGTH as Condition

See the results set in Table 7.98 and note that the WHERE condition worked properly and returned only customers with long names.

id	name
73	Charlie Brown
74	Diana Prince

Table 7.98 Customers with Long Names

7.4.4 LOWER and UPPER

We use this pair of keywords to convert a string to either lowercase or uppercase. See their usage in Listing 7.111.

```
SELECT
    id,
    LOWER(name) AS low_name,
    UPPER(name) AS up_name
FROM
    customer;
```

Listing 7.111 Query to Convert Customer Names to Lowercase and Uppercase

The results set of this query is not hard to guess, and it can be seen in Table 7.99.

id	low_name	up_name
71	alice smith	ALICE SMITH
72	bob johnson	BOB JOHNSON
73	charlie brown	CHARLIE BROWN
74	diana prince	DIANA PRINCE
75	eve adams	EVE ADAMS

Table 7.99 Customer Names in Lowercase and Uppercase

Ignoring the performance cost, let's get a bit more adventurous! Listing 7.112 showcases a query in which two familiar string functions are nested in a WHERE condition.

```
SELECT
    id,
    name
FROM
    customer
WHERE
    RIGHT(UPPER(name), 1) = 'N';
```

Listing 7.112 Combining String Functions in WHERE Condition

For each row, the database engine will execute the UPPER inner function first and build the uppercase name. Then, using the uppercase value, the database engine will apply the RIGHT outer function and determine the rightmost character. Finally, it will apply the filter regarding the N value.

You can understand this approach better by looking at Table 7.100, where you can follow the execution order of the condition from left to right.

7　Data Query Language

Customer Name	Uppercase	Rightmost Char.	Is 'N'?
Alice Smith	ALICE SMITH	H	false
Bob Johnson	BOB JOHNSON	N	true
Charlie Brown	CHARLIE BROWN	N	true
Diana Prince	DIANA PRINCE	E	false
Eve Adams	EVE ADAMS	S	false

Table 7.100 Execution Schema

Only the second and third rows match our condition, so the query will return only those customers.

> **Merged Functions**
>
> When functions are nested as in our latest example, the execution will start from the innermost function and move toward the outermost function.
>
> If you've a nested call like *f1(f2(f3(f4(x))))*, the execution order will be as in *f4 – f3 – f2 – f1*, just like in math!

7.4.5　LTRIM, RTRIM, and TRIM

We use these functions to get rid of the leading or trailing spaces of a string. LTRIM stands for *left trim* and removes any leading spaces, whereas RTRIM stands for *right trim* and removes any trailing spaces.

If you want to apply both simultaneously, you can simply use the function TRIM and be done with it.

Listing 7.113 demonstrates the usage of one of these simple functions, which remove any leading or trailing spaces in custom order notes. Naturally, this removal affects the results set only—not the original data in our customer_order table.

```
SELECT
    id,
    custom_note,
    TRIM(custom_note) AS trimmed_note
FROM
    customer_order;
```

Listing 7.113 Usage of TRIM in Query

366

The results set of this query will be as in Table 7.101. Note that TRIM affected the rows for 101, 103, and 105, where leading spaces were present. It didn't have any effect on 102 and 104, where leading spaces weren't present.

id	custom_note	trimmed_note
101	Special gift for friend.	Special gift for friend.
102	Urgent order.	Urgent order.
103	Thanks for your business.	Thanks for your business.
104	Order for special event.	Order for special event.
105	Gift for a birthday.	Gift for a birthday.

Table 7.101 Trimmed Custom Notes

Here's a little exercise: if you want to calculate the net length of a string, excluding leading and trailing spaces, you can nest LENGTH and TRIM functions as in Listing 7.114.

```
SELECT
    id,
    LENGTH(custom_note) AS gross_note_len,
    LENGTH(TRIM(custom_note)) AS net_note_len
FROM
    customer_order;
```

Listing 7.114 Nesting LENGTH and TRIM

The results of this query can be seen in Table 7.102. Note the difference between gross and net lengths. The gross LENGTH() value contains leading and trailing spaces, while the net LENGTH(TRIM()) value doesn't.

id	gross_note_len	net_note_len
101	24	23
102	12	12
103	26	24
104	23	23
105	20	19

Table 7.102 Gross and Net String Lengths

7.4.6 REVERSE

This simple and eccentric function can reverse strings. Self-explanatory, right? An example query can be seen in Listing 7.115.

```
SELECT
    id,
    name,
    REVERSE(name) AS rev_name
FROM
    customer;
```

Listing 7.115 Query for Reverse Customer Names

The results of this query are exactly what you'd expect. See Table 7.103.

Id	name	rev_name
71	Alice Smith	htimS ecilA
72	Bob Johnson	nosnhoJ boB
73	Charlie Brown	nworB eilrahC
74	Diana Prince	ecnirP anaiD
75	Eve Adams	smadA evE

Table 7.103 Reverse Customer Names

7.4.7 SUBSTRING

SUBSTRING has a functionality that's similar to that of LEFT and RIGHT. We've used LEFT to extract leading characters from a string and RIGHT to extract trailing characters from a string. On the other hand, we use SUBSTRING to extract characters from the middle of the string.

To see SUBSTRING in action and compare and contrast the differences between these similar functions, check Listing 7.116.

```
SELECT
    id,
    name,
    SUBSTRING(name, 7, 3) AS mid_7_3
FROM
    customer;
```

Listing 7.116 Query Containing SUBSTRING

SUBSTRING will take three parameters: string input, starting position for extraction, and number of characters to extract. In our query, we've provided the values (name, 7, 3) for that. If you check the results set in Table 7.104, the behavior of the function should become clear.

id	name	mid_7_3
71	Alice Smith	Smi
72	Bob Johnson	hns
73	Charlie Brown	e B
74	Diana Prince	Pri
75	Eve Adams	ams

Table 7.104 Strings Extracted from Customer Names

For each name, the database engine determined three characters, starting from position 7, and extracted them into a new results set column. You can count the character positions under the name column (including spaces) and come to the same conclusion.

> **Substring Offset**
>
> If you provide offset/length values that exceed the actual length of the input string, the database engine will silently return empty of cutoff values that may be shorter than what you'd expect.
>
> For example, SUBSTRING('KEREM', 5, 9) will merely return the value M because there are no further characters beyond the fifth character. SUBSTRING('KEREM', 6, 9) will return an empty value for the same reason.
>
> In this example, if your client application expects nine characters in return, it may be disappointed (but hopefully not crash) in some cases. It's a best practice to check the length of the input string in critical cases.

7.4.8 Regular Expressions

Regular expressions are some of the staples of string processing. Some programmers love it, some dislike it, but everyone has to use it eventually. DQL is no exception to that.

In a nutshell, *regular expressions* (regexes) are sequences of characters that define a search pattern. They are typically used to test whether a string matches a certain pattern. This mechanism makes many mundane tasks easier, including input validation (like email formatting), string matching, and data extraction.

7 Data Query Language

Each regex is a formula of its own and signifies a string pattern. For example, the regex `^[abcde]+$` asserts a formula that the string should contain only the characters a, b, c, d, and e—and nothing else. Comparing the `bad` string to it returns true because it contains only those characters. On the other hand, comparing the `draft` string to it returns false because it contains different characters as well.

Some further regular expression samples can be seen in Table 7.105.

Regular Expression	Explanation	Matching String	Nonmatching String
`^[a-zA-Z0-9]+$`	Alphanumeric string with no special characters	abc123	abc_123!
`^[A-Z].*$`	String starting with a capital letter	HelloWorld	helloWorld
`^\d{5}$`	Five-digit number	12345	1234
`[aeiou]{2}`	Two consecutive vowels	cooperation	corporate
`\.com$`	String ending with .com	example.com	example.org
`^[a-zA-Z0-9._%+-]+@[a-zA-Z0-9.-]+\.[a-zA-Z]{2,}$`	Email format	info@example.com	info example
`^(?=.*o)(?=.*n).+$`	String containing o and n	Bob Johnson	Alice Smith

Table 7.105 Sample Regular Expressions

> **Regular Expressions**
>
> Teaching you how to build regular expression formulas is beyond the scope of this book. Instead, we'll focus on how to use regular expressions in DQL. If you want an in-depth understanding of regular expression formulas, you can consult your favorite search engine; there are countless online tutorials and playgrounds in which to learn this subject.

Let's learn how to use a regular expression in DQL. We'll use the last row of Table 7.105 to run a query, looking for customers with the letters *o* and *n* in their names. Check Listing 7.117.

```
SELECT
    id,
    name
```

370

```
FROM
    customer
WHERE
    name ~ '^(?=.*o)(?=.*n).+$';
```
Listing 7.117 Regular Expression Query

In this common-looking query, we use our regular expression in the last line. Table 7.106 breaks it down into parts.

Token	Description
name	Name of column
~	Regular expression operator, instead of =
'^(?=.*o)(?=.*n).+$'	Regular expression in quotes

Table 7.106 Regular Expression Query Line in Depth

Clear, right? Once you have a regular expression in hand, applying it to DQL is not difficult. Instead of using the common expression = { value } for value checks, we used the expression ~ { regex }.

When you execute this regular expression query, the result set will be as in Table 7.107. Note that we only have customers with names matching our regular expression.

id	name
72	Bob Johnson
73	Charlie Brown

Table 7.107 Customers Containing the Letters o and n in Their Names

Cool, right? But wait, there's more.

We use the ~ operator to run a case-sensitive regex match. In the example above, we would miss customers with a capital *O* and *N* in their names. To mitigate that potential problem, we can also use the ~* operator to run a case-insensitive regex match. Listing 7.118 contains an example in which we query customers having the letters *a* and *s* in their names, in either lowercase or uppercase.

```
SELECT
    id,
    name
FROM
    customer
```

7 Data Query Language

```
WHERE
    name ~* 'a.*s|s.*a';
```

Listing 7.118 Case-Insensitive Regular Expression Query

See the result set in Table 7.108, where it's clear that the regular expression of case-insensitive pattern worked fine.

id	name
71	Alice Smith
75	Eve Adams

Table 7.108 Customers with Letters a and s in Their Names (Case Insensitive)

A cool built-in function related to regular expressions is called regexp_matches. We use this function to expose how a string matches the given regular expression. Check Listing 7.119 to see it in action. We've used the previous regular expression, but this time, it's case sensitive.

```
SELECT
    id,
    name,
    REGEXP_MATCHES(name, 'a.*s|s.*a')
FROM
    customer;
```

Listing 7.119 Usage Example of regexp_matches

The results of this query can be seen in Table 7.109, which clarifies the usage of regexp_matches. The ams substring was extracted from the Eve Adams string because it's the part that matches the regular expression. This functionality is especially useful in testing complex regular expressions against test datasets.

id	name	regexp_matches
75	Eve Adams	{ams}

Table 7.109 Results of regexp_matches

Another useful regex function is regex_replace, which we use to execute a find-and-replace operation using regex patterns. Substrings matching the given regex will be replaced with another value. We'll use the same example as before to demonstrate this function. See Listing 7.120.

```
SELECT
    id,
    name,
    REGEXP_REPLACE(name, 'a.*s|s.*a', '#')
FROM
    customer
WHERE
    id = 75;
```

Listing 7.120 Usage Example of regex_replace

This function takes three parameters, which are broken down in Table 7.110.

Parameters	Descriptions	Sample Values in Query
1	String to process	name
2	Regular expression to search	'a.*s|s.*a'
3	New value to set	'#'

Table 7.110 Parameters of regex_replace

The results set of this query will be as in Table 7.111. Note how the substring matching the regular expression has been replaced with #, just as we intended.

id	name	regexp_replace
75	Eve Adams	Eve Ad#

Table 7.111 Results of regex_replace Query

This concludes our chapter on string functions. Our DQL journey will continue with a similar topic: numbers instead of strings.

7.5 Math and Numeric Functions

In this section, we'll review mathematical functions in DQL. These are useful for running calculations and using the numerical results however necessary. We'll go over significant math functions and review examples together.

7.5.1 Math Operators

Let's get the obvious out of the way first. Basic math operators for addition, subtraction, multiplication, and division are naturally supported by DQL. These operators are,

7   Data Query Language

in the same order, +, -, *, and /. Listing 7.121 showcases a demonstration in which multiple math operations are used together to calculate VAT amounts.

```
SELECT
    invoice_id,
    invoice_item_no,
    amount,
    vat_rate,
    amount * (vat_rate / 100) AS vat_amt
FROM
    invoice_item;
```

Listing 7.121 Math Operators in Query

Note that we've used parentheses alongside math operators, just as you would in basic trigonometry. That's a good approach to leaving no room for errors regarding the priority of operators. The results set of this query can be seen in Table 7.112.

invoice_id	invoice_item_no	amount	vat_rate	vat_amt
501	1	18.99	20.00	3.798
502	1	105.00	20.00	21
502	2	50.00	20.00	10
503	1	105.00	20.00	21
504	1	40.00	20.00	8

Table 7.112 Results Set with Calculated vat_amt Column

We can use math operators in WHERE conditions as well, as demonstrated in Listing 7.122.

```
SELECT
    invoice_id,
    invoice_item_no,
    amount
FROM
    invoice_item
WHERE
    amount * (vat_rate / 100) > 20;
```

Listing 7.122 Math Operators in WHERE Condition

In this query, the database engine will calculate the value of amount * (vat_rate / 100) for each invoice_item row, and if the value is greater than 20, the row will be added to the results set. The results set of this query will be as in Table 7.113, which is a natural subset of Table 7.112.

invoice_id	invoice_item_no	amount
502	1	105.00
503	1	105.00

Table 7.113 Results Set of Query

> **Math in WHERE Conditions**
>
> You saw a performance warning regarding string functions in where conditions in Section 7.4.2. The same warning applies to math functions.
>
> You can use many math functions as conditions, but you should be aware of the performance cost. In the previous example, the database engine must compute the numeric value for each row in the table and can't leverage indexes efficiently, leading to a slow full-table scan.
>
> If you expect such read operations to occur frequently, you may consider precalculating the query value (like vat_amt) in a trigger and storing it in a separate indexed column. That enables you to query the table via this new column, which will be much faster—especially as the table grows.

There are two further operators we're going to address that are used less frequently but are very useful when needed.

We use the % operator to calculate the remainder of a division. We typically use it to check whether the remainder of an operation is zero—that way, we can find out whether a number is odd or even, for instance. Listing 7.123 showcases this operator in action.

```
SELECT
    id,
    name,
    id % 2 AS id_odd_even
FROM
    customer;
```

Listing 7.123 Separation of Customers by Their IDs as Odd or Even

The results set of this query can be seen in Table 7.114. Note how the id_odd_even column can be determined to differentiate customer IDs as odd or even. Values of 1 point out odd customers, while values of 0 point out even customers.

id	name	id_odd_even
71	Alice Smith	1
72	Bob Johnson	0
73	Charlie Brown	1
74	Diana Prince	0
75	Eve Adams	1

Table 7.114 Results Set of % Query

We use the ^ operator to calculate exponentiations, and it raises the left operand to the power of the right operand. Listing 7.124 demonstrates the usage of this operator to calculate the squared value of product prices.

```
SELECT
    id,
    name,
    price,
    price ^ 2 AS price_squared
FROM
    product
WHERE
    category_id = 'ACC';
```

Listing 7.124 Sample Query Showcasing ^ Operator

The results set of the query will be as in Table 7.115. Note how the price values have been squared using the price ^ 2 expression.

id	name	price	price_squared
BAG	Bag	60	3600
BELT	Belt	25	625

Table 7.115 Prices Squared with ^ Operator

7.5.2 ABS

We use this simple function to calculate the absolute value of a given number. ABS(-5) would return a result of 5, and naturally, ABS(5) would return a result of 5 as well. In a query, we typically use the ABS function with columns.

To see this function in action, we'll review orders and products. Figure 7.27 contains a memory refresher regarding the order_item and product tables. The order_item table contains the items in customer orders, while the product table contains the master data for each available product.

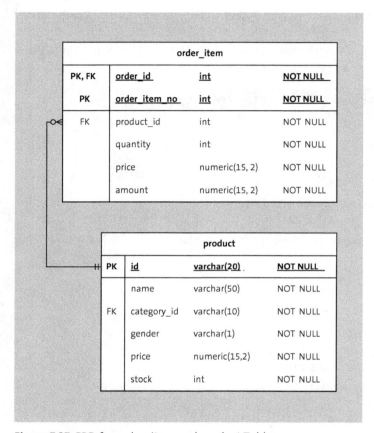

Figure 7.27 ERD for order_item and product Tables

In this design, order_item.price contains the historical product price on the date of the order, while product.price contains the current price of a product. As prices of products change over time, these values are bound to differ, eventually. Clear, right?

Listing 7.125 contains a query that detects order items with prices that deviate from current product prices.

```
SELECT
    o.order_id,
    o.order_item_no,
    o.price AS order_price,
    p.price AS current_product_price
FROM
    order_item AS o
    INNER JOIN product AS p ON p.id = o.product_id
```

```
WHERE
    o.price <> p.price;
```
Listing 7.125 Query to Find Order Items with Prices that Deviate from Current Product Prices

The results set of this query can be seen in Table 7.116. Note that we've increased prices in some rows and decreased prices in others.

order_id	order_item_no	order_price	current_product_price
101	1	18.99	19.99
102	1	105.00	100.00
103	2	40.00	45.00

Table 7.116 Order Items with Deviating Product Prices

If we were to calculate the price difference for each row, we could initially do it using math operators as in Listing 7.126.

```
SELECT
    o.order_id,
    o.order_item_no,
    o.price AS order_price,
    p.price AS current_product_price,
    o.price - p.price as price_diff
FROM
    order_item AS o
    INNER JOIN product AS p ON p.id = o.product_id
WHERE
    o.price <> p.price;
```
Listing 7.126 Calculation of Price Deviations

The results set of this query will be as in Table 7.117. Note that `price_diff` contains a negative number for decreased prices and a positive number for increased prices.

order_id	order_item_no	order_price	current_product_price	price_diff
101	1	18.99	19.99	−1.00
102	1	105.00	100.00	5.00
103	2	40.00	45.00	−5.00

Table 7.117 Calculated Price Deviations

What if we don't care whether the price has been decreased or increased, and we simply need the absolute value of the price deviation? You guessed right: we'll use the ABS math function, as in Listing 7.127.

```
SELECT
    o.order_id,
    o.order_item_no,
    o.price AS order_price,
    p.price AS current_product_price,
    ABS(o.price - p.price) AS abs_price_diff
FROM
    order_item AS o
    INNER JOIN product AS p ON p.id = o.product_id
WHERE
    o.price <> p.price;
```

Listing 7.127 Calculation of Absolute Price Deviations

The results set containing the absolute values will be as in Table 7.118.

order_id	order_item_no	order_price	current_product_price	abs_price_diff
101	1	18.99	19.99	1.00
102	1	105.00	100.00	5.00
103	2	40.00	45.00	5.00

Table 7.118 Calculated Absolute Price Deviations

7.5.3 RANDOM

As its name suggests, the RANDOM function is used to generate random numbers. It will return a value between 0 and 1, which is ideal for many machine learning enthusiasts!

To generate a single random number, you can use the query in Listing 7.128. The result can't be expressed, because every time you execute this query, it will return a random number—so you need to execute it yourself.

```
SELECT RANDOM() AS rnd_no;
```

Listing 7.128 Generation of Single Random Number

A typical use case for RANDOM is to shuffle rows of a table. Imagine that you want to send a gift to three random customers. Lucky customers can easily be determined by Listing 7.129, which would return different customers every time you execute it.

7 Data Query Language

```
SELECT
    id,
    name
FROM
    customer
ORDER BY
    RANDOM()
LIMIT
    3;
```

Listing 7.129 Query Returning Three Random Customers

7.5.4 ROUND, FLOOR, and CEILING

Rounding numbers is one of the core requirements of programming, and DQL naturally empowers us with the typical functions for that: `ROUND`, `FLOOR` and `CEILING`.

To build our case study, we'll use Listing 7.130, which calculates the average price and VAT amount for each product category.

```
SELECT
    p.category_id,
    AVG(o.price) AS avg_price,
    AVG(i.vat_amount) AS avg_vat
FROM
    invoice_item AS i
    INNER JOIN delivery_item AS d ON d.delivery_id = i.delivery_id
    AND d.delivery_item_no = i.delivery_item_no
    INNER JOIN order_item AS o ON o.order_id = d.order_id
    AND o.order_item_no = d.order_item_no
    INNER JOIN product AS p ON p.id = o.product_id
GROUP BY
    p.category_id;
```

Listing 7.130 Calculation of Average Price and VAT Amount by Product Category

Although the query is a bit comprehensive, we aren't really interested in the details of it. All that matters is that we have some decimal numbers at hand. See Table 7.119.

category_id	avg_price	avg_vat
TOP	52.99	15.26
ACC	25.00	10.00
BOT	40.00	8.00

Table 7.119 Average Prices and VAT Amounts by Product Category

Now that we have our core results set, we can review how rounding functions affect the results. Let's start with ROUND. See the enhanced query in Listing 7.131.

```
SELECT
    p.category_id,
    ROUND(AVG(o.price)) AS avg_price,
    ROUND(AVG(i.vat_amount)) AS avg_vat
FROM
    invoice_item AS i
    INNER JOIN delivery_item AS d ON d.delivery_id = i.delivery_id
    AND d.delivery_item_no = i.delivery_item_no
    INNER JOIN order_item AS o ON o.order_id = d.order_id
    AND o.order_item_no = d.order_item_no
    INNER JOIN product AS p ON p.id = o.product_id
GROUP BY
    p.category_id;
```

Listing 7.131 Query Enhanced with ROUND

See the enhanced values in Table 7.120 and note that 52.99 has been rounded up to 53 and 15.26 has been rounded down to 15. That's the natural behavior of ROUND—it rounds decimals to the nearest whole number.

category_id	avg_price	avg_vat
TOP	53	15
ACC	25	10
BOT	40	8

Table 7.120 Values Enhanced with ROUND

If you want to force the ROUND operation strictly towards the higher number, you can use the CEILING function instead, as in Listing 7.132.

```
SELECT
    p.category_id,
    CEILING(AVG(o.price)) AS avg_price,
    CEILING(AVG(i.vat_amount)) AS avg_vat
FROM
    invoice_item AS i
    INNER JOIN delivery_item AS d ON d.delivery_id = i.delivery_id
    AND d.delivery_item_no = i.delivery_item_no
    INNER JOIN order_item AS o ON o.order_id = d.order_id
    AND o.order_item_no = d.order_item_no
    INNER JOIN product AS p ON p.id = o.product_id
```

```
GROUP BY
    p.category_id;
```

Listing 7.132 Query Enhanced with CEILING

Note how the values have been strictly rounded up in Table 7.121.

category_id	avg_price	avg_vat
TOP	53	16
ACC	25	10
BOT	40	8

Table 7.121 Values Enhanced with CEILING

In contrast, you can use the FLOOR function to round values strictly down, as in Listing 7.133.

```
SELECT
    p.category_id,
    FLOOR(AVG(o.price)) AS avg_price,
    FLOOR(AVG(i.vat_amount)) AS avg_vat
FROM
    invoice_item AS i
    INNER JOIN delivery_item AS d ON d.delivery_id = i.delivery_id
    AND d.delivery_item_no = i.delivery_item_no
    INNER JOIN order_item AS o ON o.order_id = d.order_id
    AND o.order_item_no = d.order_item_no
    INNER JOIN product AS p ON p.id = o.product_id
GROUP BY
    p.category_id;
```

Listing 7.133 Query Enhanced with FLOOR

Note how the values have been strictly rounded down in Table 7.122.

category_id	avg_price	avg_vat
TOP	52	15
ACC	25	10
BOT	40	8

Table 7.122 Values Enhanced with FLOOR

7.5.5 SIGN

This function tells us whether a number is negative or positive. SIGN(42) would return 1 because the number is positive, whereas SIGN(-42) would return ?1 because the number is negative.

To see this function in context, we'll revisit the case study in Section 7.5.2 and evaluate the differences between historical order prices and current product prices. In Listing 7.134, we use the SIGN function to determine whether a product price has been increased or decreased.

```
SELECT
    o.order_id,
    o.order_item_no,
    o.price AS order_price,
    p.price AS current_product_price,
    o.price - p.price AS price_diff,
    SIGN(o.price - p.price) AS price_diff_sign
FROM
    order_item AS o
    INNER JOIN product AS p ON p.id = o.product_id
WHERE
    o.price <> p.price;
```

Listing 7.134 Usage of SIGN in Context

See the price_diff_sign column in Table 7.123, where 1 indicates that the price difference is positive and ?1 indicates that the price difference is negative.

order_id	order_item_no	order_price	current_product_price	price_diff	price_diff_sign
101	1	18.99	19.99	−1.00	−1
102	1	105.00	100.00	5.00	1
103	2	40.00	45.00	−5.00	−1

Table 7.123 Product Price Change of Direction

This concludes our section on math functions. Leaving string and math functions behind, we'll move forward with a topic in the same family: temporal functions.

7.6 Temporal Functions

The topic of temporal functions covers date manipulations. In this section, we'll inspect commonly used functions in this category.

7.6.1 Interval Calculations

As you would naturally expect, you can execute date calculations in DQL, where you add or subtract values to or from base dates. Listing 7.135 contains an example in which we add three days to req_dlv_date by using the INTERVAL keyword. Note that INTERVAL is followed by a natural language input, and PostgreSQL is able to handle that.

```
SELECT
    id,
    req_dlv_date,
    req_dlv_date + INTERVAL '3 days' AS dlv_date_deadline
FROM
    customer_order
WHERE
    req_dlv_date IS NOT NULL;
```

Listing 7.135 Adding Three Days to Base Date

The results set can be seen in Table 7.124, which lists the original dates and calculated dates next to each other.

id	req_dlv_date	dlv_date_deadline
102	2024-10-01	2024-10-04
103	2024-10-05	2024-10-08
105	2024-09-20	2024-09-23

Table 7.124 Calculated Dates

We can use INTERVAL for time values as well. Take a look at Listing 7.136, where we add 10 minutes to existing timestamp values.

```
SELECT
    id,
    order_ts,
    order_ts + INTERVAL '10 minutes' AS order_ts_plus_10
FROM
    customer_order;
```

Listing 7.136 Using INTERVAL for Time Calculation

The results set in Table 7.125 is how you expect it to be—10 minutes have been added to the original order timestamp.

id	order_ts	order_ts_plus_10
101	2024-09-23 15:47:22	2024-09-23 15:57:22
102	2024-09-23 15:47:22	2024-09-23 15:57:22
103	2024-09-23 15:47:22	2024-09-23 15:57:22
104	2024-09-23 15:47:22	2024-09-23 15:57:22
105	2024-09-23 15:47:22	2024-09-23 15:57:22

Table 7.125 Calculated Timestamps

As an exercise, you can try further natural language INTERVAL values. It's fun, and most of your attempts will produce valid results!

7.6.2 Current Date and Time

Our DQL toolbox contains three practical keywords we use to fetch the current temporal values, and they are demonstrated in Listing 7.137.

```
SELECT
    CURRENT_DATE AS cda,
    CURRENT_TIME AS cti,
    CURRENT_TIMESTAMP AS cts;
```

Listing 7.137 Keywords to Determine Current Temporal Values

Although the results set will be similar to the one in Table 7.126, the exact values will differ in your attempt. You'll get the temporal values of the date and time you're executing in the sample code.

cda	cti	cts
2024-10-07	13:57:12.224930+03:00	2024-10-07 13:57:12.22493+03

Table 7.126 Current Temporal Values

We'll use some of these keywords in the upcoming examples.

7.6.3 Date Differences

We can calculate the difference between two dates as well. In Listing 7.138, we calculate two values using that technique. The req_dlv_span entry will represent the duration between the requested delivery date and the order creation date, whereas req_dlv_delay will represent any delay of the delivery.

```
SELECT
    id AS order_id,
    req_dlv_date - order_ts AS req_dlv_span,
    CURRENT_DATE - req_dlv_date AS req_dlv_delay
FROM
    customer_order
WHERE
    req_dlv_date IS NOT NULL;
```

Listing 7.138 Date Difference Calculations

Check the result set in Table 7.127. The req_dlv_span entry contains days and hours, simply because order_ts is a timestamp column containing the date and time, so the result contains high granularity including the time difference as well. On the other hand, req_dlv_delay contains a simple day difference because both CURRENT_DATE and req_dlv_date are dates without time.

order_id	req_dlv_span	req_dlv_delay
102	7 days 08:12:37	5
103	11 days 08:12:37	1
105	−3 days −15:47:22	16

Table 7.127 Calculated Date Differences

Here's a practical tip: you can combine aggregate functions with date differences as in Listing 7.139, where we calculate average values for previous values.

```
SELECT
    AVG(req_dlv_date - order_ts) AS avg_span,
    AVG(CURRENT_DATE - req_dlv_date) AS avg_delay
FROM
    customer_order
WHERE
    req_dlv_date IS NOT NULL;
```

Listing 7.139 Date Difference Aggregation

The results set in Table 7.128 is exactly what you'd expect.

avg_span	avg_delay
5 days 00:12:37.655131	7.33

Table 7.128 Calculated Date Difference Averages

7.6.4 Extracting Date Parts

Using the EXTRACT keyword, we can extract day, month, year, hour, etc., values from a given date. Listing 7.140 showcases a query in which many extraction options are demoed. Most are self-explanatory, but DOW stands for the day of the week and retrieves a value of 1 for Monday, 2 for Tuesday, etc.

```
SELECT
    id,
    invoice_ts,
    EXTRACT( DAY FROM invoice_ts ) AS dy,
    EXTRACT( MONTH FROM invoice_ts ) AS mo,
    EXTRACT( YEAR FROM invoice_ts ) AS yr,
    EXTRACT( HOUR FROM invoice_ts ) AS hr,
    EXTRACT( MINUTE FROM invoice_ts ) AS mn,
    EXTRACT( SECOND FROM invoice_ts ) AS sc,
    EXTRACT( DOW FROM invoice_ts ) AS dw
FROM
    invoice
WHERE
    id = 501;
```

Listing 7.140 Date Part Extraction

The results of the query will be as in Table 7.129. Note how the date has been sliced and diced into different columns.

id	invoice_ts	dy	mo	yr	hr	mn	sc	dw
501	2024-09-23 15:47:22	23	9	2024	15	47	22	1

Table 7.129 Extracted Date Parts

As in many other DQL functions, we can use extracted date parts in WHERE conditions as long as we ignore the aforementioned performance penalty. Listing 7.141 showcases such a query, which calls invoices created on a Monday.

```
SELECT
    id,
    invoice_ts
FROM
    invoice
WHERE
    EXTRACT( dow FROM invoice_ts ) = 1;
```

Listing 7.141 Querying Invoices Created on Monday

The results of the query will be as in Table 7.130. Since 2024-09-23 is a Monday, we get invoices created on that date.

id	invoice_ts
501	2024-09-23 15:47:22
502	2024-09-23 15:47:22
503	2024-09-23 15:47:22
504	2024-09-23 15:47:22

Table 7.130 Invoices Created on Monday

7.6.5 Time Zones

Time zones can be a rather important subject, especially if you're dealing with international data from different continents. In PostgreSQL, we have two primary data types for handling time zones that are explained in Table 7.131.

Data Types	Descriptions
timestamp	This is a timestamp without a time zone. It stores date and time values without any time zone information.
timestamptz	This is a timestamp with time zone. It stores both date and time values along with the time zone information. Internally, it's stored in Coordinated Universal Time (UTC) and converted to the specified time zone when displayed.

Table 7.131 Time Zone Data Types

Now that you understand your data type options, let's move on to common functions related to the subject.

To set the time zone of the current session, we can use the SET TIMEZONE command as in Listing 7.142. Natural language inputs are supported for time zone names, and this is a convenient and clear approach.

```
SET TIMEZONE = 'America/New_York';
```

Listing 7.142 Setting Time Zone to New York

> **Time Zone Names**
>
> Usable time zone names are stored in the pg_timezone_names table. You can query this table to get a list of usable expressions.

To convert an existing timestamp to another time zone, we use the AT TIME ZONE expression. For instance, our `delivery.delivery_ts` is a `timestamp` field (without a time zone). Listing 7.143 demonstrates the time zone conversion in that field.

```
SELECT
    id,
    delivery_ts,
    delivery_ts AT TIME ZONE 'America/New_York' AS ny_to_local
FROM
    delivery
WHERE
    id = 301;
```

Listing 7.143 Applying AT TIME ZONE in timestamp Column

The time zone conversion results can be seen in Table 7.132. The database engine has assumed that the original timestamp of `2024-09-23 15:47:22` was recorded at `America/New_York` and has converted it to the session time zone as `2024-09-23 22:47:22+03`. The output value may be different depending on your local time zone, but note that `ny_to_local` has a time zone suffix of +03.

id	delivery_ts	ny_to_local
301	2024-09-23 15:47:22	2024-09-23 22:47:22+03

Table 7.132 Time Zone Conversion Results

If your input timestamp is of the `timestamptz` type (with a time zone), the database engine already knows the source time zone. AT TIME ZONE simply converts the source time zone to the provided target time zone.

Having just completed a set of lightweight topics, we should be rested enough for a relatively heavyweight topic: window functions! But don't be disheartened; now that you know about multitable queries, the concept should be easy for you to follow.

7.7 Window Functions

We've arrived a topic that will make your life as a developer much easier. Window functions offer the benefit of reducing some calculations into a single query instead of multiple related queries.

In a nutshell, we use *window functions* to perform calculations across a set of rows that are related to the current row. Window functions are different from aggregate functions in that related rows won't collapse into a single aggregate row. Instead, each row stays intact and becomes a new calculated column.

7 Data Query Language

This may be hard to imagine before seeing it in action, so let's review all the window functions to make them understandable.

7.7.1 RANK

For starters, let's take a look at our product prices via Listing 7.144.

```
SELECT
    id,
    category_id,
    name,
    price
FROM
    product
ORDER BY
    price DESC;
```

Listing 7.144 Initial Query for Product Prices

That's a simple one without any bells and whistles (yet)—we're just pulling product prices and ordering them from the most expensive to the least expensive. The output can be seen in Table 7.133.

Id	category_id	name	price
BLZ	TOP	Blazer	100.00
JKT	TOP	Jacket	100.00
BAG	ACC	Bag	60.00
PNT	BOT	Pants	50.00
SKT	BOT	Skirt	45.00
SHIR	TOP	Shirt	35.00
BELT	ACC	Belt	25.00
TEE	TOP	T-shirt	19.99

Table 7.133 Products Sorted by Price

Now, what if we need a new column to rank our products? In this new column, the most expensive product will get the value 1, the second most expensive will get the value 2, etc.

Some approaches could be as follows:

- Adding a `price_rank` column to the database table and keeping it up-to-date with a trigger could work, but this approach would bring a performance overhead on every DML command.
- Following the initial query, we could do a manual rank calculation via cursors, but this would lead to us having a complex and possibly slow code.

Actually, a window function is all we need to achieve this goal! It will add the new column, calculate the rank of each product, and put in the appropriate rank number automatically—in a single query, with a single command. See the enhanced query in Listing 7.145, where the RANK window function has been added.

```
SELECT
    id,
    category_id,
    name,
    price,
    RANK() OVER (ORDER BY price DESC) AS price_rank
FROM
    product
ORDER BY
    price DESC;
```

Listing 7.145 Query Enhanced with RANK Window Function

Before discussing the syntax, let's see the results set first. See the new `price_rank` column in Table 7.134.

id	category_id	name	price	price_rank
BLZ	TOP	Blazer	100.00	1
JKT	TOP	Jacket	100.00	1
BAG	ACC	Bag	60.00	3
PNT	BOT	Pants	50.00	4
SKT	BOT	Skirt	45.00	5
SHIR	TOP	Shirt	35.00	6
BELT	ACC	Belt	25.00	7
TEE	TOP	T-shirt	19.99	8

Table 7.134 Ranked Product Prices

7   Data Query Language

Isn't that beautiful? The RANK function did all the hard work for us and assigned a rank number to each product row. Note that two products sharing the same price became the same rank of 1, rank 2 was skipped, and the next most expensive became the rank of 3. That's just the natural behavior of the RANK function. Shortly, we'll see alternative window functions that behave slightly differently.

Now that you've seen the output, the syntax of RANK should be rather self-explanatory. Let's put it under the magnifying glass in Listing 7.146.

```
RANK() OVER (ORDER BY price DESC) AS price_rank
```

Listing 7.146   RANK Under Magnifying Glass

We started with the RANK() OVER expression, which is the standard. Following that, we provided the ranking formula in parenthesis as (ORDER BY price DESC). This tells the database engine to sort the intermediate results set by price in descending order and conduct the ranking accordingly.

To get a clearer overview of the execution order, take a look at Table 7.135.

Execution Order	Operation
1	The first four columns were prepared.
2	The window function was executed over the first four columns and the price_rank was calculated.
3	The final output with five columns was published.

Table 7.135   Execution Order of Query

> **Window Function Execution Order**
>
> Window functions execute after WHERE, GROUP BY, and HAVING clauses, but before ORDER BY.

In our latest example, we built a price rank among all product rows. It's also possible to build ranks within subgroups of rows. For instance, we can rank products by price *within their product category*. To achieve that goal, we have to make a small extension to the RANK window function, as in Listing 7.147.

```
SELECT
    id,
    category_id,
    name,
    price,
    RANK() OVER (PARTITION BY category_id ORDER BY price DESC) AS
cat_price_rank
```

```
FROM
    product
ORDER BY
    category_id,
    price DESC;
```

Listing 7.147 Usage of PARTITION BY to Rank Among Subgroups

We've simply added the PARTITION BY category_id expression to tell the database engine to make the ranking by category_id instead of ranking the entire list of products. Check the results set in Table 7.136 to see the independent price ranking of each product category.

id	category_id	name	price	cat_price_rank
BAG	ACC	Bag	60.00	1
BELT	ACC	Belt	25.00	2
PNT	BOT	Pants	50.00	1
SKT	BOT	Skirt	45.00	2
JKT	TOP	Jacket	100.00	1
BLZ	TOP	Blazer	100.00	1
SHIR	TOP	Shirt	35.00	3
TEE	TOP	T-shirt	19.99	4

Table 7.136 Ranked Product Prices by Category

ACC, BOT, and TOP have their own independent price rankings, and each restarts with rank 1. Cool, right?

Now, let's move forward and get to know some other window functions.

7.7.2 DENSE_RANK

DENSE_RANK is closely related to RANK, with one difference: RANK may leave blank rank values among rows, while DENSE_RANK doesn't. To demonstrate the difference, let's execute both in the same query in Listing 7.148.

```
SELECT
    id,
    category_id,
    name,
    price,
```

```
        RANK() OVER (ORDER BY price DESC) AS price_rank,
        DENSE_RANK() OVER (ORDER BY price DESC) AS price_drank
FROM
    product
ORDER BY
    price DESC;
```

Listing 7.148 RANK and DENSE_RANK in Same Query

Now check the results set in Table 7.137, where `price_rank` contains the RANK result and `price_drank` contains the DENSE_RANK result.

id	category_id	name	price	price_rank	price_drank
BLZ	TOP	Blazer	100.00	1	1
JKT	TOP	Jacket	100.00	1	1
BAG	ACC	Bag	60.00	3	2
PNT	BOT	Pants	50.00	4	3
SKT	BOT	Skirt	45.00	5	4
SHIR	TOP	Shirt	35.00	6	5
BELT	ACC	Belt	25.00	7	6
TEE	TOP	T-shirt	19.99	8	7

Table 7.137 RANK and DENSE_RANK Results in Contrast

The difference stands out in the first three rows. The first two products have the same price and also the highest price, so they've both been given a RANK and a DENSE_RANK of 1. The product on the third row has the second-highest price, so it's been given a RANK of 3 and a DENSE_RANK of 2. As stated, DENSE_RANK leaves no gaps between rank values, so depending on your requirement at hand, you can use either window function.

Now that we're familiar with window functions, let's get a bit adventurous! One of the typical use cases of window functions is to combine them with aggregate functions. For instance, we can build ranks among customers based on their total order amounts so far. We need a two-step plan for that:

1. Aggregating order amounts per customer
2. Ranking those aggregate values

The solution for that requirement will be as in Listing 7.149. Although we've used DENSE_RANK here, RANK would work equally well.

```
SELECT
    hd.customer_id,
    SUM(it.amount) AS sum_amt,
    DENSE_RANK() OVER (
        ORDER BY SUM(it.amount) DESC
    ) AS amt_rank
FROM
    customer_order AS hd
    INNER JOIN order_item AS it ON it.order_id = hd.id
GROUP BY
    hd.customer_id
ORDER BY
    sum_amt DESC;
```

Listing 7.149 Query to Rank Customers

The database engine will follow our two-step plan:

1. The intermediary list containing `customer_id` and `sum_amt` will be prepared.
2. The `sum_amt` will be dense-ranked into the `amt_rank` column.

The results set will be as in Table 7.138. Now we know the rank order of our most valuable customers!

customer_id	sum_amt	amt_rank
72	155.00	1
73	145.00	2
75	100.00	3
71	87.98	4
74	60.00	5

Table 7.138 Customers Ranked by Total Order Amounts

7.7.3 ROW NUMBER

ROW_NUMBER is another window function that's closely related to RANK and DENSE_RANK. There's a slight difference, though: ROW_NUMBER offers a unique set of rank values, even in rows with the same base value.

To demonstrate the difference, let's put all three window functions into the same query. See Listing 7.150.

7 Data Query Language

```
SELECT
    id,
    category_id,
    name,
    price,
    RANK() OVER (ORDER BY price DESC) AS price_rank,
    DENSE_RANK() OVER (ORDER BY price DESC) AS price_drank,
    ROW_NUMBER() OVER (ORDER BY price DESC) as price_row
FROM
    product
ORDER BY
    price DESC;
```

Listing 7.150 RANK, DENSE_RANK, and ROW_NUMBER in Same Query

Check the `price_row` column in Table 7.139 to see its behavior. The database engine ensured that each row got a unique rank value—even rows with the same price didn't share the same rank and got different values of 1 and 2.

id	category_id	name	price	price_rank	price_drank	price_row
BLZ	TOP	Blazer	100.00	1	1	1
JKT	TOP	Jacket	100.00	1	1	2
BAG	ACC	Bag	60.00	3	2	3
PNT	BOT	Pants	50.00	4	3	4
SKT	BOT	Skirt	45.00	5	4	5
SHIR	TOP	Shirt	35.00	6	5	6
BELT	ACC	Belt	25.00	7	6	7
TEE	TOP	T-shirt	19.99	8	7	8

Table 7.139 RANK, DENSE_RANK, and ROW_NUMBER Results

How about some more adventures? A typical use case for window functions is to use them in subqueries.

Suppose we need to find the bestselling product in each product category. To achieve that result, we can follow a three-step plan:

1. Calculate the total order quantity of each product.
2. Rank them by total order quantity.
3. Pick the product with the highest rank.

Let's start with step 1, which is rather straightforward given the DQL knowledge we have at hand. Listing 7.151 contains the query we use to calculate total order quantities per product.

```
SELECT
    pr.category_id,
    oi.product_id,
    SUM(oi.quantity) AS quan_sum
FROM
    order_item AS oi
    INNER JOIN product AS pr ON pr.id = oi.product_id
GROUP BY
    oi.product_id,
    pr.category_id
ORDER BY
    category_id,
    quan_sum DESC;
```

Listing 7.151 Calculation of Total Product Sales

The results of the query can be seen in Table 7.140. Our final goal is to extract the ACC – BELT, BOT – PNT, and TOP – SHIR rows from this raw list; they are the bestselling products of each category.

category_id	product_id	quan_sum
ACC	BELT	2
ACC	BAG	1
BOT	PNT	1
BOT	SKT	1
TOP	SHIR	3
TOP	TEE	2
TOP	BLZ	1
TOP	JKT	1

Table 7.140 Total Sales Quantities per Product

To achieve this goal, let's advance to step 2 and rank these entries using ROW_NUMBER. Depending on your requirements, you could also use another window function like RANK or DENSE_RANK. The extended query can be seen in Listing 7.152, and all we did was add a ROW_NUMBER window function to rank total product sales by category.

```
SELECT
    pr.category_id,
    oi.product_id,
    SUM(oi.quantity) AS quan_sum,
    ROW_NUMBER() OVER (
        PARTITION BY
            category_id
        ORDER BY
            SUM(oi.quantity) DESC
    ) AS row_no
FROM
    order_item AS oi
    INNER JOIN product AS pr ON pr.id = oi.product_id
GROUP BY
    oi.product_id,
    pr.category_id
ORDER BY
    category_id,
    quan_sum DESC;
```

Listing 7.152 Ranking Total Product Sales by Category

The results set of step 2 can be seen in Table 7.141; note the new row_no column, which is the result of our window function.

category_id	product_id	quan_sum	row_no
ACC	BELT	2	1
ACC	BAG	1	2
BOT	PNT	1	1
BOT	SKT	1	2
TOP	SHIR	3	1
TOP	TEE	2	2
TOP	BLZ	1	3
TOP	JKT	1	4

Table 7.141 Total Product Sales Ranked by Category

Finally, in step 3, we'll turn Listing 7.152 into a subquery and select only the highest-ranking products per category. Check Listing 7.153 for the final query and note that the outer query is merely used to select entries with row_no values of 1, which indicates the bestselling products.

```
SELECT
    category_id,
    product_id
FROM
    (
        SELECT
            pr.category_id,
            oi.product_id,
            SUM(oi.quantity) AS quan_sum,
            ROW_NUMBER() OVER (
                PARTITION BY
                    category_id
                ORDER BY
                    SUM(oi.quantity) DESC
            ) AS row_no
        FROM
            order_item AS oi
            INNER JOIN product AS pr ON pr.id = oi.product_id
        GROUP BY
            oi.product_id,
            pr.category_id
        ORDER BY
            category_id,
            quan_sum DESC
    )
WHERE
    row_no = 1;
```

Listing 7.153 Selecting Most Popular Products per Category

And voila! The final results set in Table 7.142 gives us the answer we were looking for.

category_id	product_id
ACC	BELT
BOT	PNT
TOP	SHIR

Table 7.142 Bestselling Product in Each Category

Although the results set looks like a success, there's a catch. Check the BOT category in Table 7.141. Products PNT and SKT have the exact same sales quantity but are ranked as 1 and 2 due to the behavior of the window function ROW_NUMBER. Therefore, our final

7 Data Query Language

results set in Table 7.142 says PNT is the bestselling product in the BOT category when in fact, SKT sells equally well.

That's one of the typical cases in which you need to make a smart decision on which window function to use. If you want both bestselling products to be included in the final results set, you may prefer to use the RANK or DENSE_RANK window function. These window functions will assign a rank of 1 to both products, so both will be included in the final results set.

Listing 7.154 contains the modified query, in which ROW_NUMBER has been replaced by RANK.

```
SELECT
    category_id,
    product_id
FROM
    (
        SELECT
            pr.category_id,
            oi.product_id,
            SUM(oi.quantity) AS quan_sum,
            RANK() OVER (
                PARTITION BY
                    category_id
                ORDER BY
                    SUM(oi.quantity) DESC
            ) AS row_no
        FROM
            order_item AS oi
            INNER JOIN product AS pr ON pr.id = oi.product_id
        GROUP BY
            oi.product_id,
            pr.category_id
        ORDER BY
            category_id,
            quan_sum DESC
    )
WHERE
    row_no = 1;
```

Listing 7.154 Selecting Most Popular Products per Category via RANK

Check the results set in Table 7.143. Under the BOT category, both PNT and SKT are listed because both were given a rank of 1 by the RANK function.

category_id	product_id
ACC	BELT
BOT	PNT
BOT	SKT
TOP	SHIR

Table 7.143 Bestselling Product(s) in Each Category

Now, which results set is right and which is wrong? It depends on the requirement! If you must ensure category uniqueness in your final output, then going forward with ROW_NUMBER is inevitable, and you must make the compromise of leaving some equally bestselling products in the shadows. If you don't have such a constraint and are interested in seeing all bestselling products to start a promotion or something, going forward with RANK is preferable.

7.7.4 LEAD

LEAD is an occasionally useful window function. It enables us to fetch values from upcoming rows in the results set. Check Listing 7.155 to see the syntax right in the example.

```
SELECT
    id,
    name,
    stock,
    LEAD(stock, 1) OVER (ORDER BY stock) AS next_stock
FROM
    product
ORDER BY
    stock;
```

Listing 7.155 Query with LEAD Window Function

To understand what the LEAD expression did, check Table 7.144. It generated a new column called next_stock, which contains the stock value of the upcoming row. In the last row, this column contains null simply because there are no more upcoming rows.

id	name	stock	next_stock
BLZ	Blazer	25	30
JKT	Jacket	30	40

Table 7.144 Product Stocks Listed with Next Stock

id	name	stock	next_stock
SKT	Skirt	40	50
SHIR	Shirt	50	60
PNT	Pants	60	70
BAG	Bag	70	100
TEE	T-shirt	100	120
BELT	Belt	120	null

Table 7.144 Product Stocks Listed with Next Stock (Cont.)

Using LEAD, we can access other upcoming rows as well. In our last query, we used the expression LEAD(stock, 1), which indicates that the database engine should skip one row and bring the value from there. If we used the expression LEAD(stock, 2), the database engine would skip two rows and bring the value from there. Check Listing 7.156 to see it in action.

```
SELECT
    id,
    name,
    stock,
    LEAD(stock, 1) OVER (ORDER BY stock) AS next_stock,
    LEAD(stock, 2) OVER (ORDER BY stock) AS next_stock_2
FROM
    product
ORDER BY
    stock;
```

Listing 7.156 Using LEAD Twice to Access Different Upcoming Rows

Now check the results set in Table 7.145. In each row, we not only have the stock value of the upcoming row but also the stock value of the upcoming second row. Null values are exactly where we expect them to be.

id	name	stock	next_stock	next_stock_2
BLZ	Blazer	25	30	40
JKT	Jacket	30	40	50
SKT	Skirt	40	50	60
SHIR	Shirt	50	60	70

Table 7.145 Product Stocks Listed with Next Stocks

id	name	stock	next_stock	next_stock_2
PNT	Pants	60	70	100
BAG	Bag	70	100	120
TEE	T-shirt	100	120	null
BELT	Belt	120	null	null

Table 7.145 Product Stocks Listed with Next Stocks (Cont.)

Now, if we use LEAD in a subquery, we can easily calculate the stock delta between each row—which is a typical use case of this window function. See Listing 7.157 for a demonstration.

```
SELECT
    id,
    name,
    stock,
    next_stock,
    (next_stock - stock) AS stock_delta
FROM
    (
        SELECT
            id,
            name,
            stock,
            LEAD(stock, 1) OVER (ORDER BY stock) AS next_stock
        FROM
            product
        ORDER BY
            stock
    );
```

Listing 7.157 Using LEAD in Subquery to Calculate Delta Values

See the `stock_delta` column in the results set in Table 7.146. It contains the stock difference between each row and the following row. Cool, right?

id	name	stock	next_stock	stock_delta
BLZ	Blazer	25	30	5
JKT	Jacket	30	40	10
SKT	Skirt	40	50	10

Table 7.146 Stock Delta Values in Results Set

7　Data Query Language

id	name	stock	next_stock	stock_delta
SHIR	Shirt	50	60	10
PNT	Pants	60	70	10
BAG	Bag	70	100	30
TEE	T-shirt	100	120	20
BELT	Belt	120	null	null

Table 7.146 Stock Delta Values in Results Set (Cont.)

7.7.5　LAG

LAG is the mirror image of LEAD—it brings values from the preceding row(s) instead of the upcoming ones. The rest should be pretty intuitive; see Listing 7.158 for an example.

```
SELECT
    id,
    name,
    stock,
    LAG(stock, 1) OVER (ORDER BY stock) AS prev_stock,
    LAG(stock, 2) OVER (ORDER BY stock) AS prev_stock_2
FROM
    product
ORDER BY
    stock;
```

Listing 7.158 Query Containing LAG Window Function

The results set in Table 7.147 is exactly how you'd expect it to be.

id	name	stock	prev_stock	prev_stock_2
BLZ	Blazer	25	null	null
JKT	Jacket	30	25	null
SKT	Skirt	40	30	25
SHIR	Shirt	50	40	30
PNT	Pants	60	50	40
BAG	Bag	70	60	50
TEE	T-shirt	100	70	60
BELT	Belt	120	100	70

Table 7.147 Product Stocks Listed with Previous Stocks

7.7.6 NTILE

NTILE fulfills a purpose that's similar to that of ABC analysis. You can use this function to cluster rows into sets. Suppose you need to categorize your products as premium, mid-tier, or affordable, based on their prices. You can easily achieve this goal via Listing 7.159, where you use NTILE to cluster rows into three sets.

```
SELECT
    id,
    name,
    price,
    NTILE(3) OVER (ORDER BY price DESC) AS price_cat
FROM
    product
ORDER BY
    price DESC;
```

Listing 7.159 Using NTILE to Cluster Products into Three Sets

The results set will be as in Table 7.148. Note that price_cat indicates the category of each product: 1 is assigned to the most expensive category, 2 is assigned to the mid-price category, and 3 is assigned to the least expensive category.

Id	Name	Price	price_cat
BLZ	Blazer	100.00	1
JKT	Jacket	100.00	1
BAG	Bag	60.00	1
PNT	Pants	50.00	2
SKT	Skirt	45.00	2
SHIR	Shirt	35.00	2
BELT	Belt	25.00	3
TEE	T-shirt	19.99	3

Table 7.148 Products Clustered into Three Categories

We can adjust the granularity of our categories easily. If we need two categories, all we have to do is to modify the NTILE expression as in Listing 7.160.

```
SELECT
    id,
    name,
    price,
```

7 Data Query Language

```
        NTILE(2) OVER (ORDER BY price DESC) AS price_cat
FROM
    product
ORDER BY
    price DESC;
```

Listing 7.160 Using NTILE to Cluster Products into Two Categories

Check the results set in Table 7.149, where we have two categories instead of three.

id	name	price	price_cat
BLZ	Blazer	100.00	1
JKT	Jacket	100.00	1
BAG	Bag	60.00	1
PNT	Pants	50.00	1
SKT	Skirt	45.00	2
SHIR	Shirt	35.00	2
BELT	Belt	25.00	2
TEE	T-shirt	19.99	2

Table 7.149 Products Clustered into Two Categories

If we need only the expensive half of products from this list, we can get that simply by making use of a subquery as in Listing 7.161.

```
SELECT
    id,
    name
FROM
    (
        SELECT
            id,
            name,
            price,
            NTILE(2) OVER (ORDER BY price DESC) AS price_cat
        FROM
            product
    )
WHERE
    price_cat = 1;
```

Listing 7.161 Selecting Expensive Half of Product List

The results set will be as in Table 7.150.

id	name
BLZ	Blazer
JKT	Jacket
BAG	Bag
PNT	Pants

Table 7.150 Expensive Half of Product List

7.7.7 FIRST_VALUE

We can use this self-explanatory window function to fetch the first value in the intermediary results set that matches the given sorting condition. In Listing 7.162, we made use of FIRST_VALUE to fetch the highest price in the results set and list it as max_price and also fetch the lowest price in the results set and list it as min_price.

```
SELECT
    id,
    name,
    price,
    FIRST_VALUE(price) OVER (ORDER BY price DESC) AS max_price,
    FIRST_VALUE(price) OVER (ORDER BY price ASC) AS min_price
FROM
    product;
```

Listing 7.162 Usage of FIRST_VALUE to Fetch Highest and Lowest Prices

The results set can be seen in Table 7.151. Note how the same max_price and min_price values have been copied to all rows.

id	name	price	max_price	min_price
TEE	T-shirt	19.99	100.00	19.99
BELT	Belt	25.00	100.00	19.99
SHIR	Shirt	35.00	100.00	19.99
SKT	Skirt	45.00	100.00	19.99
PNT	Pants	50.00	100.00	19.99
BAG	Bag	60.00	100.00	19.99

Table 7.151 Listing Highest and Lowest Prices in Each Row

id	name	price	max_price	min_price
BLZ	Blazer	100.00	100.00	19.99
JKT	Jacket	100.00	100.00	19.99

Table 7.151 Listing Highest and Lowest Prices in Each Row (Cont.)

To make the example more entertaining, Listing 7.163 has transformed the former query into a subquery. In the main query, we're calculating the difference between each product's price from the most expensive to the cheapest product's price.

```
SELECT
    id,
    name,
    price,
    ABS(max_price - price) AS max_delta,
    ABS(min_price - price) AS min_delta
FROM
    (
        SELECT
            id,
            name,
            price,
            FIRST_VALUE(price) OVER (ORDER BY price DESC) AS max_price,
            FIRST_VALUE(price) OVER (ORDER BY price ASC) AS min_price
        FROM
            product
    );
```

Listing 7.163 Price Delta Calculation from Highest and Lowest Prices

The results set can be seen in Table 7.152, which we can use for analytical and visualization purposes.

id	name	price	max_delta	min_delta
TEE	T-shirt	19.99	80.01	0.00
BELT	Belt	25.00	75.00	5.01
SHIR	Shirt	35.00	65.00	15.01
SKT	Skirt	45.00	55.00	25.01
PNT	Pants	50.00	50.00	30.01

Table 7.152 Product Price Delta Values

id	name	price	max_delta	min_delta
BAG	Bag	60.00	40.00	40.01
BLZ	Blazer	100.00	0.00	80.01
JKT	Jacket	100.00	0.00	80.01

Table 7.152 Product Price Delta Values (Cont.)

Our example so far has showcased only one feature of FIRST_VALUE, which is working over the entire results set. However, like many other window functions, it can be used with partitions as well. If the requirement was to determine the highest price in *each product category*, we can easily achieve that by throwing in a PARTITION BY expression as in Listing 7.164.

```
SELECT
    id,
    name,
    category_id,
    price,
    FIRST_VALUE(price) OVER (
        PARTITION BY
            category_id
        ORDER BY
            price DESC
    ) AS max_price
FROM
    product
ORDER BY
    category_id,
    id;
```

Listing 7.164 Determination of Maximum Price per Product Category

Check the results set in Table 7.153 and note that the max_price values represent the maximum price in each product category now.

id	name	category_id	price	max_price
BAG	Bag	ACC	60.00	60.00
BELT	Belt	ACC	25.00	60.00
PNT	Pants	BOT	50.00	50.00

Table 7.153 Maximum Price per Product Category

id	name	category_id	price	max_price
SKT	Skirt	BOT	45.00	50.00
BLZ	Blazer	TOP	100.00	100.00
JKT	Jacket	TOP	100.00	100.00
SHIR	Shirt	TOP	35.00	100.00
TEE	T-shirt	TOP	19.99	100.00

Table 7.153 Maximum Price per Product Category (Cont.)

That concludes our section on window functions. They provide very useful calculation options for use with intermediary results sets, and they negate the need to achieve a results set via multiple queries in many cases. Now, we'll get familiar with a handful of the remaining functions offered by DQL.

7.8 Miscellaneous Functions

In this section, we'll get familiar with some supplementary functions to help you empower and simplify your queries. Mind you that they are not exactly syntactic sugar; instead, they may fulfill critical roles in the right scenarios.

7.8.1 CAST

Data type conversion is a natural part of nearly all programming platforms, and DQL is no exception. We use the CAST keyword to convert a value from one data type to another. The basic syntax is as in Listing 7.165.

```
CAST(expression AS target_type);
```

Listing 7.165 Syntax for CAST Function

Some simple CAST operations are demonstrated in Listing 7.166.

```
SELECT
    CAST('123' AS INTEGER) AS v1,
    CAST(CURRENT_DATE AS VARCHAR(10)) AS v2,
    CAST(99 AS VARCHAR(2)) AS v3;
```

Listing 7.166 Some Simple CAST Operations

The resulting values can be seen in Table 7.154. Although the output values seem identical to their respective input values, their types have been changed. For instance, v1 is an INTEGER now and can be used in mathematical calculations.

v1	v2	v3
123	2024-10-09	99

Table 7.154 Results of CAST Operations

As a practical example, Listing 7.167 showcases a query in which CAST has been used in a table column. Numeric vat_rate values have been converted to characters and concatenated with % to build the final VAT rate text.

```
SELECT
    invoice_id,
    invoice_item_no,
    vat_rate,
    CAST(vat_rate AS VARCHAR(2)) || ' %' AS vat_rate_txt
FROM
    invoice_item;
```

Listing 7.167 Using CAST in Table Columns

The results set will be as in Table 7.155. Note that vat_rate_txt contains a string now.

invoice_id	invoice_item_no	vat_rate	vat_rate_txt
501	1	20.00	20 %
502	1	20.00	20 %
502	2	20.00	20 %
503	1	20.00	20 %
504	1	20.00	20 %

Table 7.155 VAT Rates Converted to Text

Data Type Compatibility

When converting data types with CAST, it's your responsibility to ensure that each input value is compatible with the target type. Otherwise, you may receive errors.

7.8.2 CASE

Using CASE expressions gives us the possibility of determining conditional output values in our queries. You can consider these as the IF … THEN equivalent in DQL. The syntax of CASE is showcased in Listing 7.168.

7 Data Query Language

```
CASE
    WHEN { condition_1 } THEN { result_1 }
    WHEN { condition_2 } THEN { result_2 }
    ...
    ELSE { fallback_result }
END AS { column_name }
```
Listing 7.168 Syntax for CASE Function

As a practical example, Listing 7.169 contains a query in which CASE is used to categorize product price values. Prices up to 35 are categorized as Low, those between 35 AND 75 are categorized as Mid, and the rest are categorized as High. The CASE condition in the query reflects this logic accurately.

```
SELECT
    id,
    name,
    price,
    CASE
        WHEN price < 35 THEN 'Low'
        WHEN price BETWEEN 35 AND 75  THEN 'Mid'
        ELSE 'High'
    END AS price_cat
FROM
    product;
```
Listing 7.169 Categorization of Product Prices

The results set of this query can be seen in Table 7.156. Note how price_cat values were built dynamically, based on price values going through the CASE condition.

id	name	price	price_cat
TEE	T-shirt	19.99	Low
SHIR	Shirt	35.00	Mid
BLZ	Blazer	100.00	High
JKT	Jacket	100.00	High
PNT	Pants	50.00	Mid
SKT	Skirt	45.00	Mid
BAG	Bag	60.00	Mid
BELT	Belt	25.00	Low

Table 7.156 Categorized Product Prices

Like many other functions, CASE conditions may be combined with other DQL mechanisms, such as nested functions and subqueries. Listing 7.170 showcases such an example, in which we use a subquery in a CASE condition. If an order has a corresponding delivery, the CASE condition will generate the text **Has delivery**; otherwise, it will generate the text **No delivery**. The resulting condition value will be listed in the generated dlv_state column.

```
SELECT
    co.id AS order_id,
    CASE
        WHEN EXISTS (
            SELECT
                id
            FROM
                delivery_item
            WHERE
                order_id = co.id
        ) THEN 'Has delivery'
        ELSE 'No delivery'
    END AS dlv_state
FROM
    customer_order AS co;
```

Listing 7.170 Using CASE with Subquery

According to the results set in Table 7.157, order 105 doesn't have any deliveries yet while others do.

order_id	dlv_state
101	Has delivery
102	Has delivery
103	Has delivery
104	Has delivery
105	Does not have delivery

Table 7.157 Delivery State of Orders

> **WHEN to Stop**
>
> It's important to know that the database engine will stop at the first valid condition it finds. If you have five WHEN conditions and the third condition is fulfilled, the engine will output the result of the third condition and ignore the rest.

> Therefore, the order of conditions is not a trivial matter. You have to sort the conditions by their priorities instead.

7.8.3 COALESCE

We addressed this function in Section 7.4.1, but we'll give the formal explanation of it here. COALESCE is a function that returns the first nonnull value out of a given set of values.

To build our example, let's take a look at our customer contact information using Listing 7.171.

```
SELECT
    id,
    name,
    phone,
    mobile
FROM
    customer;
```

Listing 7.171 Query for Customer Contact Information

Now check the results set in Table 7.158. Some customers have valid landline phone numbers, while others have valid mobile phone numbers.

id	name	phone	mobile
71	Alice Smith	null	555-1234
72	Bob Johnson	555-5678	null
73	Charlie Brown	null	555-4321
74	Diana Prince	555-8765	null
75	Eve Adams	555-9876	null

Table 7.158 Customer Contact Information

If the customer service department asks for a list of callable phone numbers, they won't like this dirty list with null values. Instead, they'll prefer a cleaner list that includes just the first valid phone number for each customer.

This is a case in which we can make use of COALESCE. Check Listing 7.172, where COALESCE has been used to pick the first nonnull value for mobile or phone, in that order. If mobile is not null, it will be assumed as the valid_phone value; otherwise, phone will be assumed as the valid_phone value.

```
SELECT
    id,
    name,
    COALESCE(mobile, phone) AS valid_phone
FROM
    customer;
```

Listing 7.172 Picking First Valid Phone Number

The results set of the COALESCE query will be as Table 7.159. If you compare that with the previous results set in Table 7.158, the effect of COALESCE becomes evident: the first non-null phone number has been picked.

id	name	valid_phone
71	Alice Smith	555-1234
72	Bob Johnson	555-5678
73	Charlie Brown	555-4321
74	Diana Prince	555-8765
75	Eve Adams	555-9876

Table 7.159 Customer Contact Information with Nonnull Phone Numbers

> **Number of Values**
>
> Although the foregoing example featured only two value candidates within the COALESCE function, it can accept more than two values if needed.

7.8.4 Common Table Expressions

We can use common table expressions (CTEs) to make queries that contain complex subqueries more readable. Let's take a second look at the subquery in Listing 7.82, which we've relisted as Listing 7.173.

```
SELECT
    c.name AS customer_name,
    c.email AS customer_email,
    o.total_orders
FROM
    customer AS c
    INNER JOIN (
        SELECT
            customer_id,
```

7 Data Query Language

```
            COUNT(*) AS total_orders
        FROM
            customer_order
        GROUP BY
            customer_id
    ) AS o ON o.customer_id = c.id;
```

Listing 7.173 Query with Subquery

Although the query is syntactically correct, the readability could be a little better, don't you think? It's not very easy to determine where the main query ends and the subquery starts, and vice-versa.

But no worries! We're about to take care of that. In Listing 7.174, the same query has been refactored using the WITH keyword.

```
WITH
    order_count AS (
        SELECT
            customer_id,
            COUNT(*) AS total_orders
        FROM
            customer_order
        GROUP BY
            customer_id
    )
SELECT
    c.name AS customer_name,
    c.email AS customer_email,
    o.total_orders
FROM
    customer AS c
    INNER JOIN order_count AS o ON o.customer_id = c.id;
```

Listing 7.174 Subquery Refactored using WITH

We coded the subquery at the beginning of the statement and gave it an alias of order_count. That's a clear distinction of the subquery. Following that, the main query was able to refer to the subquery using the order_count alias and became much more readable.

For a more complex example with multiple WITH aliases, we'll revisit Listing 7.86, which we've relisted below as Listing 7.175.

```
SELECT
    cg.id,
    cg.gender,
```

```
        SUM(oi.amount) AS amount_sum
FROM
    (
        SELECT
            customer_order.id,
            g.gender
        FROM
            customer_order
            CROSS JOIN (
                SELECT DISTINCT
                    gender
                FROM
                    product
            ) AS g
    ) AS cg
    INNER JOIN product AS p ON p.gender = cg.gender
    LEFT OUTER JOIN order_item AS oi ON oi.order_id = cg.id
    AND oi.product_id = p.id
GROUP BY
    cg.id,
    cg.gender;
```

Listing 7.175 Query with Two Subqueries

The refactored version of this long query can be seen in Listing 7.176. The innermost query has been given an alias of g, while the inner query has been given an alias of cg—just like the original subquery aliases. Both have been predefined in the WITH section of the statement.

```
WITH
    g AS (
        SELECT DISTINCT
            gender
        FROM
            product
    ),
    cg AS (
        SELECT
            customer_order.id,
            g.gender
        FROM
            customer_order
            CROSS JOIN g
    )
```

```
SELECT
    cg.id,
    cg.gender,
    SUM(oi.amount) AS amount_sum
FROM
    cg
    INNER JOIN product AS p ON p.gender = cg.gender
    LEFT OUTER JOIN order_item AS oi ON oi.order_id = cg.id
    AND oi.product_id = p.id
GROUP BY
    cg.id,
    cg.gender;
```

Listing 7.176 Subqueries Refactored using WITH

Following these predefined queries, the main query becomes much simpler and easier to read. Any programmer can initially read the main query and jump to the WITH section if they need to see more details about any subquery.

> **A Common Table Expression or a Subquery?**
>
> The choice between using a CTE or a simple subquery depends on the query.
>
> CTEs are preferable in complex queries containing multiple subqueries. They can help improve readability, and they are also useful in cases where you need to reference the same subquery multiple times.
>
> Subqueries are preferable if they are very simple and only used once, like an in-line calculation.

7.9 Summary

This chapter has been the most comprehensive part of the entire book. This is for good reason, too—DQL offers powerful tools for data extraction, and it's arguably the most intensively used sublanguage of SQL.

After building the database of an imaginary online apparel store called Retro Loom, we learned about single table queries and multi table queries. We also covered table joins, subqueries, and set operations in depth.

We followed that with string, math, and temporal functions, which enable field calculations in data queries. We also covered powerful window functions that which empower us with the ability to conduct numeric calculations on intermediary results sets before building the final output.

Finally, we covered miscellaneous but useful functions.

One thing worth remembering is that each database product may have its own set of SQL keywords. Although ANSI SQL is mostly supported, different products "spice up" the standard syntax to improve functionality. DQL is no exception to that. The concepts you've learned here should be present in any major database product, but their syntax may differ from PostgreSQL slightly.

Now that you know how to read and write data, you can start thinking about limitations on data access, meaning limiting who can do what. This is the topic of our next chapter on data control language (DCL), which helps us determine limits to the access users or groups have to our sensitive data.

Chapter 8
Data Control Language

Data control language (DCL) is the language we use to organize data access authorizations. This chapter will discuss the necessity of DCL, explore its use cases, and provide SQL code examples to configure database authorizations.

Welcome to the final SQL chapter of the book! It's been a long journey through many SQL sublanguages, and we'll be concluding with a worthy one: DCL. "Last, but not least" is an appropriate label for DCL, as it's a topic of utmost importance.

In a nutshell, DCL is a sublanguage we use to organize data access privileges. Through DCL, we gain the ability to declare who can do what. We can, for instance, set up an authorization structure in which the following can occur:

- Certain privileged users can access any table and conduct any operation, such as `INSERT` and `SELECT`.
- Certain users can read data from most tables but write to only some.
- Certain users can only read data from certain tables.

Such a well-defined authorization structure may seem trivial in playgrounds or casual databases, but it's a crucial part of production databases—especially those that store sensitive data. Some reasons for this are explained in Table 8.1.

Reasons for Data Control Language	Explanations
Data protection	Only authorized users have access to sensitive data, which reduces the risk of data breaches and unintentional or malicious damage to important data.
Damage control	By implementing the principle of least privilege, you can ensure that users only have the minimum privileges needed for their tasks. Even if a user account is compromised, the damage will be limited by the user's authorization level.
Compliance	DCL makes it easier to comply with data regulations, either corporate or legal.

Table 8.1 Some Reasons for DCL

8　Data Control Language

Reasons for Data Control Language	Explanations
Data isolation	In a shared database environment, isolating data of distinct tenants is crucial due to typical privacy agreements, and this is possible via proper DCL implementations.

Table 8.1 Some Reasons for DCL (Cont.)

DCL enables us to set up authorization structures on two different levels:

- Privileges can be set directly to a user. This is good enough in simple cases but may become unmanageable as the number of users grows.
- Privileges can be set to a role, and all users inheriting that role would automatically inherit all privileges assigned to that role as well. This is a better choice for systems hosting multiple users who perform the same role.

In this chapter, we'll learn the appropriate DCL statements to conduct these approaches. But first, we need a playground to run our examples on. Let's start with that!

8.1　Building a Data Control Language Playground

To follow through DCL statements, we're going to create a playground like we did in previous chapters. This time, we'll assume the role of the database administrator for an imaginary company called Tombi Industries. This company has various departments, of which sales, human resources (HR), and finance will be our focus.

Each department needs access to its own tables, but for security reasons, no department should be able to access others' data. There are some exceptions, though. Company managers may need broader access, while data analysts should have read-only access to all departments.

Further requirements may arise in the future, such as creation of integration users with minimum privileges to synchronize some tables with external systems. Wearing the hat of a database administrator, we should be able to manage such access requirements through a flexible privilege structure—via DCL statements, obviously.

To cover the examples in this chapter, it will be enough to create one table per department. You can execute Listing 8.1 to create these sample tables. Note that each table name starts with its respective department name—that will help us with clarification.

```
CREATE TABLE sales_customer (
    customer_id SERIAL PRIMARY KEY,
    customer_name VARCHAR(50),
    contact_email VARCHAR(50)
);
```

```
CREATE TABLE hr_employee (
    employee_id SERIAL PRIMARY KEY,
    employee_name VARCHAR(50),
    department VARCHAR(50),
    salary NUMERIC
);

CREATE TABLE finance_transaction (
    transaction_id SERIAL PRIMARY KEY,
    transaction_date DATE,
    amount NUMERIC,
    description TEXT
);
```

Listing 8.1 Creation of Playground Tables

The columns of these tables are simplified to keep our focus on DCL. Nevertheless, to make the tables a little livelier, you can execute Listing 8.2 to fill them with some mock data to help them make sense.

```
-- Insert mock data into sales_customer
INSERT INTO
    sales_customer (customer_name, contact_email)
VALUES
    ('John Doe', 'john.doe@example.com'),
    ('Jane Smith', 'jane.smith@example.com'),
    ('Michael Johnson', 'michael.johnson@example.com'),
    ('Emily Davis', 'emily.davis@example.com'),
    ('Daniel Martinez', 'daniel.martinez@example.com');

-- Insert mock data into hr_employee
INSERT INTO
    hr_employee (employee_name, department, salary)
VALUES
    ('Sarah Connor', 'Human Resources', 75000),
    ('Rick Sanchez', 'Engineering', 95000),
    ('Morty Smith', 'Marketing', 50000),
    ('Walter White', 'Research', 120000),
    ('Leslie Knope', 'Operations', 85000);

-- Insert mock data into finance_transaction
INSERT INTO
    finance_transaction (transaction_date, amount, description)
VALUES
```

8 Data Control Language

```
('2024-10-01', 250.00, 'Office supplies purchase'),
('2024-10-03', 5000.00, 'Client invoice payment'),
(
    '2024-10-05',
    1500.00,
    'Employee travel reimbursement'
),
('2024-10-07', 320.00, 'Software license renewal'),
('2024-10-09', 2300.00, 'Office rent payment');
```

Listing 8.2 Creation of Mock Data

Unlike our previous chapters, this is enough to launch our basic playground for DCL! We'll create the rest of the database objects, such as users and roles, in due course—with the explanation of corresponding DCL concepts. We'll start with the core elements of DCL, which are users and roles.

8.2 User and Role Manipulation

So far, all code samples in this book have been executed by a single user with infinite privileges. That's fine for a playground or an offline personal database, but real-life production databases are more complex than that. There are typically multiple stakeholders who should or shouldn't perform certain actions, based on their functions.

Ideally, each stakeholder should connect to the database with their own user account, and their user account should be set up in such a way that their necessary actions are enabled while others are disabled.

Before learning how to set up privileges, we need to learn about two core elements in databases: users and roles. That's the exact scope of this section.

Initially, we need to make a distinction between users and roles.

8.2.1 Users

A database *user* is basically a registered account on the database. Like any other typical software platform, each user has a username and password, which are used to connect to the database. Each user must have a unique username, and ideally, each person or application should connect with their own user account.

Figure 8.1 demonstrates two different users (user accounts), which you can use to connect to the database as long as you know their password. The user john_doe is probably a user prepared for a human, while payroll_sys is probably a user prepared for an external system to access data automatically.

8.2 User and Role Manipulation

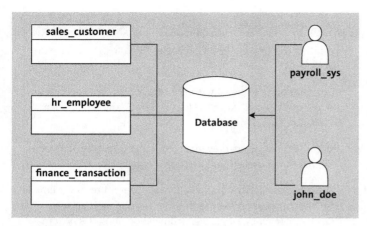

Figure 8.1 Different Users Connecting to Same Database

Now, what is the purpose of having multiple users in a database system? Can't we just create a single user and let everyone use that account?

That's a big no-no!

Most importantly, access control is a big concern in public databases. In the example above, we might want `payroll_sys` to have the ability to read `hr_employee` and do nothing else. If we give `payroll_sys` full database access, anyone with that account can read or modify sensitive data in other tables, such as `finance_transaction`. Obviously, that's not desirable.

Therefore, creating different users for different stakeholders with minimum necessary privilege sets is very important for data privacy and consistency. Figure 8.2 contains an enhanced version of our diagram, in which each user has a different set of privileges.

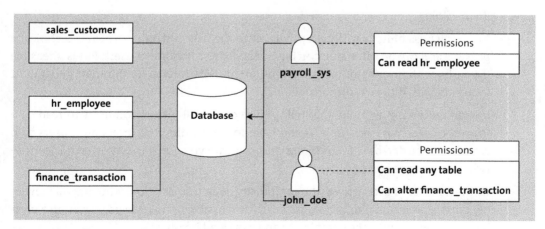

Figure 8.2 Different Privileges for Different Users

Some advantages of working with a multiuser structure can be seen in Table 8.2.

8   Data Control Language

Benefits	Descriptions
Access control	Limiting the capabilities of each user helps to protect sensitive data.
Auditing	Differentiating users allows better tracking of who accesses or modifies data, and database logs can track and report such actions per user.
Separation of duties	Differentiating users prevents conflicts of interest and reduces the risk of misuse, either intentional or by mistake.
Workload management	Database administrators can allocate different resource limits for query execution to different users, based on their roles. That can help prevent a single user from overloading the system.
Multitenant support	In multitenant platforms, having multiple users helps with data isolation and prevents tenants from accessing each other's data.

Table 8.2 Some Benefits of Working in Multiuser Structure

Focusing on the topic of access control, it's clear by now that we want to have multiple users in the database who have the necessary privileges to perform their tasks—but not more than necessary.

There's also a special user type called SUPERUSER that has unrestricted access to the database and can bypass all permission checks. Due to security reasons, such an unlimited privilege shouldn't be given to common users. It should be reserved for administrators or for use in emergency situations.

8.2.2 Roles

Now, one possibility is to assign privileges to the users directly—which is technically possible and can be a fine solution if you only have a handful of users. But is it feasible if you have thousands of users from different departments, in different geographic locations, with different responsibilities?

Imagine receiving an email that tells you to enable all integration users to read data from the `sales_customer` table. If you have forty-two different integration users who connect to the database for different purposes, are you going to have to modify forty-two accounts one by one?

As the number of users grows, the complexity of data access requirements will inevitably grow as well, and it may become nearly impossible to manage privileges on a user-by-user basis—due to the complexity and workload involved.

Luckily, database systems empower us with a concept called a *role*, which is a collection of privileges that we can assign to users or other roles. Roles are used to simplify privilege management by grouping various privileges and granting those groups to users.

See Figure 8.3 for a visual representation of how roles work.

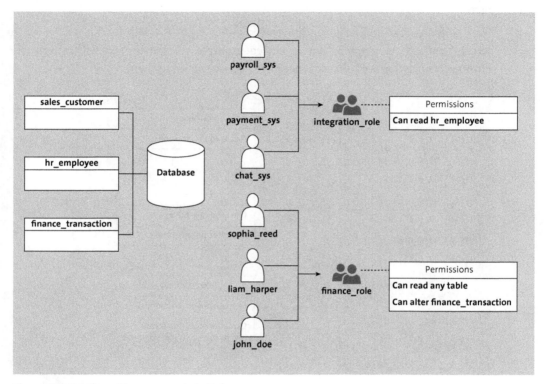

Figure 8.3 Privilege Management via Roles

Instead of assigning privileges to users directly, we've created the following two roles:

- The integration_role contains the permission to read the hr_employee table.
- The finance_role contains the permission to read any table and alter the finance_ transaction table.

In this diagram, we've assigned the finance_role to all users from the finance department—such as sophia_reed, liam_harper and john_doe. Those users automatically inherit all the privileges of the finance_role.

Here's how this approach makes life easier:

- If new people join the finance department in the future, we can simply assign the finance_role to their users. They'll inherit all existing privileges of the role.
- If someone leaves the finance department, we can remove the finance_role from their users to revoke their finance-related privileges.

8   Data Control Language

- If we modify the privileges of the finance_role in the future, then all users having that role will automatically be adjusted to inherit the new privileges set. We won't have to modify each user individually.

In the end, these benefits reduce the administration workload and room for human error.

Naturally, a user can inherit multiple roles as well. Figure 8.4 demonstrates a design in which user marcus_langford has inherited multiple roles. The user will inherit the cumulative privileges of all roles that have been assigned to them.

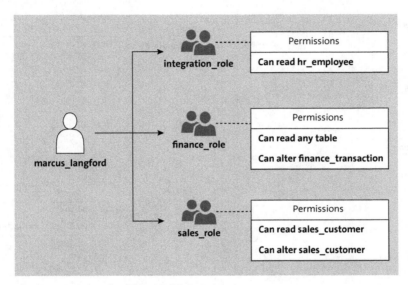

Figure 8.4 User Inheriting Multiple Roles

But what if there are multiple users like marcus_langford, who need to inherit the same set of roles? Do we need to assign all three roles to each similar user? What if the number of inheritable roles increases in the future—do we need to detect and modify all similar users?

To resolve such issues, we have a mechanism called *role inheritance*. We can grant a role to another role, allowing it to inherit the privileges of all roles it contains. This allows for a hierarchical structure in which container roles automatically gain the privileges of subroles.

Figure 8.5 demonstrates such a structure, in which the container vip_role has been set up to include the subroles integration_role, finance_role and sales_role. In such a structure, any change made to one of these roles will automatically be inherited by vip_role and its corresponding users, marcus_langford and natalie_prescott.

This way, we don't have to worry about the individual privileges of VIP users anymore. We can set up whatever they need to do in the container role vip_role.

8.2 User and Role Manipulation

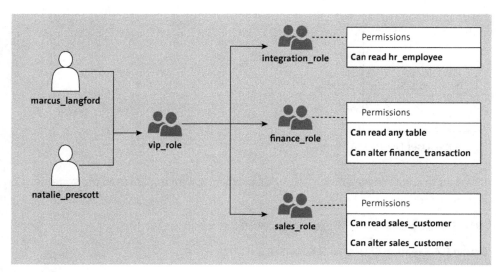

Figure 8.5 Role Inheritance Diagram

Naturally, our so-called subroles are still fully functional roles, which we can use for direct role assignments to users as well. Their subrole function in vip_role doesn't change their core characteristics.

Also, the container characteristic of vip_role is no hindrance to direct privilege assignment either. In other words, vip_role can still contain individual table privileges.

Just as we can create users with SUPERUSER privileges, we can create roles with SUPERUSER privileges.

Now that we're aware of the core concepts of users and privileges, we can venture further and see how we can manipulate them by using DCL statements.

8.2.3 User Manipulation

In this section, we'll learn how to create, modify, and delete users—which is one of the easiest sets of statements in SQL! Listing 8.3 contains an initial statement to create a new user and set a password for them.

```
CREATE USER alice WITH PASSWORD 'securePass123';
```
Listing 8.3 Creation of User

This statement creates a new user called alice. Now, any stakeholder can connect to the database with the credentials alice:securePass123. Current database users can be seen in pgAdmin under **Login/Group Roles**, as shown in Figure 8.6.

8 Data Control Language

Figure 8.6 User List in pgAdmin

If we had to create the user with SUPERUSER privileges, we could've used the statement in Listing 8.4 instead.

```
CREATE USER alice WITH SUPERUSER PASSWORD 'securePass123';
```

Listing 8.4 Creation of User as SUPERUSER

To set a new password for alice, we can use the statement in Listing 8.5.

```
ALTER USER alice WITH PASSWORD 'newSecurePass456';
```

Listing 8.5 Changing Password of User

To add or remove the SUPERUSER privilege, we can use the statements in Listing 8.6.

```
ALTER USER alice WITH SUPERUSER;
ALTER USER alice WITH NOSUPERUSER;
```

Listing 8.6 Adding or Removing SUPERUSER Privilege

And finally, when we decide that the user isn't needed any longer, we can delete it via Listing 8.7.

```
DROP USER alice;
```

Listing 8.7 Deleting User

So far, so good, right? We should be familiar with the CREATE, ALTER, and DROP keywords from the DDL chapter. They have the same functionality in DCL as well—with the difference that we've used them to manipulate users instead of database objects.

In due course, we'll set up user privileges as well.

8.2.4 Role Manipulation

We conduct *role manipulation* with nearly the same keywords we use to conduct user manipulation. Listing 8.8 showcases a statement to create a new role called manager.

```
CREATE ROLE manager;
```

Listing 8.8 Creation of Role

Current database roles can be seen in pgAdmin under **Login/Group Roles** as well, as shown in Figure 8.7.

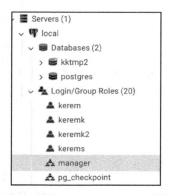

Figure 8.7 Role List in pgAdmin

If we had to create the role with SUPERUSER privileges, we could use the statement in Listing 8.9 instead.

```
CREATE ROLE manager WITH SUPERUSER;
```

Listing 8.9 Creation of Role as SUPERUSER

To add or remove the SUPERUSER privilege, you can use the statements in Listing 8.10.

```
ALTER ROLE manager WITH SUPERUSER;
ALTER ROLE manager WITH NOSUPERUSER;
```

Listing 8.10 Adding or Removing SUPERUSER Privilege

When the role is no longer needed, we can delete it as in Listing 8.11.

```
DROP ROLE manager;
```

Listing 8.11 Deletion of Role

Now that we know how to create users and roles, we're ready to set privileges for roles and users.

8.3 Granting Access

In this section, we'll get hands-on with DCL and see how to grant privileges to users—either directly or via roles, as we've learned to do, conceptually.

431

8 Data Control Language

8.3.1 Granting Access Directly

Before granting privileges to users, you need some sample users, right? Execute Listing 8.12 to create a few users. You can create different accounts if you like.

```
CREATE USER sophia_reed WITH PASSWORD 'securePass123';
CREATE USER liam_harper WITH PASSWORD 'password321';
CREATE USER john_doe WITH PASSWORD 'thompson2024';
```

Listing 8.12 Creation of Sample Users

Now, let's start with a simple requirement of letting john_doe read entries from the finance_transaction table. Jumping to the practical code sample first, the DCL statement to achieve that goal would be as Listing 8.13.

```
GRANT SELECT ON finance_transaction TO john_doe;
```

Listing 8.13 Letting john_doe Read Entries from finance_transaction

Congratulations! User john_doe can read entries from finance_transaction now! The syntax of the DCL statement that made this happen is very intuitive, but let's break it down in Listing 8.14, nevertheless.

```
GRANT { privilege } ON { object } TO { grantee };
```

Listing 8.14 Syntax for GRANT Command

In our example, we've granted the SELECT privilege for a certain table. But many other privilege types are supported, and Table 8.3 showcases some privilege types and their related objects that we can assign by using the same syntax.

Privilege Types	Granted Abilities	Objects
SELECT	Reading data	Tables, views, and sequences
INSERT	Inserting new rows into a table	Tables
UPDATE	Modifying existing rows in a table	Tables
DELETE	Deleting rows from a table	Tables
TRUNCATE	Removing all rows from a table without logging	Tables
REFERENCES	Creating foreign key constraints	Tables
TRIGGER	Creating triggers	Tables
CREATE	Creating new database objects	Databases and schemas

Table 8.3 Privilege Types

Privilege Types	Granted Abilities	Objects
CONNECT	Connecting to a database	Databases
TEMPORARY	Creating temporary tables in a database	Databases
EXECUTE	Executing a stored procedure or function	Functions and procedures
USAGE	Accessing a schema or use sequences, types, or domains	Schemas, sequences, and types
SET	Changing configuration settings for the session	Global
ALTER SYSTEM	Changing system-level settings and configurations	Global
MAINTAIN	Performing maintenance tasks	Tables (administrative)

Table 8.3 Privilege Types (Cont.)

As an exercise, Listing 8.15 contains a set of sample DCL statements we can use to assign further privileges to `john_doe`.

```
GRANT INSERT ON finance_transaction TO john_doe;
GRANT UPDATE ON finance_transaction TO john_doe;
GRANT SELECT ON hr_employee TO john_doe;
```

Listing 8.15 Assigning Further Privileges to john_doe

It's possible to see table privileges of users via system tables. Check the query in Listing 8.16.

```
SELECT
    grantee,
    table_schema,
    table_name,
    privilege_type
FROM
    information_schema.role_table_grants
WHERE
    grantee = 'john_doe';
```

Listing 8.16 Query for Table Privileges

The results set of this query will be as in Table 8.4, which contains all table privileges assigned to that user.

8 Data Control Language

grantee	table_schema	table_name	privilege_type
john_doe	public	finance_transaction	INSERT
john_doe	public	finance_transaction	SELECT
john_doe	public	finance_transaction	UPDATE
john_doe	public	hr_employee	SELECT

Table 8.4 Table Privileges for john_doe

Assigning privileges one by one is a good option for achieving a high level of granularity. However, there may be cases where we simply want to grant a user all available privileges for a specific database object, such as a table or a view. We can achieve this goal by using the GRANT ALL PRIVILEGES expression. Check Listing 8.17 to see it in action — we give all possible privileges for the sales_customer table to sophia_reed.

```
GRANT ALL privileges ON sales_customer TO sophia_reed;
```

Listing 8.17 Giving Full sales_customer Table Access to sophia_reed

To follow up this statement, let's query her current privileges via Listing 8.18.

```
SELECT
    grantee,
    table_schema,
    table_name,
    privilege_type
FROM
    information_schema.role_table_grants
WHERE
    grantee = 'sophia_reed';
```

Listing 8.18 Query for Privileges of sophia_reed

The results set of this query will be as in Table 8.5. Note that all table-related privileges mentioned in Table 8.3 were automatically assigned to her — we didn't have to mention privilege types one by one.

grantee	table_schema	table_name	privilege_type
sophia_reed	public	sales_customer	INSERT
sophia_reed	public	sales_customer	SELECT
sophia_reed	public	sales_customer	UPDATE

Table 8.5 Table Privileges for sophia_reed

grantee	table_schema	table_name	privilege_type
sophia_reed	public	sales_customer	DELETE
sophia_reed	public	sales_customer	TRUNCATE
sophia_reed	public	sales_customer	REFERENCES
sophia_reed	public	sales_customer	TRIGGER

Table 8.5 Table Privileges for sophia_reed (Cont.)

The behavior of GRANT ALL PRIVILEGES will depend on the object type included in the statement. For tables, this expression will behave as seen in Table 8.5. For other database object types, such as stored procedures and functions, the expression will give other corresponding privileges from Table 8.3.

Another cool feature of privileges is the WITH GRANT OPTION suffix. If we add this optional expression to our statement, the target user will gain the ability to delegate their privileges to other users via GRANT statements. As a result of Listing 8.19; liam_harper won't only gain read access to hr_employee but will also gain the ability to GRANT SELECT to other users as well—but only for hr_employee, obviously.

```
GRANT SELECT ON hr_employee TO liam_harper WITH GRANT OPTION;
```

Listing 8.19 Granting Privileges with Grant Option as Well

Following the execution of this statement, let's check table privileges of liam_harper via Listing 8.20. This time, we're checking the is_grantable column as well.

```
SELECT
    grantee,
    table_schema,
    table_name,
    privilege_type,
    is_grantable
FROM
    information_schema.role_table_grants
WHERE
    grantee = 'liam_harper';
```

Listing 8.20 Checking Privileges of liam_harper

This user's privileges will be as in Table 8.6. Note that is_grantable is set to YES, indicating the effect of WITH GRANT OPTION.

8 Data Control Language

grantee	table_schema	table_name	privilege_type	is_grantable
liam_harper	public	hr_employee	SELECT	YES

Table 8.6 Table Privileges of liam_harper

Now that we've learned the basics of direct privilege assignment, we can move forward to granting privileges through roles.

8.3.2 Granting Access Through Roles

Let's start by creating some fresh users for this topic. This will allow you to see the effects of role-based assignments more clearly. Execute the code in Listing 8.21.

```
CREATE USER olivia_warren WITH PASSWORD 'passOlivia123';
CREATE USER jake_peterson WITH PASSWORD 'passJake321';
CREATE USER emma_richards WITH PASSWORD 'richardsPass2024';
CREATE USER ethan_sullivan WITH PASSWORD 'ethanSecure!';
CREATE USER mia_cooper WITH PASSWORD 'cooperMia@987';
```

Listing 8.21 Creation of Fresh Database Users

We'll assume that the first three users are sales staff and the last two are finance staff.

Now, let's continue by creating two empty roles. Execute the code in Listing 8.22.

```
CREATE ROLE sales_role;
CREATE ROLE finance_role;
```

Listing 8.22 Creation of Fresh Roles

Now that we have our roles in hand, we can assign privileges to them. Actually, assigning privileges to a role isn't much different from assigning privileges to a user. All we need to do is to set the role as the GRANT target, instead of the user. Listing 8.23 contains a sample statement in which the sales_role gains some access to the sales_customer table.

```
GRANT SELECT, INSERT, UPDATE, DELETE ON sales_customer TO sales_role;
```

Listing 8.23 Granting Privileges to sales_role

Following the same approach, let's set up the privileges of the finance_role in Listing 8.24.

```
GRANT SELECT, INSERT, UPDATE ON finance_transaction TO finance_role;
```

Listing 8.24 Granting Privileges to finance_role

We can query granted privileges to roles via the `information_schema.role_table_grants` table, just as we did for users. Listing 8.25 showcases the code to query our fresh sample roles.

```
SELECT
    grantee,
    table_schema,
    table_name,
    privilege_type
FROM
    information_schema.role_table_grants
WHERE
    grantee = 'sales_role' or
    grantee = 'finance_role';
```

Listing 8.25 Query for Privileges Assigned to Roles

Check the result set in Table 8.7, which naturally corresponds to our former statements.

grantee	table_schema	table_name	privilege_type
finance_role	public	finance_transaction	INSERT
finance_role	public	finance_transaction	SELECT
finance_role	public	finance_transaction	UPDATE
sales_role	public	sales_customer	INSERT
sales_role	public	sales_customer	SELECT
sales_role	public	sales_customer	UPDATE
sales_role	public	sales_customer	DELETE

Table 8.7 Privileges Assigned to Roles

Finally, we need to assign the roles to corresponding users to make them inherit the privileges. We also execute this operation via the GRANT command! Listing 8.26 demonstrates how to assign the `sales_role` to the sales staff.

```
GRANT sales_role TO olivia_warren;
GRANT sales_role TO jake_peterson;
GRANT sales_role TO emma_richards;
```

Listing 8.26 Assigning sales_role to Sales Staff

8 Data Control Language

And voila! Our sales staff have been granted all privileges that are included in the sales_role. Let's grant finance privileges to the finance staff now. Listing 8.27 will take care of that.

```
GRANT finance_role TO ethan_sullivan;
GRANT finance_role TO mia_cooper;
```

Listing 8.27 Assigning finance_role to Finance Staff

To see the roles directly assigned to users, we can use the simple query in Listing 8.28.

```
SELECT
    r.rolname AS role_name,
    u.rolname AS member_name
FROM
    pg_roles r
    INNER JOIN pg_auth_members am ON r.oid = am.roleid
    INNER JOIN pg_roles u ON u.oid = am.member
WHERE
    r.rolname = 'sales_role' OR
    r.rolname = 'finance_role';
```

Listing 8.28 Query for User Roles

The results set of this query should be as in Table 8.8, which naturally matches our former statements.

role_name	member_name
sales_role	olivia_warren
sales_role	jake_peterson
sales_role	emma_richards
finance_role	ethan_sullivan
finance_role	mia_cooper

Table 8.8 Roles Assigned to Users

> **The PUBLIC Role**
> You'll be pleased to know that PostgreSQL has a built-in role called PUBLIC. Any privilege assigned to PUBLIC will be available to all users of the database.

8.3.3 Granting Access through Role Hierarchies

Now, we'll deal with the case of a manager who needs to inherit the privileges of both the sales_role and the finance_role. Our final structure should be as in Figure 8.8.

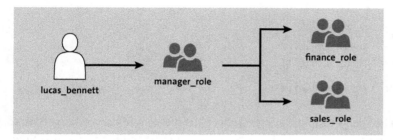

Figure 8.8 Target Role Hierarchy

Let's create the manager's user via Listing 8.29 first.

```
CREATE USER lucas_bennett WITH PASSWORD 'securePassword123';
```

Listing 8.29 Creation of Manager's User

The next step is to create a managerial role via Listing 8.30, exactly as we've created other roles before.

```
CREATE ROLE manager_role;
```

Listing 8.30 Creation of Manager Role

Now comes the interesting part: we want the manager_role to contain all privileges of the sales_role and the finance_role. We also make this assignment is via the magic GRANT keyword as in Listing 8.31, which should be intuitive at this point.

```
GRANT sales_role TO manager_role;
GRANT finance_role TO manager_role;
```

Listing 8.31 Assigning Role Privileges to Manager Role

Finally, we'll assign the managerial role to the manager Lucas Bennett via Listing 8.32.

```
GRANT manager_role TO lucas_bennett;
```

Listing 8.32 Assigning Manager Role to User

Now, let's see how our role hierarchy turned out. We can query our latest role hierarchy via Listing 8.33.

```
SELECT
    r.rolname AS role_name,
    u.rolname AS member_name
```

```
FROM
    pg_roles r
    INNER JOIN pg_auth_members am ON r.oid = am.roleid
    INNER JOIN pg_roles u ON u.oid = am.member
WHERE
    r.rolname = 'sales_role'
    OR r.rolname = 'finance_role'
    OR r.rolname = 'manager_role';
```

Listing 8.33 Query for Latest Role Hierarchy

The hierarchy can be seen in Table 8.9. If you check the last two rows, you can see that the `finance_role` and the `sales_role` have been assigned to the `manager_role`. Now, check one row above, and you can see that the `manager_role` has been assigned to `lucas_bennett`. Following that recursion, it becomes evident that Lucas Bennett has inherited all privileges of the finance and sales staff.

role_name	member_name
sales_role	olivia_warren
sales_role	jake_peterson
sales_role	emma_richards
finance_role	ethan_sullivan
finance_role	mia_cooper
manager_role	lucas_bennett
finance_role	manager_role
sales_role	manager_role

Table 8.9 Latest Role Hierarchy

Naturally, you can build more comprehensive role hierarchies recursively using parent-child logic. But the DCL statements to do so don't change at all; it's just a matter of organization.

Now that we've concluded the topic of granting privileges to users, we should also learn how to revoke privileges—which is our next topic.

8.4 Revoking Access

Revoking privileges with DCL is nearly the same as granting privileges. All we need to do is to use the expression REVOKE...FROM instead of GRANT...TO. It's that simple!

Nevertheless, let's go through some exercises. Listing 8.34 demonstrates how to remove a privilege from a user.

```
REVOKE INSERT ON finance_transaction FROM john_doe;
```

Listing 8.34 Removing Single Privilege from User

The syntax doesn't change much for roles either. Listing 8.35 demonstrates how to remove a privilege from a role.

```
REVOKE DELETE ON sales_customer FROM sales_role;
```

Listing 8.35 Removing Single Privilege from Role

How do you remove a role from a user, then? See Listing 8.36 for a demonstration.

```
REVOKE sales_role FROM olivia_warren;
```

Listing 8.36 Removing Role from User

If you are using a nested role structure and want to remove a child role from a parent role, Listing 8.37 shows you how.

```
REVOKE sales_role FROM manager_role;
```

Listing 8.37 Removing Child Role from Parent Role

In a production database, where privileges are actively granted or revoked, it might be hard to keep track of the current state of authorizations. The next section will cover that topic and provide useful recipes accordingly.

8.5 Reporting Privileges

In this section, we'll go over some useful queries to detect the most current state of privileges. You can use them as is or modify them according to your own requirements. We've covered some of these queries previously, but we'll consolidate them here as well to keep the topic self-contained.

> **Privilege Tables**
>
> The statements refer to tables or views that are specific to PostgreSQL. Other database products offer different tables or mechanisms to report privileges.

If you need a simple list of users, you can refer to the pg_user table as in Listing 8.38.

```
SELECT
    usename
FROM
    pg_user
ORDER BY
    usename
LIMIT
    4;
```

Listing 8.38 Query for Database Users

The results of the query can be seen in Table 8.10. Note that this table has more fields, and you can review them as an exercise.

Table 8.10 Some Database Users

On the other hand, if you need a simple list of roles, you can refer to the pg_roles table. A sample query has been provided in Listing 8.39.

```
SELECT
    rolname
FROM
    pg_roles
WHERE
    rolname LIKE '%_role'
ORDER BY
    rolname;
```

Listing 8.39 Query for Database Roles

You can see the result set in Table 8.11. Note that this table has more fields, and you can review them as an exercise. One significant field is rolsuper, which indicates that the role has SUPERUSER privileges—which means that members of this role can bypass all security checks. Audit staff will probably be particularly interested in this field.

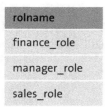

rolname
finance_role
manager_role
sales_role

Table 8.11 Some Database Roles

To list all privileges that correspond to a table, we can refer to information_schema.table_privileges as in Listing 8.40.

```
SELECT
    grantee,
    privilege_type
FROM
    information_schema.table_privileges
WHERE
    table_name = 'sales_customer'
    AND grantee <> 'postgres';
```

Listing 8.40 Query for Table Privileges

The privileges for the sales_customer table can be seen in Table 8.12. Note that both roles and users are included in the result set.

grantee	privilege_type
sophia_reed	INSERT
sophia_reed	SELECT
sophia_reed	UPDATE
sophia_reed	DELETE
sophia_reed	TRUNCATE
sophia_reed	REFERENCES
sophia_reed	TRIGGER
sales_role	INSERT
sales_role	SELECT
sales_role	UPDATE

Table 8.12 Privileges for sales_customer Table

8 Data Control Language

To list all privileges that correspond to a routine, such as a function or a stored procedure, we can refer to `information_schema.routine_privileges` as in Listing 8.41. In this statement, we're querying privileges for a subroutine that we created in the previous chapters.

```
SELECT
    routine_schema,
    routine_name,
    grantee,
    privilege_type
FROM
    information_schema.routine_privileges
WHERE
    routine_name = 'make_bad_money_transfer';
```

Listing 8.41 Query for Routine Privileges

Privileges for the `make_bad_money_transfer` routine can be seen in Table 8.13. This routine seems to be available to the `PUBLIC`, meaning that anyone may call it.

routine_schema	routine_name	grantee	privilege_type
public	make_bad_money_transfer	PUBLIC	EXECUTE
public	make_bad_money_transfer	postgres	EXECUTE

Table 8.13 Privileges for make_bad_money_transfer Routine

To list all privileges assigned to a user or a role, we can refer to `information_schema.role_table_grants` as in Listing 8.42.

```
SELECT
    grantee,
    table_schema,
    table_name,
    privilege_type
FROM
    information_schema.role_table_grants
WHERE
    grantee = 'john_doe'
    OR grantee = 'sales_role';
```

Listing 8.42 Query for Role or User Privileges

The privileges of the user `john_doe` and the `sales_role` can be seen in Table 8.14. Note that both users and roles can be queried from the same source.

grantee	table_schema	table_name	privilege_type
john_doe	public	finance_transaction	SELECT
john_doe	public	finance_transaction	UPDATE
john_doe	public	hr_employee	SELECT
sales_role	public	sales_customer	INSERT
sales_role	public	sales_customer	SELECT
sales_role	public	sales_customer	UPDATE

Table 8.14 Privileges of john_doe and sales_role

To see role-to-user and role-to-role assignments, we have to join a set of tables. Listing 8.43 showcases such as query.

```
SELECT
    r.rolname AS role_name,
    u.rolname AS member_name
FROM
    pg_roles r
    INNER JOIN pg_auth_members am ON r.oid = am.roleid
    INNER JOIN pg_roles u ON u.oid = am.member
WHERE
    r.rolname = 'sales_role'
    OR r.rolname = 'finance_role'
    OR r.rolname = 'manager_role';
```

Listing 8.43 Query for Role Assignments

The results set of this query can be seen in Table 8.15. As stated before, be mindful of recursion in the last two rows.

role_name	member_name
sales_role	jake_peterson
sales_role	emma_richards
finance_role	ethan_sullivan
finance_role	mia_cooper
manager_role	lucas_bennett
finance_role	manager_role

Table 8.15 Assignment of Custom Roles

8.6 Summary

In this chapter, we've learned about privileges in databases and how DCL statements help us manage them efficiently. Users are basically the accounts that connect to a database. In simple scenarios, we can assign privileges to users directly, and those privileges determine the users' capabilities in terms of reading and writing data or executing subroutines.

For more complex scenarios, we can make use of roles, which are containers of predetermined sets of privileges. Instead of assigning the same privileges over and over to a set of users, assigning roles is a practical shortcut that lets us create a container role instead and assign the role to the users. Roles can also work recursively—a role can contain privileges from other roles in a parent-child relationship.

This concludes our chapters on SQL sublanguages. We've nearly reached the end of the book!

Chapter 9
Conclusion

This chapter will bid you farewell and include suggestions for additional resources.

Well, congratulations on reaching the end of the book! It's sure been a comprehensive journey, and hopefully fun as well. At this point, you can consider yourself armed to tackle most typical requirements of relational database-driven development.

The core purpose of the book has been to help you learn the essential features of SQL. However, we've gone the extra mile and helped you gain insight into how to efficiently apply technical skills to real-world problems. Practicality has been one of the driving forces of our content, so we've highlighted best practices, common pitfalls, and bad habits as necessary.

Knowing the syntax is one thing, but accurately solving a problem with the correct approach is another. This book has hopefully provided the necessary input for both.

To recap our learning journey, we started with the fundamentals of relational databases and went through the steps to create a local playground database. Following that, we went through the sublanguages of SQL in their logical order:

1. Data definition language (DDL), which we use to create database objects like schemas and tables
2. Data manipulation language (DML), which we use to insert, update, and delete rows
3. Transaction control language (TCL), which we use to ensure data consistency among tables
4. Data query language (DQL), which we use to read data from tables
5. Data control language (DCL), which we use to organize data access and privileges

We combined these sublanguages to build SQL, with which you can cover any relational database task from basic table creation to complex data querying. Since relational databases are the most common type of databases, your SQL skills will surely be useful in any industry in today's data-driven world.

We didn't shy away from advanced features either. One of our challenges in writing this book has been to strike a balance between the simplicity of vanilla ANSI SQL and the extended capabilities of modern databases. Although we included both, we inevitably had to pick a sample database to build the samples on, and that's PostgreSQL.

9   Conclusion

Like any database product, PostgreSQL has its own set of commands and keywords in addition to ANSI SQL for advanced capabilities. Although code samples that cover core functionality should work well on any decent relational database product, you may need to do some code adaptation for extended features.

Software development is an ever-evolving industry, and programmers typically need to research and learn new topics all the time. Now that you have a fair amount of know-how on SQL, here are some suggestions for how you can venture further from here:

- Dive deeper into advanced topics like query optimization, performance tuning, profiling, and recursive queries.
- Explore database administration topics like database security, backup and recovery, high availability, and scalability.
- Practice database-driven development with external languages like Python.
- Obtain a SQL certification.
- Learn about other common relational databases, such as Microsoft SQL Server, Oracle Database, and MySql.
- Learn about other database types, such as NoSQL, time series, graph, and in-memory.

With those suggestions, we say fare thee well—and we encourage you to go through the appendices too!

Appendices

A	Entity-Relationship Diagrams	451
B	Tips and Tricks	471
C	About the Author	485

Appendix A
Entity-Relationship Diagrams

Entity-relationship diagrams (ERDs) are an industry-standard set of visual symbols that we used to demonstrate different relationship types between database tables. Most of the diagrams in this book use ERD notation, but many readers don't have any experience with ERDs. This appendix describes ERD symbols and explains their meanings, closing knowledge gaps that may prevent you from fully benefiting from this book.

In this section, we'll learn about ERDs, which can be considered the industry standard "sign language" for database diagrams. Many chapters in this book rely on ERDs to demonstrate database objects (such as tables) and their relationships. Therefore, we felt it would be fair to include an introductory appendix on ERDs so all readers can follow the book's examples confidently and accurately.

There are multiple notation types for ERDs, such as the following:

- **Crow's foot**
  This uses feet, lines, and circles.
- **Chen**
  This uses diamonds and numbers.
- **Bachman**
  This uses arrows and numbers.

Although we could use any of these notation types, we use crow's foot notation throughout this book—simply because it's arguably the most commonly used one. It's a very clear and readable notation type that contains symbols for detailed representation of relationship types, such as optional and mandatory constraints.

> **Crow's Foot Notation**
>
> Crow's foot notation was developed by Gordon Everest in the 1970s. This notation got its name because some symbols literally look like a crow's foot, and it's arguably more memorable and more fun than some other notations.
>
> Even though Everest preferred to call these symbols inverted arrows or forks, the name *crow's foot* stuck in the industry—possibly because it's catchier.

A Entity-Relationship Diagrams

If you're already familiar with ERD using crow's foot notation, you can skip this appendix. Otherwise, keep reading to equip yourself with the necessary skills.

A.1 Entity-Relationship Diagrams and Their Significance

Many industries have their own jargon, as well as their standardized set of symbols. Musicians communicate their songs with notes and chord symbols on staffs, electrical engineers communicate their circuits via schematics, and programmers communicate their class architectures via UML diagrams.

Having an industry-standard set of symbols enables a community to quickly and accurately express designs and ideas and understand one another correctly. It also enables us to fit many details into a small document page.

Database development is no exception in this regard. During the design phase, a developer typically plans to create a set of database objects, such as tables, columns, primary keys, and foreign keys. Most of the time, these database objects also have relationships—for example, a database table containing customer orders will most definitely have a relationship to the customer master table.

> **Database Terminology**
> If such database terms are foreign to you, don't worry! We'll go over them throughout the book, and you'll end up having the necessary grasp of such concepts.

Alternatively, the developer may want to document their database design *after* completing the development—so that other team members can understand the data structure accurately.

In both cases, the developer needs a language to express their logic. If they picked free text as the language of choice and wrote everything down in plain English, it would take many paragraphs to explain all the details. That documentation would also be very hard for other team members to follow accurately. We'll intentionally demonstrate this difficulty in the upcoming examples.

Imagine a musician describing the harmony of a song in plain text instead of using chord symbols and notes on a staff. It would be very hard—or next to impossible in some cases—for another musician to follow the song by reading plain text. However, a trained musician can sight-read a musical staff with note symbols and play a song they never heard before on the spot! Why? Because both the writer and the reader know and agree on the same symbols.

In our case, ERD enables database developers to easily share their ideas via common symbols—just like musicians share their music.

This book is no different from that. We're sharing database ideas from developer to developer, and we're using industry-standard ERD symbols to do it. In the following sections, we'll get to know ERD symbols and their meanings, making sure to equip you with the necessary knowledge to follow through.

> **Producing Entity-Relationship Diagrams**
>
> There are a handful of different ways to produce your own ERDs. You can use pen and paper or any basic drawing tool to manually draw a diagram, but that could be impractical in many cases. Instead, you can pick and use a dedicated ERD app to speed up the process—and there are even web-based tools for that. Many database management apps can also automatically generate ERDs from existing database objects, and using them is a practical approach to creating post-development documentation.

Before delving into ERDs, we need to agree on the term *entity* and what it represents to us database developers.

A.2 Entities

Within the scope of this book, when we talk about an *entity*, we're mostly referring to a database table time. In other words, to express a database table within a diagram, we'll draw an entity.

Let's assume that we have a retail store selling different categories of products—such as apparel, food, stationary, and electronics. To keep track of our stocks, the natural initial step would be to create a database table to define these categories. Table A.1 demonstrates what the contents of such a table might look like.

id	description
APP	Apparel
FOO	Food and drinks
STA	Stationary
ELE	Electronics

Table A.1 Sample Table of Product Categories

In this example, we've set the `id` column as unique texts for the sake of simplicity—it's not the main concern of this chapter.

Our concern is the expression of such a table as an entity in our diagram. It's simple, though! Let's see how in Figure A.1.

A Entity-Relationship Diagrams

```
                product_cat
    PK | id            char(3)  NOT NULL
         description   char(50) NOT NULL
```

Figure A.1 Product Category Table as ERD Entity

Depending on your database background, the content of this entity may be completely self-explanatory or somewhat confusing. No worries, we'll inspect each element in detail now.

The top section of the entity indicates the name of the table. In our case, we've named our table product_cat.

The following entries indicate the columns of the table. For each table column, we ought to have a separate entry in the entity visualization. The best practice is to list primary keys first and regular value columns afterward.

Let's demystify these entries and find out what each symbol means. See the breakdown in Table A.2.

Key Type	Column Name	Data Type	Null State
PK	id	int	NOT NULL
	description	char(50)	NOT NULL

Table A.2 Breakdown of ERD Entity Elements

In a typical ERD entity, it's assumed that the recipient already knows the title of each element. Therefore, the titles Key Type, Column Name, Data Type, and Null State are excluded from the diagram. Otherwise, entities would get too crowded and the resulting big diagrams would be hard to follow. But now that you have seen these titles, it should be intuitive to follow through!

In our case, product_cat has only one primary key: id. This primary key appears as the first entry, and the indicator PK symbolizes the fact that it's a primary key. PK is the abbreviation of *primary key* anyway, so it's an easy symbol to catch.

> **Primary Keys**
>
> Chapter 2 covers the basic elements of relational databases and explains this concept in detail. In terms of ERDs, it's enough to know this: a primary key is a special column type that contains a unique value for each entry in the table. That value identifies the entry uniquely and is used to pinpoint it accurately when needed.

> It's also possible to define a primary key out of multiple columns. We'll see such examples in due course.

Our next (and last) entry corresponds to our sole value field, which is called description. Please note that this entry doesn't have a key indicator like a PK, simply because the column is not a key. Regular value columns won't have PK indicators.

Easy, right?

Let's inspect another table and create a further entity. Our next table contains a list of products being sold in the retail store. Table A.3 contains a snapshot of what our table contents might be.

id	description	price	currency	product_cat_id	brand_id
1	Jeans	100	USD	APP	LEVIS
2	Cap	25	USD	APP	LEVIS
3	T-shirt	50	USD	APP	DIESEL
4	Chips	2	USD	FOO	DORITOS
5	Soda	1	USD	FOO	PEPSI
6	Bubblegum	1	USD	FOO	EXTRA
7	A4 paper	5	USD	STA	FABER
8	Pencil	7	USD	STA	FABER
9	USB-C cable	20	USD	ELE	APPLE

Table A.3 Sample Table of Products

Easy and intuitive, right? Each row in the table contains a distinct product which will be sold in our retail store. Although the table is simplified, the main logic is evident.

You may have noticed that our product table has a special column called product_cat_id. If you inspect that column, you'll see that it contains values from our previous table, product_cat. Since the values in this column would logically refer to the values in the product_cat table, they have a foreign key relationship.

Following the same logic, the special brand_id column would refer to another table containing brands. Therefore, this column would have a foreign key relationship to a table possibly named brand.

Following our experience from the previous table, we can easily visualize the entity of our product table. See Figure A.2.

A Entity-Relationship Diagrams

product			
PK	id	int	**NOT NULL**
	description	char(50)	NOT NULL
	price	numeric	NOT NULL
	currency	char(3)	NOT NULL
FK	product_cat_id	char(3)	NOT NULL
FK	brand_id	char(10)	NOT NULL

Figure A.2 Product Table as ERD Entity

> **Foreign Keys**
>
> If you don't have experience with foreign keys, don't fret! Chapter 2 covers the basic elements of relational databases and explains this concept in detail. In terms of ERDs, it's enough to know this: a foreign key indicates that the values in a column refer to values in another database table.

So far, so good! The product entity in our diagram should be completely intuitive at this point. Just as in the previous example, each column has a distinct entry containing its name, type, and null state. We can also easily see whether a column is a primary key or whether it refers to another database table as a foreign key.

Now, let's see all our entities (tables) as a single ERD in Figure A.3.

product_cat			
PK	id	char(3)	**NOT NULL**
	description	char(50)	NOT NULL

brand			
PK	id	char(10)	**NOT NULL**
	name	char(50)	NOT NULL

product			
PK	id	int	**NOT NULL**
	description	char(50)	NOT NULL
	price	numeric	NOT NULL
	currency	char(3)	NOT NULL
FK	product_cat_id	char(3)	NOT NULL
FK	brand_id	char(10)	NOT NULL

Figure A.3 All Entities in Single Diagram

Voila! Now, it starts to look like a real ERD.

But there's a missing crucial element. Although we've visualized all our tables, we have not visualized the relationships among the tables. That's the exact topic of our next section.

A.3 Relationships Among Entities

Since we've built a handful of tables and diagrams ourselves, it's obvious *to us* that the `product.product_cat_id` column refers to the `product_cat.id` column. It's also obvious *to us* that `product.brand_id` refers to `brand.id`. Picking self-explanatory and intuitive column names helps with that.

However, we can't assume that everyone looking at the diagram can intuitively figure out such relationships, and don't let the simplicity of our humble example make you think otherwise. Most users would need to have industry and/or process knowledge to understand many database schemas intuitively.

Therefore, it's a good practice to draw table relationships in ERDs. While drawing relationships, it's typical for us to include their cardinality as well. That way, we can ensure that a much wider audience can grasp our diagrams with less prerequisite knowledge, and we don't leave much room for wrong assumptions either.

> **Cardinality**
>
> *Cardinality* is the numerical relationship between entities.
>
> For example, someone may have zero, one, or many laptops, so there can be a "zero to many" cardinality between a person and their laptops. On the other hand, each person must have a mother and only one mother, so there can only be a "one and only one" cardinality between a person and their mother.
>
> There are more cardinality types, and we're about to cover them and draw them as ERD relationships.

Without further ado, let's jump into it and make use of crow's foot notation to demonstrate table relationships.

A.3.1 Zero to One

To understand this relationship type, we'll assume a loyalty card system in our retail store. In this system, some high-ranking customers receive a private loyalty card that they can use to gain special discounts on some occasions. But a customer can't receive multiple cards—only one card per customer is allowed.

So, we need the following two database tables to store the corresponding data:

- A table to store customer data
- A table to store loyalty cards that references the owner of each card (who is also a customer)

Table A.4 and Table A.5 demonstrate what the simplified table contents would look like.

A Entity-Relationship Diagrams

id	Name	email	mobile
1	Emily Johnson	ejohnson@mail.com	123-758-4955
2	Michael Brown	michael@mbrown.com	123-874-6594
3	Sarah Davis	sarah33@gmail.com	123-874-9355

Table A.4 Sample Data in Customer Table

id	customer_id	card_no
101	1	LC123456
102	3	LC654321

Table A.5 Sample Data in Loyalty Card Table

At this point, we are experienced enough to draw the initial ERD for these tables. So, let's do it. See Figure A.4.

customer			
PK	id	int	NOT NULL
	name	char(50)	NOT NULL
	email	char(50)	
	mobile	char(20)	

loyalty_card			
PK	id	int	NOT NULL
FK	customer_id	int	NOT NULL
	card_no	char(10)	NOT NULL

Figure A.4 Initial ERD for Loyalty Cards

So far, so good! We've prepared the framework for our example, so let's jump to the *zero or one* relationship type.

You've probably noticed that `loyalty_card` has a foreign key: `customer_id`. This foreign key obviously points to the `customer` table, and that will be the relationship in our scope at this time.

Now, how many loyalty cards can a customer have? Remember our rules:

- Only some high-ranking customers have loyalty cards
- A customer can't have multiple loyalty cards

This brings us to the conclusion that a random customer may have zero or one loyalty cards, so zero or one is the cardinality type of our scope!

In other words, the `customer` table has a zero or one cardinality to the `loyalty_card` table. This makes sense, both logically and technically.

Now, the only thing left to do is to use crow's foot notation to demonstrate this relationship.

Note in Figure A.5 that the connection begins in the `customer.id` field and ends in the `loyalty_card.customer_id` field. It also has an unusual symbol at its destination. This very symbol indicates a *zero to one* relationship.

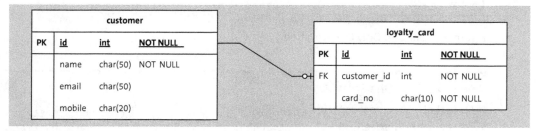

Figure A.5 Zero to One Notation

Zero to One Symbol

Note that the symbol contains a pair of icons—the circle looks like a *0* and the line looks like a *1*. This is what makes the crow's foot notation so popular and practical: each symbol is intuitive and easy to understand. We'll see the same practicality in other relationship types as well.

If we read this ERD aloud, it would sound like this: "If I pick a random `customer` entry and search for it in the `loyalty_card` table, I may find either zero corresponding `loyalty_card` entries or a single `loyalty_card` entry." That's exactly the business rule itself!

Zero to one cardinality is not assertive by nature, and it expresses optionality. A customer may not have a loyalty card or may optionally have a loyalty card, and the same flexibility applies to the database relationship.

Let's continue with our next cardinality type.

A.3.2 One and Only One

So far, we've evaluated the relationship and cardinality from `customer` to `loyalty_card`. How about the reverse relationship: from `loyalty_card` to `customer`?

Since a loyalty card is assigned to a single customer, it obviously has a cardinality of *one and only one*. Let's see it in our diagram.

If we follow the relationship in Figure A.6 from `loyalty_card` to `customer`, we'll find a new symbol close to the customer table. This symbol indicates a one and only one relationship.

A   Entity-Relationship Diagrams

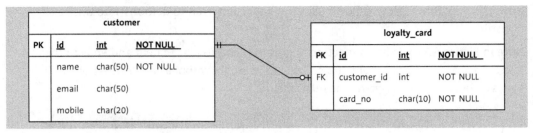

Figure A.6 One and Only One Notation

> **One and Only One Symbol**
> Note that the symbol contains a pair of parallel lines, each of which looks like a 1. This symbol works perfectly like a pictogram and makes us intuitively understand the one-to-one nature of the cardinality.

If we read this ERD aloud, it would sound like this: "If I pick a random `loyalty_card` entry and search for it in the `customer` table, I must find a single `customer` entry—no more, no less." That's exactly the business rule itself.

In contrast to zero to one cardinality, one and only one cardinality asserts a mandatory situation:

- Just like a physical loyalty card can only belong to a single customer, a `loyalty_card` table entry can refer to only a single `customer` table entry.
- Just like a physical loyalty card can't exist without its owner, a `loyalty_card` table entry can't exist without having a corresponding entry in the `customer` table.

So far, we've inspected cardinalities ending with *one*. Now, we'll continue with cardinalities ending with *many*.

A.3.3   Zero to Many

Our former examples have provided a certain level of insight. Therefore, you can probably tell intuitively what *zero to many* cardinality means. Nevertheless, we'll go over a dedicated example.

After producing and distributing loyalty cards, our retail store will surely want to track the usage statistics of those cards. Our business rules state that a card can be used only once per order, and its discount rate is applied to the entire order.

Assuming that we have a database table for orders already, we can add some new fields to this table to keep track of loyalty card usage. Let's make up a simplified snapshot of the corresponding table contents in Table A.6, leaving irrelevant order columns out.

order_id	loyalty_card_id	loyalty_discount_rate
1083	101	0.12
1084	102	0.11
1085	101	0.14
1086	NULL	NULL
1087	NULL	NULL

Table A.6 Sample Loyalty Data in Order Table

Moving forward, we can express our table structures in the form of an ERD. Relationships will come later.

If we inspect the fields in Figure A.7 a little closer, we see the following:

- Our primary key is order_id, and it corresponds to an order created for a customer.
- The ID of the card used for that order is loyalty_card_id.
- The special discount applied to that order due to the loyalty card is loyalty_discount_rate.

	loyalty_card					order		
PK	id	int	NOT NULL		PK	order_id	int	NOT NULL
FK	customer_id	int	NOT NULL		FK	loyalty_card_id	int	
	card_no	char(10)	NOT NULL			loyalty_discount_rate	numeric(3, 2)	

Figure A.7 Initial ERD for Loyalty Card Usage

If you check orders 1086 and 1087, you'll notice that the loyalty fields have null values. This means that those orders weren't created by providing a loyalty card, so no discount was applied. Remember, an order may or may not have an applied loyalty card.

If we reverse this sentence, a loyalty card may have zero to many corresponding orders. As you've probably noticed, this is also the title this section: "Zero to Many."

In more technical terms, the loyalty_card table has zero to many cardinality to order table.

Now, let's see the correct symbol to express this cardinality type in ERDs.

Following the relationship in Figure A.8 from loyalty_card to order, we find the symbol indicating a zero to many relationship.

A   Entity-Relationship Diagrams

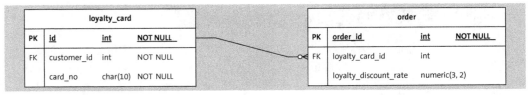

Figure A.8 Zero to Many Notation

> **Zero to Many Symbol**
>
> Note that the symbol contains a pair of icons—the circle looks like a *0* and the three lines look like a crow's foot, quite literally! Now, you have seen how this notation got its name.
>
> We already know that a circle icon stands for *0*, and now, we've learned that a crow's foot icon stands for *many*. So, to express zero to many cardinality, all we have to do is to put the two icons next to each other.

If we read this ERD aloud, it would sound like this: "If I pick a random `loyalty_card` entry and search for it in the `order` table, I might find no entries, just one entry, or multiple entries." This is exactly what the business rule states.

Like zero to one cardinality, zero to many is not assertive by nature and expresses optionality. A loyalty card may not have been used at all, or it optionally may have been used in multiple orders. The same flexibility applies to the database relationship.

But this diagram is incomplete. As a further exercise, we can also examine the cardinality from `order` to `loyalty_card`. There are two possibilities in this regard:

- An order may have no loyalty card discount at all.
- An order may have a single loyalty card discount.

The cardinality speaks for itself. It's a cardinality type we've already covered: zero to one. Let's put that symbol into our diagram as well.

The relationship between these tables is now complete in Figure A.9, cardinalities and all!

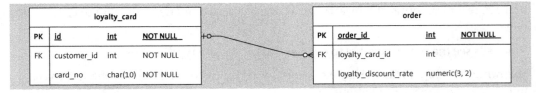

Figure A.9 Additional Notation for Zero to One

Let's continue with the next *many* cardinality type.

462

A.3.4 One to Many

As its name suggests, *one to many* cardinality is very similar to zero to many cardinality, with a small but important difference: the target table is expected to have at least one corresponding entry. This logic and necessity will become clearer in our next example.

We've already seen the order table, where a new entry is created for each new order. But what about the products included in the order? We would certainly need to store the cart contents and order items in a distinct database table, because an order may include multiple products.

Let's create a snapshot of a simplified order item table. See Table A.7.

order_id	item_no	product_id	quantity
1083	1	7	4
1083	2	8	2
1083	3	3	1
1084	1	5	6

Table A.7 Sample Product Data in Order Item Table

If we look more closely at our sample data, order 1083 has three items that correspond to products 7 (A4 paper), 8 (pencil) and 3 (t-shirt). These products were already mentioned and defined in Section A.2, so we're just referencing the product table as we should.

Now, let's put the order and order_item tables next to each other, building our initial ERD. Inspecting our fields in Figure A.10 a little more closely, we can see the following:

- Our first primary key field is order_id, which refers to the order itself.
- Our second primary key field is item_no. For each item in the order, this field will become a sequential number.
- The product_id field stores the ID of the purchased product and has a foreign key reference to product table.
- The quantity field stores the count of purchased items.

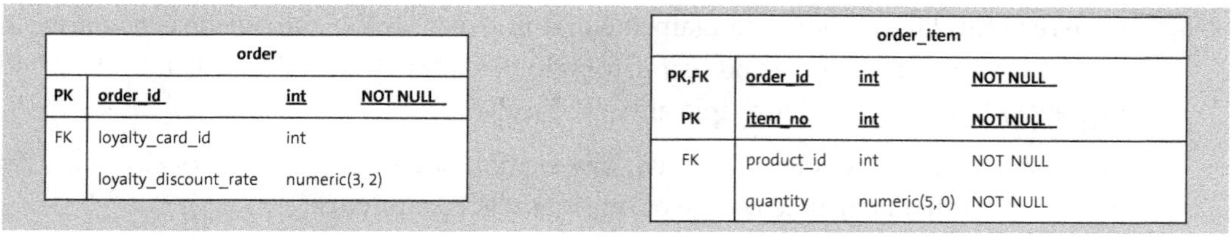

Figure A.10 Initial ERD for Order Items

A Entity-Relationship Diagrams

> **Two Primary Key Fields**
>
> Note that the `order_item` table has two primary keys: `order_id` and `item_no`. This is perfectly natural because entry uniqueness can only be ensured when those fields are combined. Primary keys can consist of multiple fields in such cases.
>
> In our sample dataset, check order 1083. It has multiple items, so we can't ensure entry uniqueness by `order_id` alone. Therefore, we mark the combination of `order_id` and `item_no` as our primary key.

Logically, an order can include multiple products and order items. However, there can't be a case where an order is placed without it including any products. It just doesn't make sense—a customer has to buy at least one product to place an order. In other words, an order ought to have one to many items, and it should be no surprise that this is the title of this section: "One to Many."

If we express the same idea technically, the `order` table has one to many cardinality to the `order_item` table.

We're confident that you could correctly guess the correct symbol for this kind of cardinality, but let's see it in the ERD anyway. Following the relationship in Figure A.11 from `order` to `order_item`, we find the symbol indicating a one to many relationship.

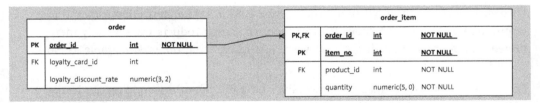

Figure A.11 One to Many Notation

> **One to Many Symbol**
>
> Note that the symbol contains a pair of icons we've seen already. The singular line looks like a 1 and means *one*, and the crow's foot stands for *many*. So, to express one to many cardinality, all we have to do is to put the two icons next to each other.

If we read this ERD aloud, once again, it will sound exactly like the business scenario: "If I pick a random `order` entry and search for it in the `order_item` table, I will definitely find one entry but might find multiple entries as well."

Like the one and only one cardinality, one to many asserts a mandatory situation. An `order` entry must have *at least* one `order_item` correspondence.

To complete our diagram, we'll go through a further exercise: cardinality from order_item to order. An order item logically can't exist without an order, and an order item belongs to one order only. Therefore, for each order_item entry, there must be one and only one order entry.

We've already seen this cardinality, so without further ado, let's put it into our diagram. This final cardinality symbol in Figure A.12 concludes our ERD.

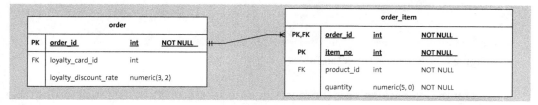

Figure A.12 Additional Notation for One to One

A.4 Entity-Relationship Diagrams Exercises

During our ERD journey, we've sat on the production side of the desk. We've acted as the main developer, who designed their data structures first and produced corresponding ERDs afterwards.

However, you may very well be the recipient of an ERD. Another developer, whom you've never met before, may send you an ERD and expect you to understand their data structure and business logic.

In the near future, as the reader of this book, you'll encounter many ERDs. They won't be too complex, but you'll need to understand them accurately to follow through on them.

So, it's good idea for us to run through some exercises together. We'll inspect a final ERD diagram and decipher the data structure and logic behind it.

Let's start with a familiar case.

A.4.1 Retail Store

We've learned our ERD symbols via a retail store example, so it makes sense to build our first exercise on that. We haven't gotten a bird's eye view of all the tables yet either, despite using crow's feet notation!

Look at Figure A.13! Isn't it beautiful? Time to be proud of ourselves—we've learned how to prepare ERDs while preparing a basic table structure for a retail store.

This final figure hopefully makes our initial justification for ERD evident. If we send this diagram to a fellow developer, who has absolutely no notion of the business scenarios of the retail store, they can still figure out the data structure and the logic behind it.

465

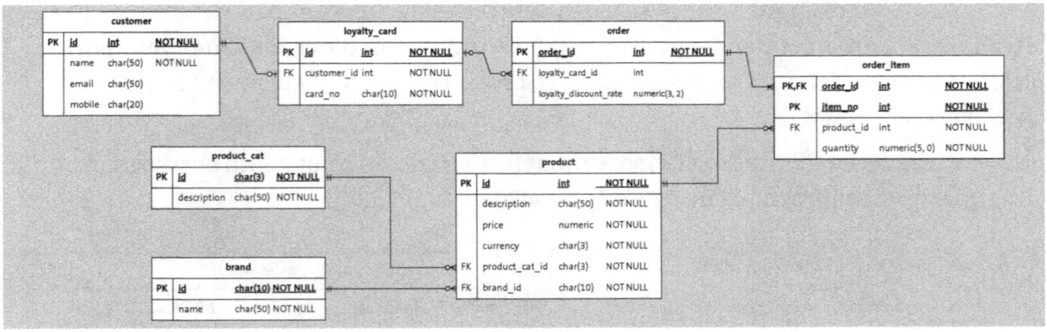

A   Entity-Relationship Diagrams

Figure A.13 Entire ERD of Retail Tables

As for the exercise, let's see the most significant features of our data structure in Table A.8.

Source	Target	Cardinality	Interpretation
customer	loyalty_card	Zero to one	Only some customers earn a loyalty card, and a customer can possess only one card.
order	loyalty_card	Zero to one	An order can optionally involve a loyalty card, but not more than one.
brand	product	Zero to many	It's possible to define brands in advance, before receiving any products from them.

Table A.8 Significant Relationships

ERD has enabled us to communicate such business rules by using appropriate symbols without writing a single letter, just like a musician communicating their piece by using musical notes.

The next exercise will also be familiar to most readers.

A.4.2   Social Media Platform

In this exercise, we'll put a partial section of a social media platform database under the magnifying glass. In reality, social media platforms deal with colossal quantities of data, and they use a diverse array of data storage technologies. Relational databases are one of many tools they use, so for the sake of simplicity, we'll assume otherwise and go forward with a small relational database snapshot.

Figure A.14 is the ERD we've received, without further explanation.

It's evident that user is the central table of this design—it has the highest number of relationships. Let's start our analysis there. Judging by its fields, each user has a unique

A.4 Entity-Relationship Diagrams Exercises

ID, and their master data is stored in corresponding fields. That's simple and straightforward, with nothing out of ordinary.

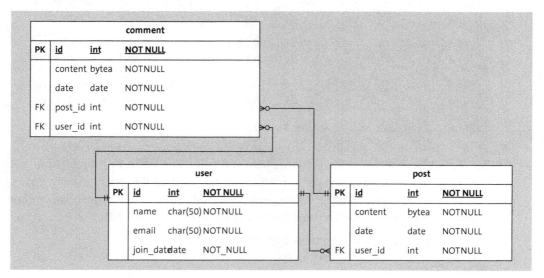

Figure A.14 Social Media Platform ERD

Next comes the post table. Judging by its name, this table stores comments made on the platform. Each entry has a unique ID like it should, and content is stored in binary format while the ID of the user who made the post is stored in the user_id field. Let's cumulate its relationships into Table A.9.

Source	Target	Cardinality	Interpretation
post	user	One and only one	The author of each post must be defined as a singular user, and collaborative posts are not supported.
user	post	Zero to many	A user may stay passive without posting anything at all, or they can post multiple entries at will.

Table A.9 Relationships of Post

Next comes the comment table. The name and relationships of this table make it clear that it stores the comments made in posts. Each comment has a unique ID, content is stored in binary format, and the IDs of the corresponding post and commenting user are stored in their respective fields: post_id and user_id. Everything seems intuitive and in order, so let's cumulate the table's relationships into Table A.10.

Source	Target	Cardinality	Interpretation
comment	post	One and only one	A comment belongs to a singular post.

Table A.10 Relationships of Comment Table

A   Entity-Relationship Diagrams

Source	Target	Cardinality	Interpretation
post	comment	Zero to many	A post may have no comments at all or multiple ones.
comment	user	One and only one	A comment can only be made by a single user, and collaborative comments are not supported.
user	comment	Zero to many	A user may stay passive without commenting at all, or they can post multiple comments at will.

Table A.10 Relationships of Comment Table (Cont.)

Most of us have social media accounts here and there, and we know roughly how they function. We've used social media in our example intentionally, because we can often learn a new skill by studying an example we know well. The thought process we've gone through would mostly be the same to get familiar with a foreign ERD.

Moving forward, we'll use the same approach in further examples.

A.4.3   Hospital

This time, we'll go over an ERD in Figure A.15 that visualizes part of a hospital database.

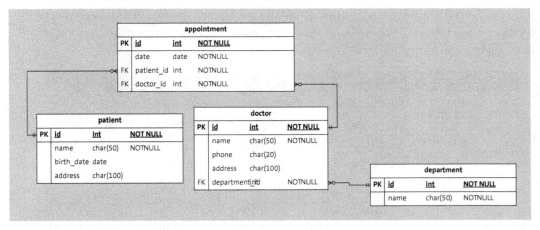

Figure A.15 Hospital ERD

Let's start our analysis with one of the tables with the highest number of connections: doctor. Thankfully, the developer has followed a basic best practice and picked self-explanatory names for tables and columns, so we can see clear as day that this table stores doctors working in the hospital. Each doctor has a unique ID, and their master data is stored here.

Following the first relationship, we arrive at the appointment table. Each appointment has a unique ID, some details, and two relationships: `doctor` and `patient`. This makes it evident that an appointment involves a doctor and a patient. Check the cumulated relationships in Table A.11.

Source	Target	Cardinality	Interpretation
appointment	doctor	One and only one	An appointment must have an assigned doctor, even during booking.
doctor	appointment	Zero to many	There may be doctors not accepting appointments (such as lab staff), but a doctor may have multiple appointments.
appointment	patient	One and only one	An appointment must have an assigned patient, even during booking.
patient	appointment	Zero to many	There may be patients who have made an appointment yet, but a patient may have multiple appointments.

Table A.11 Relationships of Appointment

While checking out appointments, we've mostly completed the analysis of the `patient` table, so, let's move forward.

Following the next relationship, we arrive at the `department` table. This table seems to store the departments of the hospital, such as cardiology, neurology, and dermatology. Let's look at its sole connection with doctors in Table A.12.

Source	Target	Cardinality	Interpretation
department	doctor	Zero to many	A department might be empty without any doctors (yet), or it may have multiple doctors working.
doctor	department	One and only one	A doctor must be assigned to a single department. There are no generic or multi-disciplinary doctors.

Table A.12 Relationships of Department

That concludes our hospital analysis. It's bewildering how much information can be fit into a single diagram with four boxes and a few crow's feet here and there, right? Even at the most basic level, explaining the diagram took many paragraphs—while an educated eye can see them all in the ERD with a quick look.

A.5 Summary

In this appendix, we've covered the important subject of ERD, which is arguably the industry standard language to communicate database table designs.

You've probably read this chapter because you either had no previous ERD experience at all or needed to refresh your memory. In either case, reading this chapter before going forward with the book's main content (as suggested) was a good time investment for sure! You'll be able to follow examples and understand diagrams much more accurately and smoothly.

In your career as a programmer, you can use ERD to quickly sketch a database design to discuss with your colleagues or get approval of it from involved parties. Alternatively, you can use it to create an overview map of an already developed set of database tables.

Appendix B
Tips and Tricks

This chapter will provide tips and tricks from a seasoned developer to database freshmen, to help them improve their initial database designs. The topics are not SQL, but rather satellite concepts revolving around SQL.

In this appendix, we're going to pay attention to some satellite subjects related to SQL and database driven development. These considerations would naturally be expected from senior developers, so we recommended that they be part of your future learning journey. Instead of a deep dive, we'll provide introductory overviews of them here.

B.1 SQL Injection

Although we don't want to encourage malicious hacking, a book on SQL ought to include a heads-up regarding SQL injection. Consider it a short course on defending yourself against potential attackers.

SQL injection is a type of attack in which a malicious user tricks a website or app by manipulating input fields like text boxes. For example, on a login form, they could enter tailored values that would enable them to log in without having the necessary credentials.

Here's a basic attack: imagine a website having a simple login page, as shown in Figure B.1.

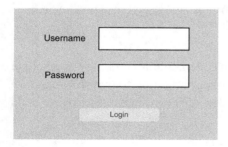

Figure B.1 Simple Login Page

Now, when a user enters credentials like `my_user` and `my_password`, an unsecure backend code would concatenate those values to build up a query like in Listing B.1.

471

B Tips and Tricks

```sql
SELECT
    *
FROM
    user_acccount
WHERE
    username = 'my_user'
    AND password = 'my_password';
```

Listing B.1 Regular Query for Credential Check

It all looks good so far—if the query returns a value, it means that the user is valid.

Here's how the SQL injection risk arises. Imagine that the malicious visitor has entered the value ' or 1 = 1 as their password. When the unsecure backend code does the string concatenation, the resulting query will be as in Listing B.2.

```sql
SELECT
    *
FROM
    user_acccount
WHERE
    username = 'my_user'
    AND password = ''''
    OR 1 = 1;
```

Listing B.2 SQL Injected Query for Credential Check

This query would return all users in the `user_account` table, which could be wrongly interpreted as a successful login. That way, the malicious visitor would be able to access the website without having valid credentials.

> **Don't Attempt SQL Injection**
> Having learned the basic logic of SQL injection, please don't go to websites and try this attack. Most websites already have security measures against SQL injection, and such attempts may get you into legal trouble.

Now, there are more complex forms of SQL injection, and attacks may happen via applications and API's as well. The main idea is to pay attention to that risk and make sure that your software is robust against it. Any code that concatenates strings to build SQL statements may be at risk.

Here are some common measures against SQL injection.

Using parameterized queries ensures that user inputs are treated strictly as data, not code. Listing B.3 showcases a Python code snippet using the `psycopg2` library, which implements this approach. The %s value is a placeholder, and the username and password values are safely passed as parameters. No raw concatenation takes place.

```
cursor.execute("SELECT * FROM user_account WHERE username = %s AND password = %s", (username, password))
```

Listing B.3 Python Code with Parameterized Queries

Any decent development framework or database library ought to provide a similar mechanism for parameterized queries, and you can make use of it.

Although it's a controversial decision, if you're using an object-relational mapper (ORM) like SQLAlchemy or Hibernate, it typically provides mechanisms to handle safe query construction, preventing risks of raw SQL generation.

On the database backend, you may prefer to take parameters like username and password as parameters to a stored procedure and run the SQL code within the procedure. In some cases, this simple approach could negate the need for string concatenation.

If, for some reason, you must use string concatenation eventually, you can make use of string escape mechanisms. For example, PHP has a built-in function called pg_escape_string that targets PostgreSQL and escapes potentially harmful characters in user input before using them in a query. That way, risky characters like quotes are replaced to prevent SQL injection.

Limiting database privileges to the absolute minimum also helps with damage control related to SQL injection and similar vulnerabilities. Even if someone gains unintended access to the database, they would be limited by the capabilities of the active database user.

Another important aspect is to suppress technical database error messages and not show them to end users. It's OK to log them to review later, but they may contain critical backend information that could be invaluable to malicious users.

B.2 Application-Level Authorization

In Chapter 8, where we covered data control language (DCL), we learned how to handle privileges on the database level, which is a sound and solid approach for authorization management.

However, in many cases, backend applications connect to the database with a single user, which has enough (but still limited) privileges to access all tables related to the application, as shown in Figure B.2.

In such cases, authorization management is not made via distinct database users. Instead, each "application user" has an entry in a custom database table (like member) and their credentials and authorizations are stored in further custom database tables.

B   Tips and Tricks

Authorization management is handled on the application level accordingly (using Python, Java, etc.).

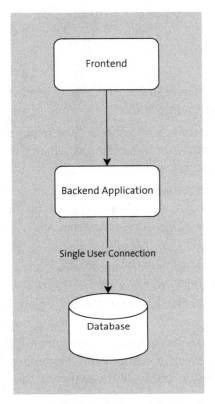

Figure B.2 Diagram for Single User Connectivity

This common approach has its own set of pros and cons. Some typical pros can be seen in Table B.1.

Pros	Descriptions
Flexibility	Authorization logic is part of the application and can be mapped to business rules more easily.
Dynamism	More complex rules involving business logic can be implemented easily. These include conditional access based on the state of the process.
Integration	When authorization is handled at the application level, it's easier to integrate with identity providers (such as OAuth, SAML, etc.).
Independence	Taking the authorization logic out of the database makes us less reliant on just one database product.

Table B.1 Some Pros of Application-Level Authorization

Some typical cons of can be seen in Table B.2.

Cons	Descriptions
Security	Although any commercial application can pose vulnerabilities from time to time, fresh custom code is a common culprit for creating security gaps, and authorization mechanisms are no exceptions to that.
Boilerplate code	If authorization checks are skipped or forgotten at certain entry points, some operations may be left unprotected.
Multiple apps	If multiple applications are accessing the same database, enforcing a common authorization logic among them may be a challenge.

Table B.2 Some Cons of Application-Level Authorization

So, when is database-level authorization favorable, and when is application-level authorization favorable? Those questions don't have easy, straightforward answers. It depends on the situation, but here's a general guideline.

Database-level authorization use cases include the following:

- Environments where security is top priority (financial institutions, sensitive data, etc.)
- Multitenant applications where tenants need to be strictly isolated
- Situations where data security is the responsibility of the database administrators (DBAs)

Application-level authorization use cases include the following:

- Web or mobile applications with many users, where permissions are tied to business logic rather than low-level database structures
- Applications dealing with multiple data storage mechanisms, instead of a single relational database
- Applications with dynamic authorization schemas requiring flexible role management

You can also use a hybrid approach, in which core data access restrictions are enforced at the database level while top-level permissions are handled at the application level. In this approach, the application would connect with a database user having privileges limited by to the application user's position. Further limitations would be enforced at the application level, depending on business rules. For each possible position, there would be a different corresponding database user.

But the challenge of this approach would be the complexity of the authorizations. When a user encounters an authorization problem, it may be difficult to pinpoint the source—whether it's at the application level or the database level.

As you can see, there's no one-size-fits-all approach to this subject. But this mental exercise should provide you with a good starting point for evaluating possible options.

B.3 Sensitive Data

Sooner or later, you may find yourself in a situation where you'll need to store sensitive data, such as passwords, salaries, health records, or confidential content. In some cases, a data breach may have corporate or even legal consequences. In this section, we'll go through some basic considerations regarding such situations.

First of all, it's crucial to identify what qualifies as sensitive data. You may have to consult with management to clarify this, and the next step is to apply appropriate security measures to protect the data.

B.3.1 Encryption

A typical approach is to use *encryption*, in which sensitive data is encrypted before storage and decrypted when shown to an authorized user. It's preferable to keep data encrypted in transit as well (when it's sent over the network). Using a strong industry-standard algorithm is recommended.

In the case of passwords, we prefer hashing. In contrast to encryption, *hashing* is a one-way operation. Typically, you wouldn't store the password of a user directly. Instead, you'd generate an irreversible hash value and store the hash in the database. Given that you've used a strong industry-standard algorithm, no one can guess the password by analyzing the hash value. When the user attempts to log in, you'd hash the submitted password as well and compare it to the hash value in the database.

You can also take advantage of *salting*, which is a technique used to enhance the security of hashed values. Basically, you'd add a random, unique string to the password before hashing it. That way, even if an attacker gains access to your hashed values, they can't easily figure out plain passwords by hashing and comparing common passwords.

Storing sensitive data without any kind of encryption is asking for trouble. Someone might reach your table contents eventually, and when they do, they shouldn't be able to make any sense of what they see.

It may be tempting to use homemade algorithms for encryption or hashing, but compared to industry-level algorithms, they'll probably be weak and relatively easy to crack. Outdated algorithms are equally inefficient.

Never store keys or API secrets as plaintext! Source codes are meant to be shared, and eventually, someone will read your code or configuration files. Having access to secret keys is the same thing as having access to database contents, so store them accordingly. Secure key management systems or environment variables are some possible options.

B.3.2 Anonymization

Data *anonymization* is another approach to privacy. When dealing with data like health records, you can anonymize the data by removing any identifying information. This approach can be particularly useful for machine learning purposes, where you don't really care about the identity of the patient. If you do care, then another option is *pseudonymization*, in which you use patient identifiers that are reversible by the hospital staff but not by the public.

In any case, implementing a strict authorization plan regarding sensitive data is naturally expected. Even when you have encrypted or hashed values, there's no need to take the risk of exposing them and opening yourself up to attacks, such as brute force, dictionary, and rainbow table attacks.

B.3.3 No Storage

Avoiding data storage altogether is also sound plan! For instance, there are many online platforms that take care of credit card management securely. You can work with such a vendor and handle transactions over their APIs, leaving the financial heavy lifting to them.

B.3.4 Database Features

You can also purge obsolete, sensitive information from the database. That would reduce the extent of the damage in case of a data breach.

Note that backups of sensitive data deserve the same care as the main database. If your backups get stolen, it's still a valid data breach.

B.4 Logical Deletion

When managing data, there are two common strategies for deleting rows from a database.

The first option is physical deletion, which occurs via a `DELETE` statement. We went over that option in Chapter 5, which covered data manipulation language (DML).

Another option is logical deletion, in which the row is not deleted physically. Instead, a column like `is_deleted` is set to `true`. The entire application takes this column into consideration and evaluates rows with `is_deleted=true` as deleted rows, ignoring them in most cases.

Both approaches can be valid in different scenarios. Table B.3 showcases a general comparison.

B Tips and Tricks

Feature	Physical	Logical	Comments
Storage efficiency	Yes	No	As entries are physically deleted, storage requirements are kept under control.
Compliance	Yes	No	If regulations mandate that personal data should be permanently removed, physical deletion should be preferred.
Query simplicity	Yes	No	Logical deletion brings complexity to queries by throwing in a new column to consider.
High performance	Yes	No	Logical deletion inevitably reduces performance as the number of rows grows.
Reversibility	No	Yes	Logical deletion can be easily undone by updating the deletion flag.
Audit history	No	Yes	Logical deletion provides a readable history for audit purposes, making it ideal in ERP-like systems.
Constraint preservation	No	Yes	Logical deletion enables the preservation of rows related by constraints.

Table B.3 Comparison of Physical and Logical Deletion

In summary, physical deletion can be preferable when you're legally bound to do it, when you're deleting noncritical data (like logs), or when storage space is a concern. On the other hand, logical deletion can be preferable when historical data is needed, when undoing should be an option, or when constraints are critical.

A hybrid approach is to summarize big chunks of data into smaller summaries and physically delete the "big data" afterward. That saves storage space while preserving historically critical information.

B.5 Indexes versus Summary Tables

We've already learned about indexes and how they may speed up data queries. There's a second, similar approach though: using summary tables.

Basically, a *summary table* is a secondary satellite table that lives next to your big main table. Typically, a periodic job reads data from the big table, runs some calculations, and summarizes the results into the summary table. The summary table can be considered a data cache.

If the summary data is frequently queried, summary tables offer performance benefits. Instead of recalculating the same values over and over via the big main table, you can simply access the precalculated and cached values from the summary table.

Summary tables have also proven to be useful for web API calls, in which you can be racing to return results quickly before a timeout occurs. Reporting, analytics, and data warehousing are some other typical use cases.

Summary tables inevitably bring storage overhead, because even though the data is summarized, it will still occupy some space. Therefore, you should make the removal of obsolete summary rows part of your plans.

There's also the risk of data staleness. Summary tables inevitably offer historical data—even if they're merely five minutes old! It's a good practice to store the timestamp of any summarization so the client can take the age of the data into consideration.

As a comparison, we can say that using indexes is a good choice for speeding up searches, filters, and lookups on relatively small sets of rows. On the other hand, summary tables are useful for accelerating complex queries involving the aggregation of large datasets.

B.6 Legal Concerns

When you're storing data in a database, there may be numerous legal and regulatory requirements that you must take into consideration. Different countries or industries may have different rules, and laws change over time. Therefore, how you explore this subject is best left up to you, and your best option in many cases is to consult with your legal department.

Some typical legal concerns revolve around the following:

- Minimization of stored data
- Obtaining explicit consent from users
- Individual rights regarding data access and erasure
- Data breach notifications
- Disclosure of data collection and the possibility to opt out
- Security measures for sensitive data (encryption, access control, etc.)
- Credit card management
- Data anonymization
- Deletion of expired data
- Keeping audit logs
- The physical location of the data center
- Cross-border data transfers

B Tips and Tricks

One thing you shouldn't overlook is third-party risks. Even if you do everything in your power to comply with legal requirements, if there's a weakness in a third-party component, it may become the weak link in the chain and you may be the one facing penalties.

B.7 Primary Key Determination

Determining PKs is a critical decision in database design, as they must uniquely identify an entity, such as an employee, a purchase, or a product. There are multiple methods to ensure PK uniqueness, which we'll cover in the following sections.

B.7.1 External Values

You can use external values as PKs. These include Social Security numbers, email addresses, serial numbers, etc.

This method comes with the benefits of being already unique and human-readable most of the time. However, the risk lies in the fact that external values can change. Once a user changes their email address, you can't identify them uniquely anymore.

Another risk is security. If you store a sensitive value like a Social Security number as plaintext because it's a PK, a data breach will expose this value, leading to security issues and possible penalties.

If such risks are avoidable, external values can be an excellent source of PKs.

B.7.2 Manual Values

It's also a common practice to use manually generated values as PKs. Sometimes, business rules force us to use a certain format to build keys, and that's a typical use case.

This approach comes with the benefit of you being in full control of value generation. You can implement custom business logic for key generation if necessary.

The risk is that if a weakness in the algorithm causes duplicate value generation, you may end up with data inconsistencies. Concurrency is another potential issue: if data is stored in multiple systems, a key value generated in one system may conflict with a key value in another system.

Still, a requirement that custom IDs follow string business-specific formats can be enough of a reason to justify preferring manual values.

B.7.3 Autoincrementing Values

We've used autoincrementing values in many examples using the SERIAL data type, where a new number is generated for each new row. That's a simple and efficient solution to ensure the uniqueness of each row.

However, concurrency risks of manual values are also valid for autoincrementing numbers. The same number (like 00002) is nearly guaranteed to be generated by other systems as well, which may lead to key conflicts.

A possible approach is to attach a unique system ID to the generated key in distributed systems. That way, SYS_A_00002 will never equal SYS_B_00002, due to their unique prefixes.

Despite the challenges, autoincrementing values is a typical choice for single-node databases with no distributed requirements.

B.7.4 Globally Unique Identifiers

A globally unique identifier (GUID, also known as UUID) is a computer-generated value that is globally unique. All decent development platforms provide built-in functions to generate GUID values on the fly, and you can be nearly sure that the generated value will be unique around the globe. No other electronic system will ever generate the same value again—probably.

A generated GUID value would look like this: e83d5696-ac34-4860-bb32-acd42daa231e.

While generated GUIDs can't be objectively guaranteed to be unique, value duplication is a very slim risk, as there are 2^{128} possible GUID values. Electronic systems typically make a combination of random values, the current date and time, hardware ID's (like MAC addresses), and content hashes to generate GUIDs—which increases the chance of their uniqueness.

The benefits of using GUIDs is that they're globally unique—even among distributed systems. That way, you can have a decentralized key generation logic and not worry about key conflicts.

The main disadvantage of GUIDs is that they're hard to read. Imagine a business user trying to pinpoint a certain value in a spreadsheet of GUID values like e83d5696-ac34-4860-bb32-acd42daa231e or a customer trying to pronounce the GUID of their order on the phone. Due to such difficulties, GUIDs are best used as internal keys.

GUIDs also bring a store overhead due to their length. Especially when you use GUIDs as foreign keys, you have to repeatedly store the same long GUID values in multiple tables.

B.8 Logging

Keeping data logs is a common practice to keep track of events. In essence, most database products provide built-in mechanisms to keep logs, in which the granularity can be configured via system settings.

Databases can be configured to log errors, crashes, and startup and shutdown events only. That would be a narrow scope of logging, so you can widen the scope as needed, up to the point where all table traffic is recorded.

Obviously, database logs have storage costs, so you should meticulously set up the appropriate logging strategy.

If you need a tailored log structure that the built-in logging mechanisms can't handle, you can always create your custom log tables and fill them via triggers. Naturally, the lifecycle of such log data will also be your responsibility—and you probably can't keep them forever if you're logging a high-traffic table.

Some benefits of database logs are listed in Table B.4.

Benefits	Descriptions
Auditing	In a mission-critical database with sensitive data, tracking data changes is necessary for auditing purposes so that you can easily detect the accountable users for questionable actions.
Troubleshooting	In case of data issues, logs can help developers trace the data history and pinpoint the sources of the issues.
Performance	Logs can help determine query execution times, which can help developers identify slow queries and take measures to speed them up.
Forensic Analysis	In case of a data breach attempt, logs can help administrators pinpoint the vulnerability and detect the damage at hand.
Crash Recovery	In case of a system crash, the database can use logs to restore itself to a consistent state. Note that backups provide an alternative way to do that.

Table B.4 Benefits of Database Logs

B.9 Backup and Recovery

In today's world, even personal computer owners are aware of the importance of backups. For better or worse, most users have a system to back up their data—on an external disk, in the cloud, or in a hybrid solution. It's an essential part of data protection—in case of a data loss, a recent backup can restore most of the data.

Databases are subject to the same risks and also require backups. Plus, it's a sound plan for a quick recovery, as production databases usually have low tolerance for downtime.

Typically, a backup and recovery plan is the responsibility of database administrators instead of developers. However, as a developer, you may be the one to raise a red flag if the current plan doesn't match the criticality of the dataset and process at hand.

Some database log types are listed in Table B.5.

Backup Types	Descriptions
Full	This creates a complete copy of the entire database. It's easy to restore but time consuming, and it requires significant storage space.
Incremental	This captures only changes made since the last full or incremental backup. It's slower to restore but faster to back up, and it requires less storage space.
Differential	This captures only changes made since the last full backup. It has moderate backup and restore times.
Transaction Log	This backs up the transaction log containing all data changes. It supports point-in-time recovery, but it requires additional storage continuously.

Table B.5 Some Database Log Types

In some cases, database administrators may choose to use a hybrid approach, like weekly full backups and daily incremental backups. On mission critical systems, transaction logs can be activated on top of that to minimize data loss in case of a crash.

Here's an important reminder: as stated in Section B.3, if you're backing up sensitive data, your backups should be well protected. A data breach in backups may have the same consequences as a data breach in the production database.

Finally, here are some tips:

- Backup and restore methods should be tested and proven to work.
- Never store backups locally. In case of a physical disaster, backups should be accessible offsite or from the cloud.
- Adjust backup frequency to the point where a crash at any point in time won't cause significant data loss.

Appendix C
About the Author

Dr. Kerem Koseoglu is a seasoned software engineer, author, and educator with extensive experience in global projects and commercial applications.

With over twenty years of experience in SAP ABAP, he's also proficient in database-driven development using Python and Swift. He is the author of *Design Patterns in ABAP Objects* (SAP PRESS, 2017) and several bestselling technical books in Turkey.

He holds a PhD in organizational behavior and is renowned for his work in time management. He conducts a variety of technical and soft-skill trainings. He speaks Turkish, English, and German fluently.

When he's not coding or teaching, you're likely to find him onstage, playing his bass guitar. You can visit his website at *www.keremkoseoglu.com* or contact him at *kerem@keremkoseoglu.com*.

Index

A

ABS 132, 376, 379, 408
ADD COLUMN 135, 138, 139, 247
ADD CONSTRAINT 143, 144
AFTER 199, 201, 208, 210
Aggregation 321
Alias 322, 323, 337, 416
ALL PRIVILEGES 434, 435
ALTER COLUMN 137, 138, 141, 142
ALTER DATABASE 102, 105
ALTER ROLE 431
ALTER SCHEMA 109, 111
ALTER SEQUENCE 186, 193, 270
ALTER SYSTEM 433
ALTER TABLE 24, 134–138, 140–144, 218, 247
ALTER USER 430
ALTER VIEW 151
American National Standards Institute Structured Query Language (ANSI SQL) 16
AND 283
API 42, 192, 476, 477, 479
AS 323, 324, 345, 347, 349
ASC 293–295, 297
Atomicity, consistency, isolation, and durability (ACID) 18, 230
AT TIME ZONE 389
Audit 70, 254, 278, 426, 442, 478, 479, 482
Authorization 23, 26, 68, 110, 421, 422, 473, 477
AVG 306, 349, 380–382, 386

B

Backup 482, 483
BEFORE 199, 201, 204, 206, 210
BETWEEN 287, 288

C

CALL 195, 196, 198, 228, 231, 234, 237, 238, 240, 273
Cardinality 457, 458, 461, 462, 464, 466, 467, 469
CASCADE 112, 146, 219
CASE 132, 182, 183, 412, 413
CAST 139, 410, 411
CEIL 132

CEILING 380, 381
CHECK 129–131, 144
COALESCE 132, 344, 360, 414, 415
COMMIT 25, 230, 233, 234, 237, 239, 241, 242, 244–247, 251
Common table expression (CTE) 415, 418
Compliance 34, 71, 202, 254, 278, 421, 478–480
Concatenate 358–360
CONNECT 433
Constraint 20, 115, 118, 124, 127, 129, 133, 141, 145, 161, 168, 478
Conversion 45
COUNT 232, 310, 311, 416
CREATE 432
CREATE DATABASE 100
CREATE OR REPLACE FUNCTION 205, 209, 216
CREATE OR REPLACE PROCEDURE 193–195, 197, 227, 232, 270
CREATE OR REPLACE VIEW 152
CREATE ROLE 431, 436, 439
CREATE SCHEMA 107
CREATE TABLE 24, 90, 96, 116, 119–124, 127, 129, 131, 133, 143, 157, 159, 160, 225, 226, 255–257, 260, 264, 268, 270, 422, 423
CREATE TRIGGER 206, 210, 216
CREATE USER 103, 111, 429, 430, 432, 436, 439
CREATE VIEW 150, 212
CROSS JOIN 342, 344, 417
CROSSTAB 342, 344–346
CURRENT_DATE 132, 385, 386
CURRENT_TIME 385
CURRENT_TIMESTAMP 132, 193, 385

D

data_exception 197
Database 74
Data control language (DCL) 421
Data definition language (DDL) 99
Data manipulation language (DML) 155
Data query language (DQL) 253
Data type 43, 54, 74, 117, 158, 165, 388, 410, 411
DATEDIFF 132
Declarative programming languages 21

487

Index

DEFAULT 133
DELETE 25, 186, 188–190, 193, 201, 218, 228, 242, 245, 246, 432
Deletion 153, 185, 477, 479
DENSE_RANK 394–396, 400
DESC 296, 297
DISABLE TRIGGER 218
DISTINCT 299–301, 342, 417
division_by_zero 197
DROP 142
DROP COLUMN 136, 140
DROP CONSTRAINT 144, 145
DROP DATABASE 106
DROP FUNCTION 219
DROP PROCEDURE 198
DROP ROLE 431
DROP SCHEMA 112–114
DROP TABLE 24, 92, 97, 119, 143, 146
DROP TRIGGER 219
DROP USER 430
DROP VIEW 153

E

ENABLE TRIGGER 218
Encryption 476
Entity-relationship diagram (ERD) 26, 47, 208, 222, 225, 260, 263, 264, 266, 269, 451, 452, 465, 470
EXCEPT 356, 357
EXCEPTION 197, 198
EXECUTE 433
EXECUTE FUNCTION 206, 210, 216
EXISTS 216, 341, 342, 350–352, 354–357
EXTRACT 387

F

FIRST_VALUE 407–409
FLOOR 132, 380, 382
foreign_key_violation 197
Foreign key 52, 120, 122, 123, 144, 158, 159, 226, 312, 316, 456, 463, 481
FOR UPDATE 244–246
FROM 338, 339
FULL OUTER JOIN 332
Function 203, 206, 444

G

GET DIAGNOSTICS 232, 233
GRANT 26, 432–439

GROUP 304–307, 309–311, 322–324, 329, 343, 345, 380–382, 397–400, 416–418
GROUP BY 305

H

Hashing 476, 477
HAVING 307, 311

I

IDE setup 83
IF 198, 205, 209, 216, 232
IF EXISTS 146, 198, 219
Imperative programming languages 21
IN 289, 290, 342
Index 55, 74, 478
IN EXCLUSIVE MODE 247
INNER JOIN 213, 315, 316, 320–324, 327–329, 336, 338, 343, 345, 377–383, 395, 397–400, 415–418
INSERT 25, 91, 96, 162, 164–166, 168, 169, 171, 173, 186, 193, 195, 197–199, 201, 216, 227, 228, 232, 236–238, 240, 241, 271, 423, 432
IN SHARE MODE 247
INSTEAD OF 201, 212, 214, 216, 218
INTERSECT 354, 355
INTERVAL 384
ISOLATION LEVEL 248–250

J

Job 224, 478
JOIN LATERAL 346, 348

L

LAG 404
LEAD 401–403
LEFT 361–363, 368
LEFT OUTER JOIN 326, 329
LENGTH 132, 364, 367
LIKE 291, 292
LIMIT 298, 315, 347
Local database 75
Lock 242, 244, 246–248, 251
LOCK TABLE 247
Log 202, 426, 482, 483
LOWER 132, 365
LTRIM 366

Index

M

MAINTAIN	433
Math operator	373
MAX	308, 309
MIN	307

N

NEW	205, 209, 216
Normalization	59
NOSUPERUSER	430, 431
NOT	285–288, 290, 292
not_null_violation	197
NTILE	405, 406
NULL	120, 124, 128, 134, 166, 167, 302, 332, 359, 461
NUMBER	186, 399

O

Operation	62
Operator	281, 374–376
OR	282
ORDER	293–298, 301, 309, 320–324, 326, 328, 329, 331, 345, 346, 349, 391, 393–406, 409
ORDER BY	293
OUTER JOIN	325–330, 333, 334, 339, 343, 345, 417, 418
OWNER TO	103, 111

P

Parenthesis	283, 284, 287
PARTITION	392
Password	83, 87, 94, 424, 429, 430, 476
Performance	34, 36, 57, 62, 202, 248, 250, 251, 275, 277, 278, 339, 341, 363, 375, 478, 482
pgAdmin	74, 84
macOS installation	84
Windows installation	84
PostgreSQL	73
macOS installation	81
Windows installation	75
Primary key	49, 52, 56, 61, 119, 123, 126, 143, 158, 160, 175, 225, 226, 454, 461, 463, 467, 468, 480, 481
Privilege	68, 421, 422, 425–427, 431, 436, 438, 440, 441, 443, 444, 473, 475
PUBLIC	438, 444

R

RAISE EXCEPTION	198, 205, 232
RAISE NOTICE	197, 198
RANDOM	379
RANK	391, 392, 394, 396, 400, 401
READ COMMITTED	249
READ UNCOMMITTED	248
REFERENCES	144, 432
regexp_matches	372
REGEXP_REPLACE	373
Regular expression (regex)	369, 371, 372
Relational database	17, 20, 24, 30, 42, 52, 59, 62, 113, 122, 170, 202, 457, 459, 462, 467, 468
RENAME COLUMN	135, 140
RENAME TO	102, 109, 134, 151
Renaming	153
REPEATABLE READ	250
RESTRICT	114, 147, 219
RETURN	205, 209, 216
REVERSE	368
REVOKE	26, 441
RIGHT	361, 362, 365, 368
RIGHT OUTER JOIN	330
Role	69, 422, 424, 427–430, 436, 439, 442–444, 475
ROLLBACK	25, 230, 232–235, 237, 239, 241, 242, 251
ROUND	380, 381
Round	132
ROW_COUNT	233
ROW_NUMBER	194, 396, 398, 399, 401
RTRIM	366

S

Salting	476
SAVEPOINT	25, 235, 238–240
Schema	34, 71, 89, 99, 107, 135, 157
Security	20, 34, 73, 83, 421, 426, 471, 472, 475–477, 479, 482
SELECT	22, 25, 56, 57, 149, 150, 171, 173, 181, 186, 193, 213, 216, 244–250, 274–277, 288, 364, 375, 389, 432–435, 437–439, 442–445
Self-join	334, 337
Sensitive data	34, 36, 68, 73, 223, 426, 476, 477, 483
SERIALIZABLE	250
SET	141, 270, 433
SET DATA TYPE	137
SET TIMEZONE	388
SET TRANSACTION	248–250

489

Index

SIGN 383
SQL injection 471, 472
Storage 18, 58, 475–480
Stored procedure 25, 63, 67, 191, 193, 196, 227, 228, 233, 444, 473
Structured Query Language (SQL)
  definition 20
Subquery 180, 181, 337–339, 341, 398, 403, 406, 408, 415, 418
SUBSTRING 368
SUM 303–306, 322–324, 328, 329, 342, 344, 395, 397–400, 417, 418
SUPERUSER 426, 429–431, 442

T

Table 38, 59, 99, 115, 145
Temporal functions 383
TEMPORARY 433
Transaction 20, 22, 229, 247, 249, 251
Transaction isolation 248
Trigger 25, 65, 191, 192, 199, 201–206, 208, 218, 432, 482
TRIM 132, 366, 367
TRUNCATE 432
TRUNCATE TABLE 147, 189, 227, 270

U

UNION 186, 194, 350–352
UNION ALL 352
UNION DISTINCT 352
UNIQUE 127, 129
unique_violation 197, 198
UPDATE ... 25, 139, 174, 175, 177–180, 182, 183, 190, 201, 228, 232, 233, 242–246, 432
UPPER 132, 365
USAGE 433
User 68, 83, 87, 94, 103, 111, 421, 422, 424, 425, 427, 428, 431, 436, 437, 439–441, 443, 444
USING 141

V

View 46, 147, 149, 151, 152
Visual Studio Code (VS Code) 84
  installation and setup 92

W

WHEN 197, 198
WHERE 279, 281, 299
WHERE EXISTS 341
WHERE IN 341
Wildcard 291
Window function 25, 389, 391–393, 395
WITH 186, 193, 416, 417
WITH GRANT OPTION 435